Hospitality and Catering

A Closer Look

URSULA JONES and SHIRLEY NEWTON
with PAULINE DIXON

Foreword by PRUE LEITH

CASSELL

Also available from Cassell

N. Johns (editor), *Productivity Management in Hospitality and Tourism*

P. Jones (editor), *Introduction to Hospitality Operations*

R. Kotas, R. Teare, J. Logie, C. Jayawardena and J. Bowen, *The International Hospitality Business*

R. Lucas, *Managing Employee Relations in Hotel and Catering*

M. Olsen, R. Teare and E. Gummesson (editors), *Service Quality in Hospitality Organizations*

R. Teare, D. Adams and S. Messenger (editors), *Managing Projects in Hospitality Organizations*

R. Teare and A. Boer (editors), *Strategic Hospitality Management*

R. Teare, S. Calver, J. A. Mazanec and S. Crawford-Welch, *Marketing in Hospitality and Tourism: A Consumer Focus*

K. Webster, *Environmental Management for the Hospitality Industry*

Cassell
Wellington House, 125 Strand, London WCR2R 0BB
PO Box 605, Herndon, VA 20172

First published 1997

British Library Cataloguing-in-Publication Data
A catalogue for this book is available from the British Library

Library of Congress Cataloging-in-Publication Data
    Jones, Ursula
      Hospitality and catering : a closer look / Ursula Jones and Shirley Newton.
        p. cm.
      Includes index.
      ISBN 0–304–33182–1 (alk. paper). — ISBN 0–304–33184–8 (pbk. : alk. paper)
      1. Restaurant Management. 2. Caterers and catering—Management.
      I. Newton, Shirley. II. Title.
  TX911.3.M27J67 1996
    647.95'068—dc20
                                                    96–14292
                                                               CIP

ISBN 0-304-33182-1 (hardback)
       0-304-33184-8 (paperback)

Typeset by Ben Cracknell Studios

Printed and bound in Great Britain by The Bath Press

Contents

Acknowledgements

The authors would like to especially thank Whitbread PLC Education Partnership; Martin Sykes, who was instrumental in arranging for their visits to Whitbread retail outlets in order to include details of these in the text, Tony Allan, who arranged for the illustrations and photographs to be included in the book, and the Whitbread employees, who gave their support and comments to the authors.

Other sources of assistance were freely given and gratefully received from:

Mr WRC Culshaw (Bass Taverns Ltd)	William Murray
Alan Jones – ARA Services PLC	Sico (Europe)
Northamptonshire Police (Crime Prevention)	Simon Jersey
Leith's	Wittenborg UK
AA Publishing	Martin Richardson
Microsoft	Rachel Ellis
Marolow Foods	Robert Mason

Foreword

At first blush, this book looks slightly alarming! Weighty, worthy and perhaps not a great deal of fun.

But students should not be misled by first impressions. Our best friends are not generally the loudest or the jolliest, and this book will, I am sure, be the very best friend of anyone lucky enough to own it.

It is clear, practical, detailed and reliable. *Everything* is in it. Long after trainees and young cooks have passed their exams and lost their nervousness when boiling lobsters or spinning sugar, *Hospitality and Catering: A Closer Look* will still be on the kitchen shelf and will still be consulted, trusted and very well thumbed.

Prue Leith
August 1996

Preface

This text is designed to provide a foundation to new and future employees in the hospitality and catering industry for underpinning knowledge upon which to build a range of competence-based skills.

The reader will find an explanatory text interspersed with summary charts and diagrams.

It is important to remember that this is an introductory text. It does not set out to give the reader all the answers but rather aims to give the reader the principles and outlines that can be applied to their working environment, bearing in mind the diverse nature of the industry.

In order to help the reader to gain the necessary foundation knowledge for their portfolio of evidence, a series of work-based activities have been included within the text. These enable the reader to work at their own pace, and offer evidence-building support for those working on their own or in a group.

It is envisaged that candidates following both GNVQ and NVQ programmes will find this text a valuable source of reference and study, and it will be of great assistance to candidates following a modern apprenticeship programme.

ONE

Investigating the hospitality and catering industry

The hospitality and catering industry is a thriving and diverse sector of the UK economy. It includes establishments that are owned by international companies, those owned by UK-based companies and those owned and managed by individual persons. It ranges from the smallest kiosk that sells icecream to the largest luxury hotel, the corner fish and chip shop to the smartest city restaurant. All types of tasks and methods of service are catered for by the industry in all types of establishments.

The residential sector caters for campers using licensed sites, residents of guest houses or public houses and guests in luxury hotel suites. In the welfare sector boarding schools, university halls of residence, hospitals and homes for the elderly are all part of the hospitality and catering industry.

The industry is so diverse and flexible that it can cater for all types and ages of customer from the cradle to the grave, offering both sustenance and accommodation as required.

Imagine that you are a foreign visitor who has just arrived in the UK. You do not know where to stay for the night. You decide to go to the tourist information office and ask for accommodation. The information clerk could ask you the following questions in order to find out the type of accommodation that you require. You can see from this example that there are a great many factors to consider and a large number of options.

Money?	Little as possible	Youth hostel, guesthouse, public house
	Limited	Small hotel, guesthouse
	Unlimited	Luxury hotel, large hotel
Facilities?	Basic	Youth hostel, guesthouse
	Some	Small hotel, country hotel
	Luxury	Large expensive hotel
Company?	Little	Hotel
	Sociable	Public house, city hotel
	Discrete	Hotel suite, country hotel
Food?	No choice	Youth hostel, guesthouse
	Some choice	Hotel, public house
	Large choice	Luxury hotel

Entertainment?	None	Guesthouse, Small hotel
	Limited choice	City hotel, public house
	Wider choice	Luxury city hotel
Sports facilities?	None	Guesthouse, small hotel
	Limited	City hotel
	Wider choice	Luxury hotel, country hotel

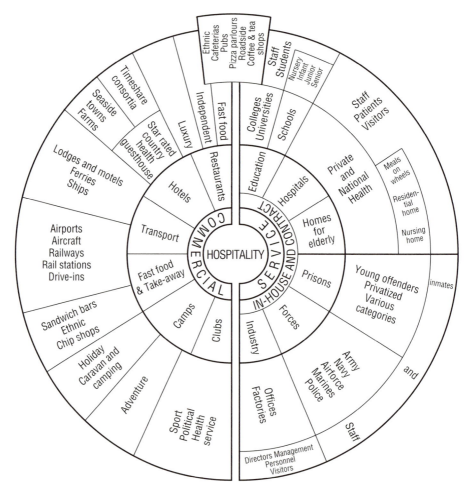

Figure 1.1 The hospitality industry

ACTIVITY

Working in small groups, select a town near your home and investigate its hospitality and catering establishments. Each group should choose a different town.

1. Obtain a map and indicate the position of the establishments using a colour or numerical key system.

2. List the total numbers of each of the following:
   (a) hotels
   (b) guesthouses
   (c) boarding schools
   (d) homes for the elderly
   (e) hospitals
   (f) schools
   (g) in-store catering
   (h) in-house catering
   (i) fast food outlets
   (j) take-away units

3. Compare your findings with those of other groups.

COMMERCIAL SECTOR: ACCOMMODATION

Luxury hotels

Luxury hotels are not widespread. Most are set in the heart of London, in large cities such as Edinburgh or tourist areas such as the Cotswolds. Accommodated in large elegant buildings, the luxurious surroundings appeal to royalty from around the world, diplomats and the famous. The more notable of these hotels have offered service for over 100 years and employ very well trained staff. This type of hotel can give guests the very best of everything.

- high ratio of staff to guests
- excellent service
- formal atmosphere
- peace and quiet
- luxurious surroundings
- superb food
- total privacy
- every need catered for

Town and city hotels

Throughout Britain there is a wide variety of hotel types and sizes to meet every customer's needs and pocket – hence the need to devise systems to inform prospective customers of the choice (see Figure 1.2).

Published guides vary according to the organization that has developed them. Figure 1.2 displays some of the most familiar ratings.

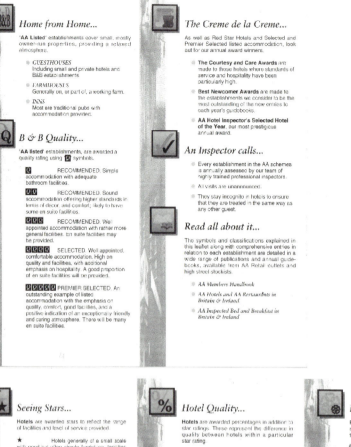

Home from Home...

'AA Listed' establishments cover small, mostly owner-run properties, providing a relaxed atmosphere.

- GUESTHOUSES
  Including small and private hotels and B&B establishments.

- FARMHOUSES
  Generally on, or part of, a working farm.

- INNS
  Most are traditional pubs with accommodation provided.

B & B Quality...

'AA listed' establishments, are awarded a quality rating using Q symbols.

Q   RECOMMENDED. Simple accommodation with adequate bathroom facilities.

QQ   RECOMMENDED. Sound accommodation offering higher standards in terms of decor, and comfort; likely to have some en suite facilities.

QQQ   RECOMMENDED. Well appointed accommodation with rather more general facilities. En suite facilities may be provided.

QQQQ   SELECTED. Well appointed, comfortable accommodation. High on quality and facilities, with additional emphasis on hospitality. A good proportion of en suite facilities will be provided.

QQQQQ   PREMIER SELECTED. An outstanding example of listed accommodation with the emphasis on quality, comfort, good facilities, and a positive indication of an exceptionally friendly and caring atmosphere. There will be many en suite facilities.

The Creme de la Creme...

As well as Red Star Hotels and Selected and Premier Selected listed accommodation, look out for our annual award winners.

- The Courtesy and Care Awards are made to those hotels where standards of service and hospitality have been particularly high.

- Best Newcomer Awards are made to the establishments we consider to be the most outstanding of the new entries to each year's guidebooks.

- AA Hotel Inspector's Selected Hotel of the Year, our most prestigious annual award.

An Inspector calls...

- Every establishment in the AA schemes is annually assessed by our team of highly trained professional inspectors.

- All visits are unannounced.

- They stay incognito in hotels to ensure that they are treated in the same way as any other guest.

Read all about it...

The symbols and classifications explained in this leaflet along with comprehensive entries in relation to each establishment are detailed in a wide range of publications and annual guide-books, available from AA Retail outlets and high street stockists.

- *AA Members Handbook*
- *AA Hotels and AA Restaurants in Britain & Ireland*
- *AA Inspected Bed and Breakfast in Britain & Ireland*

Seeing Stars...

Hotels are awarded stars to reflect the range of facilities and level of service provided.

★   Hotels generally of a small scale with good but often simple furnishing, facilities and food. This category sometimes includes private hotels where requirements for public access and full lunch service may be relaxed. Not all bedrooms will necessarily have en suite facilities. These hotels are mostly managed by the proprietor and there may well be a more personal atmosphere than in larger hotels.

★★   Small to medium sized hotels offering more in the way of facilities such as telephones and televisions in bedrooms. Like one star hotels, this category can also include private hotels. At least half the bedrooms will have full en suite facilities. These can be proprietor managed or group owned.

★★★   Medium sized hotels offering more spacious accommodation and a greater range of facilities and services. Generally these will include a full reception service as well as more formal restaurant and bar arrangements. You can expect all rooms to provide en suite facilities, most of which will include a bath. Though often individually owned, this category encompasses a greater number of company owned properties.

★★★★   Generally large hotels with spacious accommodation including availability of private suites. This category of hotel normally provides a full range of formal services including room service, reception and porterage and may well offer more than one dining operation. En suite facilities in all rooms should include both bath and shower. High standards of comfort and food are expected at this level.

★★★★★   Large luxury hotels offering the highest international standards of accommodation, facilities, services and cuisine.

Lodges...

Lodges offer reasonably priced accommodation catering for overnight stops and offering good, functional bedrooms with private facilities. They are usually situated adjacent to a motorway or roadside restaurant. They are of fairly standard quality and are not star rated.

Hotel Quality...

Hotels are awarded percentages in addition to star ratings. These represent the difference in quality between hotels within a particular star rating.

50%-59%
A sound hotel which meets all the minimum standards for AA star rating and which overall provides modest but acceptable levels of accommodation, facilities and service.

60%-69%
A particularly sound hotel which exceeds the minimum requirements for its star rating by offering higher standards in certain areas.

70%-85%
Overall a very good hotel which can be strongly recommended for providing a high level of service, food and accommodation often with excellent standards in certain areas of its operation.

AA inspectors routinely assess each hotel for a percentage rating. Paying particular attention to quality, comfort and standards generally, they are awarded marks under the following headings

- *Hospitality*
- *Service*
- *Bedrooms*
- *Cleanliness*
- *Food*
- *Public Areas*
- *Overall Concept*

Red Stars...

The AA recognises hotels which consistently provide outstanding levels of hospitality, service, food and comfort through its prestigious red star award scheme. These are given to a select group of hotels considered to be of the very best within their star rating. In such cases, a percentage score for quality is considered unnecessary.
Red stars range from one ★ to five ★★★★★

Food Quality...

Restaurants and Hotels can be awarded rosettes to denote the quality of food they serve.

Enjoyable food, carefully prepared that reflects a high level of culinary skills.

A high standard of food that demonstrates a serious, dedicated approach to cooking.

Very fine food prepared with considerable flair, imagination and originality.

Excellent standards of cuisine, service and wine consistently achieved.

Outstanding cuisine, service and wine that reaches the highest international standards

Table talk...

Restaurants, too, have their own classification scheme, using 'Knives and Forks' to denote the level of amenities and service.

X   Simplicity is generally the keynote, as evident in both service and decor.

XX   Generally, a higher standard of service, decor, furnishings and amenities will be found in this type of establishment. A small lounge or cocktail bar may be available.

XXX   Often of a type where it is usual to sit in a bar or lounge for an aperitif and to order your meal. You can expect a higher standard of comfort and more formal service.

XXXX   Normally found only in the larger cities, a very well appointed, sizable restaurant with bar or lounge, and formal service.

XXXXX   The height of luxury and good living this category of establishment should be comparable in decor and service with the best 5 star hotel.

Figure 1.2 The AA's Hotel Services brochure

Large hotels with many amenities are usually to be found in inner city areas. They appeal to business people for conferences and stop-overs, to organizations requiring banqueting, to foreign and British tourists and to the famous, and offer comfort and style. Very often there is a separate 'in-house' restaurant, serving non-residents as well as residents. Sometimes they are difficult to access by car due to their location. Most needs are catered for and customers expect excellent facilities:

- good ratio of staff to customers
- excellent customer care
- excellent food
- very comfortable accommodation
- accommodation suites available
- all other rooms with ensuite bathrooms

- swimming pool
- gym and sauna
- live music for dancing
- business services, e.g. fax
- lifts if multi-storey, with an attendant
- car parking

There are also large hotels on the outskirts of big towns and cities. These are usually frequented by business people who require conference facilities and stop-overs, and by passing tourists. Buildings are often set on larger sites than within the towns and so are very rarely multi-storey. Car parking is easy and access is from main arterial routes. Facilities vary and are rated accordingly, but customers still expect excellent service, good food and comfortable surroundings.

Smaller hotels may be found in inner towns and cities and often don't have quite as many facilities. Appealing to passing business people, local trade and some tourists, they offer good value for money, wholesome food and friendly atmosphere.

Country hotels

The range of hotels available in the country regions is as broad as within the towns and cities of Britain. Some situated on arterial routes and others in far-away places, they range from the smaller friendly hotel with a modest range of facilities, to the larger hotel with separate restaurant and excellent range of facilities meeting most needs. One particular type of hotel is worthy of a mention.

Country house style hotels are being developed in many tourist areas, often created by converting a stately home or manor house. They provide for those who are looking for a quiet, luxurious comfortable break away from it all. Huge sums are spent on renovating these magnificent buildings and excellent facilities offer the guest the same that can be found in the luxury hotels of our big towns and cities. There is the added luxury of beautiful surroundings and magnificent views over rolling countryside.

Consortia

A consortium is a group of independent hotels who purchase sales, marketing and corporate image ideas from a specialist company giving the public an expected standard of service. Membership of a consortium provides members with access to international, even global, reservations systems. Joining a consortium can be an attractive proposition to an independent hotelier, as it can result in an improvement in bookings and consequently more business. Moreover, it is cost-effective for tourist organizations to work closely with groups of hotels rather than with individual establishments. But at the heart of the consortium concept there is a contradiction: against the advantage of being able, as a group, to compete against the big chain hotels there is the disadvantage of losing individuality to the corporate image. Some consortia set membership criteria based on certain standards of product and increased emphasis on quality control. This may not work well if it means all hotels adhering to particular brands of product. However, since consumers are in fact looking for the same product, but packaged differently, consortia can be extremely successful in exploiting this fact to create return custom.

It is important for a hotelier to be realistic when considering buying into a consortium. It can be expensive, so the benefits must be weighed against the economic potential of the establishment. Joining does not necessarily represent a wave of the magic wand. Benefits include a rise in bookings through a central reservation system, exposure in consortia brochures and group purchasing of food and liquors. A possible further benefit can be the training and advice which some groups offer to break down the barriers of isolation.

For consumers, consortium membership provides a seal of professionalism and the security of the wider management to complain to, should there be a need.

Motels

These establishments, set alongside motorways and arterial routes are typically known as 'lodges', and suit the business motorist who needs an overnight stop, or the tourist who is driving around Britain. It may be necessary to book in advance in high season and in popular areas.

Motorists may pull into the spacious car park and be offered a good standard of accommodation at a set price. The building is modern and consists of bedrooms only, each room exactly the same and sleeping up to four people. The price includes en-suite facilities, coffee and tea-making, television and telephone. At the entrance there is a security door and reception to ensure the guests' welfare, and payment may be taken in advance for early leavers. Departing guests are expected to leave by noon so that rooms may be prepared by 3 p.m. for the following bookings. Staffing is minimal as no food is available on the premises. However, motels are always situated adjacent to other services, managed by the same company, where travellers may eat – at extra cost.

Timeshare villas/apartments/rooms

A timeshare owner purchases the right to occupy a self-catering apartment, a suite or a room in an hotel or leisure club for a specified number of weeks per year, over a period of years, or possibly indefinitely.

A one-off payment and modest annual maintenance fee secures annual holiday accommodation, perhaps for a lifetime. Nowadays this does not mean being tied to one resort. Today's timeshare buyers, if they fancy another destination, temporarily swap their holiday through one of the international exchange organizations.

For hotels there are many advantages to be gained through investing in timeshare:

- inclusion on a national, even global, register
- opportunities to increase occupancy
- extend the holiday season
- increased use of restaurant
- improved bar takings
- up-front monies are generated
- provides funds for refurbishment and development

There are, however, a few disadvantages:

- timesharers will rightly feel that they own the place
- a receptionist will be expected by the client to remember them from one year to the next
- after sales care may be difficult to arrange yet is essential as it has been paid for

Timeshare is now established world-wide, despite early problems caused by unscrupulous operators using hard-sell tactics. This problem has been eased by the introduction of legislation and by the entry of large hotel corporations on to the scene. Consumer confidence has been revived and the industry is booming. Units of timeshare tend to be developed in resorts or centres alongside big hotels. Until now America has dominated the market but a few hotel chains in Britain have been operating quietly and successfully for several years. The UK is a high-demand area, especially with Americans, so it is worth British companies taking up the opportunities available.

Table 1.1 Commercial establishments

Type of establishment	Typical location	Brief description	Target clientele	Facilities/Customer expectations	Purpose of stay
Luxury hotel	Inner cities Inland tourist resorts	Large (often old) buildings World famous High-ratio staffing Well-trained staff Very formal Access to main arterial routes	Royalty Diplomats The famous Tourists Executives	Excellent standard of customer care Luxurious and comfortable Stylish and elegant Every need met Private and confidential Quiet Extensive leisure facilities Garage and car park Conference and banqueting	Conventions and meetings Conferences Holiday Tours
4/5 star hotel	Edge of large cities and towns Town centres	Large buildings, both old and modern Well trained staff Many facilities Formal	Conference delegates Business people Tourists Families	High standard of customer care Comfortable Most needs met En suite, room service Leisure facilities Car park Conference and banqueting	Sales conventions and product launch Conferences Holiday Leisure and recreation
2/3 star hotel	Town centres Edge of towns Country Tourist/seaside resorts	Polite and efficient staff Friendly atmosphere	Business people Tourists Families	Good standard of customer care Comfortable Leisure facilities Children's facilities Arranged tours Car park	Sales conventions Conferences Holiday Leisure and recreation Travellers
Country house hotels	Tourist resort Country	Converted historical buildings High-ratio staffing Well-trained staff Gardens	Tourists Mature couples The famous	Excellent standard of customer care Luxurious and comfortable Stylish and elegant Private and confidential Every need met Extensive leisure facilities Car park	Leisure and recreation Touring
Guesthouses Farms	Town and country Tourist areas	Small buildings Converted houses Farm houses Family run	Tourists Travellers Families	Bed and breakfast basis Friendly atmosphere Relatively inexpensive	Journey break Holiday Recreation and leisure
Motels	Arterial routes Motorway services	Modern buildings Usually low-level Adjacent fast-food restaurant	Business people Travellers Families	Comfortable En-suite, television Tea-making facilities Pay on registration Single price per room Car park	Easy access Journey break
Public houses	Town and country	Few rooms to let Similar to guesthouse Family-run	Families Travellers	Bed and breakfast basis Friendly atmosphere Relatively inexpensive	Touring Journey break

Health farm

Converted stately homes in magnificent settings, health farms provide a cosseted atmosphere for those able to meet the charges, and who feel in need of a 'get away from it all' break. Clients will be largely royalty, the famous, foreign visitors and stressed business people.

Physicians, therapists, consultants and a high number of well-trained service staff are on hand to restore and relax the clientele, who may be suffering from stress or overwork. A week or even a month or more at a health farm offers a feeling of relaxation and well being. Clients will expect:

- excellent food, possibly following specific diets
- a full range of exercises and activities such as water aerobics and horse riding
- extensive health and beauty treatments
- meditation
- peace and quiet
- luxuriously comfortable surroundings
- polite but friendly staff

Guesthouses

Typical of seaside and small towns throughout Britain, guesthouses tend to be converted larger houses with a few guest bedrooms. The owner usually lives on the premises and is responsible for:

- shopping
- preparation and service of food
- cleaning and maintenance of rooms
- bar service
- reception

Guests may be given a front door key as well as their room key to enable them to come in and out freely. In most establishments the meals are home cooked and are taken on either a bed and breakfast basis or with evening meal included, but occasionally full-board is offered for those who do not wish to be out and about all day, such as older people. Full board obliges the owner to cook at a time when rooms need to be serviced. There is usually a small dining room and guest lounge as reception rooms. Accommodation offered may be double or twin room, single or even family rooms, with up to four beds. These rooms are particularly good value as a reduction is usually made for sharing.

Standards vary and bookings are usually undertaken through recommendations. Prices also vary, although they are never high. Establishments with less than six letting beds are exempt from fire and food hygiene regulations and can also avoid the payment of business rates. There have been calls for action to close these loopholes as they are allowing standards to decline, but the government wishes to encourage small businesses by not imposing 'red tape'.

In post-war years the guesthouse was extremely popular, but latterly there has been a decline as more people take holidays abroad. The British climate does nothing to help the tourist industry and so owners must look towards other areas for their business:

- the businessman
- links with larger hotels offering conference facilities
- low-priced, short out-of-season breaks
- breakfast service to coaches and travellers

Farms

Farming and horticulture together form one of the largest industries in Britain producing 65 per cent of all the food we eat. There are nearly 250,000 farms of differing types, dependent upon the type of soil, climate and size. In general, grassland farms are in the west and north, crop growing in the east and south, mountain farms (known for their sheep and beef) in Wales and Scotland. The West country is noted for dairy farming and East Anglia for cereals.

In 1983 an association was formed between the Royal Agricultural Society of England, the English Tourist Board, the Ministry of Agriculture and the farming magazine *Farmers' Weekly*. Difficult times have obliged the farmer to diversify in order to promote business. Recognizing the importance of tourism in the countryside, farmers formed a national organization called the Farm Holiday Bureau. This has 75 local groups in the UK, constantly working together to improve the service offered. Most members have outlayed heavily to transform basic bedrooms to meet the required standards and visitors can expect an abundance of home-produced food. The National Tourist Board inspects every member property to ensure the reputation of offering good value and quality accommodation, alongside a warm welcome.

In most cases the establishments are working farms, so where it is impractical for visitors to stay in the farmhouse during the day they may be asked to be 'out' from breakfast till teatime. Not always dependent upon tourists, some farms are open for business travellers and for the unusual wedding reception. Often guests can be shown round the farm and even help with the chores and some farms have special nature trails, but it must be remembered that a farm can be a dangerous place and so children must never be left to roam. With supervision, they can enjoy the animals, machinery, flora and fauna.

Youth hostels

The YHA (Youth Hostels Association) runs as many as 260 youth hostels in various locations in England and Wales, housed in converted castles, mansions, historic houses, barns and country cottages. The YHA is allied to a further 5,000 establishments world-wide in approximately 60 countries.

A friendly welcome is always available at these hostels, which appeal to single people, families or groups who wish to 'travel on a budget', especially for those who enjoy an activity holiday. There may be available at or near a hostel activities ranging from abseiling, rock climbing, horse riding, hill walking, and wind-surfing to canoeing. For the less adventurous there may be painting, photography or yoga. In the country, hostel guests may expect to see bicycle sheds and in the city hostels sightseeing is often catered for. Close to or within some hostels, especially those in far away places, there is a shop stocking basic items for the self-caterers.

Prices are reduced for those who have already paid a membership fee but even without, the fees are modest. Accommodation may be in bunk-bedded rooms and guests are expected to make up their own bed and clear up after themselves. This is in order to keep staffing costs to a minimum. Guests also have the use of public rooms – lounge or common room, dining room and self-catering kitchen and laundry. A few hostels (their location specified in the YHA guide) do accommodate the disabled. However, it would be necessary for a disabled person to travel with a companion, as staff are not always available to assist.

Some hostels do provide food and drink and this is usually offered in a cafeteria style operation, often serving wholesome homemade food with vegetarian and ethnic dishes. Packed lunches may be available on request.

In order to boost out of season trade, there is a scheme whereby private groups may rent a hostel between October and Easter. During the summer months, the hostels are at their busiest and employ many casual staff to cope.

COMMERCIAL SECTOR: RESTAURANTS

Luxury restaurants

Set both in large city centres and out in the depths of the country, these restaurants are providing food and service to an exceptionally high standard. Either owned by well-known chefs or famous names employing excellent chefs, these restaurants appeal to the rich and famous for their expertly produced and presented menu of delicious food, quiet atmosphere and polite and efficient service. Expectations are very high with, of course, prices to match.

It may be considered an honour to obtain employment in one of these establishments and once experience is gained, doors within the industry are easily opened.

Hotel restaurants

Set within hotels, these restaurants offer service to non-residents as well as residents at lunchtimes and dinner. Service varies according to the size and type of hotel but most offer high standards of food and excellent waiter/waitress service. Conference and banqueting facilities may be available and employment in this sector usually offers variety and a good career progression. Very many hotels and restaurants of this nature belong to hotel groups or chains.

Public houses

Many of our public houses have in-house restaurants offering a separate service from any residential facilities and bars. Appealing to a very broad range of customers, these establishments offer an evening or lunchtime meal either on the basis of a carvery, grill room, formal restaurant or bar service. To produce cost-effective and appealing dishes is important. In order to meet target profits, maintain regular standards, save labour costs, improve portion control – all without necessarily employing highly skilled staff – most opt for convenience products.

Pub meals represent a growth industry, with nearly four million meals being served every day. Pubs are part of our native culture and owe little to American or European influences. The relaxed and informal atmosphere has remained even though we have seen 'beer outlets' change

to lounges, restaurants and bars serving good food and wine, and family restaurants where formerly there was an adult-only domain. There is no doubt that the British public do expect the traditional surroundings of a pub to remain and even though many establishments are undergoing major refurbishments, companies are making great efforts to maintain an informal atmosphere along with comfort and good value. Generous helpings are served at moderate prices, and not all accompanied with chips and peas. To tempt consumers, many establishments write up a daily menu on a chalk board behind the bar, complementing the printed menu. Whilst table service is expected in the more formal pub-restaurants, in most the order is placed at the bar and paid for in advance, the waiter/waitress then serves the food. Each meal is prepared to laid-down standards, especially when the establishment is part of a group.

Ethnic restaurants

In this instance, ethnic refers to vegetarian as well as to Indian, Chinese, Italian, Greek and Thai restaurants. Usually set in town and city centres, these ethnic restaurants offer many styles of cuisine all over Britain, relying upon opening during the evenings and at weekends to offer the public a chance to try dishes from around the world.

Public tastes have changed as the population has become a mixed community. New styles of cooking and tastes have been introduced and this has encouraged us to try new foods at home as well as in restaurants. During this century, it has been customary for the typical English meal at Sunday lunch time to be a 'roast'. More recently, the public have ventured out of home for Sunday lunch and in fact at any time of the week. Popular venues are the ethnic restaurants providing dishes such as lasagne, chicken tikka and sweet and sour pork. These dishes now seem quite commonplace and we are becoming quite discerning in the standards of cuisine we expect.

Occasionally, restaurants such as Italian or Greek will create an atmosphere by offering entertainment as well as good food and drink. This is popular for parties and functions, ensuring the guests a good evening's fun and the restaurant a promise of return trade. Prices in all ethnic restaurants are usually good value for money and the service friendly, polite and efficient.

In-store restaurants

Large departmental stores now provide a service for the tired shopper within the store, usually on one of the upper floors. These facilities are mostly self-service although there are some with waiter/waitress service in towns and cities much visited by tourists.

In recent years spending on eating out has increased and the stores have cashed in by providing catering facilities right where they are needed. A discreet area is set aside were shoppers are able to obtain a variety of snacks, main meals and drinks often at prices that are high for the standards offered. During very busy times it is almost impossible for staff to supply food and clear tables quickly enough, and long queues may form. As the introduction of these facilities is quite recent most of the equipment is state of the art, but employers tend to employ part-time untrained staff during busy times, who are ill-equipped to cope with the rush.

Quick service restaurants (QSRs)

Very familiar to all of us as part of our high street and shopping malls, quick service (or fast food) restaurants offer their customers:

- an efficient service when time is limited
- good value for money
- a relaxed family atmosphere

The fast growth of these establishments over the last few years still continues, due to the style and pace of our busy lives, especially in:

- town and city areas
- leisure centres
- university campuses
- motorway service areas

Influence has come from the USA and menus vary, with pizzas, hamburgers and fried chicken being some of the most popular dishes offered.

In some QSRs customers are greeted and seated, others expect their customers to order at the service desk. Food is produced to order but there is little waiting time. Crockery and cutlery may be disposable or cleared by service staff.

Take-away service

Many of the QSRs also include a take-away service from their service bar and some offer take-aways as their only service. Also part of our fast-moving society, after a busy week we enjoy a meal at home without having to prepare it. Overheads in these businesses are lower than in traditional style restaurants as customers do not stay on the premises to eat and of course less space is needed. Menus vary and ethnic take-aways give us the opportunity to try new dishes in private! Types of establishment include:

- burger bars
- southern fried chicken
- pizzerias
- Indian, Chinese, Thai and Malaysian foods
- fish and chip shops
- sandwich bars

Some offer a telephone order service so that the food may be collected in the minimum time, others offer a delivery service. It is important that the food is always cooked well and maintained at the correct temperature before consumption. This is a factor to be reckoned with, as is the problem of litter. If customers eat in the street there is every possibility that packaging

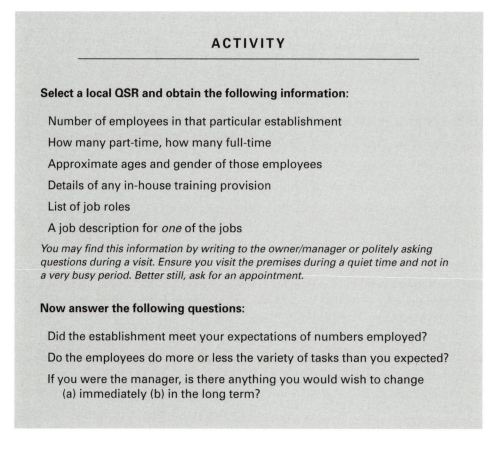

ACTIVITY

Select a local QSR and obtain the following information:

Number of employees in that particular establishment

How many part-time, how many full-time

Approximate ages and gender of those employees

Details of any in-house training provision

List of job roles

A job description for *one* of the jobs

You may find this information by writing to the owner/manager or politely asking questions during a visit. Ensure you visit the premises during a quiet time and not in a very busy period. Better still, ask for an appointment.

Now answer the following questions:

Did the establishment meet your expectations of numbers employed?

Do the employees do more or less the variety of tasks than you expected?

If you were the manager, is there anything you would wish to change
(a) immediately (b) in the long term?

will be discarded in the wrong place. Within close proximity of each establishment there should be a refuse bin.

Coffee and tea shops

These provide an informal atmosphere in which customers can sit and relax awhile to enjoy a snack or light meal with a very welcome beverage. They are usually situated in sight of passers-by in busy streets and shopping malls, sometimes with tables and chairs on the pavement, at which relaxing customers provide a lure for further custom. Occasionally set within a retail baker's shop, they can increase trade for that aspect. Service may be a basic table service or simply self-service with staff clearing and maintaining cleanliness. Foods are usually good value.

LEISURE OUTLETS

Sports clubs

The main concern of these establishments is providing entertainment in the form of sport. Just a few years ago, the only refreshments available on site would be fast-food style snacks and drinks. Now clubs around the country have invested large sums of money on new catering facilities and are realizing the potential for extra revenue.

There is demand for tables in lavish dining suites overlooking sports arenas, or even in luxurious private boxes. Fans may book their meal in advance and in some instances caterers are asked to serve as many as 500 guests within a relatively short space of time. Alongside this restaurant style of service there is the provision of fast food, and on match or special days there may be as many as 2000 lunches served.

In most sports there are limited periods of use when teams are 'at home', at other times marketing plays an important part in realizing the full potential of the catering facilities. Banqueting suites provide additional function rooms for exhibitions, wedding receptions and conferences as well as for club business. In some clubs the sheer variance in the size of available rooms and a competitive pricing structure encourages as many as 25 reception and functions each week.

Social clubs

This type of club exists throughout the country to provide an informal setting in which employees or the general public may enjoy entertainment, social and sporting activities. Bingo clubs are also run on very similar lines. Many are operated by leisure chains, although smaller clubs may be run by a husband and wife team.

Staff may number as many as 60 in larger clubs – managers, cashiers, cooks, bar staff, maintenance teams and cloakroom attendants. In smaller clubs staff have to be very versatile and take on more than one role. All staff are in contact with members and so must be:

- of smart appearance
- be helpful and polite
- enjoy being with people

ACTIVITY

If you or any of your family visit a sports club, organize and produce suitable questionnaires that may be used by your club to analyse their catering facilities.

Discuss with your tutor the type of questions you would need to ask and ensure that the club is happy with your proposal. Here are some example questions.

Ask of the club management:

How many full-time and part-time staff are employed for catering at the club?

Does the club advertise the availability of its catering facilities to the general public?

Are there any problems experienced in staffing irregular functions?

Do you offer conference/banqueting facilities and, if so, are you able to arrange for overnight stays?

Ask of the clientele:

How often do you visit the club?

Do you come alone to the club, or with family and friends?

If available, would you use the club catering facilities at any other time, say for a party?

Do you prefer to stand, be seated or dine whilst the game is in progress?

Collect all the information from your questionnaires and present the results to the rest of your group.

Apart from the fact that managers may need to be able to do most jobs in the clubs in order to provide cover for absent staff, they also need to have a range of attributes such as:

- friendly and outgoing personality
- showmanship
- leadership
- stamina
- organizational ability
- bar experience/customer contact work
- simple accounting
- marketing

Very many social club staff undertake on-the-job training, experiencing the work in several departments. Employees must be highly motivated as hours are unsociable and long. Young, qualified people may take rapid promotion and become managers in their early twenties.

Sports centres

Built and run by local authorities for community use, or by private profit-making organizations, there are now more than 3000 sports centres throughout the country, reflecting public preoccupation with health and fitness. Staff in these centres tend to fall into different categories:

- instructors or coaches giving specialist training in various sports and activities
- administrative or clerical staff taking bookings, selling time and equipment
- maintenance and ground keepers working to keep the surroundings in good order
- hospitality and catering staff offering good food and beverages, comfortable atmosphere and, in some centres, an entertainment programme.

Overseeing these people are managers, who co-ordinate, plan, promote and work for the success of the centre for both public and staff. Reports are constantly prepared to identify level of use and financial viability of the various areas.

Marketing plays an important role in promoting the centre, which will experience its busiest times during school holidays and on evenings and weekends, when extra part-time staff may be employed.

Sports centre assistants are chosen for their ability to get on with people and for their enthusiasm. Instructors and swimming pool attendants must possess the relevant specialist qualifications and be over 18. Styles of catering outlet may range from fast food bars and cafés to up-market restaurants appealing to those using the entertainment facilities. Jobs in these centres are popular and competition can be fierce.

ACTIVITY

Research in leisure journals and trade press to find out how sport and leisure centres have grown in recent years.

Working in groups, find out:

- How many centres there are in your county

- Average number of employees in each establishment and altogether in the county

- The location of these establishments

List the provision of activities and hospitality offered generally, using the format exemplified below to display your results.

Mytown	Yourtown	Littlemuddling	Greatmuddling
Olympic swimming pool	Aqua-splash centre	No swimming pool	School pool for public use
Multi-screen cinema and theatre	Three-screen cinema centre	Family-run cinema	No cinema
Countryside park	Small park with bowling green	Community park with tennis courts	Pocket park and community centre
Tennis courts Badminton courts Golf course	Leisure centre with sports facilities Laser quest	Skateboard ramp Roller skating rink Go-carting arena	Skateboard ramp

Event catering

Function areas to offer hospitality and catering are built around places such as racecourses, golf courses, tennis centres and stately homes. Most of the time these areas can cope with a normal trade of as many as 1000 people, but on special occasions there may be a requirement for facilities to cope with a huge influx of people who wish to enjoy a great day out. For example:

- Ascot and Gold Cup races
- golf tournaments
- open air operas and concerts
- tennis tournaments
- Grand Prix racing
- new opening of factory

These special occasions usually occur outside and so mobile units, caravans and tented villages are used to provide extra space. Stacking glass-fronted mobile units can be used in the case of racing or other spectator sport to allow customers to watch the proceedings whilst enjoying a meal. These units are usually fully furnished with carpets and curtains and seat up to 12 people. As much as £1000 per day each may be charged for their hire.

Food served at events ranges from simple snacks and meals, such as jacket potatoes and bar meals, to more elaborate sit-down banquets and dinners. There are facilities to suit every taste and pocket.

Space is hired to firms specializing in event catering. Understanding all the problems and overcoming them is an important factor in offering an efficient and professional service. More than one company may be represented at an event and there may be a different menu in each mobile suite, according to standards expected.

Each company will have a nucleus of permanent employees, who travel to different events, and then there will be the regular site staff. Further help can be obtained on a casual basis from:

- local job centres
- college students
- employment agencies

Standards are set prior to each event but the diversity of staff abilities can make these difficult to maintain. Some uniform may be offered to standardize the image and basic training in food hygiene may be given on an in-house training programme.

Employment on a casual basis may lead to a permanent role if commitment and ability are proven. For students, working at events can be good experience, although for everyone the hours are long and the work tiring. Tips make extra effort worthwhile and food is usually free to those on duty. Accommodation is not offered but temporary staff are bused in from a large area.

Potential problems lie in the correct storage of foods, transport of equipment, bad weather and lack of fittings. Normally adequate power supplies can overload with the surge in use. It is important to thoroughly plan for this, as every other, eventuality and so generators are often used to run refrigeration and lighting.

Kitchens located in a main marquee can provide a central production for many satellite areas. This central location also helps with security, which can be a major problem. Food stocks are checked regularly and full food costing and control operated. In the bars there is strict control of alcohol by daily stock-taking and removal of stocks to a secure place overnight.

Holiday centres

The great British holiday camp was pioneered before World War II to provide reasonably priced holidays for the masses. The first camp was opened in Skegness in 1936. Holiday centres are still popular but they meet the more sophisticated demands of the modern public and are a far cry from the Hi-de-hi image portrayed on television. Many centres can cater for up to 10,000 people at busy times, two-thirds of which will be self-catering but requiring facilities on demand, the other third at half of full board.

Millions of pounds have been spent in an effort to bring quality to the experience. On site there may be:

- sub-tropical pools with snack bars and cafés
- various styles of restaurants including ethnic and vegetarian
- supermarkets
- bars in several entertainment areas

Service in the dining room provides a set menu, polite and friendly service and speed, an important factor where children are concerned, as they don't have time to become bored. Up to 1500 people are served in a one-hour sitting, the food is wholesome and the menu extensive enough to provide adequate variety during a seven-night stay. The kitchen employs as few catering staff as possible, using suitable large-scale cooking equipment. The meals are then plated and placed into computer-controlled holding ovens ready for the waiters to collect. Strict attention is paid to hygiene rules as, with such large numbers, the risk of food poisoning has to be carefully guarded against.

A wealth of special measures are now tempting British holidaymakers to take a break 'at home', with those of particular importance being the provision of all-weather and open-all-year centres. About 40 per cent of the resorts' visitors are under the age of 15, which indicates that care and safety considerations are as important as the fact that most of the attractions are free of charge.

Whenever possible, the companies running holiday centres use their own managers to provide relevant coaching or formal training for staff. Only when such expertise is not available, do they call upon external bodies.

ACTIVITY

If possible, pay a visit to a holiday centre near you, or else obtain a brochure, and investigate the following possible problems that may be involved in providing a good service to customers.

1. Identify when holidays begin and when they finish. Is this on any particular day, at any particular time?

2. If it is possible for as many as 10,000 people to be on site, how many do you think could arrive at one time to be booked in?

3. Discuss and write down any problems that may be encountered by the following staff in dealing with large numbers of people leaving and entering the site on one day (some ideas have been given to get you started):

   Receptionists (bookings, issue of keys)

   Housekeeper (staffing, times)

   Chambermaids (late leavers, large number of rooms)

   Security staff (car and coach parking, money handling)

   Dining room staff (new customers, seating arrangements)

In recent years a new style of holiday village has hit the British scene. From villas, usually set in a wooded area, clients make their way across the campus to a large domed area for all indoor pursuits. This all-weather centre provides for swimming, shopping and eating, while a further selection of pursuits for all ages is available out of doors, e.g. archery, tennis, water sports of all descriptions, riding and golf. Evening entertainment (shows, bars and dancing) takes place in the domed area. This style of holiday village is different from the others, with clients expecting higher standards of service and the chance to participate in serious outdoor pursuits, rather than 'games'. Most activities require extra payment and are not included in the cost of the villa.

All holidaymakers are expected to be self-catering, so there are no large dining rooms on site. However, the profits to be made in catering are recognized by providing a selection of fast-food establishments, such as burger bars, pizzerias and pancake houses, as well as luxurious restaurants for customers to use if and as they wish.

Camp sites

As the economic situation has altered in recent years in this country, more people are holidaying 'at home' and there has been an increase in the number of caravan and camping holidays. This applies to touring and static sites. Gone are the days when the only water supply was from a tap in the centre of a field and the nearest toilet block meant a long trek in the mud. Caravan and camp sites now attempt to provide sufficient home comforts within easy reach of all camping areas to ensure a return of clientele. Static caravans with as many as eight berths can be hired, or the holidaymaker can park their own touring vans. Luxurious tents may also be available, or areas provided for clients to put up their own. Daily hire charges are made, which include the use of all amenities on the camp site. These vary (brochures will give details) but in general there may be:

• entertainment areas
• swimming pools
• sports facilities
• shops
• toilet and shower blocks

COMMERCIAL SECTOR: TRANSPORT

Motorway service areas

Britain's first motorway service area (MSA) opened at Newport Pagnell on the M1 in 1960. Until 1992 government regulations restricted the building of sites, but now it is possible to apply to local authorities for planning permission with only a minimum distance of 15 miles necessary between sites. Difficulties arise, however, due to the Department of Transport restrictions on slip roads and signs and for this reason some motorways are devoid of services. An MSA can cost between £15m and £30m to build and so a company must be certain of good returns. The number of customers attracted to this type of service each year is about 140 million and this is expected to increase by as much as 100 per cent in the next 25 years due to the growth in motor vehicle traffic. Some of this increase may be retarded due to the expected imposition of charges for motorway use. In order to make the best of sites, catering facilities must move towards the food 'court' style with a wide variety of services:

• 24-hour service
• restaurants for a quick meal
• table service restaurants
• takeaways and sandwich bars
• shops
• toilets and baby changing facilities
• separate coach and lorry park
• telephones and emergency services

For information regarding hotels for travellers see page 7: Motels.

Drive-ins

Until recent years drive-in catering services meant solely those provided for the long-distance lorry driver. Somewhere was needed to park a huge vehicle when the driver needed to take a break or stop overnight. Expectations were not high. As long as a good hearty meal was offered and a clean bed – all at good value – the driver would proceed happily and return again on the next journey.

Now we have the ultimate in convenience, a style inherited from America and the most notable name being McDonald's. Customers stay in their vehicles and drive up to a microphone in order to place a request. This is then relayed to a fast-food service point and as the car moves forward in the queue the order is ready and waiting at the window. Of course, food and drink must be well packed in order to travel and stay at its best, as customers are expected to leave the paypoint before consuming their purchase. They may of course stop in adjacent car parks. All wrappers are disposable and it is hoped that they will be disposed of correctly and not thrown from moving cars. Very often a drive-in service is available at the rear of a fast-food restaurant providing seating, thus employing staff and facilities more economically. This type of fast-food establishment will be open quite early in the morning till very late at night with continuous service throughout the day provided by staff on a rota basis. It ought to be added that it is *not* a service for lorry drivers. Facilities for large vehicles are not offered.

Sea ferries

From Britain's south-eastern ports ferries cross the seas to various destinations in Europe: Spain, France, Holland and Scandinavia; from the south-western ports to Eire. Rarely are they equipped to venture further. Night and day, fleets of ferries have been necessary to carry all types of vehicles and passengers from these shores to keep our economy healthy and to maintain links with our European neighbours. Freight carriage, coaches, caravans, motorcycles, cars and pedestrians are all catered for.

Now with competition from the Channel tunnel rail link, ferry services are continuing to improve. Some longer journeys warrant the use of luxury cabins. Each operator must market their service to provide flexibility for most needs. Some offer packages for a complete holiday, including return travel fare and accommodation in apartments, country houses, hotels or even theme parks.

The shortest journey across the Channel is from Dover to Calais (1.5 hours). Journeys to Santander in Northern Spain or north to Scandinavia can take 24 hours or more. The flexibility of fares, sailing times, accommodation and combined vehicle tours, added to the fact that on some occasions there is no need to make a booking, increase the attraction of ferries over that of the tunnel.

Staff are expected to offer a polite and efficient service. On board the areas provided are:

• fast-food restaurants
• a formal dining room
• duty-free shops
• bars
• lounges

Cruise liners

Ships designed as a home away from home attempt to provide a special place that is tranquil and relaxing as well as exciting and entertaining. Customers expect:

• first rate accommodation
• friendly and efficient service
• superb food
• comfort

With an extensive variety of itineraries, cruises range from a few nights to several weeks and from the breath-taking fjords of Norway to sun-drenched holidays on the other side of the world. Appealing to all types of people as a much needed rest far away from the pressures of everyday life, a cruise holiday is flexible enough to suit families and single travellers alike. Families can share accommodation for economy and there are usually on-board activities for children. The sheer romance of a cruise makes it suitable for honeymooners, and for those keen on sport some cruises are programmed to cater for specialist excursions, such as golf tours.

Flights are available from all over Britain to connect with a cruise liner if desired. Fully inclusive prices offer some packages that cover everything from connecting flights to tips for the cabin staff.

Passenger capacity ranges from medium-sized cruise liners accommodating around 800 passengers to larger liners with upwards of 2500 passengers. These larger ships require a staffing of around 830 employees to provide every comfort for their clients. Ensuring a wide range of employment opportunities for the hospitality and catering industry, ship facilities may include:

- luxurious staterooms as well as a range of cabin standards
- swimming pools
- gymnasium
- sauna and spa
- library
- beauty parlour
- casino
- cinema
- boutiques
- hairdressers or barber shop
- activity centre for children
- facilities for the disabled

Airline services

Catering services in this sector can be divided into two distinct areas:

AT THE AIRPORT

Millions of consumers each year pass through airports all over the United Kingdom for various destinations around the world. The ability to offer customers a quality service, 24 hours per day, is very important for the success of increased and repeat custom. Rigorous standards must be maintained to meet the individual needs of a broad range of customer types and to remain competitive in the market place. Up-to-date equipment and continuous staff development training programmes are a key to that success. Airport customer services now tend to come under one or two specialist companies that operate in several locations. Customers expect:

- fast food and waiter/ess service restaurants
- coffee bars and vending machines
- comfortable departure lounges
- duty free bars
- duty free shops
- childcare facilities

- car hire service
- banking and currency exchange facilities

ON BOARD THE AIRCRAFT

Services in one of our biggest airports may require the production of as many as 12,500 meals per day, providing for many different airlines. Stringent standards must be maintained along the line – from the commodity supplier, through expert care in preparation, to delivery to the aircraft. Good timing and rigorous hygiene standards are essential. Pre-departure checks ensure that each meal is prepared and presented according to pre-arranged specifications. During their flight customers expect:

- polite and efficient steward/ess service
- good food
- beverage service

STATE SECTOR

Schools

Since the 1980 Education Act there has been no statutory obligation on local authorities to provide catering facilities for any child other than those who qualify for free school meals. A number of authorities have now reduced their service to this minimum and have abolished the bulk of their catering services. When the supply of food has to compete with books and teaching on a limited budget, it generally loses out, as the local authority subsidy goes on teaching rather than food when funding is short. Around 80 per cent of school meals catering operations are now run by direct service organizations. These are local authority in-house catering teams which have been re-structured to enable them to bid for contracts. The other 20 per cent are commercial contract caterers.

Many factors have influenced the changes in school meals catering:

- the state of the equipment and whether it needs replacing
- the responsiveness of staff to changes
- the amount of disposable income available to the children

Taken as an average across the country, the number of children buying school meals had declined steadily, but where an authority has marketed heavily there is a marked increase in uptake. Grant-maintained schools view catering as part of the package which will attract children to their school rather than another.

Links with the management of facilities in schools are predicted for the future, combining catering with cleaning, security, ground maintenance and other services providing a more profitable and secure future for contractors. Another possibility is for authorities to combine their education, welfare and civic catering, providing scope for sidelines such as weddings and functions. Such co-operation would present opportunities for joint purchasing and discounts.

Schools (private sector)

For day schools, catering services are very similar to those in the state sector. Many private schools, however – famous and set in idyllic surroundings in some of our most picturesque towns – are boarding schools and require catering services for three meals per day, seven days a week during term time. Holiday periods are used for the maintenance of equipment and buildings, menu planning and ordering, organization of exit balls for pupils leaving and welcome parties for new ones and their parents.

The schools are often divided into small units of 'houses' (with perhaps 80 to 100 pupils in each house) for ease of organization. Pupils have more a sense of belonging and are not as overwhelmed. Providing services is also simplified when dealing in smaller numbers. Small and large dormitories have to be regularly cleaned, meals organized for both staff and pupils, nursing facilities made available and tutorial support made available.

Contract caterers may be given responsibility for the supply of a total catering service for a fixed fee. This saves the school the worry of staffing rotas, ordering ingredients, preparation of food and menu planning. But the cost involved in hiring contract caterers is usually higher than in-house staffing, so the advantages and disadvantages must be carefully considered.

Colleges

Many non-residential colleges offer break-time, luncheon and evening service. The service is usually in-house and provides snacks or full meals at reasonable cost to the students. All colleges became independent of local education authority control in 1993, and now, as businesses, are considering the financial implications of offering catering services to students. Many have introduced a complete service offering vending, stationery and shop facilities as well as fast-food or restaurant style service, accommodation and conference facilities.

Others, especially those that offer courses in Hospitality and Catering, have combined educational with real experience by organizing food outlets of various styles for the public and students throughout the college which are run by the students, guided by lecturers.

Agricultural colleges, which are residential because students need to be on campus at unusual hours to look after animals, usually enjoy idyllic surroundings in the countryside. Many of them hire out facilities to organizations to ensure a steady income throughout the year. Income from these facilities may be increased by diversifying into any of the following:

- production of food from the farms
- garden centres
- ice-cream production
- farm shops
- farm 'attractions'
- cafeteria facilities for the public

Universities

A revolution is occurring in student restaurants, with improved facilities reflecting well on the universities, helping to attract valuable conference business as well as more students to the campus. Most catering is in-house but contract caterers are taking an increasing interest. There has been a move away from charging live-in students an all-inclusive board and lodgings price.

Students are now able to eat breakfast, lunch and dinner when and where they wish. Dependent as they are for funding on student numbers the universities' attempts to attract entrants is likely to include the provision of excellent catering facilities as well as attractive study courses. With several thousand students on most university campuses, the sheer volume can pose catering difficulties. However, by luring famous name franchises into a high-street operation, various styles of service can be offered alongside a food-hall style restaurant. Sophisticated point-of-sale technology accurately records best-selling lines, busy periods and stock requirements as well as speeding up the service to students. Prices on campus must be kept to a minimum due to student poverty. There is potential on sites for the public to use the dining facilities and for caterers to diversify using the facilities for functions, but for this a two-tier pricing structure must be introduced.

When students are not on campus between terms, universities are offering their facilities for block bookings in order to gain income from the residencies. Some of the buildings and their surroundings are of course very attractive. Travel agents, religious groups, businesses and sporting bodies are just a few of the organizations who book holidays, meetings and conferences of this type for a few days or maybe weeks. This enables the university to keep staffing levels and income steady throughout the year and avoid lean periods.

Prisons

All prison catering is financed by public funds. Until recently the service, including the food suppliers, was run completely 'in-house'. But now new prisons are interested in introducing contracted private caterers, although these are still rare in prisons.

Traditionally, chefs are prison officers who have come to specialize in catering. They must have a minimum 12 months' service as an officer before their catering training. This training is then completed in three months in the service's own training establishment. Once into the kitchen an officer will then work under the guidance of a senior officer who will check their suitability for the work.

There are approximately 130 prisons in Britain with an average of 300 to 500 inmates in each and an average of 300 officers working a shift system. Kitchens are staffed by prison officers and inmates who have 'earned' the right to work there. Inmates are paid and so this encourages them to do a good job and maintain standards. They are also able to obtain qualifications. Security can be difficult within the kitchen and in the disposal of waste. Prisons have lost their 'crown immunity', which prevented prosecution through negligence should someone become ill through foods consumed. The board of visitors acts as an independent watchdog in maintaining standards, and every day a doctor and one of the governors will check the menu book for nutritional content.

A senior officer will be designated as an inspector to maintain standards. In most establishments the following factors have an effect on the menu:

- there is often a demand for 'chips with everything'
- usually there are three choices on the menu
- waste must be minimized and so advance choice is offered
- special diets, e.g. ethnic, vegetarian or those prescribed for medical reasons, are catered for although it is known that inmates tend to change their diets at will
- a home-style of cooking is preferred
- the young usually eat large quantities

- limit on food cost spend per head per day
- three meals per day each and every day of the year
- changes may only be introduced gradually to avoid breaks in routine

There is a major refurbishment programme in operation for many of the kitchens to upgrade equipment and meet the needs of environmental health. The austerity and discipline of mealtimes is easing. Service is from one point only and prisoners collect a complete meal on a specially designed tray so that it can be carried in one hand with a drink in the other. Prisoners may return to their cells or to the wings. Officers go to the staff mess for their meals.

To reduce costs to the service some prisons are involved in food production, such as the preparation of whole carcasses from beef that has been reared on prison farms. This also employs the inmates in meaningful tasks. One prison is also involved in convenience food packaging. All supplies are distributed throughout the country from a central depot at Corby, Northamptonshire.

The armed forces

The Royal Logistics Corps feeds and supports all members of the British armed forces, based all over the world. Within Britain, training centres also have army chefs, either supporting or substituting for civilian staff.

To give you some idea, here is a list of a few of the areas of the world in which there is a British military presence (as at 1996)

- England, Scotland and Wales
- Northern Ireland
- Norway
- Canada
- Belize
- Bosnia
- Falkland Islands
- Brunei
- Rwanda
- United States of America
- Italy
- Germany
- Cyprus

It is very difficult to be specific when quoting the numbers employed in the forces as this is constantly changing. However, there is possibly a personnel of 140,000 in the army, with an average unit size of 500, in approximately 280 bases. Not all bases have the same size of personnel, as this depends upon the need for their presence: some are on peace-keeping duty, others preventing aggression, some on mercy missions. Numbers may range from as few as 30 to as many as 1000 or more. An average unit would probably have up to 15 chefs, indicating that there could be as many as 4200 catering personnel required for all the forces.

IN BARRACKS

Some of the forces personnel are married and therefore whilst not on duty will take their meals at home, whilst the remainder are entitled to eat within their mess (dining room). This applies to all three meals of the day although not everyone takes their entitlement. Some fail to get up in time for breakfast, and others, when free to do so, go out in the evening, missing a meal. Eating in the mess does seem very much part of the social scene in the forces and a time that most look forward to.

The mess in which you eat depends on your rank: all military personnel fall into three categories:

- Commissioned officers (COs): maybe 10-20 in one camp
- Senior non-commissioned officers (SNCOs): approx. 30-40 in one camp
- other ranks and junior non-commissioned officers (JNCOs and privates): 300-400 in one camp

Each category of rank has its own accommodation and feeding arrangements. All single personnel pay for their food and accommodation out of their wages and so do personnel who are married and live on camp. The quality of food offered by service caterers is superb irrespective of rank:

- in the COs Mess the standard is of a very good class hotel, with a server or steward on duty and silver service
- in the SNCOs Mess the style would be more of a carvery or quick-service restaurant with server assistance
- in the JNCOs Mess the standard is a quick-service operation mainly due to the fact that there are far larger numbers to be served in this rank

IN THE FIELD

When on exercise or on active service all personnel, irrespective of rank, eat together although seating, dining areas and timings may be separate. Food is generally fresh but when this is impossible, then composite or 'field' rations are used to supplement the menu. Emergency rations are composed completely of composite rations which are available in different sizes of packet: 10-man, 4-man, and single. They are designed to feed over a 34-hour period and may be vacuum-packed, canned or dried rations. They are nutritionally balanced and designed in different packs to suit either hot conditions or very cold conditions, in which a man would require a much higher intake of calories to survive.

Chefs whilst on exercises generally work as many hours as are required of them to fulfil their tasks, but on ordinary duty they work approximately 40+ hours per week.

Entry into forces catering can be in one of two ways:

Apprenticeship at 15–17 years old, without qualifications but with a reasonable standard of education. Training at Aldershot, lasting for 18 months, includes intensive military and basic training or craft and field training.

Adult entry at 17.5 years with preference of basic catering training and basic food hygiene. Intensive military and basic training is done at one of the army's training establishments, then the craft and field training is completed at Aldershot, normally taking six to eight months.

Qualifications and training offered range from basic in-house and certificated course to NVQ Level 3 in food preparation and service to training awards. Within the services there is a broad range of jobs in hospitality for which recruits can be trained, including:

- hospitals
- stewards
- butchers
- teachers
- larder chefs
- VIP chefs to senior officers and embassies
- bakers
- storeman

Progression in rank can be comparatively speedy. In order to keep a young and active force, retirement is deemed to be at the age of 40. It is many a service person's dream to run their own unit and so an average dedicated individual could go up a rank every three to four years, gaining good managerial skills on the way. The military is renowned for its managerial qualities and professional standards. Adherence to procedures in every discipline within the forces ensures a smooth running and efficient operation, paramount in importance for success.

WELFARE SECTOR

Homes for the elderly

These homes are available for private care as well as through the National Health Service. They are divided into two distinct categories.

NURSING HOMES

Clients require nursing care due to infirmity. These establishments resemble hospitals, with full nursing care provided by qualified nurses.

RESIDENTIAL CARE HOMES

These are for clients who do not require constant nursing though care assistants are available. Residents will have a room of their own, or share with another, and use communal rooms for leisure and dining. In some establishments the residents have independent accommodation but with an emergency bell, should it be necessary to call a warden.

In providing hospitality in homes for the elderly there are certain considerations:

Food

As residents are, perforce, eating in all the time, the food must be interesting and appetising. As people become older, their appetite and ability to taste may fail and in losing interest in food, they may well lose their health also. Meeting any specific dietary needs is an equally important factor in maintaining health.

Residencies

Although it may be difficult, it is important to provide as much privacy as possible, in order to ensure comfort and peace of mind. Staff will need to clean and check rooms regularly, although some residents may prefer some independence. During the design of the building, planners should consider that light switches need to be lower so those in wheelchairs can reach them. Rails are needed to assist and give confidence with walking, especially in a long hall or corridor. Stairs can be a problem, so stair-chairs and lifts are a must. Emergency call buttons are usually placed within easy reach in all rooms. Bathrooms must be designed so that staff are able to assist residents into and out of baths without discomfort for either party and to minimize risk of accidents.

Visits

In order to avoid the onset of ill-health due to boredom and inactivity, it is a good idea to involve the more able residents in accepting visitors and going on organized outings. Making visits to the local hairdresser, theatre, community centre or receiving visits from family and friends can be the highlight of the week.

Meals on wheels

Hot meals delivered seven days a week to the old and infirm from central kitchens could be a thing of the past as local authorities turn to frozen ready-meal suppliers in an attempt to reduce costs, widen choice and maintain standards. The mainstay of the service is the Women's Royal Voluntary Service (WRVS), which has just completed 50 years' involvement with meals on wheels.

One frozen ready-meals supplier has recently won a contract to supply 8500 meals a week to two London boroughs. This growth in demand for its services may be due to the average cost per meal of approximately £2.75 compared to between £3 and £4 per meal under the traditional system. Customers are supplied with a freezer and a steamer to heat their meals. They choose their menu from a brochure and receive their choices just once a week. The scheme offers wider choice, flexibility of eating times and a better quality product that has not been kept warm for a long time.

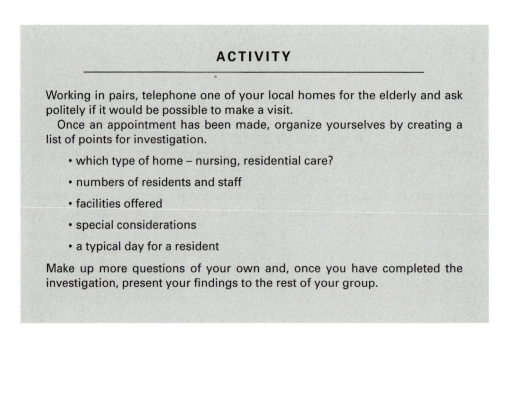

ACTIVITY

Working in pairs, telephone one of your local homes for the elderly and ask politely if it would be possible to make a visit.

Once an appointment has been made, organize yourselves by creating a list of points for investigation.

- which type of home – nursing, residential care?

- numbers of residents and staff

- facilities offered

- special considerations

- a typical day for a resident

Make up more questions of your own and, once you have completed the investigation, present your findings to the rest of your group.

ACTIVITY

1. In the *commercial sector* of the industry, research and find out as much as you can about one of the following areas:

- a mainline railway station
- an airport
- a seafront area
- ferry terminal
- leisure centre
- indoor shopping complex
- holiday camp

In the *service sector* of the industry, research and find out as much as you can about one of the following areas:

- hospitals
- homes for the elderly
- boarding schools
- industrial catering

Present your work as professionally as possible, including maps, diagrams, photographs, lists, graphs and charts where possible, as well as text.

2. Key to services

Draw a map of your area and indicate, using a 'key', where commercial and service establishments can be found.

In order to research this information, you may need to visit your local library, study publicity material and local newspapers, and visit the local tourist office. Include with your map a list of sources of information.

EMPLOYMENT IN HOSPITALITY AND CATERING

The industry is the largest employer in the UK, representing more than 10 per cent of the workforce. It is difficult to include details of every employment opportunity within the widely differing aspects of the industry, as careers within the sectors will vary according to the type and size of establishment. Most organizations will provide any or all of the following areas for employment:

- service of food and drink
- accommodation services
- leisure facilities
- support administration
- reception

Each area will open differing career paths for the trainee, and new roles and opportunities in this fast-moving service sector are increasing.

Without qualifications
NVQ 1
GCSE (any grade)
NVQ 2
or GNVQ Intermediate
GCSE (4 at A–C)
GNVQ Advanced
NVQ 3
HND
University degree

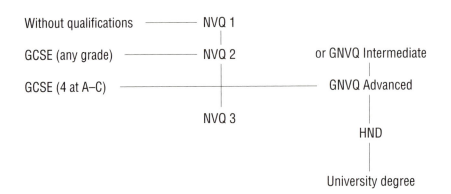

Key: GCSE: General Certificate of Education; NVQ: National Vocational Qualifications (levels 2, 3, 4 and 5); GNVQ: General National Vocational Qualifications (Intermediate and Advanced); HND: Higher National Diploma in Hospitality

Figure 1.3 Qualifications path in the hospitality and catering industry

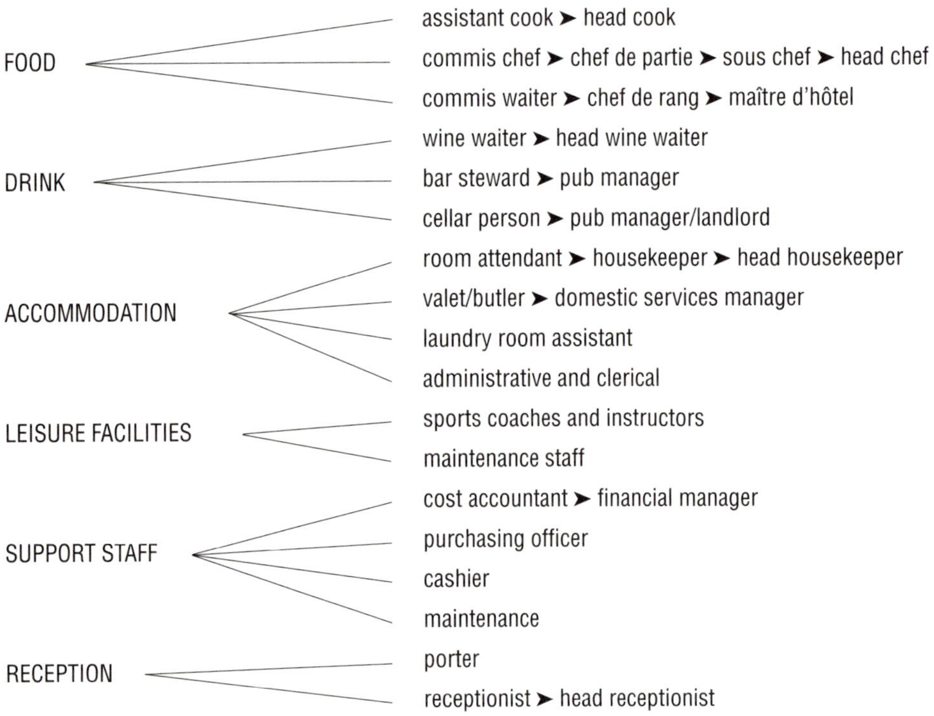

FOOD
assistant cook ➤ head cook
commis chef ➤ chef de partie ➤ sous chef ➤ head chef
commis waiter ➤ chef de rang ➤ maître d'hôtel
DRINK
wine waiter ➤ head wine waiter
bar steward ➤ pub manager
cellar person ➤ pub manager/landlord
ACCOMMODATION
room attendant ➤ housekeeper ➤ head housekeeper
valet/butler ➤ domestic services manager
laundry room assistant
administrative and clerical
LEISURE FACILITIES
sports coaches and instructors
maintenance staff
SUPPORT STAFF
cost accountant ➤ financial manager
purchasing officer
cashier
maintenance
RECEPTION
porter
receptionist ➤ head receptionist

Figure 1.4 Some typical careers

Employment opportunities

The section below will describe a selection of job roles and employment opportunities available (see Figure 1.4) within the commercial and service sectors of the hospitality and catering industry. Qualifications, training, and personal attributes are briefly described, together with working conditions and possible routes for progression. The jobs described may be found in the following sectors of the industry:

- holiday centres
- hotels and guesthouses
- clubs
- restaurants
- hospitals
- education
- travel organizations

HOLIDAY CENTRE STAFF

Both full- and part-time, casual or career opportunities are available. Positions vary due to the range of facilities offered at centres: kitchen work, restaurant service, bars, reception, accommodation and entertainment organization. A general manager will be in overall charge of staffing, finance and the daily operations.

Ideal qualifications	Experience/qualities	Progression

A level or HND
Degree for larger companies
	Possible sporting experience.
	Motivation
	Outgoing personality
	Organizational flair.
	Ability to forward plan
		Through ranks to management
		  or via training programmes
		Basic training at start of season
		  for casual staff

Working conditions	Work role
Long hours Shift work Possibly seasonal (some open all year) Live-in accommodation Entertainment and shops	Responsible to supervisor Versatile diverse range of jobs Food preparation and service

HOTEL HOUSEKEEPER

This post in larger hotels is a separate job role. Within a smaller establishment and guesthouse the owner or hotel manager may well undertake the responsibilities of accommodation. (The responsibilities of the hotel housekeeper are described on page 157.)

Ideal qualifications	Experience/qualities	Progression
4 GCSEs GNVQ A levels City & Guilds 708 HND	Organizational skills Ability to motivate staff Desire for cleanliness Smart appearance	After a full or part-time course or thorough in-house training

Working conditions	Work role
May begin as early as 6.30 a.m. Often shifts, weekend work – requiring live-in status Office work, but mostly on move all day	Responsible to manager Care of all public areas Ordering cleaning materials Organization of staff

CONFERENCE AND BANQUETING MANAGER

In many larger establishments, such as hotels, restaurants, university halls and leisure centres, there is a specific responsibility for someone to organize special functions. These events range from a special luncheon to weddings and even a seminar that may last for several days. Often there are large numbers of guests involved and to ensure smooth running of events the occasion has to be thoroughly organized in every detail.

Ideal qualifications	Experience/qualities	Progression

GNVQ Advanced
HND
Degree
	Previous experience in related career
	    (e.g. restaurant post; manager
	    catering admin.)
	Meticulous attention to detail
	Outgoing personality
	Accounting experience
		An important specialist
		There is continued expansion
		    in event catering and large
		    organizations offer a range
		    of opportunities

Working conditions	Work role

Flexibility – long summer months
Event catering may involve working
    in unfamiliar surroundings
Long hours – clients expect their
    'personal contact' to be at their event
	Organize staff and equipment
	Ordering requirements
	Customer care
	Handling of payment
	Overseeing whole operation

WAITER AND WAITRESS

Whether in a hotel or restaurant, on a liner or at a railway station, the exact job role depends upon the type of outlet. A greater level of skill and knowledge will of course be necessary in a luxury restaurant as opposed to a cafeteria or pub. In smaller establishments the role may well be undertaken by an owner or manager as part of the versatile nature of hospitality and in a larger hotel some cooking skills may be required for gueridon service. The responsibilities of the waiter and waitress are described on pages 278–80.

Ideal qualifications	Qualities	Progression
Youth Training	Well spoken	Can be fast with staff turnover high
Commis waiter/ess	Organized	Promotion is usually through experience
GNVQ or NVQ 2	Engaging personality	
Restaurant and bar service	Unflappable	

Working conditions	Work role
Hours vary and include weekend work	Responsible to maître d'hôtel or manager/owner
7 a.m. start (hotel or guesthouse)	Customer service of food/drink
Lunchtime until after midnight (restaurant)	Taking orders/payment
Food provided whilst on duty	Preparing starters/desserts

CHEF AND COOK

The basic difference between a chef and cook is that in a hotel the title is usually chef whereas in most other catering establishments the term is cook. In most positions cooks are expected to be as skilled as chefs and so there is little difference in reality. Call-order cooks work in fast-food establishments. There are many different types of chef and their responsibilities are explained in more detail on pages 180–1.

Ideal qualifications	Qualities	Progression
NVQ 2 or 3	Genuine interest in food	Part or full-time training at college/with
Food prep. and cooking	Methodical	employer
GNVQ Intermediate	Individual flair	Demand high, promotion rapid
	Sense of timing	
	Highly skilled	

Working conditions	Work role
Start at 6.30 a.m. in a hotel or airport	Preparation of food
Restaurant /takeaway finish after midnight	Cleaning duties
Five shifts worked then two days off	Menu planning and costing
Some posts accommodation and meals	Food ordering
Shop hours in a sandwich bar	Stocktaking

RECEPTIONIST

Wherever the reception, this role is the hub of activity for the whole establishment. Constantly in touch with guests, administration and hospitality staff in hotels, leisure centres, hospitals, welfare establishments, holiday centres, industry and many many more. The extent of the duties will vary according to the type and size of the reception; these are described on pages 112–14.

Ideal qualifications	Experience/qualities	Progression
NVQ 2 Hotel reception and front office GNVQ Advanced HND University degree Over 18 years old	Patient and friendly Outgoing personality Organizational skills Computer literacy Numeracy	Receptionist duties can lead to front office (FO) supervisor then FO manager

Working conditions	Work role
Long hours Evening and weekend shifts Usually uniform is worn Emphasis on smart appearance Accommodation provided Meals may be taken on duty	Telephonist duties Customer service Handling payments Booking rooms Computing

ACTIVITY

Keep a scrapbook or create a file.

Throughout your training, collect information with regard to career paths in the hospitality and catering industry. In an ever-changing industry this will keep you up to date with opportunities open to you.

Sources of information may be:

Newspapers
Trade journals
Your college/school library and staff
Local library
Job centres
Career conventions
Trade exhibitions
Visits and tours to various establishments during your course
Hotel, Catering and Institutional Management Association
Hotel and Catering Training Board
Hotel and Catering Training Company

PUBLICAN

The role of publican has changed to more than just the keeping of a good cellar. Services he or she may need to provide are good food in bars and restaurants, family rooms and play areas for children. The publican may be:

- a self-employed owner of the public house with no ties to a specific brewery (a free house)
- a tenant who rents his property from a brewery and keeps the profits
- a manager who runs the public house for one of the bigger breweries and is salaried

Ideal qualifications	Experience/qualities	Progression
CGLI Pub Catering	Restaurant/catering/	60 per cent of publicans are
HCTC Introductory	social club management	now self-employed
The Brewers' Society	Sociable and friendly	Some take positions as bar
– Licensed Trade Diploma	Firm manner	managers in large hotels/clubs
British Institute of	Organizing ability	
Innkeeping membership	Good numeracy	

Working conditions	Work role
Unconventional hours	Service of alcoholic beverages
– most of the day and evening	Service of food (maybe also food preparation)
Much preparation outside opening hours	Handling of payment
Living accommodation	Organization of staff

STEWARD AND STEWARDESS

Traditionally thought of as working on an airliner but now also part of other transport – trains, ferries, hovercraft and cruise liners. Working in bars, restaurants, shops and offering a trolley service, the role is primarily involved with ensuring passengers are comfortable and happy.

Ideal qualifications	Experience/qualities	Progression
In-service training	Sea steward or hotel work an advantage	Rail – many openings but
National Sea Training	Outgoing personality	most based in London
Catering award	Smart appearance	Sea – limited openings on ferries,
NVQ 2	Good sense of balance (sea or air)	better on cruises
GNVQ Advanced	Good at working with others	Air – strict entry rules
		Promotions to chief steward

Working conditions	Work role
Long shifts, working in uniform,	May be some food preparation
at sea or in flight, then a long break	Food service
Time off for exploring foreign places	Drink preparation and service
Accommodation and food provided	Cleaning duties
Cleaning duties add to the workload	Handling payments
Free uniform	Customer care
Reduced-rate travel when off duty	

ROADSIDE CATERING STAFF

There are a wide variety of opportunities provided by motorway service stations, budget lodges and public house restaurants on busy intersections, not to mention the kerbside cafeterias and heavy transport stops. On smaller sites all staff tend to be involved with more than one job.

Ideal qualifications	Experience/qualities	Progression

On the job training
NVQ 2
Supervisors –
  GNVQ (Advanced)
  HND
	Adaptability
	Outgoing personality
	Unflappable
	Numeracy
		Little opportunity for advancing
		  in a small business
		Large hotel and leisure chains
		  offer in-service training

Working conditions	Work role
Long shifts, sometimes 24 hours in one day (but under-18s must not work after 10 p.m.) Meals on duty Service every day of the year Most staff wear uniforms	Food preparation/service Customer care Some cleaning duties Responsible to manager Handling cash/payment

The following job descriptions are kindly provided by the Prue Leith Organisation.

A job description describes precisely the role and responsibilities of a particular job title.

SAMPLE JOB DESCRIPTIONS

JOB TITLE:	**Cashier**
RESPONSIBLE TO:	Catering manager
RESPONSIBLE FOR:	N/A
JOB SUMMARY:	To operate the tills and assist with the recording and banking of all takings to the satisfaction of Leith's management and the client.
MAIN DUTIES:	— To operate a pre-programmed till during service recording items sold accurately and in accordance with Leith's standards.
	— To handle money efficiently and accurately so the till reading and money balance at the close of every shift.
	— Ensure floats and till drawers are secure before banking takings.
	— To serve customers and behave in a pleasant and courteous manner at all times.
	— Assist customers with problems or queries.
	— To be familiar with portions, ingredients of dishes and prices.
Cleaning	— To carry out designated cleaning duties ensuring the highest possible standards of cleanliness and hygiene.
General	— To assist the catering assistants with food production and service when required.
	— To carry out any other reasonable duties.

ACTIVITY

Everyone has strengths and weaknesses and it is essential for these to be identified in individuals to ensure the correct career path has been chosen.

Within small groups develop a list to investigate your own strengths and weaknesses. Ask you friends and colleagues to offer opinions as well as indentifying you own feelings. These are points to get you started:

	POOR	EXCELLENT	GOOD
Communications: verbal			
written			
Calculations			
Working with people			
Dislike of shift work/ unsociable hours			
Timekeeping			
Problem solving			
Managing people			
Outgoing personality			
Quiet personality			
Enthusiastic			
Determined			
Lack of confidence			
Impatience			

Identify the areas of the hospitality and catering industry that you are interested in and write down the possible requirements for several positions. Complete this exercise at the beginning of your course and again nearing the end. Note any changes in your capabilities and career aspirations.

JOB TITLE:	Conference rooms waiter/waitress
RESPONSIBLE TO:	Conference rooms supervisor
RESPONSIBLE FOR:	N/A
JOB SUMMARY:	To provide a service of teas, coffees and lunches to conference rooms, in a discreet and courteous manner, to meet the standards set by Leith's management and the client.

MAIN DUTIES:

Food preparation and service

— Ensure that the conference rooms are serviced quickly and efficiently to the required standards.

(continues overleaf)

— Provide conference rooms with tea and coffee as required.

— Prepare and serve working lunches to the standards set by Leith's management.

— Maintain strict portion controls in accordance with the standards set by the Catering Manager and Leith's management.

— To be familiar with menus and ingredients.

— Maintain stock levels and ensure the Conference Room supervisor is informed of any stock requirements.

— Assist with clients' problems and queries.

Cleaning — To carry out designated cleaning duties, in the preparation, service and dining areas ensuring the highest standard of cleanliness and hygiene.

General — To carry out any other reasonable duties.

JOB TITLE:	**Head chef**
RESPONSIBLE TO:	Catering manager
RESPONSIBLE FOR:	Kitchen staff and porters
JOB SUMMARY:	To work closely with the catering manager to ensure the highest standard of food is produced and presented in the staff restaurant and dining rooms to meet the standards set by Leith's management and the client.
	To deputize in the catering manager's absence.

MAIN DUTIES:
Food production and service

— Liaise with the catering manager on a daily basis regarding food production and service.

— To ensure production and presentation of menu items on the daily menu by service times.

— Ensure that preparation, presentation and portion control are kept to the standards set by Leith's.

— Monitor food levels and presentation during service periods.

Menu Planning — Advance weekly menu planning for the staff restaurant in conjunction with the catering manager.

— Liaise with the client regarding requirements in absence of catering manager.

Staff supervision and training

— Manage the kitchen staff to ensure all tasks are completed to the required standards.

— Ensure staff are familiar with the preparation and presentation of all food items.

(continues overleaf)

Ordering	— Maintain tight control of stock, keeping levels to a minimum and implementing good stock rotation.
	— Control costs to keep within budget guidelines.
	— Daily ordering of supplies in accordance with Leith's purchasing policy.
	— Monitoring of orders i.e. checking deliveries for quality, quantity and reporting any problems. Liaising with suppliers for best market prices and produce.
Hygiene, health and safety	
	— To carry out hygiene and temperature checks at specified intervals and record them on the company documentation.
	— In conjunction with the catering manager establish cleaning schedules and ensure the staff follow them.
	— Ensure the kitchen and related work areas are left clean and tidy at the end of each day.
	— To pay attention to all aspects of health and safety within the operation. Report any problem areas to the catering manager.
General	— To carry out any reasonable request from the client or Leith's management.

Jobsearch support

There are several organizations who are able to assist with finding the right employment for you.

CAREERS CENTRES

A central point of communication for many businesses and all educational establishments who have places to offer. These centres employ specialists called careers officers who use computerized systems to support their information gathering. They visit schools and colleges to give guidance in careers with advice for further education or employment prospects. A valuable source of information.

JOBCENTRES

For those ready for employment, jobcentres advertise any vacancies available in their local area even though they are run nationally. Jobclubs have evolved from these centres, where prospective employees can meet on a weekly basis to swap ideas and gain confidence in writing their curriculum vitae and applications.

TRAINING ENTERPRISE COUNCIL

A government-funded organization offering free advice and guidance to assist clients in the setting up of new businesses. It is involved also with training programmes and innovations in education in their local area.

TRAINING ENTITLEMENT CREDITS

Offered to all school leavers who wish to take up training whilst in a place of work. Employers are given financial support to allow an employee time to attend a college course on a part-time basis. The employee is given 'training credits' to a specific value to be spent on a course and at an educational establishment of their choice, but of course one which will progress their career choice. Help can also be given towards travelling costs.

Useful organizations

Brewers and Licensed Retailers Association, 42 Portman Square, London W1H 0BB

British Institute of Cleaning Science, Whitworth Chambers, George Row, Northampton NN1 1DF

British Hospitality Association, 40 Duke Street, London W1M 6HR

British Institute of Management, Corby, Northamptonshire. 01536 204222

British Safety Council, 70, Chancellors Road, London W6 9RS

British Standards Institution, 2 Park Street, London W1A 2BS

Catering Managers Association, Mount Pleasant, Egton, Whitby, Yorkshire YO21 1UE

Coffee Information Centre, 21 Berners Street, London W1P 4DD

Cookery and Food Association, 1 Victoria Parade, 331 Sandycombe Road, Richmond, Surrey TW9 3NB

Department of Trade and Industry, 123 Victoria Street, London SW1E 6RB

English Heritage, 23 Savile Row, London W1X 1AB

English Tourist Board, Thames Tower, Blacks Road, Hammersmith, London W6 9EL

Flour Advisory Bureau, 21 Arlington Street, London SW1A 1RN

Fresh Fruit and Vegetable Information Bureau, Bury House, 126–128 Cromwell Road, London SW7

Health and Safety Executive, Broad Lane, Sheffield, Yorkshire S3 7HQ

Health Education Authority, Hamilton House, London WC1H 9TX

Hospital Caterers Association, St James University Hospital, Beckett St, Leeds LS9 7TF

Institute of Food Science and Technology, 5 Cambridge Court, 210 Shepherd's Bush Road, London W6 7NL

Institute of Meat, Churchill Building, Langford, Bristol BS18 7DY

Leisure Studies Association, Chelsea School Research Centre, University of Brighton, Eastbourne BN20 7SP

London Tourist Board, London Visitor and Convention Bureau, 26 Grosvener Gardens, London SW1V 0DV

Ministry of Agriculture Fisheries and Food, Great Westminster House, Horseferry Rd, London SW1P 2AE

National Association of Master Bakers, Confectioners and Caterers, 21 Baldock Street, Ware, Hertfordshire SG12 9DH

National Trust, 36 Queen Anne's Gate, London SW1H 9AS

Nutrition Society, 10 Cambridge Court, 210 Shepherd's Bush Road, London W6 7NJ

Pizza and Pasta Association, 29 Market Place, Wantage, Oxfordshire OX12 8PG

Royal Institute of Public Health and Hygiene, 28 Portland Place, London W1N 4DE

Royal Society of Health, RSH House, 38a St George's Drive, London SW1V 4BH

Sea Fish Industry Authority, 18 Logie Mill, Logie Green Road, Edinburgh EH7 4HG

Sports Council, 16 Upper Woburn Place, London WC1H 0QP

Tea Council, Sir John Lyon House, 5 High Timber Street, London EC4V 3NJ

Vegetarian Society, Parkdale, Dunham Road, Altringham, Cheshire WA14 4QG

Educational organizations

British Institute of Innkeeping, 42 Portman Square, London W1H 0BB

Business and Technician Education Council, Central House, Upper Woburn Place, London WC1H 0HH

City and Guilds of London Institute, 1 Giltspur Street, London EC1A 9DD

Council for National Academic Awards, 344–54 Grays Inn Road, London WC1X 8BP

Hotel Catering and Institutional Management Association, 191 Trinity Rd, London SW17 7HN

Hotel and Catering Training Company, International House, High Street, Ealing, London W5 5DB

Wine and Spirit Education Trust, 5 Kings House, Kennet Wharf Lane, Upper Thames St, London EC4R 1QS

Useful trade journals and magazines

Most are available from newsagents, although some are publications printed specifically for professional associations and available directly from the publisher. An extensive list of periodicals is available in the HCIMA reference book. Researching in current publications plays a vital part for all interested in the hospitality industry in keeping up to date with recent developments.

A la carte, IPC Magazines Ltd, Kings Reach Tower, Stamford St, London SE1 9LS

Brewing Review, Brewers' Society, 42 Portman Square, London W1H 0BB

British Hotelier and Restaurateur, Economist Publications, 40 Duke St, London W1A 1DW

Caterer and Hotelkeeper, Reed Business Publishing, Quadrant House, The Quadrant, Sutton, Surrey SM2 5AS

Catering, Dewberry Publication Services, 161–5 Greenwich High Road, London SE10 8JA

Catering Update, Reed Business Publishing (as above)

Chef, Reed Business Publishing (as above)

Hospitality, HCIMA Publications, 119 Trinity Rd, London W17 7HN

Hotel Catering Review, Jemma Publications, 22 Brookfield Avenue, Blackrock, Co. Dublin

Leisure Management, Leisure Publications, 40 Bancroft, Hitchen, Herts SG5 1YL

International Tourism Quarterly, Economist Publications (as above)

Marketing, Haymarket Magazines, 22 Lancaster Gate, London W2 3LY

Nutrition and Food Science, Forbes Publications, 120 Bayswater Road, London W2 3JH

Popular Foodservice, Reed Business Publishing (as above)

Pub Caterer, Reed Business Publishing (as above)

Publican, 29–31 Lower Coombe Street, Croydon CR9 1LX

Travel and Tourism Analyst, Economist Publications (as above)

Travel Trade Gazette, TTG Ltd, Morgan Grampian House, 30 Calderwood Street, London SE18 6QH

Which, The Consumer's Association, 14 Buckingham Street, London WC2N 6DS

Wine, EVRO Publishing, Thames House, 5–6 Church Street, Twickenham, Middlesex TW1 3NJ

THE ESTABLISHMENT IN CONTEXT

Beefeater (Part of Whitbread PLC)

Halfway House
Dunstable
Bedfordshire

Beefeater
Restaurant & Pub

Set on a very busy corner between Dunstable and Luton, close to Junction 11 of the M1, this house obviously gets its name from its position between the two towns. The building has been decorated on the outside with trellis, hanging baskets and window canopies to catch the eye and create a welcome. The area in front of the building is devoted to car parking and due to the busy crossroads there is a separate entrance and exit gate so that customers can leave safely into the flow of traffic. Inside, a small reception area is situated just in the doorway from where customers are directed to their table or to the bar lounge. Interiors are designed to create an 'olde worlde' atmosphere of niches, plants and wooden beams with historical artefacts dotted on

shelves to created a talking point for customers. Subtle lighting, music and an occasional games machine add to the atmosphere.

At present there are 280 Beefeater Restaurant and Pubs nationwide with an aim to expand this number to 500 by the year 2000. Many Beefeaters have a Travel Inn on the same site offering budget accommodation.

MANAGEMENT

Management staff are recruited nationally. Beefeater like to employ a management team of two, one male and one female, for joint responsibility in the day-to-day running of a busy pub-restaurant. An area manager offers advice and support. A few restaurants are designated as 'training houses' with selected teams being responsible for the training of potential managers before they can take on their own establishment.

The marketing of each restaurant is very much at local level. Gaining a reputation in their own area, managers are responsible for meeting company targets and good business levels. This can be assisted by:

• local newspaper advertising
• vouchers through doors
• in-house draw for free dining

Managers are at liberty within company guidelines to offer other services, such as breakfast and afternoon tea, but this would vary from one area to another as each is trying to meet local needs. Different sites demand different service when some are in-town and others in drive-out locations. In maintaining standards Beefeater customers are offered an opinion card to comment on their visit. This is then put into a free monthly draw. Other methods of quality control include the employment of an agency to provide 'mystery diners' who then submit a report each month on establishments visited. Managers never know the identity of these people.

SERVICE NICHE

The unique selling points include

- individual character of establishments
- customer care, friendly service
- comfort
- menu for all tastes and occasions at affordable prices

All age groups are welcome but the target customers include:

- couples and those in the older age bracket, who enjoy their food served in traditional surroundings
- young people for functions and parties
- families with young children who are made to feel at ease
- in some establishments, stopover customers from Travel Inn

FRONT OF HOUSE

Typical of the Beefeater chain, this type of restaurant has an approximate capacity of 130 covers. For this number there would be possibly one full-time server and many permanent part-time servers, who work various shifts of four or five staff at a time. Lunchtime and evening service must be covered every day of the week and busy times such as Saturday evening and Sunday lunchtime command a higher staffing ratio. Three staff in the front of house operation have specific duties:

- at the desk
- seating customers and re-setting of tables
- service support and progress chaser

On entering a Beefeater, customers will be shown to their table and introduced to their server by name. A drinks order is taken immediately, bread offered and the information entered immediately into a point of sale terminal where an invoice number is automatically raised. Automatic despatch of this order and subsequently a food order, saves time and improves efficiency, as one copy goes directly to the bar for drinks service and another to the kitchen for the food to be produced. It is hoped that customers may be seated at 15 minute intervals to ensure a smooth flow in service. Management expect a party of four to take approximately 1.5 hours to complete a meal and a party of eight 2 hours. In this way it is possible to control booking, use facilities to the full and ensure good service. Each server would expect to serve between 35 and 40 covers on a busy shift and in the bar as much as £5,000 could be taken in one evening. It is important that servers should wear comfortable clothing which portrays the correct company image and so a standard uniform is provided of short-sleeved blouse or shirt and navy skirt with a red print or navy trousers. A navy neck apron with pink edges completes the ensemble for the ladies. At the point of sale terminal the length of time it takes for a server to complete service to a group of customers is measured. When customers are ready to pay, the bill is easily retrieved and offered to them. Method of payment is recorded for future reference. All details from this terminal are used for detailed reports on each service session, in maintaining business records for head office and for predicting future business trends.

Very many staff are employed through recommendations, some through the local job centre and some by company transfer. Staff are usually local people who may take full- or part-time work and are happy to work shifts. There are no specific entry requirements for employment with Beefeater, apart from an ability to get on well with people and work as part of a team. Also, flexibility of skills is a useful asset when asked to transfer from the restaurant to the bar, or from reception duties to the kitchen. Training is completed all in-house and the company do not offer sponsorship for external qualifications. However, staff are encouraged to progress and, with ability and confidence, there is every opportunity to work up to the post of manager and beyond. On-the-job trainers are staff who are given extra responsibility within each establishment. New staff are immediately put on to a basic training programme called the 'silver award', which covers such areas as:

- establishment and personal hygiene
- conduct
- dress codes
- service of food and beverages
- handling cash

A departmental supervisor is designated as a 'gold award' trainer. This award is offered when the silver award basic skills are extended and marketing skills are added.

BACK OF HOUSE

Behind the scenes in the kitchen, a printer by the grill will automatically receive customer orders and these are processed as they are received. Hot starters and main courses are produced within the grill area, cold starters and sweets are prepared (traditionally by the servers themselves) on a chilled table in a separate area. Other equipment may include a deep fat fryer, microwave and oven. Nothing is pre-cooked in a Beefeater although some convenience products are used. Staff requirements are for approximately three chefs on each shift. A full complement of chefs may be two commis and four grill chefs working split shifts to cover the weekdays and as many as four chefs employed all day at weekends. There is little room for individual flair as company recipes and service standards must be strictly adhered to in order to maintain the same menu nationwide. Minimal changes to the menus occur about four times a year to encourage repeat custom and occasionally there is a major change. A head chef is responsible to his manager for adhering to laid down percentage profits, stock levels and ordering of commodities from designated suppliers.

HOUSEKEEPING

Cleaning of all public areas is carried out by contracted personnel who arrive very early in the morning. Cleaning staff are expected to be honest and trustworthy as well as thorough, as they are often in the establishment when no one else is on duty. Chefs are responsible for the cleaning of the kitchen and bar staff for behind the bar. Every six months the contract cleaners carry out a 'deep clean'. It would be expected that total refurbishment of the restaurant and bar would take place every five years.

Pizza Hut (Part of Whitbread PLC)

555 Midsummer Boulevard
Milton Keynes
Buckinghamshire

Holding a prime site, centrally located within a very busy city centre shopping mall of Milton Keynes, Pizza Hut here has an added advantage of two entrances. The one from the shopping mall appeals to tired and hungry shoppers as they pass and the other from the car park appeals not only to shoppers during opening hours, but to cinema-goers and others coming into the city centre for evening entertainment.

Classed as a quick service restaurant on an American Diner theme, Pizza Hut (in common with others in the chain) has a series of bench seats along the walls and several free tables in the centre area. A central service bar is easily accessed from both ends of the service area for servers and take-away customers. In this particular establishment the bench seats have been upholstered in an attractive fabric due to the amount of trade in the evenings. In other establishments there may be a leather-like finish for heavy daytime usage, or niched alcoves for more privacy. In this way, Pizza Hut can meet the demands of local trade with more effect. Tables are of polished dark wood which is easy to maintain and tables are set with napkins and cutlery alongside the cruet and menus. To finish setting the scene, there is subtle ceiling lighting and popular music playing.

MANAGEMENT

The restaurant manager has overall control of the day-to-day running of the establishment from a business point of view and of directing the labour force. The deputy manager assists in the running of the establishment during duty time and has added responsibility for recruitment. There are two assistant managers, who are able to operate the establishment in the absence of the others but have no added responsibilities.

Managers are recruited both centrally, nationally and locally. This shows the many ways possible for advancement with this company. Having been recruited locally into an establishment as a crew member, you may work your way up to management through the in-house training programme. Others may find that in gaining management skills as a deputy manager, they will then be able to take on full responsibility in another branch.

A personal identification card held by the manager allows access to different programmes on the electronic point of sale computer which offers instant information about sales, product cost analysis, stock control, ideal usage and actual usage.

SERVICE NICHE

The unique selling points include:

- convenience and accessibility of stores
- value for money
- children made welcome, parents feel comfortable
- quick service meal especially during lunchtime
- special offer meals advertised locally and nationwide
- full on-licence serving bottled beers and wines only

All age groups find Pizza Hut enjoyable for different reasons.

There are three distinct types of service

- dine in
- take-away
- delivery (some Pizza Hut are delivery only units)

Target customers include

- local office personnel and shoppers at lunchtimes
- families, late shoppers and cinema goers in the evening
- children's parties
- young people at good value times

There are often national promotions alongside any that the manager has put forward locally. A popular current one is the 'Hit the Hut' promotion, whereby customers may enjoy as many visits as they like to the buffet bar for a very reasonable set price. The selection of six types of pizza slices, pasta and salad are a big attraction and the staff constantly replenish to meet demand. Another, especially for the children, is the 'Icecream Factory'. For a set price the customer can pay as many visits as they like, helping themselves to icecream with many different toppings. These promotions not only bring in customers who will buy other products at the time, but they ensure a good return trade through customer satisfaction.

FRONT OF HOUSE

There are 162 covers in this Milton Keynes Pizza Hut, with approximately 60 tables to be served. Arranged all on one level with two entrances, the restaurant is able to serve disabled customers easily. On arrival at Pizza Hut, guests are requested to wait a few moments before being shown to their table. Occasionally, during peak periods, a queue may form but customers are usually quite happy to wait. Once at the table an order is taken for beverages, which are served whilst the food items are chosen. Time standards are set by head office and crew are expected to ensure that the wait for food is no longer than eight minutes. The turn around for a table of eight customers is approximately 1 hour.

The crew member takes all orders to an electronic point of sale and keys in the table number and own identity. From then on all items are entered under that identification will be held on a stored order receipt. Orders are despatched (in this instance by hand) to the kitchen for the production of the food. The points of sale are at the service bar and so the bar person can immediately prepare any drinks ordered. Crew members carry an order pad (of which one copy goes to the customer) and money pouch with them, so they only approach the point of sale when time permits. Thus they are able to present the bill at the table and give change without waste of time, which is especially useful for customers in a hurry.

When the customer leaves then the bill is called up, the information about money tendered is entered and the table number logged off. Credit for the service is automatically awarded to that member of staff.

In dividing the workload for the crew, the restaurant is divided into sections of either four tables with twelve covers or eight tables with twenty covers. The distance from the service bar, traffic flow, number of covers and popularity of the table position has an effect on whether an experienced member of staff or a trainee works it. In the more popular section there tends to be more tips from customers and so this area will be allocated in rotation.

At Milton Keynes there are eight full-time crew working 32–39 hours per week on a split shift basis (mornings and evenings). There are, in addition, 35 permanent part-time servers offering a broad availability of from 5–10 hours per week on shifts as the restaurant is open every day. In recruiting, the manager will be looking for people who are considerate and able to communicate well. Those who have a bubbly personality and character, rather than someone with experience. Working as part of a team is also important.

At interview, prospective employees are given the opportunity to come into the restaurant for three to four hours during service to see whether it really is a job they will enjoy. This process usually works in finalizing selection for both parties. The new employee is given 14–28 days of training with a designated member of staff. The company use the 'buddy' system, whereby the experienced crew member will pair with a trainee who will be given advice and support and will not have to bother management all the time. In developing confidence, the trainee is soon taking more initiatives.

Progression can be:
Crew — Trainer — Shift supervisor — Trainee manager — Manager — Area manager

BACK OF HOUSE

The type of production at Pizza Hut is referred to as a 'scud' operation. This means that most of the preparation is done before the restaurant opens, then food is produced to order in a very short time. The pizzas used to be prepared on the premises, but now they are bought into the premises already in the required shape and size. They are then held in a retarder (under refrigeration) until preparation time, when they are proven (allowed to lift) and retarded again ready for production. The pizzas offered are 'deep pan' which are thick-based, and 'Neapolitan', which are thin-based with a risen edge and are prepared from cornmeal.

The familiar toppings for pizzas are available: pre-cooked meats (e.g. salami, pepperoni); tuna, sweetcorn, olives (canned); fresh onions, peppers, mushrooms (all pre-prepared).

Fresh salad items, coleslaw and potato salad are prepared on the premises.

The work in the kitchen then involves preparation for the shift and organizing a good workflow to ensure fast service. This is done by turning the 'make' table around to face the oven. It has all the required ingredients to hand in a refrigerated unit above and below the table. There is a wall chart which shows all the products, the quantity of ingredients and the order in which to place them to ensure standardization. The crew then take the orders as they are presented, prepare the items on the order and place them straight into the oven. Running at a constant temperature of 275°C, the oven has two conveyor belts which deliver the cooked food through to the service bar in 6 minutes 30 seconds precisely. Starter items and garlic bread, which do not require as long to heat, are placed in the oven through a side door, either three-quarters or half way through the standard cooking period. All the food passing through the oven should match with the orders as they are passed back to the service bar, where a crew member cuts pizzas into portions and the very next person along will deliver to the table. It is vital that food arrives for the customer piping hot.

Time before service also includes preparation for the salad bars. In this restaurant there are two chilled self-service bars. Only one visit to the bar is allowed per payment, but these bars are usually refilled four times on a quiet shift! There are ten kitchen crew working straight shifts, each attending four or five of the busiest sessions during the week to reach a total of 39 hours. Staff must be dextrous and have good product knowledge.

HOUSEKEEPING

Cleaning of all public areas including the toilets is done by contract cleaners, who work before service time for three hours every day. Kitchen staff are responsible for the clearing of foodstuffs and cleaning of the kitchen after every shift.

T.G.I. Friday's (part of Whitbread PLC)

The American
Restaurant & Bar

Rugby Road,
Binley Woods,
Coventry

Purpose-built as an American style bistro and bar, the building stands out as colourful and modern on a very busy crossroad just ten minutes from Junction 2 of the M6 on the eastern edge of Coventry. One of only fifteen T.G.I. (Thank God It's) Friday's in this country, the corporate image of bold red and white stripes catches the eye in signs and window canopies. There is ample parking, surrounded with flowers and shrubs, and a patio, only used in fine weather! Inside the two-storey building, referred to as the 'store', a square central cocktail bar is the focal point. This area accommodates 80 people and a further 260 seats are available in various areas of the restaurant. These areas are set on different levels: the floor, the conservatory and the gallery. The atmosphere is created by low-level dark lighting, loud music and decorative paraphernalia typical of America. Tables are covered with thick, oilcloth-type covers in red and white stripes. Napkins, paper place mats and cutlery are set ready, and an air of relaxation ensures a warm welcome.

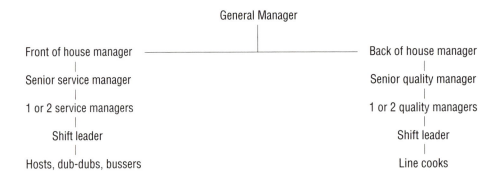

What can FRIDAYS do for you

Childrens face Painting Every Saturday and Sunday Afternoons

Business Lunch CLUB. See your Server.

MAGICIAN EVERY SUNDAY Afternoons

Over 500 COCKTAILS

take away service

MERCHANDISE HATS SWEATERS T-SHIRTS

T.G.I. FRIDAYS

CLUB Crayons drawing sheets young diners menu. and merchandise.

WATCH THIS SPACE

SPECIALTIES

PASTA

FETTUCINI ALFREDO WITH CHICKEN & HERBS
Sautéed slices of chicken breast, fresh mushrooms and red bell peppers tossed in our Alfredo sauce with basil pesto. Served with a Friday's House Salad. £9.10

BLACKENED CHICKEN ALFREDO
Friday's classic fettucini, topped with chicken breast blackened in spicy Cajun seasonings. Garnished with diced tomatoes and sliced green onions. Served with Friday's House Salad. £9.10

FETTUCINI IN MUSHROOM & HAM CREAM SAUCE
Fettucini smothered in a cream sauce with sliced mushrooms, ham and fresh Parmesan cheese. Served with a Friday's House Salad. £8.00

PASTA SANTA FE
Breast of chicken, sautéed with fresh hot peppers, mushrooms, green onions, red bell peppers, pecan nuts and pesto sauce atop steaming fettucini pasta. Served with a Friday's House Salad. £9.10

SZECHUAN SHRIMP ALFREDO
Shrimp, broccoli, water chestnuts and mushrooms tossed with fettucini and Alfredo sauce. Seasoned with garlic, ginger, sun-dried tomatoes, Hoisin and pepper sauces. Served with Friday's House Salad. £9.10

WARM GARLIC BREAD £1.50

BLACKENED-CAJUN CHICKEN
Breast of chicken seasoned with Cajun spices and blackened on a cast iron skillet. Served over brown rice pilaf and topped with a herb cream sauce. Accompanied by spicy black beans. £11.15

MUSHROOMS, CHICKEN AND MUSHROOMS
Deep-fried and topped with sautéed mushrooms and Mozzarella cheese. Served with fried mushrooms and a loaded baked potato. £11.15

SWEET AND SOUR CHICKEN
Breast of chicken lightly battered, fried golden, and tossed in a tangy sweet and sour sauce with pineapple, stir-fried snow peas, celery, onions and green and red bell peppers. Served with crisp Chinese noodles and brown rice pilaf. £10.70

SPICY THAI CHICKEN & NOODLES
Spicy Thai chicken stir-fried and tossed in fine noodles, hot peppers, mushrooms, green onions, red bell peppers & cashew nuts. £8.95

SOUTHWESTERN

...HILADAS
...n breast, green chillies and cheeses, ...n corn tortillas. Covered with ranchero ...ed Monterey Jack and Colby ...with diced tomatoes, guacamole, ...black beans with brown rice. £9.55

...d chicken breast, served on a bed ...ed bell peppers. Served with ...am, pico de gallo, fresh salsa, ...rm flour tortillas. £10.95

...oice cut beef steak on a bed ...ll peppers. Served with ...pico de gallo, fresh salsa, ...flour tortillas. £11.15

...on featuring slices of ...n on a bed of grilled ...wed with guacamole, ...sh salsa, Colby cheese ...£11.05

...ETABLE FAJITAS V
A selection of fresh seasonal vegetables, chargrilled and served on a bed of grilled onions and bell peppers. Served with guacamole, sour cream and pico de gallo, fresh salsa, Colby cheese and warm flour tortillas. £8.65

CHICKEN CHIMICHANGA
A flour tortilla filled with spicy chicken with mushrooms and Monterey Jack cheese, fried crisp and golden. Topped with ranchero sauce and melted Monterey Jack cheese. Served with guacamole salad and black beans with brown rice. £9.65

BEEF CHIMICHANGA
A flour tortilla filled with spicy beef, refried beans and Colby cheese, fried crisp and golden. Topped with ranchero sauce and melted Colby cheese. Served with guacamole salad and black beans with brown rice. £9.70

VEGETABLE CHIMICHANGA V
A flour tortilla filled with a selection of fresh seasonal vegetables, lightly spiced, fried crisp and golden. Topped with ranchero sauce and melted Monterey and Colby cheese. Served with guacamole salad and black beans with brown rice. £7.20

SIDE ORDERS

FRIDAY'S FRIES £1.35

WARM GARLIC BREAD £1.50

FRESH SEASONAL VEGETABLES £1.95

FRIDAY'S HOUSE SALAD £3.00

COLESLAW £1.95

BROWN RICE PILAF £1.70

BLACK BEANS AND BROWN RICE £2.60

BAKED POTATO £1.35

LOADED BAKED POTATO £1.95

Management

There is a general manager, who is responsible to Whitbread for the smooth running of the establishment as a whole. The management line is shown on page 52. The senior service manager is responsible for the everyday running, quality standards and training in front of house; the senior quality manager is responsible for the production from the kitchen and quality control at back of house. Since the opening of the new Travel Inn next door, service is now breakfast from 7 to 9 a.m. as well as lunchtime through to evening dinner, 12 noon till 12 midnight!

SERVICE NICHE

The unique selling points include:

- informal and personalized style of service provided by staff
- relaxed and friendly atmosphere
- busy location
- good value and good portion size
- exciting bar service and extensive cocktail menu
- late opening and evening entertainment
- each menu item produced from scratch

Target customers include:

- age group 20–45 years, who enjoy lively atmosphere
- business people for lunch
- family parties and celebrations, children especially welcome

FRONT OF HOUSE

At T.G.I. Friday's they have a theory call GET, which stands for the Guest Experience Time theory. This time is the expected experience time for guests from their arrival to be fully served, which is estimated, including eating time, to be 40 minutes. At the door guests are greeted by a host and seated within 30 seconds of arrival, when tables are free. However, as there is a 'no booking' policy, on busy occasions it is usual to seat guests at the bar to be entertained whilst waiting for a vacant table. It has been known for customers to wait for up to two hours to be seated, the restaurant is so popular. Hosts then act as the buffer between the queue and the servers, taking out nibbles and keeping guests posted on the table situation. On weekdays, there will be one host on duty during daytime and two or three in the evening. On Saturday as many as four hosts are needed with two spare to act as runners. This role is an important one of co-ordinating proceedings during hectically busy periods.

Once seated, the guests are introduced to their 'dub-dub' or server. This is a name imported from T.G.I. Friday's in America along with other unfamiliar words. The store philosophy is that the starter should be received by the guest within seven minutes of being seated, the dub-dub takes the order in a 'puppy-dog' position crouched to eye level with the table. This is a very unfamiliar stance to us, and yet it immediately puts the guest at ease as the server is not looming over whilst making choices. The dub-dub then uses an electronic point of sale with a touch screen system to identify and despatch the order for drinks straight to the bar, and for starters straight to the kitchen. By the time the next table has been seated and orders taken, the orders from the first group have been produced. The order for main course, which is expected to take only ten minutes to produce, is then despatched. When the dub-dubs are very busy and find it difficult to find time to serve desserts, there is a 'dessert weedie' to assist. A ticket accompanies all food and beverages produced so that there is no mix-up. This cycle of ordering and service ensures the dub-dubs constant service whilst on duty, which allows them to earn the commission which is paid on top of basic rate. Each will have a station of about five tables or 20 covers, the more experienced in the busier areas. A central cashier produces the guests' bill, which is presented for payment in a folded courtesy card. After leaving the table, guests may like to be seated at the bar and at this point a 'busser' assists the dub-dub in clearing the table to the bus-stand (sideboard) and replenishing for the next guests.

At the cocktail bar, the bartenders are good lookers, flamboyant and fun entertainers as well as servers. Anyone familiar with the film 'Cocktail' will realize that the idea of the service is to throw most of the glassware, bottles and ingredients in the air before putting them together. In fact, T.G.I. Friday's boasts that the film was based on their establishments in America. These bartenders undergo rigorous training as all alcohol is served on a free-pour basis instead of our usual method of measurement. If challenged by management during quality control, the alcohol is measured and should be very accurate to the designated amount. There are several hundred cocktails to be learnt, all written in a 46-page drinks menu. The bartenders take their own money rather than relying on a cashier and the till at the end of shift must be reconciled to within £3. There is an age rule of 21+ for guests at the bar but no shortage of crowds! As the bar is set in a square, there are four bartenders, each covering a corner. The guests are encouraged then to chat across the corner to one another and to the barman.

All employees are trained in 'sensitivity'. That means being sensitive to the guests' needs by 'reading' them and being totally familiar with company standards. It takes approximately six weeks to train a dub-dub because of the wide product knowledge needed. It takes about three months to train a bartender for similar reasons. Employees are encouraged to follow the style of dress in black skirt or trousers, red and white stripey t-shirt, red waiter's cloth and black boots. But from then on, each develops their own style of dress and can wear any style of hat with decorations and badges on braces. This identifies their own personality immediately and they are expected to be themselves, not what someone else expects of them. Employees are very outgoing and constantly smiling, sales people as well as servers. For employment here they must be able to get on with people, be adaptable and work well in a team. It is only the bussers who may be under 18 years of age as T.G.I. Friday's employs at 21+ years to ensure integrity and maturity in employees. Progression in employment is usually from the floor through in-house training. Experienced employees are given added responsibility of trainer and in some cases go to different establishments to train a whole team. In both front and back of house there is friendly rivalry and competition offered by management to maintain standards, improve sales on specific items and speed up service. The menu is changed slightly every six months to ensure continued interest by frequent guests.

BACK OF HOUSE

A purpose-built store and reception area is discreetly positioned at the back of the building. A quality manager will sign for all goods inwards. Groceries are delivered three times a week from a head office-approved supplier. Fresh produce is delivered daily from a local supplier. To ensure quality, at the opening of arrangements with a supplier, head office will supply to them a sample pack of the establishment's requirements so that there is no question as to the standard expected. There is a store steward on duty to maintain records and supply specified ingredients to the kitchen as they are required. The senior quality manager is responsible for an accurate weekly check of stores and of foods left in the kitchen. In general, only extra stock for two and a half days is held. The senior quality manager will also read computer data to accurately estimate the requirements for the next shift, comparing with previous sales. The computer will issue a broken-down list of ingredients for the steward to put out for line cooks to prepare their suggested numbers of dishes. In the refrigerators all foods are labelled with a coloured dot denoting day of placing in store so that the storage time can be identified quickly. The steward is also responsible for ensuring all foods are covered and in suitable containers.

KITCHEN ORGANIZATION

Kitchen employees, who wear loose white cotton clothing, with a white cap and black boots, must stay on the 'tiled' area and never cross the threshold on to the boarded area. There are five stations where the line cooks work. Each is responsible for a specific part of the menu and the orders from the dub-dubs are arranged so that they are easy to read for each section:

- broiler – steaks, burgers and fajitas
- fry station – potatoes, seafood
- sauté – eggs, pasta, cajun blackened items
- plate nacho – salads, sandwiches (a person with artistic flare for all those fussy bits!)

The very small galley kitchen consists of compact refrigerated drawers and bain-marie, burners, deep fryers and heated cabinets. Before the service shift begins, all foods are prepared and portioned before being shifted into the correct storage area, in the correctly sized container for each order. This speeds up preparation time during service.

The leader at the serving window is responsible for the workflow and when food is produced he groups dishes from each area to ensure the order is complete. He then adds garnishes before passing to the expediter through the window, who will add salads and sauces before despatch. When 'hands' is called, any dub-dub in the vicinity will collect the order, as it is important to deliver hot food immediately to the table.

The whole process is organized by a ticket-timing tracker, a computerized system which can be controlled by the senior quality manager or expediter. Table numbers appear on a screen and timing shows from the moment an order is received in the kitchen. The number glows red when 'time up' is near. This is to ensure that no order is lost and that all are despatched within ten minutes. A record is kept of all orders produced on a shift and this can be researched at any time for estimating purposes.

It takes approximately two weeks to train a line cook, then a test is undertaken and from then on the cook is watched but working solo until fully competent. After gaining confidence in one area, training may be undertaken in another area because flexibility is useful. A line cook may work 56 hours per week, if they wish.

HOUSEKEEPING

In the restaurant dub-dubs and bussers are expected to keep all areas in their own section clean and tidy and complete the work before the service shift begins. The floor is cleaned by contractors early in the morning. The toilets are checked every half-hour by a dub-dub and the check sheet signed to ensure they are clean and tidy. After closing at 12 midnight, the bar staff are expected to clean their bars, reconcile the tills and replenish stocks for the following shift. In the kitchen, the line cooks are responsible for the cleaning and replenishing in their own section and for cleaning the floor.

A maintenance man, who is on duty at the Coventry store, at the Travel Inn next door and is also shared with the Birmingham store, will undertake minor repairs where necessary to maintain all public and private areas. Refurbishment is completed as an on-going programme of maintenance.

Coventry Travel Inn (part of Whitbread PLC)

Rugby Road
Binley Woods
Coventry CV3 2TA

The Coventry Travel Inn is a purpose-built, two-storey budget accommodation and conference complex, situated next to T.G.I. Friday's (pp. 52–7) with ample car parking, adorned with shrubs and low plants. Its location is 10 minutes from Junction 2 of the M6, 5 minutes from the centre of Coventry and a 15-minute drive from the National Exhibition Centre. It has 48 bedrooms and one conference room that will accommodate up to 30 delegates.

Places of interest near the Travel Inn include:

- Coventry Cathedral
- the Georgian spa town of Royal Leamington Spa
- the park at Drayton Manor, Tamworth
- Drayton Manor park zoo
- Warwick Castle
- Stratford upon Avon
- entertainment at the National Exhibition Centre

The Travel Inn has a peaceful, friendly atmosphere, which is immediately apparent upon entering. Just what a tired motorist requires. The reception area is immediately opposite the entrance, so booking in is easily accomplished. This area is decorated in warm hues of creams and pinks with light oak wood fittings, creating a bright clean appearance.

MANAGEMENT

The Travel Inn shares a management team with T.G.I. Friday's. The senior service manager of T.G.I. Friday's has overall responsibility for the daily running of the complex and is responsible to Friday's general manager. He maintains the smooth running of the Travel Inn and the guest facilities. This includes quality checks of the accommodation areas and the provision of breakfast, evening meals, drinks and conference facilities, as required.

SERVICE NICHE

The unique selling points include:

- standard of service provided by the staff
- geographical location near the M6 and Coventry

- Whitbread central reservations service
- one fully equipped conference room
- en suite rooms with TV, tea- and coffee-making facilities
- family accommodation for no extra charge
- a flat rate budget charge for each room
- T.G.I. Friday's next door for the evening's entertainment and refreshment, as well as breakfast in the morning
- payment made when booking in, so guests are free to leave as early as they wish in the morning
- ample car parking adjacent to the accommodation

The target customers include:

- business people who need to stay away from home
- groups of business people who need to hold a small meeting
- families who wish to have budget priced accommodation
- leisure guests who wish to combine a visit to T.G.I. Friday's with accommodation

FRONT OF HOUSE

The front office

This area is well signposted from the car park. Once inside the glass door, the reception desk is immediately opposite. Friendly cheerful reception staff are there to register the guest and to take payment for accommodation. They wear a smart dark blue suit with a green, blue and white shirt. A name badge identifies them and helps to make the guest feel welcome. The pre-pay system enables guests to make an early start in the morning if they so wish and eliminates the necessity to queue up in the morning to pay the bill. The rooms are charged at a standard price, so pre-payment is easily calculated.

There is a receptionist on duty all day, and a night porter at reception during the night. The doors are locked at 23.00 hours but guests have a door key to let themselves in if they are out after this time. A security camera monitors the exterior areas 24 hours a day. The reception system is computerized, with guests' registration card details keyed straight in by a quick and simple process. Guests are offered the choice of a smoking or non-smoking room, asked the length of their stay and if they require a newspaper at breakfast time. There is a lead receptionist, two full-time receptionists and a part-time receptionist who works from 17.00 to 20.00 hours during the week and who will also cover staff leave days if necessary. Bookings can be made in advance either directly to the Travel Inn or through the Whitbread central reservations system. Rooms, once booked, are held until 18.00 after which time they may be sold. The occupancy list is updated every two hours to ensure that it is current should there be an emergency.

Public telephones are available for guests to use. These are in soundproof booths with a chair and good light to make communication and note-taking easy. These booths are phone card operated and situated on both the ground and first floor. A credit card phone facility is available in the conference room for the guests' use when the room is not in use.

In the reception area there is a wall-mounted message board next to the leaflet rack that displays the Travel Inn maps and information. This board is used to make the receiving of messages more efficient, as guests can check for themselves upon their arrival.

Services available to the guests from the front office include:

• fax transmissions
• photocopying of documents
• sale of telephone cards
• sale of gift vouchers
• loan of an iron for clothing
• loan of a hair dryer
• additional sachets of tea, coffee or hot chocolate
• toiletries travel pack for emergencies
• additional bedclothes, in case of need
• reservations facility for another Travel Inn or hotel within the Whitbread group
• advice about the location of local industries
• advice about motorway and road routes
• use of a baby alarm system
• child's cot and bedding
• heating of baby food and bottles

Conference facilities

There is a fully equipped conference room that will hold up to twenty delegates for a boardroom-style meeting, and a maximum of thirty-five delegates for a theatre-style meeting. The room includes use of a flip chart and pens, overhead projector and screen and TV/video player.

Refreshments for delegates can be provided if they are pre-booked by the conference organizer: tea, coffee and biscuits, sandwiches, or a light buffet meal. All refreshments are served in the conference room. Meals are available at the adjacent T.G.I. Friday's complex should these be required.

Other facilities include, fax transmissions, photocopying facilities and a message-taking service. There is a public toilet adjacent to the conference and the use of a credit card telephone in the room itself. Overnight accommodation can be booked for delegates, if required. Ample car parking is provided.

Conference bookings, which include the cost of the room hire, the services used and refreshments ordered, are paid for at the time of departure.

Food service

Because of the nature of the Travel Inn provision, there is no food served on the premises other than light buffets for conferences. Some Whitbread Travel Inns do have a coffee shop type provision on their premises. In the case of the Coventry Travel Inn, all breakfasts and evening meals and drinks are provided by the adjacent T.G.I. Friday's complex. In order to use these facilities, the guest books their breakfast requirements and newspaper upon their arrival. In the morning they walk under a short covered way from the Travel Inn to T.G.I. Friday's, where they are shown to their table, their newspaper is delivered and their breakfast is served. A choice of either continental or full English breakfast is offered, with a buffet style service for all cold items and table service for the hot items and beverages. Payment is taken at the end of the meal by the table service staff. Breakfast service is provides between the hours of 07.00 and 09.00 during the weekdays and between 08.00 and 10.00 at the weekends.

Should guests require an evening drink and/or a meal, they can use the T.G.I. Friday's provision, either for a full meal or for a drink and a snack. All payments here are made at the time of service. There is no billing system to the Travel Inn accounts. This facility provides the guest with an enjoyable lively atmosphere in which to relax during the evening. T.G.I. Friday's is also available for lunchtime drinks and meals, from 12 noon onwards.

BACK OF HOUSE

The Travel Inn bedrooms all lead off light, well-lit corridors, decorated in creams with light oak wooden fittings. Framed modern prints hang upon the walls to provide interest and relief. Each bedroom is en-suite with a double bed and duvet. Some rooms are for families, and have a (single) sofa bed in addition to the double bed, with a child's pull-out bed as well. The bathroom contains a bath and shower unit, a hand basin and a WC. All these are fitted with light oak-coloured panels and shelves so that no plumbing is visible and cleanliness is easily maintained. A heated towel rail is wall-mounted to provide comfort and space. Two glass tumblers, complimentary soaps and an overmirror light complete the provision. Ventilation is provided by an integral light and extractor fan system to ensure freshness at all times.

The decor and fittings of all the rooms is identical. Warm hues of creams peaches and blues create a restful yet welcoming atmosphere. The furniture (hanging shelf and drawer provision and a spacious desk area) is all of light oak-coloured melamine-finished units. The desk area is provided for the benefit of business people. Wall and table lamps provide good lighting and tea- and coffee-making facilities are provided for the guests' use. A wall-mounted heater can be switched on if required, and all rooms have a remote-controlled TV and radio alarm placed at one end of the desk. Window locks and door spy holes provide guests with an extra feeling of personal security.

Three of the 48 bedrooms are especially fitted for use by disabled guests. These rooms are all on the ground floor near to the reception area, so that evacuation difficulties would be minimized in event of an emergency. The doors to the rooms are wide, as is access to the bed and the furniture. The electrical switches are positioned at a low level. The bathroom has a low-line bath/shower and basin, and WC with hand rails and an emergency pull alarm.

A full-time housekeeper has responsibility for the room provision. There are eight chambermaids who work on a rota basis so that all rooms are served as dictated by the bookings. They work from a cleaners' room and use a trolley that carries all their equipment and clean linen, a sack for soiled linen and another for refuse. The linen is stored in a linen room and is supplied by a linen hire company. A handyman is employed for the whole complex – T.G.I. Friday's and Travel Inn – and is available to carry out maintenance as requested by the housekeeper.

Brewers Fayre (part of Whitbread PLC)

World's End
Main Road
Ecton
Northamptonshire NN6 0QN

World's End is a modern public house and restaurant complex, incorporating an ancient building that was used as a hospital during the Battle of Naseby. This original building is now the lounge bar with the manager's accommodation above, and the cellars below. New extensions accommodate the kitchen, reception area and restaurant. World's End is situated half a mile west of Earls Barton on the A4500 and is two miles from the Northampton road. It has prominent signs that direct travellers into a tidy car park with ample parking spaces, surrounded by beds of shrubs. A children's outdoor play area is well protected from the traffic and comprises activity frames built on safety ground cover and a tidy lawn area.

Places of interest that are near the World's End include:

- caravans, leisure and sailing at Billing Aquadrome
- leisure and sailing at Overstone Solarium
- private flying at Sywell airport
- Country Park at Sywell
- entertainment, plays, snooker at Northampton's Derngate Centre and the Royal Theatre
- ancient battle grounds around the village of Naseby
- traditional town market at Northampton

The atmosphere at the World's End is one of friendliness and hospitality, with a feeling of warmth generated by the staff and the decor.

The reception area doubles up as a waiting area for the restaurant at busy trading periods, so it is comfortably furnished with dark oak varnished tables and chairs of traditional style with panelling on the lower part of the walls. A central fireplace provides a focal point to both the reception and restaurant area. Photographs, and prints of the Battle of Naseby scenes are displayed on the walls, and a traditionally styled short flight of stairs leads up to the lounge bar area. The furniture is on the same traditional style with maroon tapestry-style upholstery and curtains. The area is carpeted throughout in a maroon self-pattern design. The bar is wood panelled with traditional style stained-glass panels above the service counter, and a brass foot-bar around the bar counter. The back bar is well lit, with a mirror backdrop to create more light. Spotlights in the ceiling give an intimate yet sufficient level of illumination to the customer areas. The bar will seat up to sixty people. For those who smoke, a cigarette vending machine is situated in the reception area.

MANAGEMENT

The World's End is managed by a resident manager, who is responsible for the entire operation. He is assisted by a full-time assistant manager. There are five team leaders, all of whom are full-time employees: two chefs, two food service staff and one barman. The rest of the staff, twenty-one in total, are part-time employees.

The maintenance of quality and successful trading is the manager's responsibility through the Standards of Achievement Awards system. Each achievement is awarded with a badge and a pay increase. Within three months, all employees must have attained their silver badge, which is tested by a multi-choice test paper and by an on-the-job assessment. It comprises job knowledge, food hygiene and knowledge of the Whitbread Inns aims, service standards and provision of value for money to the customers. The staff are encouraged to progress to a gold award, which is work-based assessment, with support of a work book to study and complete. Training sessions are given to support this programme and more in-depth knowledge is gained.

A further level of achievement may be gained through the diamond award, this is supported by a work book and tested by an examination as well as work-based assessments. In the alcohol sales section there is the opportunity to study for NVQ level 2 Liquor Service Award. Supervisory responsibility will follow for diamond award holders, and Whitbread external courses support this training together with a log book and work-based assessments.

The manager and his assistant are responsible for the work-based training and assessment. A district manager has the overall responsibility for the management of the World's End. The Whitbread Inns staff motto is 'Share in Success'. There is regionally run competition, based upon target sales. If these targets are met points are awarded. Points mean prizes. As a way to motivate staff it is effective and very popular.

SERVICE NICHE

The unique selling points include:

- value given for money
- speed of service
- friendliness of the staff
- good home cooked food
- informality

- family room for drinking
- children's indoor and outdoor play areas
- traditional comfort for an evening out
- ability to cater for children's parties
- well-signed ample car parking

The target customers include:

- families with children
- older retired people
- visitors from the local leisure parks
- business people at lunch times

FRONT OF HOUSE

Reception

One food service member of staff will greet the customers and ask them if they wish to eat in the restaurant, bar or garden area. If the restaurant is full their name will be taken and when a table is free this will be called out in the bar area. No advanced bookings are taken with the exception of Christmas meals and children's parties.

Food service

This service is designed with speed as the main objective. Customers will be shown to their table, and given a menu. Once they have made their choice, they go to the service area themselves and place their order with the cashier. Payment is made at the time the order is placed, or a table bill is opened if switch, credit card or cheque payment methods are to be used. Once the customer has placed their order for food they may proceed to the dispense bar area and order and pay for their drinks. The customer returns to their table and food service staff will bring their orders as soon as they are ready. The service is quick, 4–5 minutes for a starter or sweet, and 3–4 minutes for a main course. Staff will clear away all used plates, glasses and cutlery whilst the customer is ordering their next course. On a busy summer bank holiday, the

World's End can serve 2.000 meals in a day. On the average Sunday 400 meals are served, with 600 on Mothering Sunday. The restaurant is open for meal service from 12 noon until 10 p.m. and can seat 100 persons on tables of two or four. High chairs are available for babies. The tables are laid with a place mat, knife and fork and napkin. Cruets and menus are also on each table. There are additional menu items displayed on a chalk board displayed above the cashier.

The electronic point of sale system is used by the cashier to record customers' orders. The soft pad keys record all the menu choices and these are instantaneously printed out in the kitchen. This speeds up the ordering and the service. Staff are logged into the system at the beginning of their shift, so it is possible for the manager to analyse each employee's productivity rate as well as carry out the usual sales analysis. At present this system is not able to automatically adjust stock levels. A similar EPOS system is used in the bar.

The food service/order area is equipped with a display counter for chilled sweets, as well as the dispense bar and the cashier/order section. Other equipment includes an electrically heated soup cauldron, microwave for hot sweets, deep freeze for ices, and a press-button coffee machine.

The food service staff wear a heather-coloured skirt with a blue and pink striped shirt, with a waist apron.

BACK OF HOUSE

Food preparation

This area works from 11.30 a.m. to 8 p.m. each day. There is a set menu and a manual of standard specials that can be put on the chalk board on a daily basis. These specials are all produced from standard recipes, with standard products and presentation procedures, yielding predetermined costs and profit margins. All commodities are purchased from suppliers who have been head office-approved. Fresh meat and frozen foods are delivered three times a week and vegetables are delivered daily. Groceries and bread are delivered weekly.

The kitchen leads from the service area, with a large dust control mat laid between the two areas. It is a small rectangular kitchen with a range, grill, griddle, microwaves, deep fat fryers, and a bain marie. The washing up area is also in the kitchen. All dishes are finished to order and presented to the standard specifications.

Housekeeping

As this is not a residential establishment the only cleaning required is in the customer food and drink areas. The bar staff are responsible for the bar and cellar cleanliness. The kitchen staff are responsible for the cleanliness of the kitchen and food storage areas. There are two part-time cleaners who work from 8.30 a.m. to 10.30 a.m. every day and who clean all the customer service areas. Food service staff have this responsibility during service times.

TWO

Customer service

Customer care

Customer care is all about looking after your customers. How do you relate to the following statements? Ring round the appropriate number (3 is 'Yes'; 2 is 'Unsure'; 1 is 'Not much')

ACTIVITY				
I enjoy talking to customers	**3**	**2**	**1**	I prefer not to talk to customers
I like meeting people	**3**	**2**	**1**	I feel uncomfortable when meeting people
Different types of customers are interesting	**3**	**2**	**1**	All customers are the same
I try to help a customer if I can	**3**	**2**	**1**	If a customer needs help I look the other way
Working in a service industry is fun	**3**	**2**	**1**	Working in a service industry is boring
I like wearing my uniform	**3**	**2**	**1**	I try to adapt my uniform to my taste
I'm able to recognize regular customers	**3**	**2**	**1**	I never remember regular customers
I am happy at work	**3**	**2**	**1**	I am not happy when at work
My team members are my friends	**3**	**2**	**1**	I do not really know the members of my team
I apologize if I make a mistake	**3**	**2**	**1**	I cannot apologize if I make a mistake

Score 25–30   You have the ability to be a good team member and have excellent customer relation skills.

Score 24–15   You have the potential to serve customers well, try harder to like and communicate with them, and your fellow team members.

Score below 15   Oh dear! You have a long way to go. Think how you would feel if you were the customer.

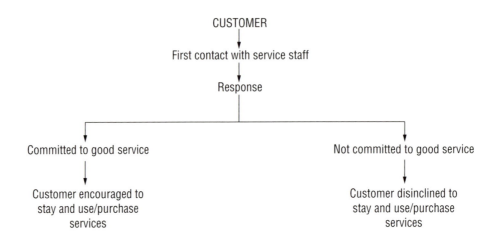

Figure 2.1 The customer and the service staff

Customer care policy

Every establishment that serves the public needs to have a customer care policy. This will take the form of a series of positive specific and achievable statements on customer care; it will help to ensure that customer care standards are implemented by the entire work force. The customer care policy does not only apply to the staff who serve the customers personally, it concerns the entire organization: all departments and all staff (see pp. 112, 157, 180 and 279).

The prime concern must always be to ensure that customers feel welcomed, that they are served and they are bid farewell in clean, pleasant and safe surroundings with the best possible quality and type of product. However, four different establishments might not have an identical focus, as the following examples show.

Public house	*Leisure Centre*
Service	Facilities
Premises	Toilets and changing areas
Toilets	Service and advice
Hotel	*Fast-food take-away*
Service	Welcome and goodbye
Premises	Service
Other facilities	Premises

When thinking about customer care it is essential to start by putting yourself in the customer's place and imagine what they will think of the facilities, premises and service. If you remember this then you will be well on the way to establishing a good customer care attitude.

When you enter a burger bar, what do you expect? Probably the following:

• clean, safe, hygienic and attractive premises
• friendly and efficient staff
• good quality food and drinks

This would be a normal customer expectation and indicates the areas to concentrate on when thinking about a customer care policy.

How would you react to poorly maintained toilet facilities in a café? Would an uncleaned toilet, with empty toilet roll holders and a broken-down electric hand-dryer suggest an establishment which is likely to be unhygienic and badly maintained in other areas?

Before writing a policy

Before reaching the stage of writing a policy there are various aspects to consider.

MAIN FOCUS

As indicated above, different establishments need to focus on different aspects of service. It depends on who your customers are and what they expect of your kind of establishment. A further aspect of this is that you may be offering products and services that other similar establishments do not offer. These are known as unique selling points (USP). Before you start compiling a customer care policy you need to be clear on these matters.

With regard to USP, for example, your leisure centre might have a club membership scheme whereas your nearest rival leisure centre does not. It would therefore be essential to focus on the services available to club members and ensure that the customer care policy gives these appropriate attention.

INVESTIGATING HOW THE ESTABLISHMENT FUNCTIONS

Obviously it is essential to identify exactly how your establishment functions with regard to procedures (systems and work flow) and face-to-face delivery of services. Looking at how things are functioning (or not) at the moment suggests what a customer care policy should cover and how much emphasis should be given to various aspects. Below are some examples of the kind of questions that need to be asked.

Questions on procedures, systems and work flow

- Are there time constraints?
- Is time important?
- Are there peak periods?
- Is the service time hindered by poor work flow?
- Are the premises efficiently maintained so as to avoid breakdowns?
- Can we cope with reasonable customer requests?
- Are service routines a help or a hindrance to the customer?
- Are staff flexible enough to provide a quality service?
- Can the equipment cope with customer demands at peak times?
- Are the service areas co-ordinated with the supply areas?

Questions on personal contact, i.e. communication and appearance

- Are we friendly yet efficient when speaking to the customers?
- Do we speak clearly and effectively to the customer?
- Can we anticipate the customers' needs?

• Do we treat all customers exactly the same?
• Can we be of personal help to our customers?
• Do all staff wear a clean, well-fitting uniform?
• Do we deal effectively with customer complaints?
• Do all staff listen to customers?
• Do all staff maintain eye contact with customers whilst speaking to them?

SETTING CLEAR AND ACHIEVABLE STANDARDS

The way in which customer care standards are set down in a policy document and communicated to staff is of utmost significance. The statements representing the policy must be clear and precise, with definite outcomes, and must also be achievable. Such statements will cover:

• procedures used to provide service to customers
• the quality of staff's personal contact with customers (manner of speaking, looking, gesturing and presenting oneself, i.e. style of dress, neatness, cleanliness etc.)

ACTIVITY

The following pairs of statements refer to customer care in a coffee shop; three of them focus on procedure and three on personal contact. One of each pair is worded positively, the other vaguely.

Using only the positive statements, list them with the statements on procedure as 1–3, and those on personal contact 4–6.

Customers' complaints are resolved by staff as soon as possible.
Customers' complaints should be listened to.

The telephone should be answered as soon as possible
All telephone calls must be answered within 45 seconds

Clean, correct uniform must be worn by all staff on duty.
Staff must be neatly dressed.

All customers must be greeted as soon as they enter the premises.
All customers must be greeted promptly.

Telephone callers should be asked to hold on if their query cannot be answered immediately.
The caller's name, telephone number and the nature of the query should be noted and a reply call given within one hour, if the matter cannot be dealt with straight away.

The effects of the customer care policy

GOOD QUALITY SERVICE

The effects of a good customer care policy will be apparent in quality of service: the two things are interdependent. If the customer care policy has been well thought out and is being put into operation by staff, then inevitably service will be good.

For example, suppose a customer telephones with a query. If she/he is
answered promptly
spoken to in a clear confident manner
given the correct information within a minimum time
bid 'goodbye' in a friendly manner
then the customer care policy standards will have been fulfilled, and the customer will have received good quality service.

CUSTOMER SATISFACTION

The customer in the above circumstances will have formed a favourable impression of the business through the efficient and courteous way in which his/her query was resolved. This is what we refer to as customer satisfaction. The likely result is that this customer will continue to use the services offered by this establishment.

Obviously, customer satisfaction depends on good quality service in the way that quality of service depends on customer care. This dependency can be graphically illustrated as in Figure 2.2.

Figure 2.2 The relationship between policy, service and customer satisfaction

INCREASED PROFITABILITY

This is another positive effect of an effective customer care policy, but it also depends on customer satisfaction being maintained – the subject of the next section. Assuming that the customer continues to be pleased with the service s/he receives, then she/he will return (known as return trade) or recommend others to become customers (referred trade). Such increases in trade mean an increase in turnover. As long as this increase is accompanied by correct pricing structure (see p. 316), and correct purchasing and preparation specifications then there will also be increased profitability.

Maintaining customer care standards

In either the case of repeat trade or of referred trade the maintenance of the customer care policy and the good quality service is imperative. The customer has formed a first, favourable impression. If the customer satisfaction is to be maintained, then this impression must also be maintained.

For example, a couple go to a steak restaurant for a meal. Upon arrival they are greeted, shown to a table in an alcove and asked what they would like to drink, while studying the menu and deciding what to order. They place their order, finish their drinks and select a bowl of salad from the central chilled salad bar. Then their steak meals are placed before them without having to wait at all. Upon leaving they remark to each other about the friendliness of the staff, the secluded alcove and the prompt service and good quality food. The entire meal has been an enjoyable, memorable experience, so much so that they plan to return in the near future and bring two friends with them.

On the return visit all four customers have positive expectations about what the experience will be like. The couple who made the original visit will have described their experience to their friends, who will have therefore been encouraged to form positive expectations too.

The meal experience will now have to be *at least* as good as it was the first time, in order to be able to satisfy these four customers. 'At least' is emphasized because there is another factor to be considered – that of customer exaggeration. A good experience may be quite unintentionally exaggerated by the customer when it is described to a friend at a later date. This exaggeration will result in a higher expectation level. It would be impossible to live up to this expectation without an effective customer care policy and good quality standards.

There are other elements – for example, standard practices, procedures and products – that will help to maintain good quality standards, but only if the staff follow the customer care policy at all times. The care underpins the quality of service.

Changing procedures so as to achieve customer care

Whilst compiling the customer care statements for the policy document, the establishment's procedures need to be analysed. They may then need to be changed to enable staff to fulfil the customer care statements.

For example: a hotel restaurant that is open to the general public for luncheon and dinner can take reservations for tables when the restaurant clerk is on duty. The clerk will answer the telephone, and take table bookings as part of his/her daily duties. But when the clerk is off duty, no bookings can be made. The customer care policy statement might read 'All customer requests are dealt with within 30 minutes', but staff cannot fulfil it. Thus the procedure for restaurant bookings needs to be changed so that front office staff can take bookings when the restaurant clerk is off duty. Now the customer care policy statement *can* be fulfilled. This change in procedure could also result in an increase in reservations for the restaurant.

Putting policy into effect

There is no point in compiling a customer care policy unless all employees within the establishment

- know the customer care statements and
- are able to achieve them

KNOWING THE CUSTOMER CARE STATEMENTS

There are various methods of ensuring that all staff know the customer care statements. These include:

- providing each member of staff with a copy of the customer care statements
- displaying copies of the customer care statements on the staff notice boards
- including a discussion of customer care statements in the staff induction programme
- compiling short checklists/questionnaires for staff, that relate to specific customer care statements, to refresh their memory of these statements

Checklists

These are often displayed in service areas, out of view to customers, to remind staff of precisely what is expected at all times. It is necessary to change these lists at regular intervals to ensure they do not become so familiar that staff ignore them. Different coloured backgrounds, or line illustrations will ensure that the same checklist is given a new look.

The example of a checklist shown below is for bar staff and relates to the customer care policy statement:

All customers will be served within three minutes.

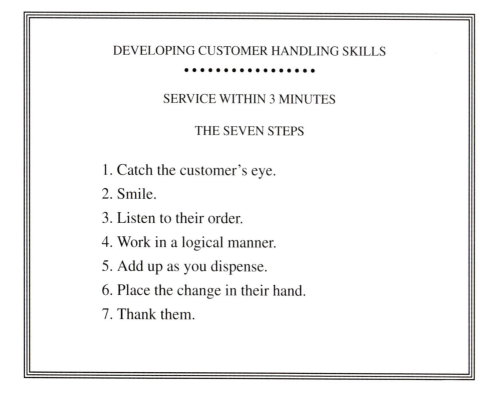

DEVELOPING CUSTOMER HANDLING SKILLS

• • • • • • • • • • • • • • •

SERVICE WITHIN 3 MINUTES

THE SEVEN STEPS

1. Catch the customer's eye.
2. Smile.
3. Listen to their order.
4. Work in a logical manner.
5. Add up as you dispense.
6. Place the change in their hand.
7. Thank them.

ACTIVITY

Compile a checklist for food service staff in a cafeteria style unit. The customer care policy statements reads:

'Customers will be served
in a clean and hygienic manner.'

Use your IT skills to produce an eye-catching checklist that could be displayed behind the service counter to act as a reminder for the service staff.

BEING ABLE TO ACHIEVE THE STANDARDS

With the best will in the world, staff will not be able to carry out the care policy if they do not have procedures to follow and equipment to use.

A customer care policy statement might read: 'The public toilets are maintained in a clean and hygienic manner.' In order to ensure that this statement is fulfilled it will be necessary to:

- make it a part of specific employees' duties to check the cleanliness of the toilets on an hourly basis
- give these staff the authority to request immediate maintenance assistance should a fault or breakage be identified
- provide adequate means for the disposal of paper hand towels and litter
- provide continuous effective air-conditioning
- provide adequate supplies of hot and cold running water
- ensure an efficient means of sanitary waste disposal
- ensure an adequate level of lighting and heating are available
- provide sufficient, appropriate cleaning equipment and agents for the staff to use

A further aid will be the thorough training given to the cleaning staff so that they are able to maintain the cleanliness of the toilets to the standards set. The use of work cards and work schedules will help maintain work standards (see p. 165).

From this example you can see that fulfilling even quite a straightforward customer care policy statement involves the entire organization.

Finding out what customers want – by questionnaires

Obviously an important ingredient of customer care is providing a service tailored to customers' needs and preferences. A standard way to find out what these are is by requesting customers to fill in a questionnaire.

SELECTING YOUR QUESTIONS

This is not as straightforward as you might at first think. First of all you need to be very clear on exactly what you wish to find out. Questions which are too general will not be of any use to you.

For example, the question 'Do you like this leisure centre?' will receive such responses as 'No', 'Yes', 'Part of it', or 'It's all right'. The customers have answered your question but you have not received any factual information on what they like or dislike about the facilities.

Examine this in more detail. The leisure centre is situated on the fringe of a town. It has facilities for football, tennis, badminton, squash, ice skating, swimming, keep fit and body building. There is a coffee shop and a garden. You want to know what your customers think about these facilities and what they would like to see changed/improved/added.

If you ask specific questions you should gain the information that you require. You must decide what aspect(s) of the facilities you need to find out about. Is it:

access to the centre
the booking systems
the facilities for group bookings
the quality of a specific facility
the times of availability
the safety of a particular sport
the reception/enquiry service
the changing facilities or
the security within the centre

MAKING REASONABLE DEMANDS ON THE CUSTOMER

Imagine that you have answered 'Yes' to all the ten points above. Look again at the facilities available at our leisure centre. There are ten areas. To receive even one answer for each, you would have to ask about 100 questions. Not many of your customers would want to answer a questionnaire of that length. It is obvious that you will need to be more selective.

You could choose two types of sport (e.g. tennis and badminton), and ask ten questions relating to these two. This would produce a questionnaire of about fifteen or twenty questions, the optimum length for most customers. You could probably include a few general questions, too, relating to the leisure centre itself.

At a later date you could compile another questionnaire on these lines for a different set of facilities.

Or you could compile a short questionnaire for each area and circulate these simultaneously. Not many of the leisure centre customers would use more than two or three of the facilities, so they will not be required to answer an impossible number of question, and you will have obtained as much information as it is possible to obtain.

For example, you could compile one questionnaire for each of the following groups:

coffee shop and gardens
keep fit and body building
football
tennis squash and badminton
swimming and ice skating

Now you have decided what you want to ask your customers, and which customers you will ask, you will need to decide how you will ask them.

GETTING ANSWERS YOU CAN ANALYSE

If you ask questions that require a written sentence as a reply, questionnaire analysis will be very difficult to carry out, because every answer might be different. If, however, you phrase your questions so that they can be answered in one or two ways, then the analysis will be simpler.

Look at these two examples and see which would be the easier one to analyse.

> How do you rate the cleanliness of the changing rooms?
> Good ...... Satisfactory ...... Poor ......

> What do you think of the cleanliness of the changing rooms?
> ....

The first is the easiest because the choices are already specified. When analysing the answers, you would simply find that you had some customers rating the changing room 'good', some 'satisfactory' and some 'poor'. These figures could then simply be converted into percentage figures for graphic display if required. Suppose 50 customers replied to the question and

    25 customers replied 'good'
    15 customers replied 'satisfactory'
    10 customer replied 'poor'

The percentage would therefore be:

    50% 'good' 30% 'satisfactory' 20% 'poor'

Useful option words for questionnaires

Good	Satisfactory	Poor
Yes	Not sure	No
Always	Sometimes	Never
Every day	3–5 times per week	1–3 times per week
Regularly	Occasionally	Never
Strong	Average	Weak
Good value	Expected value	Poor value

QUESTIONNAIRES BY POST

It may be that the manager of High Cliff Leisure Centre wishes to find out about views on facilities for group bookings. In this case she/he could post out a questionnaire to groups that are likely to use, are currently using, or have used the centre.

Let us assume that she/he wishes to investigate:

- the age ranges of the groups
- the facilities normally reserved
- the popular days of the week for group bookings
- the popular times of the day for group bookings
- the sizes of the groups
- the implications for the coffee shop trade
- the prior notice span for reservations
- the preferred payment method
- the desire for exclusive use of facilities and coaching staff
- the implications for car parking space.

The questionnaire could then look like the example given overleaf.

You will notice that space has been allowed on the questionnaire for individual comments, which could introduce further points for consideration. For example, these comments could make points about the changing or the vending facilities.

The manager might find that some new groups decide to use the High Cliff Leisure Centre after receiving the questionnaire. Thus there is an additional bonus of increased trade.

ACTIVITY

Compile a questionnaire that relates to your hospitality and catering training, perhaps the usage of a training restaurant or coffee shop.

1. Use your IT skills to present it in an acceptable format.

2. Give this questionnaire to the relevant customers/potential customers.

3. Analyse the results.

4. Use your IT skills to present these results in written and graphic formats.

In order to improve the arrangements for group bookings at the High Cliff Leisure Centre, it would be appreciated if you would complete and return the following short questionnaire. A stamped address facility is enclosed for your convenience.

For each question please tick the responses that apply to your group.

1.   Which age/s are the group members?

Under 7 yrs ☐   7–11 yrs ☐   11–16 yrs ☐
16–25 yrs ☐   over 25 yrs ☐

2.   Please tick the facilities that your regularly reserve.

Swimming pool ☐   Skating rink ☐
Football pitch ☐   Football indoor ☐
Tennis courts ☐   Squash courts ☐
Badminton courts ☐   Keep fit hall ☐
Body building gym ☐

3.   Which day/s do you /would you like to reserve facilities?

Monday ☐   Tuesday ☐   Wednesday ☐
Thursday ☐   Friday ☐   Saturday ☐
Sunday ☐

4.   Which time/s do you/would you like to reserve facilities?

8–10 am ☐   10–12 noon ☐   12 noon–2 pm ☐
2–4 pm ☐   4–6 pm ☐   6–8 pm ☐
8–10 pm ☐

5.   Does your group use the coffee shop facility?

Regularly ☐   Occasionally ☐   Never ☐

6.   How much prior notice are you able to give for your booking?

Under a week ☐   1–2 weeks ☐   more than 2 weeks ☐

7.   How would you like to pay for your reservation?

in advance by cheque ☐
on the day of the booking by cheque ☐
on the day of the booking in cash ☐
by invoice before the booking date ☐
by invoice after the booking date ☐

8.   Would your group require exclusive use of the facility booked?

Yes ☐   No ☐   Sometimes ☐

9.   Would your group require the services of a trained sports coach?

Yes ☐   No ☐   Sometimes ☐

10.   How many people would be in your group?

Under 10 ☐   10–25 ☐   25–40 ☐   more than 40 ☐

11.   Would your group require car parking spaces for :

Cars ☐   Coaches ☐   Motorbikes/cycles ☐

Please add any additional comments below

. . . .

. . . .

Thank you for your co-operation and assistance

. . . . Manager, High Cliff Leisure Centre

How was your stay?

Name _____

Address/STREET _____

_____

TOWN _____

COUNTY _____ POSTCODE _____

Room Number _____ Date of stay _____

Travel Inn stayed at _____

How would you rate us:-

At Reception

Was the service friendly and helpful?

EXCELLENT				POOR
5	4	3	2	1
☐	☐	☐	☐	☐

Bedroom & Bathroom

Were the facilities clean?

EXCELLENT				POOR
5	4	3	2	1
☐	☐	☐	☐	☐

Overall

Would you rate your stay?

EXCELLENT				POOR
5	4	3	2	1
☐	☐	☐	☐	☐

Would you be happy to stay in a Travel Inn again

Yes	No
☐	☐

If you would like to share any further views with us, about any further aspect of your stay, we would welcome your comments below:

_____

_____

_____

_____

Please hand this to reception when you leave. Alternatively if you would like to discuss your stay in more detail, either speak to me personally or provide a telephone number where we can contact you, within the next two weeks.

Telephone Number:- Code (_____) Number _____

The Manager

Travel Inn, Whitbread House, Park Street West, Luton Bedfordshire LU1 3BG
Telephone (0582) 422884 Fax (0582) 405680

Many thanks for your time

Figure 2.3 A questionnaire focusing on specific aspects of facilities

REPLIES TO LEITH'S AT THE INSTITUTE – QUESTIONNAIRE AUGUST 1992

140 questionnaires were posted and we have received 51 replies to date 25/9/92. (Some people answered twice or not at all to some of the questions, therefore replies will not all total 51.)

1. Have you ever eaten in the Restaurant at Chartered Accountants' Hall?

   yes   36

   no   15

2. If yes, how often?

   1–2 times per month   25

   3–4 times per month   nil

   more than 4 times per month   nil

   only a couple of times a year   21

3. What is normally the purpose of your lunch?

   business   35

   social   10

4. How much would you be willing to spend per head on a two-course lunch with wine at the restaurant at the ICAEW?

   less than £15   6

   £15–£19.99   19

   £20–£24.99   21

   £25–£29.99   7

   more than £30   1

5. Do you prefer a fixed priced menu or an à la carte menu?

   fixed price   25

   à la carte   8

   do not prefer either   16

6. How much would you expect to pay for a bottle of (French, appellation controlée standard) house wine?

   less than £5   1

   £5–£6.99   5

   £7–8.99   17

   £9–£10.99   18

   over £11   6

7. Would you use the wine bar facility within the restaurant at the ICAEW for lunch?

   yes   25

   no   23

8. How much would you expect to pay for a lunch-time bar snack (e.g. a salad of avocado pear, mozzarella and tomato with pesto dressing and crusty bread)

with a glass of house wine?

less than £5.00	10
£5.00–£6.99	26
£7–£9.99	8
above £10	nil

9. If the wine bar was open in the evening would you visit it after work/before concert or theatre for a drink?

yes	21
no	31

10. Would you consider having a snack as well after work in the wine bar?

yes	11
no	39

11. The restaurant will be available for parties in the evening. Would you consider using it in this way for:

staff Christmas parties	9
leaving/retirement parties	14
corporate entertainment	17
private hire	11
never	15

12. If you are entertaining at lunchtime in the restaurant at the ICAEW on business, how long would you like to spend over your meal?

less than 45 minutes	1
45 minutes–1½ hours	47
more than 1½ hours	3

13. On a three-course fixed priced menu, would you ever choose to pay a supplement for a speciality such as oysters, fillet steak or lobster?

yes	44
no	6

14. If the wine bar were to offer an evening menu including special items such as oysters and champagne, strawberries and pimms, gravadlax and vodka, etc., would you be more inclined to use the wine bar than if we offered a menu which included items like ploughman's and a pint or scampi and chips?

yes	24
no	22

15. Would you like to have suitable/appropriate background music playing during the evenings in the wine bar?

yes	19
no	29

Figure 2.4 Replies to Leith's questionnaire, August 1992

Assessing the results of a customer care policy

Various methods are used to monitor and assess the results of a customer care policy. These largely depend upon the type of business that is being run.

METHODS SUITED TO THE TYPE OF ESTABLISHMENT

A cafeteria or coffee shop-style catering operation within an industrial complex that caters for employees' meals whilst they are at work could employ any of the following methods, or a combination of some of them.

Questionnaire

This would depend upon the specific industrial climate (the likelihood of industrial disputes must be considered). It is for this reason that questionnaires are not often used in this type of establishment.

Suggestion box

This can solicit unhelpful comments, and is not usually of much benefit in assessing the results of a customer care policy.

Face-to-face interviews

This is usually effective when conducted by management level personnel. The secret is that the comments received must be seen to be taken note of, and acted upon as soon as possible after the interview. These interviews take place in the dining area of the cafeteria complex, by prior arrangement whilst the employees are eating their meals. Normally each interview will take ten to fifteen minutes. During the interview it is important to clarify comments which are not specific. For example, the comment might be: 'The food here is awful'. By careful questioning the interviewer can ascertain exactly what is causing this comment. Possible causes could be that

   the food is not hot enough

   the customer wants a less substantial meal choice

   the customer can only have lunch at the end of the trading time and therefore has very little choice of dishes

   the customer has little cash to spend so does not actually have much choice of food

   the customer would like a larger choice of pasta or stir fry-type dishes

   the customer would like the traditional meat and two veg type meal, not the large range of salads and snacks that are offered.

In all these cases careful questioning will result in a clear picture of what has prompted the original comment of 'The food here is awful'.

Comment book

This works in much the same way as the face-to-face interview, but provides a permanently available facility for comments, both complimentary and less complimentary. There is a space for the management to indicate what action has been taken (see below). This instant feedback to the customer is a vital part of the customer care policy.

Date	Comment	Signature	Management action	Date
2/5/96	Food cold	....	Temperature of hot cupboard checked	3/5/96
2/5/96	Super pudding	....	Chef says many thanks Dave	3/5/96
4/5/96	Water glasses smeary	....	Rinse aid has been checked and a new valve fitted	5/5/96

The employees can see what is being done about their grievance or compliment. This instant response is the secret to the success of the comment book. This type of comment book is a successful and appropriate method for establishments working within the welfare sector of the catering and hospitality industry. Coupled with the face to face customer interviews, it makes a good feedback strategy.

Remember everything hinges upon the managers' action taken in response to the comments made in the interview or the comment book. Often there is a simple remedial action to be taken, for instance cold plates can be rectified by putting them in to warm earlier in the morning so that they have more time to become hot, or the temperature of the hot plate can be turned up. If this type of action is recorded in the comment book, the customers will be able to see instantly that their comment has been listened to and taken note of. Greater customer satisfaction will result.

Compliments will be encouraged if a comment from the chef is written in the book.

ACTIVITY

Produce a customer comment book for use in a catering outlet. Over a period of four weeks, monitor the comments daily, and indicate the action taken in response to each comment.

At the end of the four-week period, analyse the comments into the following categories:

Maintenance faults   Quality of food

Staff hygiene standards   Temperature of food

Premises design

This analysis will be useful data when planning improvement, staff training, work flow changes and menu changes.

MYSTERY GUESTS

In the commercial sector of the catering and hospitality industry, the comment book and the face-to-face interviews are not appropriate methods to use in order to assess the results of a customer care policy. Questionnaires may be used occasionally, but the main monitoring tool is the use of mystery guests.

This strategy is used nation-wide in public houses, fast food chains, and in-store public catering areas. Some hotels also use this mystery guest monitoring method, in which case the guest may be an employee from another hotel within the same ownership or group. In some hotels the front office personnel are sometimes requested to be a customer for a night, to book into a room and sleep the night. This strategy often makes the front office personnel far more aware of the guests' needs and feelings when they arrive at the hotel.

There are commercial agencies within the UK who will employ 'mystery guests', and send these to the catering and hospitality facility in order to monitor the level of customer care received. Individual catering and hospitality organizations employ an agency to supply a mystery guest monitoring service for all their individual units. For example, a brewery with 730 public houses could employ the agency to send mystery guests to visit all its public houses and to report back to the brewery on their findings.

Mystery guests are in fact undercover customers who will watch the customer service methods and then report these back. It is important to select an appropriate age and style of the mystery guest for each type of establishment, so that they will not look out of place. They must blend into the regular clientele. For example, it would be no use sending an elderly couple to a fast food hamburger bar, or a young family couple to a public house full of middle-aged and elderly customers.

Obviously the mystery guest will not stand with a clip board and pen and mark off a checklist. They will look at the methods and time taken for the service they and others receive whilst on the premises. They will note such areas as:

(a) body language of the staff
(b) service techniques
(c) premises maintenance
(d) general aspects

(a)   Body language

This will include such aspects as:

- eye contact maintained between the service staff and their customers
- facial expressions of the service staff, both whilst serving customers and at other times
- the stance of the service staff, and their general alertness

(b)   Service techniques

These will include:

- method and types of speech used by the service staff
- time taken before being acknowledged by the service staff
- selling techniques employed by the service staff
- service techniques demonstrated, and correct use of equipment

- methods used to accept payment and to give change to the customers
- action taken when a compliment is given to the service staff
- method used to answer a simple query from a customer

(c)   Premises maintenance

The observation will take note of the:

- cleanliness and hygiene standards visible from the customer's point of view
- cleanliness of the public toilets
- tidiness of the exterior of the premises and car park area
- quality and maintenance of the interior decor

(d)   General aspects

These include the:

- speed of the trade and customer turnover rates
- atmosphere within the establishment
- staff–customer rapport
- first and last impressions of their visit

Within the hotel sector of the industry, it is very useful for staff to be encouraged to act as guests during less busy trading periods. This has many advantages, the main ones being that the staff will then be able to:

- identify with the guests' feelings when they arrive/leave
- know what it is like to be asked to register at reception
- remember what it is actually like to sleep in one of the hotel bedrooms
- understand what a guest feels like when they enter the restaurant, coffee shop, bar or lounge
- appreciate the value of customer care in the different parts of the hotel

It is apparent that there are many different methods employed to monitor the success of a customer care policy, and that different methods are useful for different sectors of the catering and hospitality industry.

Suiting care to the customer: use of profiles

In this section we give summaries of the broad categories of customer. These profiles are very general; their function is to show that staff need to be aware of the need to suit service to customer. This involves varying the approach but of course maintaining at all times the same standards of customer care. You probably wouldn't behave to your grandmother in the same way as towards your young brother. If you did your grandmother might not be best pleased. It is important to know who our customers are so that we can offer them appropriate care.

INTERNAL CUSTOMERS

These are other members of the staff who are dependent upon the service provided by a particular group or sector within the same establishment. For example, a hotel linen department serves the other hotel staff with clean uniforms, linens and laundry for their daily work. These 'other staff' are the internal customers of the linen department staff. The customer care is as important for internal customers as it is for the external customer, the hotel guest.

EXTERNAL CUSTOMERS

These are members of the general public who wish to avail themselves of the service offered for sale. For example restaurant service staff have external customers in the form of restaurant customers.

DIFFERENT AGE GROUPS

It is necessary to adjust the customer care skills to ensure that they are appropriate for customers of different ages. It is not usually appropriate to serve a group of teenagers in the same manner as a group of old age pensioners. The use of language is likely to be different, as is the speed of service and the kind of rapport. However, customer care standards should always be the same.

CULTURAL BACKGROUNDS

It may be necessary for service staff to modify the speed and complexity of their speech in order to be understood. Another consideration could be the religious customs of a particular group of guests. The customer care standards must take this into consideration and allow for staff training in order that staff may appreciate the differences in customs and behaviour.

SPECIAL NEEDS

Guests with physical or mental disabilities must be accommodated and served to the same standards as other guests. All customer care standards must be capable of achievement for these guests. Access to facilities must be considered, and so must the provision of appropriate food and drink.

GROUPS

The customer care standards for a group of customers must be the same as those for an individual. For example, if a 56-seater coach full of guests arrives at a hotel, all those 56 guests should be cared for with the same regard to the customer care standards as in the case of serving an individual guests. This requires good organization in the front office and the restaurant.

Conversely, the individual guest must not be forgotten whilst the group is being served.

RESIDENTS OF RESIDENTIAL HOMES

A customer care policy is equally important in these establishments, particularly as some residents could be there for a considerable length of time. The treatment, care and service provided by the staff should be in keeping with the customer care policy standards. Just because the residents are elderly, not very self-sufficient or not very mobile, it does not follow that they require any less customer care and individual attention.

HOSPITAL PATIENTS

Patients in hospitals will be feeling vulnerable, thus any lack of care and attention will be magnified unreasonably in their minds. Quite apart from wanting to avoid this, it is also a method of increasing patient morale, to care for and talk to the patients whenever possible. Ward orderly staff, cleaners and meal hostess staff are all involved with the hospitality customer care standards. Out and day patients will require the same customer care consideration from reception and cleaning staff during their time in the hospital.

CUSTOMERS UNDER THE INFLUENCE OF DRINK/DRUGS/ MEDICATION

These customers will require special care if they are in the establishment. They could be volatile and difficult to communicate with or control. Assistance should always be sought from the supervisory or management strata of staff. Then if necessary these staff will contact the police and/or the ambulance services. The basic customer care standards of prompt attention, politeness and concern for the customers' well being will still apply even in these circumstances.

SATISFIED CUSTOMERS

It can be tempting to relax the customer care standards for customers who are obviously content with the service that they are receiving. If the customer care standards are relaxed, then this set of customers could soon become dissatisfied. So even here the customer care standards must be maintained.

DISSATISFIED CUSTOMERS

These customers can be difficult to handle. Their attitude and behaviour can cause service staff to become harassed and agitated. All the more important to remember the customer care standards in such circumstances although it can be difficult at times. Supervisory and management staff as well as the rest of the team should be there to assist.

DIFFICULT CUSTOMERS

If you come across difficult customers, remember that they may be difficult because of something that happened before they came into the premises. It could be that:

- they are tired and frustrated by travelling problems
- they are unsure of their surroundings, it is an unfamiliar experience for them
- they are defending their ego or self-esteem
- they feel ignored or unwelcome
- they are under the influence of drink/drugs
- they do not understand or speak the language well
- they have been delayed, are late and do not want to wait for service
- they are in a bad mood and take it out on you

In these cases, remember:

- don't take it personally
- remain calm and listen
- clarify the situation
- never argue

Recognizing customers' needs

Customers will, by their body language, display their needs, attitudes and expectations. Service staff need to recognize these behavioural signs and react to them immediately. If the customer care policy is being effective, there should be no negative signs (e.g. of impatience) from the customers.

If customer care standards are adhered to, body language signs should all be positive.

Table 2.1 Customers' body language

Customer signals	Positive signs	Negative signs
Facial expressions	Smiling	Scowling
	Calm and serene	Worried
	Eyes still	Eyes darting about
	Eyes dry	Eyes moist
Hand movement	Still	Fidgeting
	Hands in pockets	Drumming fingers
	Hands on lap	Biting nails
	Arms by their side	Arms folded across their chest
Stance	Still	Pacing about
	Relaxed	Tapping feet
	Seated calmly	Sitting on the edge of the seat
Speech	Quiet	Loud
	Even	Impatient
	Unhurried	Fast
	Calm	Agitated
Group behaviour	Calm	Loud
	Friendly	Aggressive
	Still	Milling around
	Unhurried	Fidgeting

PHYSICAL NEEDS

Physical needs are easy to recognize. It only needs the staff to be able to put themselves in the customers' place, and imagine what they would be feeling like and therefore what they would require in the form of sustenance, service and amenities.

For example: in a cafeteria-style food service operation, the customer has asked for one tea and one coffee. The service staff has given the customer one individual pot of tea and one cafeteria of coffee. The customer need here is: milk, cream, sugar, cups and saucers and teaspoons. The service staff need simply to tell the customer where these are found, as they give the pots of tea and coffee to the customer. This way the customer never even has time to start worrying about such details. This is a good example of staff being aware of, and being able to recognize needs, even before the customer does themselves.

ACTIVITY

Identify four more examples of recognition of physical customer needs during your practical work.

In each case, describe in your own words, the situation as it occurred and detail what action you took as a result.

Service performance gap (SPG)

Service performance gap (SPG) means the mismatch between a customers' expectations and the actual service received. How often have you heard customers say such things as:

It was far better than I expected

The food was better than last time

I though it was going to be better than that

The service was slower than I had expected

In each of these cases, the customer had some preconceived ideas of the service before s/he entered the premises. Their experience was either of a positive service performance gap (service turns out to be better than expected) or a negative service performance gap (service is not as good as expected) (see Figure 2.5). Obviously, all the customer care policies are aimed at achieving a positive service performance gap or, at a minimum, no service performance gap at all.

There are various factors that will influence a customers' expectations, including marketing image, past experience and personal needs. In considering how to close or eliminate the service performance gap it is necessary to look at these factors.

SPG EXAMINED

Recommendations from other

Sometimes people visit an establishment as the result of an enthusiastic recommendation but are disappointed. Exaggeration is the biggest fault here. The good service experience remembered by friends could, in part, be due to the establishment's services and in part to the friends' company, their emotional state, various external factors, such as a good day at work, a birthday or a promotion. This will help to make their visit go really well. These people then all say 'What a superb evening we had' and inadvertently raise the expectations of others.

The person who visits the establishment on this sort of recommendation, might have had a poor day at work, be feeling a bit down and listless and therefore not really in the right frame of mind to enjoy an evening out. The combination of this with the effects of exaggeration will be disastrous as far as SPG is concerned.

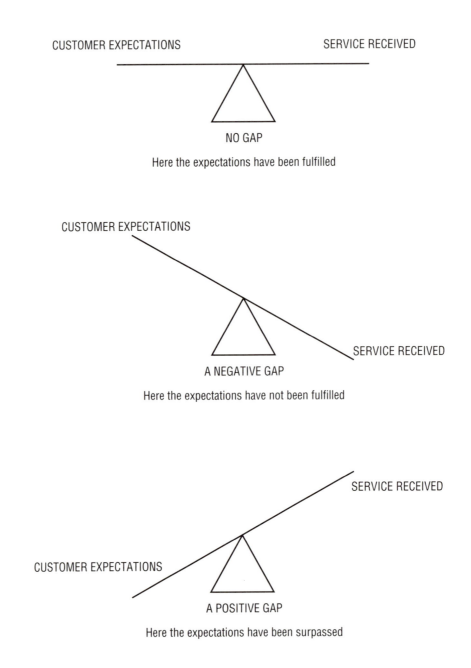

CUSTOMER EXPECTATIONS   SERVICE RECEIVED

NO GAP

Here the expectations have been fulfilled

CUSTOMER EXPECTATIONS

SERVICE RECEIVED

A NEGATIVE GAP

Here the expectations have not been fulfilled

SERVICE RECEIVED

CUSTOMER EXPECTATIONS

A POSITIVE GAP

Here the expectations have been surpassed

Figure 2.5 Service performance gaps

Concept image

The establishment will, by its very existence, project an image. By this it is meant that the premises, the staff and the facilities will enable the customer to form an instant impression of the sort of experience on offer.

An exclusive restaurant will project a different image from a corner café. The usual customer who chooses the exclusive restaurant would not necessarily be happy if he/she spent the evening in a corner café. They could end the evening with a negative service performance gap.

Marketing image

It is essential that the advertising reflects the true image of the establishment. It is against the Trades Description Act to knowingly misrepresent the facts to the public. But sometimes, the marketing image is unclear or misleading. In such a case, the customer expectations could be higher than can be fulfilled, creating a negative service performance gap.

Past experience

This is similar to the recommendations from others situation. Many factors can contribute towards a good experience at an establishment. It is necessary to realize this and to attempt to take care of all customers in the most caring way possible, thus ensuring that they have as good an experience as possible and there is no service performance gap.

Personal needs

These may vary according to the customers' situation on that day. For example, they may be very cold and need a seat in the restaurant, near the open fire. If this table has already been occupied, they could leave the premises at the end of the meal with a negative service performance gap.

The service performance gap has been looked at from the customers' point of view, but there could be service performance gaps viewed from other perspectives. These will be those gaps identified by the management and by the staff themselves. For example, the differences between:
- the management perceptions of customers' expectations and the actual customers' expectations
- the service specifications and management perceptions of customers' expectations
- the service specifications and service actually given

ACTIVITY

Look at the example described under *Personal needs* above. In this situation, what could you do to ensure that the customer leaves at the end of the evening with a positive service performance gap?

Customer research

IDENTIFYING THE SERVICE NICHE (SN)

It is important to be able to answer these two questions in order to know how to conduct relevant customer research:

Who are you marketing for?
What are you marketing?

This is called identifying the service niche (SN).

Different types of establishments will have different types of approach to the customer. For example, a fast food hamburger establishment has an assured product and delivery style: it is possible to know exactly what will be available and how it will be served. The staff can therefore be trained to deliver the products and service to a predetermined formula with standard procedures and timings. Customers know this and are happy to accept it. Not much is expected by way of interaction with the customer. A public house, in contrast, offers customers a distinctive experience. All such establishments are different in terms of ambience, atmosphere, size, style, products and service. Here the staff will be trained to be adept at serving customers, treating them as individuals, and to be polite and cheerful at all times.

In order to identify your service niche, you will need to identify your establishment's unique selling points (USP). This involves listing all the facilities, amenities, products and services that you have available and then identifying those that are not available in your immediate business rivals' establishments.

The items selected by this method will then be your unique selling points. In one hotel the swimming pool could be the unique selling point; in another the large conference facilities. The unique selling points will help you to identify the service niche:

Hotel A

USP: Swimming pool
SN: Guests who will enjoy using the pool, young athletic types or those wishing to improve their fitness

Hotel B

USP: Conference facilities
SN: Companies which require conference facilities for meetings and exhibitions

Hotel A would therefore have to target their marketing towards families or groups who would be likely to enjoy the swimming pool facility during their stay at the hotel. A swimming club membership facility for local people could also be investigated to increase local customers.

Hotel B would target their marketing towards companies and institutions who require the large conference facilities for meetings and exhibitions.

Thus there are two completely different service niches for these two hotels.

Once the service niche has been identified, the type of service required by the identified group of customers can be provided. This will result in customer satisfaction, as they will receive the type of service that they expect.

The following questions will need to be answered:

- What are you marketing?
- Is it right for your target customers?
- Is it offered at the right time?
- Is it realistically priced?

CUSTOMER/TIME ANALYSIS

The comparability of time within the same organization is an important aspect of customer research. Take a leisure complex as an example. The swimming pool closes at 9.00 p.m.; the snack bar closes at 8.30 p.m. Thus swimmers cannot obtain a hot or cold drink after their exercise. It will be necessary for the leisure centre to identify which types of customers use which types of amenities. The method used to determine this could be a questionnaire or an analysis of the bookings made and the customers' usage of the snack bar.

Look at this example:

Customer	Times	Prime facility	Additional facility
School	9 a.m.–3 p.m.	swimming pool	—
Swimming club	6 p.m.–9 p.m.	swimming pool	snack bar sauna
Individuals	All day	ice rink sauna gym	swimming pool snack bar
Keep fit club	7 p.m.–9 p.m.	gym sports hall	sauna swimming pool snack bar

From this analysis you can see which areas will be in peak demand, the times and types of customers. It is then possible to plan the staffing and the availability of the different facilities accordingly. This type of time-related customer research is very useful, as well as ensuring good customer service and customer satisfaction it will also help with necessary planning for cleaning and maintenance, and staffing levels.

CUSTOMER/SERVICE ANALYSIS

Customer research also requires you to analyse the services that you are providing. The following type of questions are usually considered:

- What type of service is available?
- Does the service require staff-customer interaction?
- What type of customer–staff contact will there be? Mental/physical?
- How much time does the service take?
- How much time do the SN customers have?
- Is the service convenient for the SN customers?
- Is the service convenient for the staff?
- What does the service look like from the SN customer's point of view?
- Is there any flexibility of service if required?
- How do the customers know what is available?
- What type of trained staff is required?

When all these questions have been answered, it will be possible to ensure that your services match your SN customers.

ACTIVITY

Select an establishment that your know well (maybe a coffee shop or a fast food establishment),

1. Identify the USP for this establishment.

2. Answer the list of questions above.

3. Identify the SN customers that would be appropriate for your selected establishment.

Interaction with customers

POSITIVE ATTITUDE

It is important for all service staff, whether serving internal or external customers, to develop a positive attitude towards their work. The catering and hospitality industry is a people-oriented business and depends on personal interaction at all levels and in all aspects of trade.

What is meant by attitude? Attitude is a state of mind influenced by feelings, thoughts and actions.

The attitude you have to your work will come across to the customer as your attitude to them. They will feel satisfied if your attitude is positive.

SERVICE PERSONNEL ──Positive attitude──▶ CUSTOMER ──────▶ Develops positive attitude

How will the customer know that you have a positive attitude towards your job and therefore towards them? It will be conveyed to the customer by some or all of the following:

- Cheerful disposition
- Enthusiastic approach
- Ability to cope with minor difficulties without hassle
- Doing all tasks well
- Being well groomed at all times
- Speaking clearly to all customers
- Maintaining eye contact with customers
- Working well within a team of staff
- Displaying a comprehensive knowledge of the job
- Being willing to help customers
- Being alert and keen to participate in all tasks

ELEMENTS OF INTERACTION

Body language

Attitude is also conveyed in body language. The signs of a positive attitude are given below.

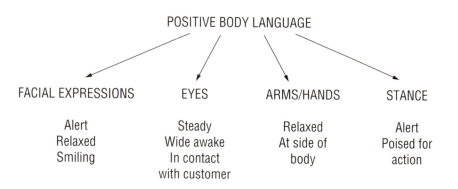

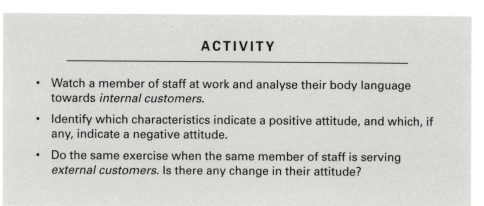

Figure 2.6 Body language conveying a positive attitude

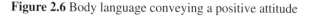

ACTIVITY

- Watch a member of staff at work and analyse their body language towards *internal customers*.

- Identify which characteristics indicate a positive attitude, and which, if any, indicate a negative attitude.

- Do the same exercise when the same member of staff is serving *external customers*. Is there any change in their attitude?

Voice

Attitude is also conveyed strongly by the voice. This applies not only in face-to-face contact but also over the telephone.

The *tone* of voice, is highly significant. *Emphasis* is also important. Different stress put on the same words can alter the meaning of the entire sentence, just as tone can indicate a difference in emphasis.

The *speed* with which you speak can be an indication of your attitude towards customers. It should not be too quick, otherwise customers cannot take in the information being given. A very quick style of speech can also indicate an impatient attitude towards the customers, whereas very slow speech can suggest a 'could not care less' attitude.

All spoken communications need to be *clear* and easily understood by all customers, both internal and external. Regional and national accents can be attractive, but they must be controlled if they cause the customer any difficulty in comprehension.

ACTIVITY

Work with a partner.
   Listen to your voice as you say the sentences below out loud. Record the attitude that your partner displayed. Is the tone of your voice:

   Authoritarian and intimidating
   Crisp and efficient
   Calm and placid
   Firm and friendly
   Quiet and unclear

1. The lift is situated round the corner, by the newspaper stand.

2. The restaurant opens at 7 a.m. for breakfast.

3. Do you wish to order a morning paper?

4. Please write your name and address in the registration book.

5. Would you like a table reservation?

6. Your taxi is here.

Effective listening

As well as speaking to both internal and external customers, it is important to listen to them, and to observe them in order to enable you to interact effectively.

   Effective listening skills can be developed with practice. To be effective you will need to listen to the customer and while taking in the meaning also analyse their tone of voice for clues as to their attitude towards you and the topic being spoken about, and maintain eye contact with them whilst they are speaking.

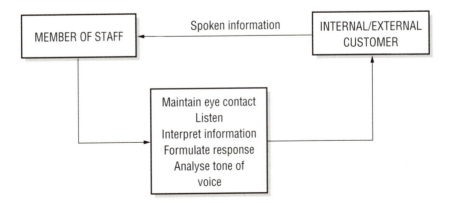

Figure 2.7 Effective listening

ACTIVITY

For this activity you need to work in pairs

1. *Person A*

Take the role of a chef speaking to a kitchen assistant.

2. *Person B*

   You are the kitchen assistant, listening to the chef. Without writing anything down, listen to what the chef is telling you.

   When he/she has finished, answer the following questions:

   • What information did the chef give you?

   • What will your response be?

   • What attitude did the chef convey?

3. Complete the exercise, only swapping roles A and B. *Person A* will be a front office clerk in a hotel; *Person B* will be a hotel guest.

Instances of interaction with customers

There are various aspects of service where *external customer interaction* is expected: in reception areas, food service areas and some housekeeping situations. *Internal staff interaction* is expected in: food preparation areas, maintenance areas and housekeeping areas. From Table 2.2 below you can see how much personal interaction could take place in a hotel.

Table 2.2 Interaction with external and internal customers

External customers

Area	Interaction	Customer	Staff
Reception Concierge	Guest arrives Bill payments Reservation enquiries	Guests Telephone queries	Receptionists Booking clerks
Restaurant and bars	Table reservation Menu selection Cash transactions Drink requests	Residents Casual customers	Restaurant staff Bar staff
Housekeeping	Bedroom supplies Extra bedding requests	Guests	Floor house-keeper Room maids
Food preparation Still room	Room service Lounge service	Guests Casual guests	Kitchen staff Lounge waiters Room service staff
Maintenance	Maintenance requests from guests	Guests	Housekeeper Maintenance staff

Internal customers

Area	Interaction	Customer	Staff
Reception concierge	Guests A/Cs Reservations Room availability Repairs	Bill clerk Front office manager Maintenance Housekeeper	Receptionist Reservations staff
Restaurant and bars	Supplies Linen Laundry	Food/beverage manager Housekeeper Linen staff	Food service staff Bar staff
Housekeeping	Linen requests Staff accommodation	Food service staff Duty manager All hotel staff	Linen staff Housekeeper
Food preparation	Staff meals	Hotel staff	Kitchen staff Head chef
Maintenance	Maintenance requests	All department managers	Maintenance staff

ACTIVITY

Using the summary in Table 2.2 to help you, compile a list of customer staff interaction for an establishment that you know well. Include both external and internal customers in your list.

Good customer care and staff loyalty

Good customer care, i.e. the caring treatment of customers by staff, is dependent on a good relationship between employer and employee, one that encourages a sense of loyalty to the organization. Good customer care is very much bound up with this loyalty: they are interdependent. Interdependence is also characterizes the relationship between management and staff, between groups of staff and between customers and staff.

Take, for example, the staff of a restaurant. You can see from Figure 2.8 that the restaurant owner/manager is dependent on staff, groups of staff are dependent on each other, and all are dependent on the external customers – for without these customers the business would not exist.

ENCOURAGING STAFF LOYALTY

Loyalty can be encouraged and developed in numerous ways. The main way is by giving staff a sense of security, self-worth and of belonging to and being a vital part of the organization (see Figure 2.9). After all without the staff, the organization could not function, and the efforts of the staff govern its success.

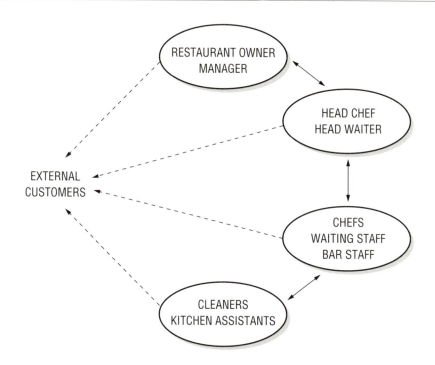

Figure 2.8 Interdependence of staff in a restaurant

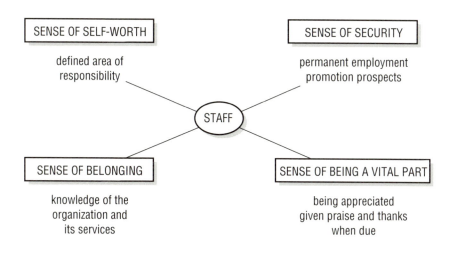

Figure 2.9 Elements of staff loyalty

Leadership

Any leader of a team of staff must be able to command that team's respect. To respect means to have a high opinion of, to look up to, to think highly of.

Leadership qualities involve the ability to:

- do the job oneself in an efficient, competent manner
- communicate effectively with staff and customers
- produce written information, checklists, work cards for staff
- take charge of a situation at a moment's notice
- understand what their staff need in order to be effective
- reward, thank and praise staff as appropriate
- help and coach staff to become more effective team members
- listen and respond to staff and customers
- use leadership authority only when necessary
- take decisions and then carry them out
- be open and honest with staff and customers
- display a positive attitude towards the job and the staff
- encourage staff to participate fully in the tasks to be completed
- show compassion and sympathy when necessary
- work in an organized and fair manner with all staff
- establish a line of authority and adhere to this
- consult with staff and give constructive feedback
- generate a feeling of well-being and a pride amongst the staff
- take responsibility for decisions and actions
- be consistent in attitude and approach to work and staff
- demonstrate a sense of humour and control bad temper at all times
- delegate responsibility to team members as appropriate

Motivating staff is an integral part of leadership. Without this it is impossible to create a climate conducive to constructive leadership. In order to increase staff motivation a team leader will need to ensure that the staff:

- appreciate the reason for the task
- have the necessary equipment to complete the task
- have the knowledge and skill to complete the task
- have the time necessary to complete the task
- feel that they and their work are valued
- receive adequate financial payment for the work achieved
- have access to training and promotion within the organization
- can use their knowledge and skill to their full potential

Teamwork

Teamwork means working effectively together with other staff. It could be a small group of three staff working in a team, or a larger group of ten or more staff. Whether the team is small or large the qualities of a good team member will be the same.

There are teams of staff in all catering and hospitality establishments, for example:

Staff Teams

Hotels	Kitchen brigades Restaurant brigades Housekeeping teams Reception teams
Hospitals	Hospitality teams Cleaning teams
Schools	Caretaking teams Cleaning teams
Leisure centres	Reception teams Coaching teams Cleaning teams Caretaking teams

Team members will have to be willing to:

• communicate effectively with others
• respect other team members
• develop a sense of comradeship with others in the team
• be helpful towards the team members
• be aware of other team members' limitations
• be reliable and punctual
• develop a selfless attitude
• delight in others' success
• demonstrate a sense of humour in a crisis
• give praise and encouragement to other team members
• be honest and open with other team members
• listen to other members of the team
• take responsibility for designated tasks

ACTIVITY

Identify a team that you work with. Keep a log (see below) of your activity as a team member, using the list above to identify relevant aspects to record.

Example of log

Team B

Situation   Restaurant service

Date	Team member attributes	Example
20.10.96	Comradeship and helpfulness	Helped John to serve a large party

Customer compliments and complaints

Compliments and complaints are both important ways of receiving customer feedback. There are two major steps to be taken whenever customers pass on to you either a compliment or a complaint.
  • The first is to thank them
  • The second is to pass this on to the appropriate department

COMPLIMENTS

These are pleasant to receive and a smile and a thank you should be an automatic response by all staff in these circumstances. A short polite conversation, customer-led, is the correct way to handle compliments from customers. Always make the customer:

  • Pleased that they took the trouble to give the compliment
  • Feel at ease whilst talking to you
  • Know that you are genuinely glad to receive the compliment
  • Aware of who you will pass the compliment on to
  • Aware of when you will pass on the compliment

The follow-up to a compliment can sometimes be to suggest a similar product or service that you think that the customer might like to try in the future. For example, a customer in a coffee shop compliments the table-clearing staff upon the excellent apple pie.

  • The staff thank the customer
  • Customer and staff hold a brief conversation
  • Staff recommends other good desserts that the customer might like
  • Staff passes compliment on to the chef

If a customer comments book is used (see p. 81) compliments must be acknowledged in the manager's action column, including a note indicating who the compliment was passed on to. Sometimes a comment from this person is added. This feedback to the person who wrote the compliment is vital to ensure success of the comments book. Customers will not use it for compliments if they do not know what happens to them.

COMPLAINTS

Whether or not you feel that a complaint is justified, it is essential that you listen to customers' comments (see Figure 2.10) and clarify the precise nature of any complaint. Then apologize and tell the customer what action you are proposing to take. In any event, the following steps should be taken:

1. Find somewhere private to speak to the complainant, they sometimes initiate a complaint to attempt to impress others around them.
2. Seat the complainant down in a comfortable chair. They will find this less stressful than being in a position to pace about, stamp their feet and bang their fists on a table.
3. Listen to the complaint. Do not interrupt whilst the complainant is speaking.
4. Establish clearly which circumstance or action caused the complaint. If the complainant is agitated, this may not at once be clear.

5. Encourage the complainant to analyse exactly what has caused the upset. It may be the 'last straw' after a difficult day.

6. Tell the complainant exactly what you propose to do about the situation

All staff should know what actions they are empowered to take in the case of complaints. For example:

A complaint about a dirty glass can be dealt with by the service staff concerned.

A complaint about a noisy bedroom may need to be investigated by the front office supervisor or manager.

Remember, all complaints must be taken seriously and follow-up action taken to ensure that similar faults do not occur again.

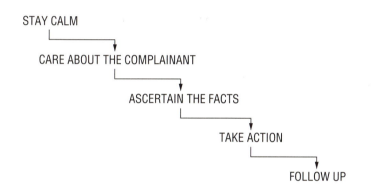

Figure 2.10 Procedure for dealing with complaints

Training for customer care

Good quality customer care will not happen of its own accord, neither will it be maintained automatically. It is necessary to include customer care aspects in both new staff induction training programmes and in existing staff update training programmes.

Customer care training will focus upon:

- staff attitudes towards others
- the product knowledge
- technical skills and related knowledge
- skills in communication
- skills in understanding the customer
- skills in recognizing customer needs
- team building strategies

INDUCTION TRAINING

Induction training is given to all newly appointed staff by their employer. It will combine the skill and technical knowledge needed for the particular job, safety and hygiene knowledge, and customer care skills.

SERVICE AUDIT

This is a way of checking that customer care skills are being practised at all times and involves using a checklist of the key indicators of quality customer care within a defined area. The management staff, guided by this checklist, will observe how well members of the customer service team carry out their duties. The checklist is often graded with numbers to provide 'scores'.

The checklist will focus upon one range of the customer care standards, or one area of the organization at any one time, so that the audit can be effective (see Figure 2.11). An effective audit will show whether there is a need to do any short follow-up training for a specific standard that is not being met.

Customer Care Standards	Above Standard 3	At Standard 2	Not Observed 1	Below Standard –
All customers greeted as soon as they enter the premises				
All telephone calls answered within 30 seconds				
Clean correct uniform worn				
Staff speak in a friendly manner whilst serving				

Figure 2.11 Assessing customer care skills: a grading chart

It is an integral part of the continuous customer care training to conduct these audits and to discuss the findings with the staff concerned. The problem may not be one of insufficient training; it could be caused by physical or material defects or shortages, in which case these can be identified and rectified.

Mystery guests (see p. 82) are also used extensively to monitor customer care standards and to identify training needs.

ACTIVITY

Compile a service audit for an area that you work in. Complete the audit and then discuss the results with the service team.

Sharing authority to act

In order to maintain the customer care standards it is necessary to delegate the authority to care for the customers to all members of the staff. This is particularly relevant when serving the customers face to face, or speaking to customers over the phone. In these circumstances staff sometimes have to give an instant decision to the customer.

There is nothing more frustrating to the customer than asking a simple question and receiving the response 'Oh, I don't know,' as an answer, or 'I'll go and ask the manager.'

Simple requests, or complaints about service or products, must be dealt with in a positive manner as soon as they are received. Some examples are listed below:

Catering:
temperature of the food
cleanliness of cutlery, crockery or glasses
damage to glassware or crockery
cleanliness of table

Reception:
wrong booking made
newspaper not delivered
change required
query on a guests' account

Housekeeping:
additional tea/coffee/milk sachets request
use of an iron
broken kettle or hair dryer
additional bedding request

All staff should have the authority, ability and knowledge to be able to deal with these types of minor queries or comments. If these are met instantly, then the customer will receive satisfaction and there will be no repercussions. If the staff do *not* deal with the request or complaint, then customer care standards will not be maintained and the customer will leave the premises with a negative service performance gap. This is obviously not a desirable situation.

ACTIVITY

List the instances that you have the authority to act upon at your place of work.

Keep a weekly log and note when you have to use this authority

Name _____ Job Title _____

Date	Instance	Action
3/6/96	Cleanliness of glasses	Replaced a smeary glass and informed the wash-up of the complaint

Assisting customers

In order to fulfil the customer care standards, it will often be necessary and desirable to take the initiative in offering assistance. This could be simply holding the door open, calling the lift or arranging a taxi. All of these small tasks are normally carried out by efficient caring staff during the course of their normal work. Assisting can also mean being aware of customer needs almost before they themselves are aware of them: in other words, being able to anticipate customers' requests and so being able to supply them at precisely the right time.

Take the case of regular customers in a public house. Good bar staff will recognize the regular customers and know what their usual drink is; so as soon as they enter the bar, their drink is just about to be poured. Or in a cafeteria-style food service unit, a customer requests a portion of fried fish, the food service staff immediately asks if chips and peas are also required.

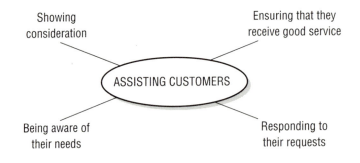

Figure 2.12 Assisting customers

Different types of customers will have different needs and expectations. It is necessary for staff in all types of hospitality and catering units to be aware of the likely needs in order to be able to respond to them efficiently and effectively. A summary of various kinds of assistance is given in Table 2.3.

Table 2.3 Ways in which staff assist customers

Establishment	Staff	Assistance
Hotel	Hall porter	Luggage, taxis, parking
	Concierge	Left luggage, papers, post
		Theatre tickets, messages
	Receptionist	Room reservations
		Guest accounts
	Room maid	Extra bedding, iron
		extra tea/coffee sachets.
Restaurant	Head waiter	Allocating/seating at a table
	Food service staff	Menu interpretation
		Dish selection/choice
	Wine waiter	Beverage selection
	Cashier	Preparation/payment of bill
Bar	Bar staff	Choice and payment of beverage

Cafeteria/coffee shop	Food service staff Cashier Table-clearing staff	Choice of foods and beverages Payment of bill Carry/disposal of tray High chair Directions to WCs
Fast food units	Food service staff Table clearing staff	Choice/payment of food and beverages Disposal of containers/trays Directions to WCs
Leisure centre	Receptionist Sports coach Pool attendant	Bookings for facilities General information Advice and general care Swimming aids Spectator seating
Hospital	Hospitality hostess Ward cleaner	Service of beverages Service of meals Comfort of patient areas
Train	Dining car stewards Buffet car attendants	Allocating/seating at table Service of alcoholic drinks Payment of bill Selection and payment of foods Service/payment of beverages
Aircraft	Steward/Air hostess	Allocation of seat Service of meals and drinks Reassurance/information Issue of pillows/blankets
Cruise liners	Cabin stewards Dining stewards	Information/cabin service Allocation to table Menu interpretation Service of meals Selection/service of drinks

The following are some observations on ways in which staff can help particular groups.

YOUNG CUSTOMERS

Children can be easily upset by unfamiliar surroundings and people. It is necessary to speak kindly and specifically to children so that they feel involved. In this way they are less likely to become upset and noisy. Young children need to be fully occupied in order to keep them out of mischief, it is useful to have some simple activity that you can use in an emergency, in order to occupy them in a quiet, unobtrusive manner.

ELDERLY CUSTOMERS

Elderly persons do not like to be hurried or hassled, patience is sometimes necessary in these circumstances. It must never be apparent that you are in a hurry when serving elderly customers.

They often like to chat to the members of staff, this is part of their enjoyment of the service experience, and staff must be prepared and able to hold a suitable conversation.

CUSTOMERS WITH IMPAIRED MOBILITY

Some customers may need to use a walking stick or a wheelchair. These are used purely to increase their mobility and do not mean that they're unable to make their own decisions. Always imagine what it would be like if you were in a wheelchair, and speak directly to these customers, never speak over their heads. There will probably be some physical help that you can give them, such as opening doors, calling lifts and generally anticipating access and handling difficulties that they might experience whilst on the premises. Any help that you can give should be given in a quiet unobtrusive manner so as not to cause any embarrassment to the customer or to the other persons.

CUSTOMERS WITH IMPAIRED HEARING

It is not always obvious that a customer is using a hearing aid. If you have difficulty getting a customer to understand/hear what you are saying, do not shout. Look directly at them and speak slowly and clearly, using simple sentences. This may enable them to lip-read the information. If any information (e.g. emergency exit procedures) is in written format show them this to make communication easier for both of you.

CUSTOMERS WITH IMPAIRED SIGHT

These customers normally have a very acute hearing abilities. It is therefore unnecessary to raise your voice when speaking to them. Their main difficulty will be one of finding their way around the unfamiliar premises. You could be requested to take them from one area to another. In this case, introduce yourself so that they know who you are, then confirm where it is that they wish to go. Lead them gently by letting them hold your arm, and speak to them while walking, telling them where you are going and warning them of obstacles – a doorway, a step, a turn in the corridor. When you arrive at your destination, tell them, and make sure that they are content before telling them that you are leaving.

CUSTOMERS ON THEIR OWN

Customers on their own need just as much attention as those who come with a companion, in fact sometimes more, since they have no one to talk to, to confer with or to turn to if uncertain about the unfamiliar surroundings. They could need reassurance in the form of a friendly helpful greeting that will instantly put them at ease and make them feel welcome. Undue familiarity, however, should be avoided. Often individual customers are quite happy to be on their own and do not readily take to idle chatter from staff. Your aim should be to make them feel that they may ask you something or pass the time of day with you, if they so wish.

FOREIGN CUSTOMERS

There could be verbal or written comprehension difficulty here. In the case of the first, speak in a slow manner and use simple sentences. There should be no need for you to raise your voice. Always try to help these customers to get as much from their visit as possible.

GROUPS

Group customers could be of any age, or even a mixed age group. Always try and speak to the courier or group leader and they will then communicate the information to everyone else. There will naturally be small groups of people within the main group when speaking/serving these small groups remember that they are all friends or family and treat them as a group, not as four or five individuals.

THREE

Front office operations

Reception area

The reception area is the first point of contact for all persons entering an establishment. It is here that the first impressions are created, including of course those of the customer. There are certain facts on which a receptionist must be well informed. These are listed below with the reason for knowing them.

Facts	Reason
The products/services for sale	To be able to sell these to customers
The facilities available	To increase sales
Local transport and car parking information	To help visitors and customers
Booking/reservation procedures	To take reservations for customers
Persons working in the establishment	To be able to make quick contact for telephone or personal callers
Internal communications systems	To be able to contact all departments and personnel
Telephone and fax systems	External communications
Special sales promotions	To maximize sales
Guest priorities	So that they can fulfil their requests promptly
Guests' apprehensions and needs	So that they can put them at their ease
Body language (own and visitors)	To realize that this displays the receptionist's attitudes, and can tell the receptionist important things about visitors
How to speak appropriately	Good verbal communication is essential to success in customer service

The reception area is the first seen by the visitor/customer. It must therefore be designed and maintained to be a welcoming and efficient area. Any reception office is like the hub of a wheel, linked to the entire establishment by information spokes (see Figure 3.1).

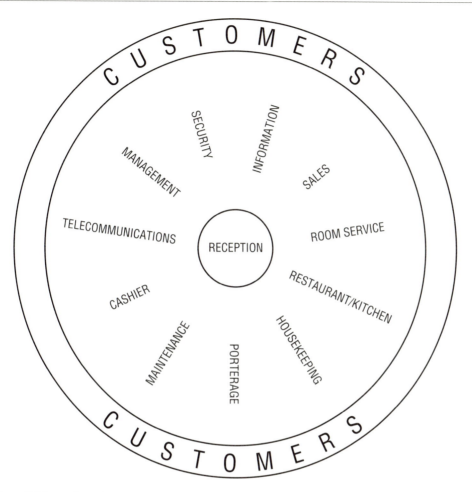

Figure 3.1 Reception wheel

- A reception area must be staffed and working whenever the establishment is open for business.
- The customer/guest must be greeted instantly and attended to as quickly as possible.
- The area should be maintained in a clean tidy manner.
- Adequate lighting, heating and ventilation should be in operation.
- There should be direct access to the main entrance of the premises.
- The atmosphere should be calm and helpful, yet businesslike and efficient.
- It should be a comfortable area for the customer/guest to be in.
- Information about services and tariffs should be visually displayed.
- Staff should be instantly recognizable by the customer/guest.
- Staff should have access to the equipment and paperwork necessary to carry out their duties, without having to leave the reception desk area.
- Staff should be able to visually monitor the main entrance to the premises whilst at the reception desk.
- The area must be used and maintained in a safe and secure manner at all times.

ACTIVITY

Using the wheel in Figure 3.1 list the items that a receptionist would have to deal with when employed in:

(a) a local leisure club

(b) a holiday camp

(c) a residential home

Study the example below to help you:

A hotel receptionist in a city hotel

Information: Facilities in the hotel and the locality. Times of meals and services.

Sales: Immediate and advanced bookings for accommodation and conference trade.

Room service: Liaise between the guest and room service department, take orders for early calls and newspapers.

Restaurant: Take restaurant bookings. Inform kitchen of all reservation numbers.

Housekeeping: Know when rooms are ready to re-let. Inform housekeeper of reservations and late room lettings.

Porterage: Liaise when guests are checking in/out.

Maintenance: Liaise with all departments and keep maintenance staff informed.

Cashier: Pass reservation and bookings information to cashier department so that accounts can be opened and updated.

Telecommunications: Take reservations and enquiries by telephone. Liaise with all other depts by use of the telephone.

Management: Keep management informed as necessary.

Security: Watch main entrance and all visitors, with premises and personnel security in mind. Be responsible for issuing and receiving mail and keys.

ACTIVITY

Investigate the reception area at your place of work or your college.

Ask yourself the following questions:

   Is it easily accessible to all persons?

   Is it easily found?

   Is it well lit and ventilated?

   Is it calm and comfortable?

   Are customers/guests attended to instantly?

Compile a short report giving your findings and recommendations for improvements.

Table 3.1 Front office functions

Establishment	Customer	Reception method
Hotel (3/4 star)	Business persons Conference delegates Tourists	Fast efficient service for booking accommodation by receptionist staff.
Luxury hotel	Overseas business persons Account executives	Individual attention by reception staff. Fast registration for account executives.
Country house hotel	Tourists Mature couples	Individual attention by reception staff. Duty manager introduced.
Conference centre	Business executives Conference delegates Visitors	Individual reception by secretarial/ conference staff.
Motels	Business persons Families Couples	Secretarial/reception clerk, collects payment in advance.
Guest house	Families Travellers	Individual registration by owner/manager.
Hostel	Students Young persons	Registration by clerical staff.
Hospital	Patients Visitors	Registration by ward clerk, then patients by medical personnel.
Leisure Centre	Young persons Groups Families Couples	Registration by clerk receptionist, then by fitness personnel.
Cruise liner	Tourists Mature couples	Registration by steward, then cabin steward.
Holiday camp	Young persons Groups Families Couples	Registration by clerk, then by camp host staff.

THE FUNCTION OF THE FRONT OFFICE

As we have discovered, there are various different types of front office. What is the function of the front office in these different establishments? Table 3.1 gives a summary of some key types of establishments and their front office functions. You may be able to enlarge this chart by looking around similar establishments your own home area.

The duties of hotel front office personnel

The exact duties of front office staff will obviously vary in each hotel, but the summary below will act as a guide to the way that the tasks and responsibilities can be distributed amongst the team in this busy area.

Front officer manager

- Control of the front office and the entire team of staff
- Supervision and training of staff
- Customer relations and the reception of VIP guests
- Liaison with other managerial staff
- Creation of the desired trading and selling atmosphere
- Sale of hotel services
- Security of the front office area
- Security of cash, cheques and vouchers
- Security of guests' property deposited for safe keeping

Supervisor/Senior receptionist

- Supervision of duty staff
- Control of working cash and vouchers
- The day-to-day running of the front office systems
- Production of sales statistics
- Administration of advanced reservations
- Reception of guests
- The promotion of the hotel services
- The creation of a welcoming atmosphere for customers/guests
- Liaison with other departments

Front office clerk

- Processing of guests' arrival and departure
- Assigning guests to appropriate accommodation
- Liaison with other staff and departments
- Responding to guest queries

Cashier supervisor

- Supervision of cashiers
- Liaison with front office team and all other departments
- Issue and receipt of cash floats
- Maintenance of accurate daily business accounts
- Preparation of documentation and cash for banking
- Maintenance of accurate guest accounts

Cashiers

- Compilation of guests' accounts
- Matching of all charges to the correct accounts
- Receipt of payments and issue of receipted accounts
- Assisting the cashier supervisor

Reservations clerk/Receptionist

- Handling all reservation enquiries
- Processing advanced bookings
- Compiling reservation statistics
- Confirming guests' reservations
- Allocating guests' accommodation
- Receiving guests and answering their queries
- Selling hotel services
- Issue of guests' keys or key cards

Concierge/Head hall porter

- Supervision of hall porters, doormen and page boys
- Arranging guests' theatre or tour tickets
- Ordering taxis for guests
- Keeping a watch on the front office area for security
- Taking orders for guests' morning papers and early calls

Porters and pages

- Carrying guests' luggage
- Showing guests to their rooms
- Looking after a left luggage facility
- Taking messages for guests and staff

Doormen

- Watching the front area of the premises
- Deterring undesirable persons from entering
- Calling taxis for guests
- Helping guests in and out of their vehicles
- Advising guests upon car parking facilities
- Liaison with staff in the concierge's department

Customer expectations

Guests/customers will have many expectations formed before they even enter the reception area of an establishment. Their prime expectations will be similar to those listed below.

- Experienced confident staff
- Exceptionally high standards
- Porter to help with luggage
- Straightforward directions to accommodation
- Comfortable surroundings

- Time spent by staff on each individual
- Accuracy of accounts
- Tourist and travel information
- Information about the establishment's facilities
- Efficient operation of equipment
- Knowledge of the job on the part of staff
- Speed of service

ACTIVITY

Working in small groups, study the list above.

Compile a checklist that could be used by newly appointed or trainee reception staff, to remind them of customer expectations.

HOTEL GUESTS' EXPECTATIONS OF THE FRONT OFFICE

The importance of the front office area from a guest's/customer's point of view cannot be over-emphasized. Thus it is worth going into some of their expectations and needs in more detail.

Speed of service

This is essential, particularly at peak booking-in times and checking-out times. It is therefore necessary to organize the work rotas with these peak times adequately staffed.

Individual recognition

Apprehensive, shy guests will appreciate recognition by the receptionist. Guests' names should be used in all conversations. Regular guests should be recognized by front office staff and their preferences noted and remembered for future visits.

Accurate billing service

It is essential that all charges are accurately and promptly charged to the guest's account. Accounts should be updated continually so that they are maintained in a current state at all times.

Comfortable surroundings

The front office area needs to be pleasant and to create an air of comfort. Often armchairs are sited adjacent to the reception desk area, so that guests may wait here or meet friends or simply pause for a while during their busy schedule.

Confidence and morale provider

Large hotels can be intimidating. It is for this reason that friendly, yet efficient, personnel can help to make the shy nervous guest feel more confident and at ease.

Information service

Guests require facts about the establishment's amenities, restaurants and bars. They frequently ask about transport problems and facilities for car parking. Tourists require facts about local sites of interest, as well as directions to a specific place or event.

General assistance

Sometimes guests require an advance booking for accommodation in another town or region. Foreign currency may need to be exchanged. Theatre or concert tickets may be required. Guests' particular needs are listed on pp. 116–17.

Message service

Guests frequently have messages left for them at the front office. These need to be recorded accurately and passed to the guests promptly.

Personal attributes of a receptionist

Whatever type of establishment you are in, there is a need for reception staff. These staff have varied duties to perform, dependent upon the house standards of the establishment where they are employed. Their personal attributes would ideally be as follows:

- Responsive to guest needs at all times
- Calm and able to handle a crisis
- Patient with guests and able to answer their queries
- Trustworthy and able to handle money safely and accurately
- Independent and able to use their own initiative
- Orderly and logical in method of working
- Neat and tidy appearance at all times
- Intuitive, able to identify guests' needs and apprehensions
- Able to speak clearly and directly to the guests
- Capable of being a co-operative team member, with a strong commitment to the team spirit

Customers with special or particular requirements

IN HOTELS

There are many groups of customers/guests that the receptionist must be aware of. In order to give the best service and attention to all persons a summary of groups with particular needs is itemized below. You will be able to add to this summary as you discuss it.

ACTIVITY

Discuss the list of personal attributes given above.

Using your word processing skills, design a page of a staff induction booklet that will remind reception employees of these attributes.

Business persons

Reception must be fast and efficient. There should be no queuing either to book in, or to settle accounts. A good message-taking facility is required. The ability to invoice head office for the account is essential.

Educational groups

A pre-registration facility is essential. Clear precise directions to their accommodation and the facilities is required. The account should be pre-paid for the accommodation and inclusive of meals. A payphone booth is required.

Tourists

Currency exchange facilities are required, as is information about local heritage sites, tours, local transport, theatres and entertainment. The ability to speak a foreign language is an asset.

Elderly persons

A lift and easy access to facilities and accommodation is required by these customers. Menus that include dishes that are easily digested, particularly in the evening, are welcome. Calm quiet surroundings away from noise and traffic are appreciated.

Families

Facilities for a child's bed or cot are often requested. Rooms with communicating doors are desirable for these guests. A child's menu served in the early evening is appreciated, as is a child-minding service during the evening. Gardens that are safe and secure will allow the children to take exercise without disturbing other guests.

Physically disabled persons

Access for wheelchairs and non slip paths and slopes with hand-rails all make the stay more enjoyable because these measures aid the guest's independence. Low-level facilities in both bedroom and bathrooms are essential. Space must be provided to manoeuvre a wheelchair around the fixtures and fittings; there must also be space enough to allow these guests to integrate with others using the same areas and facilities. The receptionist must make a note for the duty staff to escort physically disabled persons from the premises in the event of an emergency.

Sight-impaired persons

Assistance will be required to register these guests. They must be escorted to their accommodation and shown around the rooms. They should also be shown the way to the lifts, as well as to the stairs and emergency exits. The receptionist must make a note for the duty staff to escort these sight-impaired persons from the premises in event of an emergency.

Hearing-impaired persons

Clear speech that enables lip-reading should be used by the reception staff for these guests. Concise sentences without extra 'chat' is desirable. Some written information may be provided to help these guests know about the facilities, meal times and other arrangements, and they should be escorted to their accommodation and shown around the facilities. The receptionist must make a note for the duty staff to escort any hearing-impaired persons from the premises in the event of an emergency.

Non-English speaking persons

Information may be translated into foreign languages to aid these persons. Clear, concise speech should be practised at all times, and the guests should be escorted to their accommodation and shown the facilities and the emergency exits.

Persons with special dietary requirements

The receptionist must make a note of any special dietary requests. These should be passed to the catering department as soon as possible.

High security persons

Liaison with duty management and the security forces is essential in these cases. Reception staff will have to abide by any special rules peculiar to this visit. Liaison will commence prior to the visit. Extra attention to tidiness of the work area, and extra vigilance of all personnel and guests will be required.

IN OTHER ESTABLISHMENTS

Within the hospitality industry, there are organizations other than hotels where reception staff have a particular duty to their customers. These include hostels, hospitals, and homes for the elderly.

Hostels

These may be youth hostels, halls of residence or YMCA hostels. In all these establishments there will be young persons staying. In most cases they will be pre-booked for a specified length of time. Payment will have been made in advance; per stay for the youth hostel, per month for the YMCA, and per academic year for the halls of residence. Payments will be made to a clerical member of the staff.

Hospitals

There will be three completely different groups of people requiring reception assistance at a hospital.

The staff Medical staff have the facility to live in hospital-owned and -managed accommodation in a great number of UK hospitals. The nursing staff rent bed/sitting-room style accommodation, the junior doctors rent self-contained flats, whilst the senior medical staff may be able to rent a house.

When these staff first arrive at the hospital, they need to be welcomed and shown their accommodation. This is usually the duty of the domestic services manager, or the hospitality manager.

The patients At the main hospital reception, patients for admission into hospital are first of all seen by the duty reception staff who need above all to display sympathy and understanding. It is also essential to give accurate information to the patient and to their family. Patients are directed from reception to their ward or treatment area, where the ward clerk will register them and introduce them to their clinical nurse. The clinical nurse will take the reception of the patient to its conclusion by spending some time talking to the patient and obtaining all the necessary information, and putting them at ease by answering their questions, showing them their bed and introducing them to other patients.

The visitors Patients' families and friends are encouraged to visit, they will frequently arrive at the main reception area to ask where their relative is being treated and accommodated. Fast accurate directions are essential. At main visiting hours there will be a steady stream of visitors.

Maximizing sales

Every service that is sold in the hospitality and catering industry is the result of a member of staff actively making that sale. Whether the item is a meal, a newspaper, a room or a conference package, the skills necessary to sell it are in fact the same. It should be understood that it is as easy to lose a sale as it is to make one: and an important part of making a sale is letting the potential customer know what is for sale.

When customers approach a front office how do they know what services are for sale?

SELLING TECHNIQUES FOR FRONT OFFICE PERSONNEL

Remember that it is the front office personnel who can create sales and maximize potential sales. In Table 3.2 you will see a list of *positive* sales techniques that are used by effective front office personnel, set opposite a list of *negative* attitudes and habits that will have the disastrous effect of reducing sales. Study the list and then complete the activity.

ACTIVITY

Investigate the methods used to let customers know what services and products are available in *two* of the following types of front office.

(a) A three-star city hotel

(b) A large leisure centre/sports complex

(c) A holiday camp

(d) A roadside motel

When you have completed your investigation, write a short report that draws a comparison between the methods used by these two types of front office. Ask yourself:

1. What are the reasons for using the methods that you have identified?

2. Which methods were used by both types of front office?

3. Why were some methods not used by both types of front office?

4. Could you suggest any other methods that these types of front office could use?

5. Which methods did you think were most effective/least effective?

Photograph reproduced by permission of
Simon Jersey.

Table 3.2 Front office personnel as sales people: positive and negative attributes

	Positive	Negative
Personal appearance	Neat, smart uniform; clean hands and nails; tidy, clean hair.	Crumpled, ill-fitting uniform; inappropriate style of dress; dirty hands and nails; dirty untidy hair.
Speech	Clear and concise, giving definite facts. Good prompt telephone manner	Muddled facts, unclear rambling manner. Poor slow telephone manner.
Interest	Genuine concern for the establishment's services and for all potential customers. Eye contact is maintained with the customer.	Lack of interest is displayed to the potential customer. Eye contact is not maintained.
Time	Unhurried response to all customer questions and queries.	Hurried, half-hearted response. Persistent referral to the clock whilst customer is speaking.
Knowledge	Well-informed. Good level of knowledge of services, products and tariffs.	Lack of knowledge of services, products and tariffs.
Techniques	Services and products described to increase sales. Customers asked if they require/ would like any other services.	No positive additional information offered to customers.
Attitude	Cheerful, enthusiastic and interested in their job. This will increase customer satisfaction and therefore sales.	Lack of enthusiasm is evident. This will have a demotivating effect upon customers and staff.

ACTIVITY

Below is a list of positive and negative phrases that could be used by front office personnel when speaking to customers and guests.
Add at least four more of your own.

Phrases to encourage sales	*Phrases that will reduce sales*
Good morning	Hi
May I help you?	What do you want?
Just a moment, I will find out	Oh, I don't know
I will ask Mr — to have a word with you	Mr — will deal with you.
May I offer you ....?	D'you want....?

GENERATING SALES IN OTHER SECTIONS

We have been considering the sales techniques in relation to the front office. This is not the only section of the hospitality industry where sales are generated. The following is a list of some of the areas where sales can be generated, with an indication of what can be sold.

Front office
Accommodation
Private functions
Conferences
Secretarial services

Marketing department
Special accommodation promotions
Conferences and private functions
Corporate accounts.

Housekeeping
Laundry and valeting services
Mini-bar sales
Video hire

Catering and refreshment
Restaurant meals
Alcoholic beverage sales
Room service

Concierge
Postage stamps
Newspapers
Theatre tickets
Tourist guides and trips

Franchise shops
Stationery
Newspapers and magazines
Books
Confectionery
Souvenirs
Hairdressing/barber shop

Leisure suite
Mini-gymnasium facilities
Fitness classes
Swimming and sauna
Sunbed and massage services

Selling hotel facilities and services

ACCOMMODATION

The accommodation available has sales points, which need to be promoted. This involves knowing:

- the types and prices of rooms that are available at any given time, the location of each room and its capacity and special features
- the services that are available for the guests (e.g. room service meals, restaurant facilities, bistro/coffee shop services, licensed bar facilities, leisure suite services, hairdresser/barber facilities, TV and video availability, telephone and fax facilities, secretarial facilities)

SPECIAL ACCOMMODATION OFFERS

At times hotels may offer accommodation at special (reduced) rates. Staff need to know:

- the standard 'rack rate' charge for accommodation and the special tariffs, the conditions appertaining to each special tariff, the numbers of persons that it may apply to, whether children may be included, the dates or days on/between which the tariff may be applied

ACTIVITY

Imagine that you are employed in the front office area of a time share complex, comprising individual chalets and a large club house and restaurant. The chalet complex is sited in the countryside with nearby facilities for golf, bowls, tennis, and swimming.

Write a short report to cover your answers to the following questions:

1. What facilities have you to sell?

2. To whom are you able to sell these facilities?

3. What methods are you likely to use to increase your sales?

- the services included in the special promotion, transport to/from the nearest railway station or airport, the type of accommodation available; meals and beverage services
- special attractions that are included: e.g. sporting activities, heritage events, musical or dramatic entertainment, tuition in special interests or hobbies

PRIVATE FUNCTIONS AND CONFERENCE FACILITIES

In this area, staff can promote sales by knowing:

- the rooms and suites that are available, how these areas can be combined or divided to alter their shape and capacity, their maximum permitted capacity, price and billing arrangements, access arrangements to each area and car parking facilities
- the services that are available with these areas, furniture and seating arrangements, audio equipment, staging and lighting fitments, overhead projector, video and telephone facilities
- the hospitality facilities that can be provided: receptionist and secretarial support, refreshments and meals, beverages and private licensed bar facilities, special rate overnight accommodation for participants and delegates

CORPORATE ACCOUNTS

These are arranged for companies that use an establishment's facilities on a regular basis: for example, an industrial company whose executives always use a specific group's hotels whenever they have to travel away from home. Promotion of such accounts requires a knowledge of:

- the special booking-in procedures for these guests, their names and particular requirements, any special rates that apply, and the account details

LAUNDRY AND VALETING SERVICES

Hotels in the upper price bracket provide this service for guests. The staff need to know:

- which services are available, their prices, the times for collection and delivery, any special treatments that are available
- the method of allocating these guest charges to the appropriate guest accounts as soon as they are billed

IN-ROOM ENTERTAINMENT

This is in the form of a video rental service, whereby the guests select a video from a list displayed in their room. Their choice is then screened on the TV in their hotel room. Promoting sales in this area involves knowing:

- the number of 'trial' minutes that the guest may watch before incurring a charge, the method of billing the guest for this service

MINI-BARS

These are small refrigerated units placed in the guests' accommodation for their convenience. They are stocked with alcoholic and non-alcoholic beverages. For this area of sales the staff need to know:

- the charges for the full range of beverages in the mini-bars, the availability of replacements should the need arise between servicing times, the availability of savoury biscuits and nuts, and ice cubes
- the method of charging the guests for all items removed from their mini-bar

RESTAURANT MEALS

Guests and customers will often enquire at the front office when they require restaurant meals or the less formal coffee shop/ bistro style service. The front office staff will need to know about:

- the types of services (and menus) available, their cost and the service times
- the method of booking these services for the customer/guest, and how to convey this booking to the appropriate department
- the method of billing the customer/guest after they have used these services

ALCOHOLIC BEVERAGES

In the same way the customers enquire about meals they will often enquire about licensed bar facilities. The front office staff will need to know:

- the types of services available to the guests, the hours between which these service are available, the age restrictions that apply to young adults, the restrictions that apply to non-residents
- the service that is available in the lounge areas as well as those available in the guests' accommodation
- the method of billing guests for the services used

ROOM SERVICE

This service is available for hotel guests who require private, personal service in their room or suites. The front office staff will need to know:

- the menu available, the service charges and the times between which each service is available, the approximate delay time between ordering and the service being delivered to the guest
- the method of billing the guest for this service

CONCIERGE

In hotels, the front office staff will need to know which guest services are available through the concierge section. These two sections of the hotel are sited close together in the main foyer area. Guests often do not know which member of staff to speak to if they require, for example, tourist guides or information on postage rates. The front office staff will need to know:

- which services are carried out by the concierge section, and how to politely re-direct the guest
- the availability of theatre tickets, the method of booking these, the local tourist guides and events, local methods of transport and car parking arrangements
- the method used to book early morning calls and newspapers for guests
- the methods of billing guests for these services

FRANCHISE RETAIL SHOPS

These facilities are provided for the convenience of the guests/customers. The front office staff will be asked where these facilities are situated. They will need also to provide information on:

- the full range of goods and services that are supplied by these shops
- their trading times and location
- whether it is possible for the goods and services purchased to be invoiced on the customer's hotel bill

LEISURE SUITE

This service is becoming increasingly popular in hotels. The front office staff will need to know:

- the full range of facilities available, prices, opening times and any restrictions upon children's admittance
- the method of billing guests who use the facilities
- the costs and regulations for members of the public who wish to use the facilities

Security

Security means the safety of guests, staff, premises, personal belongings, equipment and fittings within the premises, and security of the grounds, car parks and outbuildings.

Premises security	Internal security
Main entrance	Public rooms
Windows/patio doors	Guest rooms
Delivery areas	Lifts
Emergency exits	Furniture
Minor/staff exits	Fittings/equipment
Gardens	Guests'/staff property
Car parks	Stock
	Cash/credit counterfoils

Always remember, security is the responsibility of all staff at all times in all types of establishments, but because the reception area is used by all members of the public and has a unique physical position within the establishment, one of the prime concerns of all front office staff must be that of security. Whether the front office staff are working in a luxury hotel, a guesthouse or a leisure complex there are certain aspects of security with which they must be familiar.

Customers and guests should have the peace of knowing that they are using safe and secure premises. It is possible to make the users of some types of premises (e.g. schools, university halls of residence, colleges of further education, leisure clubs, sports clubs) feel partly responsible for security. In these types of establishments, the users can be made to feel that they have a vested interest in the maintenance of a high yet acceptable level of security. They will not relish the prospect of fittings and equipment going missing or becoming damaged, or their area being spoilt by undesirable trouble-makers.

SECURITY POLICY

In order to maintain an effective level of security, it is necessary to have a security policy. This should be agreed between all relevant groups and employees' representatives. The security policy should identify the persons responsible to each area/unit/establishment. Although, as stated earlier, all staff must take responsibility for security, ultimately there must be someone to take specific responsibility.

For example, in the front office of a hotel there could be a duty receptionist, one or more front office clerks, a cashier and a hall porter. Who is ultimately responsible for the safety of residents' valuables deposited in the hotel safe? Or for the ejection of an undesirable person from the hotel foyer area? Or for noticing an unclaimed suitcase lying under a table in the foyer?

All staff here may have received training to make them aware of these and similar security aspects, and to teach them what to do if security-related incidents occur whilst they are working. However, the ultimate responsibility will rest with the duty manager. Thus a successful security policy relies on the vigilance and awareness of all staff but the ultimate responsibility lies with a designated individual.

EXTERNAL SECURITY

When premises are being planned or altered, it is advisable to contact the police architectural liaison officer. This officer will be able to advise on the best way to plan and use the premises from the security point of view.

The local crime prevention officer should be consulted if there are security problems, these officers have a vast amount of both local and national expertise.

Closed circuit television is often employed in premises used by members of the general public. This enables one security officer to monitor several areas simultaneously, both inside and outside the premises.

Gardens. It is necessary to survey the boundary security for all grounds and gardens. Good illumination will deter intruders. Gates should be secure and robust.

Car parks that are exclusively for the customers/guests, should be labelled as such and have good illumination. Low walls, shrubs and trees may look very attractive during daylight hours, but will provide good hiding areas for potential trouble-makers/thieves after dark.

Delivery areas need to be controlled at all times. It is unnecessary to lose stock and equipment because it has not been removed to a secure holding area upon delivery.

EXITS FROM PREMISES

Windows and patio doors should have independent locking devices fitted, so that each may be locked at night as well as during the day when the room is not in use.

Minor exits need to be closely monitored, as these could be a means of entry/exit for potential thieves or undesirable persons. It is worth analysing their usage. Are they really necessary? Are they used only as emergency exits?

Emergency exits are always labelled with green signs, which are illuminated after dark. This enables people inside the premises to leave quickly and safely in an emergency, but prevents anyone from entering by these doors.

INTERNAL SECURITY

Rooms

Public rooms should be thoroughly checked at the end of each trading period, so as to ensure that no undesirable persons are hiding, waiting for staff to leave the area. Most public areas can be locked once trading activity has ceased. This will give extra security to staff and for the fixtures and fittings within that area.

Guest rooms in any residential premises are always fitted with an individual locking device. This enables the occupant of the room to treat it as they would their own home and leave their clothes and personal items there in the knowledge that they are safe.

Changing rooms. These are provided for members of the public using sports and leisure facilities in clubs and local centres. Lockers should be provided so that personal belongings can be safely stored whilst the sporting activities are taking place. Keys are numbered to correspond with the individual lockers. A key is normally available on registration, prior to the activity. The keys are returned on departure.

Staff rooms are provided for employees at their place of work. Keys are provided for individual lockers, to enable staff to leave their outer wear and personal belongings in a safe place whilst they are at work.

Conference areas

Extra vigilance is required in these areas to ensure that no suspect packages/bombs have been hidden. This is particularly important when an exhibition or display has been set up, thereby providing many more hiding places.

When checking these areas the named person responsible will use a security checklist. The procedure is to look for anything that is out of place, upwards first, then at eye level, then at surface level, finally at floor level and below. The search is always carried out in a clockwise direction around each part of the conference complex. The crime prevention officer will always give advice and assistance with the compilation of a checklist for this.

Lifts

Passenger lifts should always be called to the ground floor at the end of the trading period. Here they may be checked and the doors left open. This ensures that no undesirable person is hiding there, and that no suspicious package has been left there.

Delivery/service lifts should be treated in a similar manner, and items inadvertently left in these lifts should be investigated and removed.

Furniture and fittings

If all areas are properly locked there should be no difficulty in protecting these items. Small items are sometimes taken, usually by departing guests or opportunist petty thieves. Prompt checking of guests' rooms upon the payment of their account can help to detect such losses. The guest could still be on the premises, having breakfast or a stroll around the grounds.

In leisure complexes small items, such as balls, shuttle cocks, towels and mats are attractive to opportunist petty thieves. To minimize such thefts, the reception staff will often issue these items upon registration for the activity, and retrieve them at the end of the session.

Property of resident guests

Valuable items can be deposited in the hotel safe deposit area. In small hotels this may simply be an envelope signed for and placed in the hotel safe. In larger hotels individual safe boxes/drawers are provided for guests to rent during their stay.

Reception staff will complete a safe deposit form and sign for the receipt of the guest's property.

Cash

This must be the responsibility of the cashier in the front office team, who will issue and retrieve cash floats and give receipts for any cash deposited with him/her. In small establishments this duty may be assigned to the manager or duty manager. The following points need to be borne in mind:

- Staff required to handle cash should be carefully selected, prior to this duty being agreed.
- Cash floats will always have to be signed for at the beginning of each working session.

- Cash receipts will be verified by the relevant till readings at the end of each working session. All cash receipts will be handed to the cashier and signed for by the staff and the cashier.
- Cash is counted, bagged and deposited in the safe as soon as it is received. This process should never be carried out in view of members of the public. It could put temptation in their way.
- Cash and cheques should be banked daily. Transporting cash to the bank should be arranged with advice from the bank and the crime prevention officer. Large businesses may use a security firm to collect and deliver their cash.

PERSONNEL SECURITY

High security visits

When such a visit is being arranged, involving, for example, a government minister, a member of the royal family or a foreign diplomat, the police will be involved. At the planning stage they will contact the management of the establishment concerned and joint planning will take place from this point.

A search of the premises and surrounding area will be carried out by the police force, prior to the time of the visit. In some cases a list of employees and contractors is required by the police force, so that security checks can be made. When a crowd is in any one confined area, such as at an exhibition or conference, it may be thought necessary to search their handbags/cases as they enter. The reception staff are often required to inform attendees that this search is being carried out.

Suspicious/undesirable persons

The front office staff in any organization will be the first people to have the opportunity of detecting such persons.

Always notice persons loitering in the reception/foyer area and ask yourself what they are doing there. It is sometimes a perfectly innocent person simply waiting for a colleague, but suspicions should be aroused if they seem to be checking security measures – eyeing closed circuit cameras, alarm systems, etc.

Visitors to the premises who will not look the receptionist in the eye whilst holding a conversation should arouse suspicion, as should potential guests who arrive with a very light suitcase or an immensely heavy bag.

Customers who wish to pay for all their services with a credit transaction or a cheque, may not in fact have the necessary money to pay for these services.

Visitors or potential customers who are wearing entirely the wrong mode of dress should arouse suspicion. Ask yourself why they want to avail themselves of the facilities and services that the establishment provides, and can they pay for them?

Accidents on the premises

If a member of the public or the staff sustains an accident and requires an ambulance, the front office staff must call one immediately.

In leisure clubs and sports areas guest safety is a very high priority. There are many potential areas for accidents. The front office staff in these areas will have a checklist to follow in event of accidents. This will include the contact number to call for the first aider, the duty manager and the senior sports personnel.

Illness

Should a guest or member of staff fall ill and request a visit from a doctor, the front office staff must inform the duty manager, who, together with the housekeeper, will ascertain the nature of the problem. Either of these senior members of staff will then request the front office staff to call the doctor.

If a guest in a hotel requests medication from a pharmacy the front office staff should contact the housekeeper. The housekeeper will ascertain if the guest is well, and if necessary ask the concierge section to fetch the item for the guest.

If a member of staff reports a suspected fatality on the premises, the front office staff will be required to telephone for an ambulance and the police. The area should be protected from any interference. If possible an emergency key must be issued to lock the area.

Fire

When a fire is discovered, the front office staff must call the fire brigade immediately (see p. 305 for telephone procedures). The register of all personnel within the premises must be taken by the front office staff to their evacuation point, so that the duty manager and the fire brigade can account for all personnel.

Suspicious packages

Letter/parcel bombs are commonly posted in a padded envelope. The address and writing could be faulty and untidy, a rectangular object the size of a cassette may be felt inside the wrapping, grease marks may be visible. If one or more of these factors is detected, the front office staff should immediately leave the area, lock the door and inform the duty manager. The duty manager will then investigate and if necessary will call the police.

All staff should be aware of the potential danger from bombs in cases or bags. In the front office area there are often bags and cases of all sizes. Front office staff should be conscious of any items that do not appear to belong to anyone. Items left under tables, in corners, by waste paper bins or in telephone booths unattended should be immediately reported to the duty manager. Like letter bombs, they should never be tampered with or touched by any front office staff. The duty manager will decide on necessary action once it has been established that the object has in fact been abandoned.

Staff training

As previously mentioned, security is a team responsibility. Thorough staff training is the key to a security-conscious business. All personnel must understand the needs for good security and to know their role in its implementation.

SECURITY DOCUMENTATION

There are various forms of documentation that front office staff in all types of hospitality establishments may be required to use. A summary of these is given in Table 3.3.

Table 3.3 Forms of security documentation

Document	Details included	Main purpose
Callers' register	Date, visitors' name, company, arrival time, person being seen, departure time	Records names of all visitors, useful for fire and security emergencies
Visitors' identity badges	As above	Instantly identifies a visitor
Staff in/out book	Date, staff name, department, time out, destination, time in	Provides an instant record of staff on the premises in the event of fire, security alert, messages, emergencies
Appointment book	Date, visitors' name, company, person being seen, time of arrival	Provides a record of the day's appointments, and of who to expect
Message form	Date, caller's name, company, message for, the message, caller's phone number, time, message taken by	Provides a reminder of all messages received, and who they are for

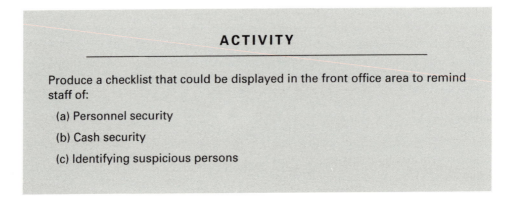

ACTIVITY

1. Using your word processing skills, design two of the security documents listed above.

2. Collect a copy of the other three types of security document from your place of training or work. Remember to mark these with the word 'specimen' to prevent them from being used by anyone.

HOTEL KEYS

Small hotels usually use the traditional manual locking system with conventional keys. Electronic systems, increasingly used, are useful in large busy hotels, where there is a constant change of room occupancies. It is an efficient system but very expensive to install. Keys can be of varying sizes and designs, but the principles of security and safety will apply to them all.

Manual locking system

The standard key suite comprises:

Grandmaster. There will only be one or two of these keys within the whole establishment, held by staff at senior management level. The grandmaster key will open all locked doors within the establishment. Security of these keys is vital; a loss would be very serious.

Floor master. These will be used by floor housekeeping and security staff. They will open all the doors on a particular floor of the building. These staff have the responsibility of checking rooms after they have been serviced and therefore need to have access to the rooms on their floor.

Submaster. These will be used by the daily room maids and servicing staff who need access to each room within their work sector. These keys will open all the doors within a work sector but no other sector. These submaster keys are handed out to the staff at the beginning of their working shift and handed back when their work is completed. The next shift of staff will then be able to use the same keys. This procedure prevents too many staff having keys to parts of the establishment.

Guest room keys. These are issued to the guest when they have completed their registration upon their arrival. They are issued in conjunction with a key card. The key card is used by the guest when wishing to log service charges from the restaurant and bars to their account. It proves that they are a bona fide guest. It is also used to regain their keys from the concierge if they have been out of the hotel.

The concierge section of the front office in larger hotels will be responsible for the issue of these keys, which are normally kept on a numbered rack/board when not in guests' possession. The numbers on the rack correspond to the room numbers so that they can be issued quickly and efficiently. It is also easy to see which keys are not there.

```
╔══════════════════════════════════════════════════════════╗
║                                                            ║
║                    ~ Crown Inn ~                           ║
║                                                            ║
║      Guest   . . . . . . . . . .    Rate   . . . . . . . . . . . .     ║
║                                                            ║
║      Room    . . . . . . . . . .    Room Type   . . . . . . . .   ║
║                                                            ║
║      Date from   . . . . . . . .    Terms   . . . . . . . . . .    ║
║                                                            ║
║      Date to   . . . . . . . . .            . . . . . . . . . . . . . . .  ║
║                                                            ║
╚══════════════════════════════════════════════════════════╝
```

Figure 3.2 Example of a key card

Supply keys. These are used within the servicing sectors of the hotel by supervisory levels of the staff to ensure that stocks and equipment are safely stored away when not in use. Examples are the linen room, equipment store rooms, offices, stationery cupboards.

Electronic locking system

This system makes use of plastic keys rather than conventional keys. Electronic systems are used for the following reasons:

- A new combination is created for each newly registered guest
- The plastic key is unaffected by humidity, dirt or temperature
- The doors are automatically deadlocked for guest privacy and security
- An interior door knob will open the door from inside the room
- The lock only opens if the correct key is inserted
- The bulky traditional keys are no longer required
- No time is taken up by collecting and distributing bulky keys to guests. The key rack is no longer required.

Key security

- All keys in the key suite must be regularly checked to ensure that none has been lost
- Staff should not be allowed to take the keys off the premises in case they are lost or stolen
- A supply of replacement lock barrels is needed in case a guest inadvertently takes their key away with them
- Conventional keys should be fitted with large tags to help prevent their loss
- The room keys should be issued to each guest after they have been registered by the receptionist, and given their key card
- The key card acts as guest identification and proves that the person is actually a resident in the hotel

Safety

SAFETY IN THE FRONT OFFICE AREA

As stated on p. 109, security must be a prime concern of front office staff. However, safety must come a close second. The list below may seem surprisingly long but it will also indicate obvious areas of potential disaster should safety precautions be ignored.

Front office safety checklist

- Unplug electrical equipment when not in use.
- Never allow flexes (telephone or other) to trail across work areas or floors.
- Never overload electrical sockets.
- Do not store or pile papers on or near heaters.
- Never leave fan heaters/coolers operating in unattended areas.
- Place the heaviest books and files on the lower shelves.
- Place bulky files in lowest drawer in filing cabinet.
- Use fireproof cabinets and cupboards.
- Keep emergency exits clear at all times.
- Never pile papers, boxes or files on the floor.
- Use good lighting that will eliminate dark areas.
- Work in a position that gives an immediate view of all callers.
- Never leave cash, cheques or counterfoils unattended.
- Keep all cash out of reach of the reception desk.
- Never cash-up in view of callers/visitors.
- Keep all keys out of view of callers/visitors.
- Empty waste paper bins regularly.
- Never allow smoking in this work area.
- Have well lit, walk-in storage cupboards.
- Arrange safe storage for OHPs, flip charts and screens.
- Work in a tidy organized manner.

ACTIVITY

Investigate the safety standards and practices in a front office area in one of the following:

(a) Hospital

(b) Leisure complex

(c) Holiday camp

Using the safety checklist above, compile a report to show your findings.

EMERGENCY EVACUATION PROCEDURES

The two usual reasons for evacuation are fire or a suspected bomb. Less common reasons could be an imminent danger from flooding or a toxic leak. In the case of these two causes, the manager will be informed by the emergency services and their instructions will therefore be followed.

For regular emergencies it is necessary to have an evacuation plan that can be put into instant effect should the need arise. The instruction to evacuate the premises should be made by the duty manager. The front office staff have the responsibility for the call to the emergency services, they must therefore have exact details of the emergency from someone in authority.

EVACUATION PLANS

The following list gives some good reasons why we have evacuation plans with which all staff and residents should be familiar:

- to enable the premises to be evacuated within the minimum time
- to ensure the safety of all persons on the premises
- to ensure the safety of all persons after evacuation
- to make known alternative routes from all areas of the premises
- to have a known way of checking that no person or group of people is trapped
- to ensure that staff know in advance the procedure for evacuation

ALARMS

These will be activated by the duty manager when the emergency has been reported. The bells are loud and will continue to ring until stopped by the fire brigade. They need to be checked at regular intervals to ensure that they are in working order, a procedure that usually involves the front office staff. The alarm is test-rung for a couple of seconds at a predetermined time on a weekly basis. Smoke alarms, sprinklers and wall-mounted extinguishers are checked every three months on average. A record of these checks should be kept in the front office files.

STAFF TRAINING

Regular evacuation training must take place in any establishment that is used by the public. It can be arranged without the public being involved or disrupted if enough thought is given to the matter.

EVACUATION PRACTICES

These need to be carried out on a regular basis. Different days and times need to be used so that all staff become familiar with the procedures.

Hotels and guesthouses

Staff need to be given an area each to be responsible for. These key staff will then check every room within their area and escort everyone outside to the allocated assembly point as quickly and safely as possible.

ACTIVITY

Investigate the evacuation procedures for the building in which you work, or attend for study such as a college.

Ask yourself the following questions:

• How do I know if there is a fire?

• How do I know how to get out of the building quickly?

• Why must I use the stairs and not the lift?

• Where do I go once outside the building?

• Do I have to tell anyone that I have come out of the premises?

• When can I go back inside?

• Can I go away, or must I stay with everyone else?

Guests of the hotel will need to be given emergency shelter until the all clear message is received. Front office staff must take the hotel register with them and check all residents against this. One member of staff will be responsible for checking all staff.

Boarding schools, halls of residence and staff hostels

Senior pupils/students or wardens will have the responsibility of checking specified areas and of marshalling the resident students and staff from the premises. The warden/matron will take the list of residents and check their whereabouts.

Schools and colleges

The class registers are used to ascertain the whereabouts of all students. One member of the staff will be responsible for checking all staff.

Leisure centres, exhibition halls, day centres

In these and other premises where members of the public are not resident, staff will be responsible for the safe evacuation of their areas. Front office staff will take their registers, or numbers, of persons within the premises, and check the evacuated persons against this.

Hospitals

Difficulties arise here because of the ill health of the patients, and in some cases because of the complex machinery that has to be moved to keep the patients in a stable position. The evacuation strategy has to be very carefully supervised. A security committee will oversee any such emergency, aided by all medical and ward staff.

Safety legislation

There are regulations on safety that apply to the front office area in particular, and legislation that applies to the hospitality industry as a whole. Full copies of relevant Acts and regulations may be studied at your local reference library. Table 3.4 gives an annotated list of the principal documents affecting the running of front office and accommodation sections of the industry.

Table 3.4 Principal health and safety legislation for the hospitality industry

Legislation	Application	Main points
Health & Safety at Work Act 1974	All places where people are employed	Employers must have safe premises and equipment. Employees have a duty to work in a safe manner. Training must be given. Local Authority can inspect premises at any time. Safety policy must be compiled and adhered to at all times.
First Aid Regulations 1981	All places where persons are employed.	Code of practice must be adhered to. Facilities, equipment and trained personnel must be provided.
Fire Precautions Act 1971	All establishments used by public	Adequate means of fire-fighting and escape have to be provided in the premises. A fire certificate is granted by the fire brigade when the premises are deemed to be safe. Maximum numbers of persons permitted in the premises are stipulated.
Trade Descriptions Act 1968		No false statements can be made about the facilities or services offered to the public. Careful wording of all advertisements and all statements about the services is essential.
Tourism Order 1977		Overnight accommodation prices in establishments with four or more rooms must be displayed. An obvious measure would be to display prices on a notice board in the main reception area, where all guests can easily see them.
Immigration Order 1972		All guests over 16 yrs of age must fill in a register giving their name and nationality. 'Aliens' must give passport details and their departure date and destination. Records must be kept for a minimum of a year. These can be inspected by the police at any time, they must be kept up to date. All persons must be individually registered.
Hotel Proprietors Act 1956		Hotels and inns (as defined in the Act) must display a copy of the 'Loss or Damage to Guests' Property' notice where it can be easily read by all guests. All other legal liabilities are covered in the Act.

ACTIVITY

1. Investigate these main health and safety regulations, using the resources of your nearest reference library.

2. Make a copy of:
   • a Loss or Damage to Guests' Property notice
   • a fire certificate

3. Find out what is meant by 'Aliens' in the Immigration order 1972.

4. Find out what is meant by the Code of Practice in the First Aid Regulations 1981.

Hotel reception procedures

	Actions	Information source
Request received	Exact requirements are ascertained	Verbal or written request
	Accommodation availability is ascertained	Bookings diary
	Provisional booking is made	Bookings diary
	Confirmation/offer of accommodation is given (by letter, fax, phone or direct)	
	Reply is received (could include deposit)	
	Provisional booking is confirmed	Bookings diary
Guest arrives	Reservation details are checked	Bookings diary, arrival sheet
	Guest enters details in register	Registration card/book
	A room is allocated	Bookings diary, rooming list
	A key card or key is given to guest	Key rack or electronic dispenser
	Guest account is opened	Accounts file
Guest's stay	Room is occupied	Rooming list
	Meals are taken	Receipts from restaurant
	Bar facilities are used	Receipts from bars
	Laundry/valeting service is used	Receipts from housekeeping department
	Telephone is used	Room telephone meter
	Mini-bar is used	Room mini-bar indicator
Guest departs	Account is requested	Accounts file
	Room is vacated, guest books out	Room list and booking diary
	Key is returned or key card invalidated	Key rack or electronic key indicator
	Account is paid or posted	Account file or ledger

USE OF COMPUTERIZED SYSTEMS

Large hotels will run a fully computerized front office system. This will enable the above processes to be completed more quickly and efficiently, less time will be taken and less staff will be required. Any computerized system will have the facility to update the master files as new information is added. There will be similar files/diaries/sheets produced as are used in the manual system.

Computerized systems will be used for a wide range of tasks, a summary of the most common ones is given below.

Administration

Reports and summaries of all types
Staff hours of work and wages records
Employee records
Standard letters compiled
Control of stocks
Word processing for written communication

Accounts

Guests' accounts constantly updated
Telephone logging
Billing for guest services
Charging for food and beverage services
Financial statistics
Nightly audit statistics
Ledger account

Sales

Daily analysis of all sales
Analysis of turnover
Block booking statistics
Conference and function statistics
Sales projection figures

Reservations

Advanced reservations
Room availability
Current rooming lists
Arrival and departure sheets
Guest history cards

ACTIVITY

Investigate the front office systems used in a local hotel and compare it with a different system used in another hotel.

Ask yourself the following questions, and compile a written comparison.

- How does the front office staff know who is expected to book in on a particular day?
- What information is recorded when a guest makes an advanced booking?
- How are the advance bookings recorded?
- What system is used to ensure that all guest charges are added to the correct account?
- How do the housekeeping staff know which guests are leaving the hotel each day?
- How does the front office staff know which rooms are vacant and ready to re-let?

ESSENTIAL INFORMATION IN THE FRONT OFFICE

The need for front office staff to be familiar with all the services and facilities that they are trying to sell cannot be stressed too much. Guests will not return to a hotel where the front office staff do not have the correct information to give as soon as it is asked for. Some establishments are small and the staff here will have no difficulty in remembering the characteristic of the individual rooms and facilities. However, in larger hotels a checklist system is used to remind staff of the facilities and characteristics in each room. The room numbering system will indicate the room's floor position. For example, all first floor rooms are numbered with a number 1 at the front, second floor rooms with a number 2 and so on. This enables the front office staff to know which rooms are on each floor. Lists are also used to remind staff of the different tariffs that apply to the various rooms and services (Figure 3.3).

Room No.	Type	Characteristics
245	Double	Pine furnishings; balcony – sea front; communicating door to 246
246	Twin	Pine furnishings; communicating door to 245
247	Single	Dark oak furnishings; side view; next to lift.

Figure 3.3 Checklist of hotel room characteristics

ROOM TARIFFS

These are described by the terms below. The front office staff must make certain that the guest knows exactly what is being included in the tariff quoted to them.

Standard rack rate

This is the standard charge for the room with no meals included and no discount of any sort. This may be the charge per person or the charge per room.

Bed and breakfast rate

This is the charge per person for one night's stay with breakfast, continental or a full English.

Half-board rate

In this case the charge is per person for overnight accommodation, breakfast and one meal – usually dinner. The type of breakfast and meal included in the tariff must be stipulated in advance.

Full board

Here the tariff includes overnight accommodation, breakfast, luncheon and dinner. As before, the type of meals included must be stipulated.

Commercial rate

This is a rate negotiated with an individual commercial company. It enables the company to use the hotel for their employees at a preferential rate.

Group rate

This is a specific tariff negotiated for a group of guests all of whom are travelling in the same party with one specified leader.

Back-to-back rate

This tariff applies to travel agents and tour operators who book a series of rooms for a specified period. Their successive clients vacate and book into the same series of rooms throughout the period.

Short break rate

A special short break tariff is charged to attract guests for short stays. These offers are often made at quiet times of their trading year, and over weekends.

Family rate

This is negotiated to provide reduced price accommodation for families with children. It is often sold in conjunction with the short break tariff.

BOOKINGS DIARY

This is often referred to as the hotel diary. It is the book that contains all the details of the reservations/bookings for each day. There will be one page per day, so that it is easy to see exactly who is booked in on any one day. In some cases the diary also indicates the numbers of the rooms that are available so that each booking is automatically allocated a specific room. This practice eliminates the risk of over-booking. Large establishments may need more than one page per day.

If the system is computerized, a grid diary page will be shown on the screen and the front office staff will simply type in the details.

Month		Day			Date		
Room number	Type of room	Name	Number guests	Rate	Number nights	Confirmation	Remarks
214	SB						
215	TB						
216	DB						
217	DB						
218	TB						

Figure 3.4 Hotel bookings diary

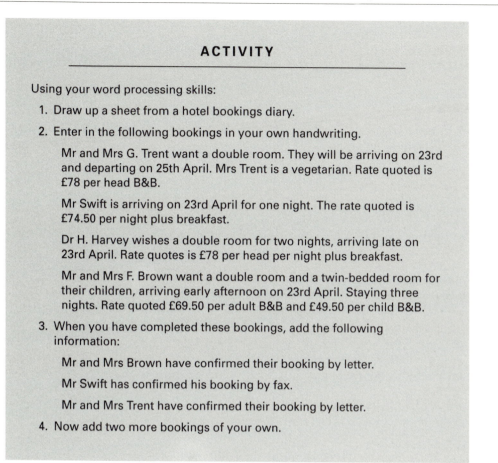

ACTIVITY

Using your word processing skills:

1. Draw up a sheet from a hotel bookings diary.

2. Enter in the following bookings in your own handwriting.

   Mr and Mrs G. Trent want a double room. They will be arriving on 23rd and departing on 25th April. Mrs Trent is a vegetarian. Rate quoted is £78 per head B&B.

   Mr Swift is arriving on 23rd April for one night. The rate quoted is £74.50 per night plus breakfast.

   Dr H. Harvey wishes a double room for two nights, arriving late on 23rd April. Rate quotes is £78 per head per night plus breakfast.

   Mr and Mrs F. Brown want a double room and a twin-bedded room for their children, arriving early afternoon on 23rd April. Staying three nights. Rate quoted £69.50 per adult B&B and £49.50 per child B&B.

3. When you have completed these bookings, add the following information:

   Mr and Mrs Brown have confirmed their booking by letter.

   Mr Swift has confirmed his booking by fax.

   Mr and Mrs Trent have confirmed their booking by letter.

4. Now add two more bookings of your own.

The remarks column is used for noting special requirements or details such as arrival times, or cancellation.

In some hotels the front office staff are required to use pencil for all reservations until they have been confirmed, after which they use ink. The diary is also marked with a simple tick in the margin when the guest has booked in. This will make it easier for the front office staff to quickly see the state of the vacant rooms.

RESERVATIONS CHART

This is a type of chart used in larger hotels, to supplement the hotel bookings diary. It shows month by month exactly which room is occupied and which is vacant and ready to be let. Again, if the process has been computerized, the information is brought up on the VDU screen.

The chart (see Figure 3.5) shows each reservation and the number of nights that the guest is to stay. On a traditional style of chart the reservations are pencilled in, and inked only when the guest books in. This way it is easy to see at a glance exactly who has booked in. The arrows at the ends of the line indicate the arrival and departure dates and must be sited in the centre of the square. This way a departure and re-let can be shown in the same square, denoting the same date.

Month _____ 199__										
Date	1	2	3	4	5	6	7	8	9	10
Room										
321 SB										
322 TB										
323 DB										

Figure 3.5 Hotel reservations chart

ACTIVITY

Produce a conventional reservations chart using your computer skills. Using the same data for the bookings as you used for the booking diary exercise, fill in your chart.

ARRIVALS SHEET

This gives details of all guests expected on a specified day. It may be easily produced from the bookings diary or the reservations chart. A computerized system will produce such a print-out list with great facility.

ACTIVITY

1. Compile a density chart like the one in figure 3.6, using your word processing skills.

2. Now complete it by hand to show the following:

Rooms booked

Monday	15 singles	20 doubles	1 triple	2 suites
Tuesday	20 singles	20 doubles	2 triple	2 suites
Wednesday	12 singles	23 doubles	0 triple	0 suites
Thursday	17 singles	14 doubles	3 triple	1 suite
Friday	11 singles	16 doubles	0 triple	0 suites
Saturday	6 singles	5 doubles	0 triple	1 suite
Sunday	14 singles	8 doubles	1 triple	0 suites

DENSITY CHART

It is often useful (for instance, when taking telephone enquiries) to be able to see at a glance how many of each type of room are free at any particular time. The density chart will give this information although it will not give the actual room numbers, which can be discovered from the bookings diary or the reservations chart. The rooms are grouped according to their type and are crossed through diagonally in pencil to indicate that they are let (see Figure 3.6).

Week Beginning _____ 199__						
Monday	Tuesday	Wednesday	Thursday	Friday	Saturday	Sunday
Singles (20)						
00000	00000	00000	00000	00000	00000	00000
00000	00000	00000	00000	00000	00000	00000
00000	00000	00000	00000	00000	00000	00000
00000	00000	00000	00000	00000	00000	00000
Doubles (23)						
00000	00000	00000	00000	00000	00000	00000
00000	00000	00000	00000	00000	00000	00000
00000	00000	00000	00000	00000	00000	00000
00000	00000	00000	00000	00000	00000	00000
000	000	000	000	000	000	000
Triples (3)						
000	000	000	000	000	000	000
Suite (6)						
00000	00000	00000	00000	00000	00000	00000
0	0	0	0	0	0	0

Figure 3.6 Hotel reservations: density chart

ROOMING LIST

This is of great value to the housekeeping department. It is a list of all rooms indicating which rooms are to be vacated that day, which are occupied and which are vacant (Figure 3.7). It is necessary for the housekeeping staff to know this so that they can service the rooms accordingly. A computerized system will produce a floor-by-floor print-out with ease.

Date 15 April									
	ARRIVALS			OCCUPIED			DEPARTURES		
Room	Name	No	Dep	Name	No	Dep	Name	No	Dep
415	Fife	2	17th						
416	Dean	1	16th				West	2	15th
417				Brack	2	20th			
418	Hill	2	19th				Ross	1	15th

Figure 3.7 Rooming list

RESERVATIONS FORMS

These are used whenever a reservation is being made. They act as a checklist to the front office staff so that they do not forget any information whilst taking a note of the guests' details and requirements. They are used for both personal and telephone bookings. When the front office staff are dealing with reservations by letter or fax, they will also fill out a reservation form to check that all the necessary information is present. A computerized system will display a reservation form on the VDU screen for the front office staff to type in the details.

Forms will need to be designed so that they will contain the following information:

From the guest

- name of guest, their address and telephone number
- the date of arrival and estimated time
- the anticipated date of departure
- type of accommodation required
- the number of persons requiring accommodation
- the date that the booking was made and by whom
- tariff agreed and confirmation requirements
- the method of payment
- any special requirements

From the front office staff

- name of the person who took the booking
- the date that the booking was made
- the length of time that the provisional booking will be held
- details of what is included in the tariff agreed

Additional information

- front office check list to process the reservation
- where the guest heard about the hotel
- if the guest is a previous or a new guest

ACTIVITY

Using the list above, and your computer skills:

1. Design a hotel reservation form, and print out two copies.

2. Write a letter to a fictitious hotel asking for a hotel reservation.

3. Using a colleague's letter, fill in your reservation form. Can all the details be included on your form or does the form need modifying?

Date 16   Month June   Year 1996   Day Tuesday

Room numbers	No. sleepers	Name	Rate	Breakfast	Lunchtime	Dinner	Liquor	Sundries	Laundry	Newspaper	Telephone	B/Forward	Total	Payment Received	Ledger Transfer	C/Forward
273	2	Mr/s Gray	220.00	–		85.00	17.50			.50	2.75	322.00	647.75			647.75
275	1	Mr Lane	85.00	7.50						.50			93.00			93.00
276	1	Mrs Brown	85.00			32.00	10.00		2.50	.75	5.00	120.00	225.25		225.25	
277	2	Mr/s Swan	170.00		32.00	55.00	15.00			.50	2.00		274.50	274.50		
278	1	Mr Lee	85.00			32.00	8.00	2.50		.60			128.10		128.10	
302	2	Mr/s Smith	170.00			67.00	18.00		7.00	.50	2.00	270.00	534.50			534.50

Figure 3.8 Tabular ledger

ACTIVITY

Using a guest bill like the one in Figure 3.8 enter the following charges for Mr Graham, Room 12.

24 April   Accommodation £45.50. Newspaper 50p. Bar drinks £3.64.

25 April   Accommodation £45.50. Laundry £2.75. Newspaper 50p. Telephone £4.76. Bar drinks £3.75.

26 April   Accommodation £45.50. Newspaper 50p. Dinner £12.00. Bar drinks £4.00.

Remember to total each day's charges and to carry these forward to the next day.

The Crown Inn

Market Square

Dutton on Edge

Room No. _____   Invoice No. _____

Guest name _____

Date				
Accommodation				
Dinner				
Telephone				
Beverages				
Bar drinks				
Laundry				
Newspapers				
Daily total				
Brought forward				
Carried forward				

Figure 3.9 Guest bill (filled in by hand)

ACTIVITY

Enter the following charges on a tabular ledger (as in Figure 3.8).

Tuesday 27 April

Mrs Green. Room no. 345. Room rate £78.00 Newspaper 50p. Dinner £23.00. Bar £2.50. Balance carried forward £230.

Mr & Mrs Todd. Room no 653. Room rate £154. Dinner £52.00. Bar £7.75. Newspapers 85p. Telephone £3.15.

Mrs Height. Room rate £65.00. Newspaper 30p. Bar £1.70.

Mr Sykes. Room rate £78.00. Dinner £45.00. Bar £25.50. Telephone £12.50. Balance carried forward £240.50.

Now add three extra guests of your own, and total the tabular ledger up.

GUEST ACCOUNTS

Whatever the size of the hotel, the principles of billing the guests' charges to their account are the same. At all times the charges must be billed to the correct account as soon as possible. If a guest is due to leave it is imperative that the account is up to date. In large hotels a computerized system will be used, which will provide an instant update on the accounts. Small hotels and guesthouses will maybe use a manual tabular ledger (see Figure 3.8) coupled with handwritten bills (Figure 3.9). Medium-sized hotels will use an electronic billing system. The billing machine automatically revises the total each time additional charges are added.

PAYMENT METHODS

Guests can pay their bill by cash, cheque or credit card (see pp. 321–3). Some guest accounts will be logged to their employer's account. In these cases the guest will be asked to sign the bill and will be given a receipt to forward to their employer.

In hotels the front office will be busy when the guests are leaving the hotel after their breakfast. Extra staff are usually on duty at these times. Some front offices are divided into reception areas and cashier areas so that incoming guests do not have to queue behind departing guests. You will find this situation in large hotels near airports and railway stations, and in hotels in capital cities, where guests will be arriving and departing at all hours of the day and night.

In hotels of whichever type, it is essential to have an up-to-date guest account ready at all times, whether a manual system or a computerized system is used. Late recording of guest charges could mean that the guest has checked out of the hotel before all the relevant charges are on the bill. This will mean a loss for the hotel.

FOUR

Accommodation operations

Accommodation areas

The diversity of the hospitality and catering industry means that there are many different types of accommodation area. The chart below summarizes these, giving the main facilities provided and any special factors the need to be taken into account.

Table 4.1 Types of accommodation area

Room/area	Establishment	Facilities provided	Special factors
Entrance hall	All	Dust control carpeting	Correct ambience
Foyer	Hotel	Seating Front office	Security Correct ambience
Lifts Stairs Corridors	All	Directions Information	Security Emergency exit signs

Conference
  halls
	Hotel
	Hall of residence
		Multi-use furniture
		  and surfaces
			Good access
			Catering facilities
			Staging
			Screens

Lounges	All	Seating Tables TV Flowers Books Newspapers	Good heating High comfort level Attractive outlook
Conservatory	Hotels Homes	Seating Tables Plants	Good heating and ventilation Blinds
Common room	Colleges Schools	Seating Tables TV Video recorder Books Newspapers	Strong, plain designs Good heating

Offices	All	Desks and chairs Bookcases Filing cabinets	Security Computers Good heating and ventilation
Bedrooms	All	Beds Storage for clothes Hand-basin Carpeting	Security High comfort level Nets or blinds Curtains
Study bedrooms	Halls of residence Schools Hostels	As bedrooms, with: Desk and chair Bookshelves	Good lighting Tea-making facilities
Wards	Hospitals	Beds Lockers Cubical curtains Chairs Hand-basin	Hygiene factors
Dormitories	Schools	As wards with: Clothes storage facilities	Safety and hygiene considerations
Changing rooms	All	Lockers Seating Hand basin Shower cubical	Security and hygiene factors
Bathrooms	All	Handbasin Bath Shower Chair	Hygiene factors
Toilets	All	Water closet Hand basin	Hygiene factors
Store rooms	All	Shelving Cupboards Receipt and issuing facilities	Security and safety
Restaurants Bars Coffee shop	Hotels Clubs	Tables and chairs Reception area Service equipment	Desired ambience Safety and hygiene High comfort level
Cafeteria	Motorway service areas	Service area Seating and tables Retail shop	Safety and hygiene Good toilet facilities Large car park
Refectory	Schools Colleges	Seating and tables Service area	Safety and hygiene

Manipulation of space

Flexibility of usage can enhance whatever accommodation space exists, but it requires careful preliminary planning. Decisions on multi-purposes need to be made only after considering the way that this can be achieved. First it is necessary to have an overall concept.

ROOM CONCEPT

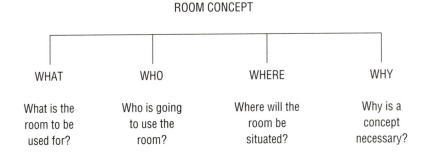

Figure 4.1 Room concept

Rooms within the accommodation sector of the hospitality industry, can be divided into categories according to purpose:

Purpose	Rooms
Sleeping	Bedrooms: en-suite, study, multi-bed, dual purpose
Reception	Entrance hall, hotel foyers
Recreation	Lounges, common rooms, conference halls, restaurants, bars
Administration	Offices: front and general, storage areas

In all these areas it is necessary to consider the users, the advantages of flexible usage, the surfaces that are required, the colour scheme, heating and ventilation requirements, soundproofing, lighting, and specialized fixtures and fittings.

As well as considering these constructively, it is helpful to look at the following aspects:

Parameters	Partitions (fixed or mobile)
	French doors leading to patios/marquees
	Staging/raised dais (fixed or mobile)
Furniture	Screens (fixed or mobile)
	Beds, folding into cupboards or standard type
	Service units (fixed or mobile), music centres
	Storage areas, cupboards or mobile units
	Tables and chairs (fixed, standard types or stackable)
Furnishings	Ancillary items, pictures, mirrors
	Lighting, central, lamps, spots, dimming facility
	Fabrics, curtains, soft furnishings, cushions
Flooring	Uses (walking, recreation, dancing, conferences)
	Surface (hard, natural or synthetic)
	Carpet, (strength, type, tiles)

USE OF COLOUR

Colour is another important element of the room concept. Colour can create perspective. The length, width, height and depth of a room can be accentuated with the use of colour. Ceilings may be 'lowered' by the use of a strong colour and large areas made to appear smaller. Light colours on walls and floor areas can emphasize the impression of space.

Furnishings can be changed to accommodate the changing seasons and hours of natural daylight. When deciding on colour of furnishings, it always advisable to colour co-ordinate with the existing features and furniture, rather than attempt to do it the other way round.

Always remember that colour co-ordination themes must complement the room's purpose and blend with any exterior view that the room might have. Never be tempted to use a colour just because it is fashionable at the moment. Such a 'fashionable' choice may not be at all suitable for the room. Colours have different effects upon the room:

Red/brown, russets	Earth colours, warm friendly, cosy
Strong pinks/reds	Vital, hot, bright, exciting
Greens	Peaceful, tranquil, restful
Blues/purples – deep	Mysterious, deep
– pale	Cool, quiet, unobtrusive, fresh

Patterns and textures can also have different effects upon the overall visual size of a room. They can be used to increase the visual interest in a section of the room, to brighten up a plain dull area or to accentuate a dominant colour theme. Borders and dado rails can be used to divide a single wall into two colour areas.

Pictures, spot lights and mirrors can all be employed to help achieve the desired tones and spatial effects; and rugs, linens, cushions, lampshades, fabrics and plants are other objects which can be used supportively.

ACTIVITY

1. Draw up a set of notes to show the concept created in two different rooms that you know well.

2. List the methods used in each of these rooms to create a feeling of space, warmth and light.

WALL COVERINGS

Here again, before making any decisions it is necessary to ascertain the intended use of the room or area. After this it is possible to choose the most appropriate wall treatment/surface.

A summary of considerations and suitability of various wall coverings is given in Table 4.2.

Table 4.2 Use of wall coverings

Surface	Considerations	Suitability
Wood panels	Initial expense high Can be sealed for ease of maintenance Half-height can be effective	Large areas, halls, libraries
Ceramic tiles	Smooth base essential Grouting needs regular maintenance	Wet or steam-filled areas, e.g. WCs, bathrooms, leisure areas, kitchens

Glass mirrors	Plate mirrors with bevelled edges,
	  or mirror tiles
		Large areas, or areas that need to be
		  enlarged by increased light

Paper	Embossed: attracts moisture and dust Standard: will tear and absorb moisture Vinyl: wipeable and fairly strong	Large areas only Normal room uses Areas where paper effect is required
Brick Stone	Attracts dust, rough Undulating finish, natural colours	Porches, conservatories, Fire places, alcoves in rustic style areas
Paint	Gloss (heavy duty) Exterior Egg shell Emulsion Vinyl (heavy duty) Anti-condensation Flame-retardant Anti-graffiti	Window frames, doors, etc. Metal surfaces Walls Walls Any surface where strong finish is required Laundries, leisure areas, food areas All public areas Areas subject to vandalism

FLOOR SURFACES

The following points need to be considered:

- *The use of the area*. For example, heavy traffic areas such as halls, foyers, conference rooms, stairs and corridors need a surface that can withstand constant use and frequent cleaning.
- *The effect to be created*. The adjacent areas and types of flooring.
- *The comfort level required*, noise factors, and the sub-floor properties.
- *Special requirements*, such as non-slip properties, flammability, resistance to insect infestation.
- *The surface strength*, its resistance to fading and staining, and its heat-resistant properties.
- *Maintenance factors* must be taken into account, the need to seal the surface, the estimated cleaning complexity and time.
- *The costs* must be considered: those of installation, maintenance and depreciation.

Varieties of floor surface

Ceramic	Tiles that are glazed and fixed with tiling mortar.
Concrete	A base surface made from cement, a filler and water. It needs to be sealed if left uncovered.
Granolithic	Granite chips mixed with cement and water.
Linoleum	Sheets or tiles, laid on a smooth surface.
Marble	Natural product cut to slabs, laid on mortar.
Metal link	Steel and rubber linked together.
PVC sheet	Can be heat-joined to produce a seam-free area.
PVC tiles	Good quality essential, laid with adhesive.
Quarry tiles	Resilient tiles laid on mortar.
Stone	Flag stones never quite smooth, fixed with mortar.
Rubber	Natural or synthetic, sheet or tiles.
Terrazzo	Marble chips mixed with cement and water.
Thermoplastic	Sheet or tiles, can crack or split.
Wood	Hard wood strips or blocks fixed to floor joists.

CARPETS

The quality of carpets is determined by the types of fibres used and the thickness and method of weave.

Carpets are graded as follows:

Light contract for domestic use only
Medium contract suitable for light industrial uses
Heavy contract suitable for commercial uses

Carpet should always be laid on top of a good quality firm underlay. This is so that the carpet is protected from pressure from both the floor below and the footwear above. It will prolong the life of the carpet and help to reduce draughts from the floor area below. It will also make the carpet feel softer and warmer. Good quality underlay is made from dense foam backed with hessian, or closewoven felt backed with rubber.

Varieties of carpet

Wool pile	Wilton or Brussels weave. Excellent quality. Close soft pile on hessian base. Most costly.
Wool tufted	Axminster weave. Good quality carpet. Tufted on a hessian base.
Wool and nylon	Can be pile or tufted. Nylon gives extra strength.
Sisal	Woven sisal thread. Very tough and firm.
Pig hair	Tiles backed onto jute. Very tough and strong.
Synthetics:	
Nylon, Polyester, Acrylic	These may be mixed or single type, carpet or tiles. A mixture gives strength and softness. May be tufted onto a foam backing. Inexpensive light contract grade carpeting.

Customer expectations

When a customer enters the establishment, certain thoughts are likely to spring to mind:

Is it safe?

Are the emergency signs easily visible?

Is it in a good state of repair?

Is it tidy and uncluttered?

Is it hygienic?

Are there any signs of dirt?

Are there any rodents or pests visible?

Are there any unpleasant odours?

Is it warm?

Does it feel stuffy and humid?

Has it a cool damp feeling?

Is it warm and dry?

Is it comfortable?

Is the furniture suitable?

Are the beds comfortable?

Is the lighting appropriate?

Are there in-room amenities?

Is there a hot beverage-making facility?

Is there adequate storage space?

Are there personal bathing facilities?

Is there in-room entertainment?

Is there a TV and radio?

Is there a video player/facility?

Is there a mini-bar?

Is there a room service facility?

Is there a personal laundry service?

Is there a baby-monitoring service?

Is there a meals and drink service?

Table 4.3 Customer expectations

	Hotels	Schools	Leisure	Hospitals
Safety	Room locks Fire certificate Establishment security	Young persons' safety Good discipline Fire certificate	Pool and sport safety Fire safety HASAWA Good organization	Fire certificate HASAWA High standards
Hygiene	High standard	High standard	Specialist standard	Specialist standard
Comfort	High-level	Average	Average	Specialist level
Room amenity	TV/video Hand-basin Tea-making facility	Basic	N/A	Locker Radio Some privacy
Room service	Comprehensive range	N/A	N/A	Specialist range

Attributes of housekeeping service staff

There are special attributes that all housekeeping service staff need to have in order to carry out their jobs well. These may be summarized as: discretion, honesty, confidentiality, communication skills, observation skills, team membership skills.

Discretion

Housekeeping staff could be in the position of seeing or hearing guests' company and conversation. It is an essential attribute of these staff to be able to take no notice of, or speak of, such things. It is, after all, not their concern.

Honesty

Guests need to feel able to treat their room as they would their own home. That is to say, it should be unnecessary to lock every single personal possession away every time they leave the room. Staff must be honest in order to be able to work amongst guests' personal effects, and to hand in any lost property.

Confidentiality

Guests could inadvertently leave private papers or company documents lying open in their room. Housekeeping staff must be able to leave these as found and never be tempted to read them or discuss them with anyone else.

Communication

Housekeeping staff are frequently asked by guests to supply them with information about the hotel services or the surrounding area. They are sometimes the first member of staff seen by the guest in the morning. They must therefore be able to speak clearly and politely to guests and have a thorough knowledge of all the hotel services.

Team spirit

If a member of the housekeeping staff cannot immediately answer a guest's query, they should refer them straight away to the front office. In this way, the guest will never be left without an answer. Should any discrepancies be noticed between the rooming sheet and the actual room status, the housekeeping staff must inform the front office immediately. An unexpected occupied room could mean a ghost guest/fraud.

Staff must be able to trust each other and be able to work together, either on a regular basis or in an emergency. The housekeeping section is usually divided into teams of staff, each team to be responsible for an allocated area or floor. The team can only be successful if all members take a pride in the standards of work achieved and have a caring attitude towards their fellow team members.

Staffing structures

Because of the diversity of residential establishments, all of which have housekeeping responsibilities, it is not feasible to compile rigid staffing charts showing lines of responsibility. There is a move within the hospitality industry to employ staff with a combination of skills who will work within a team to produce a flexible work force. This trend is taking over from the rigid structures of the past.

ACTIVITY

Visit two different residential establishments and compile a staffing structure for the housekeeping section of each. Use the job title list below to help you.

Table 4.4 Housekeeping staff by category

Category of staff	Job title	Likely establishment
Staff responsible for the organization and daily running of the housekeeping department	Executive housekeeper	Hotel
	Head housekeeper	Hotel
	Domestic bursar	Hall of residence
	Domestic superintendent	Hospital
	Hospitality manager	Hospital, home for the elderly
	Head steward	Cruise liner
	Services manager	Leisure complex, hall of residence
	Caretaker	School, university, college
	Matron	Boarding school
	House mistress	Boarding school
	Janitor	University, hall of residence

Supervisory level staff	Floor housekeeper	Large hotel
	Assistant housekeeper	Hotel
	Assistant domestic bursar	Hall of residence
	Assistant domestic superintendent	Hospital
	Hospitality supervisor	Hospital, home for the elderly
	Food supervisor	Hotel
	Section supervisor	Hospital
	Steward	Cruise liner
Staff responsible for carrying out housekeeping tasks	Room maid	Hotel, home for the elderly
	Cleaner	All residential establishments
	House porter	Hotel, school, university
	Chambermaid	Hotel
	Ward operative	Hospital
	Hospitality maid	Hospital
	Chalet maid	Leisure complex

Cleaning

PURPOSES AND PRINCIPLES

Cleaning is carried out in order to maintain an attractive environment, to preserve furnishings and surfaces and to maintain an attractive environment in which to live and work.

Table 4.5 The purposes of cleaning

Hygiene	Safety	Preservation	Standards
Removal of bacteria, dust and dirt	Provide a safe area for guests and staff	Maintenance of premises and furniture and furnishings in good condition	Ensure guest satisfaction and repeat business

The general principles are:

• to remove dirt, dust, litter and bacteria
• restore the surface to its original state at the end of the cleaning process
• remove dirt, dust and litter without harming any other adjacent surface
• use minimum equipment, cleaning agent and time that is necessary
• try the simplest method first with the mildest cleaning agent

PREVENTION OF DIRT ACCUMULATION

In most establishments measures can be taken to reduce the amount of dust, dirt and litter that enters or accumulates within the premises, by adopting some or all of the measures listed below:

• the use of dust control barrier carpets or mats in entrance halls
• the fitting of circular entrance doors to reduce draughts

- adequate exterior door mats for dirty shoes
- foot scrapers for muddy shoes
- porch areas to reduce draughts
- self-closing doors to reduce draughts
- adequate litter and waste paper bins
- regular cleaning of all barrier carpets, mats and exterior doormats
- the institution of a no smoking policy

CONSIDERATIONS PRIOR TO CLEANING

The methods used for cleaning will depend upon the type of soiling, the size of the area, the materials and surfaces to be cleaned and the standards of cleanliness to be achieved.

Usage	Accessibility of the area; time and period available for cleaning.
Materials	Types of surfaces and materials to be cleaned.
Soiling	Degree and type of dirt that has to be removed.
Area	Size of area in which the cleaning has to be completed.
Equipment	Suitable equipment and cleaning agents for the job.
Standards	Standards of cleanliness required.

CLEANING PROCEDURES

All members of the housekeeping staff work in a team and share the responsibility of maintaining cleanliness and hygiene.

Team cleaning

Sometimes staff will work in an individual capacity, at other times in pairs. This working procedure will be determined by the team supervisor.

An example of a task sometimes completed in pairs is the cleaning of hotel bedrooms, where the advantages include the ease and speed of stripping and making beds using two people and increased speed of cleaning, as one cleaner can deal with the ensuite bathroom while the other cleans the bedroom.

Many staff prefer to work in a team, as they appreciate the company. The approach has the added advantage of ensuring that all tasks are properly completed in the allocated time, as the staff will tend to keep each other working.

Block cleaning

In establishments where all the residents are out of the premises all day, for example, the bedroom areas of a boarding school or hall of residence, a cleaning routine known as block cleaning may be used. This means that one complete area of the premises is cleaned at the same time, by two or three staff. Take, for example, a floor of twenty study bedrooms, all of which need a daily clean. The procedure might be as follows:

Step	Team member	Task
1	A	Opens all doors and ventilates each room
2	B	Empties all waste paper baskets. Lifts small items off the floor
3	C	Straightens the bedding
4	A	Cleans all the hand-basins
5	B	Damp dusts all the surfaces
6	C	Suction cleans all the floors
7	A	Replaces items of furniture that have been moved
8	B	Checks each room and locks the door

This procedure is obviously not suitable for areas of high security, such as hotels, where it is not permitted to leave guests' bedroom doors open without the cleaner or cleaners being in the room.

However, block cleaning methods can be suitable for hospitals, homes for the elderly and leisure areas. In these areas, one member of the team will, for example, proceed around the premises completing all the damp dusting, followed by another team member completing all the floor buffing and a further team member cleaning all the hand-basins.

ACTIVITY

Visit two of the following types of establishment and identify which cleaning procedures are followed:

(a) Local hospital

(b) Hotel

(c) Boarding school

(d) Leisure area

In each case give the reasons and advantages of the procedures adopted in that establishment.

Table 4.6 General cleaning frequency

Frequency	Tasks
Daily (every day)	Dust removed by, suction cleaning, dry dusting, damp dusting or dust control mopping.
Weekly (once per week)	Cleaning of the following: floors, windows, paintwork. Polishing and spot cleaning. 'Below and above' cleaning.
Periodic (3-6 monthly)	All surfaces thoroughly cleaned. Furniture emptied/moved. Floors treated as appropriate. Maintenance checks completed.

HIGH RISK AREAS

Some areas require specialist care and cleaning routines that are specific risks associated with that area. An indication of these areas is given in Table 4.7 and cleaning procedures for the last three are given in Tables 4.8 to 4.10.

Table 4.7 Areas of risk requiring specialist cleaning

Area	Risks
Hospitals	Cross-infection from one patient to another via the premises or the furniture, furnishings or equipment.
Toilets	Cross-infection from one user to another due to inadequately cleaned premises.
Food preparation areas	Cross-contamination of food items due to inadequate cleansing procedures.
Food service areas	Cross-contamination due to poor standards of premises and equipment.

Table 4.8 Cleaning of toilets, washrooms and bathrooms

Order of work		
1	Ventilate	To remove air-borne bacteria.
2	Tidy	Remove litter and debris.
3	WC/urinal	Flush, brush, flush, apply acid cleanser. Clean all exterior surfaces.
4	Hand-basin Bath	Clean inside and out and the splash-back area with non-scratch/sanitizer cleanser.
5	Shower	Clean walls/panels with sanitizer and dry. Wash base tray with sanitizer. Check shower head; de-scale weekly.
6	Surfaces	Clean with sanitizer or germicidal detergent to remove bacteria.
7	WC/urinal	Flush away the acid cleanser.
8	Sundries	Replenish toilet paper, soap, towels. Adjust the ventilation.
9	Floor	Wash/clean as appropriate.
10	Check	Visual check to ensure that the area is ready for use.

Table 4.9 Cleaning food preparation areas

Order of Work		
1	Power	Turn off the power supply to all equipment.
2	Refuse	Remove all rubbish and food waste.
3	Ranges/tops	Clean with strong alkali detergent, rinse and dry well, re-assemble.
4	Deep fryers	Drain out oil. Fill with hot water and alkali-based detergent, turn on and heat. Turn off and drain. Rinse well and dry.
5	Steamers	Drain out water. Wash inside with hot detergent solution. Rinse well and dry.
6	Bain-maries	Empty, drain away water. Wash with hot detergent solution, rinse and dry well.
7	Grills	Clean with strong alkali detergent, rinse well, dry well and re-assemble.
8	Microwaves	Wash interior with mild detergent solution, rinse and dry well.
9	Surfaces	Wash with detergent solution to remove all traces of food debris, then finish with a sanitizer solution.
10	Floor	Sweep to remove all debris. Mop or scrub as appropriate, using a hot detergent solution.

Table 4.10 Cleaning food service areas

Order of work		
1	Ventilate	Adjust the ventilation to remove stale odours and air-borne bacteria.
2	Tidy	Remove all food items, litter and items to be washed.
3	Beverages	Switch off machine, empty, rinse through as appropriate. Clean exterior with sanitizer.
4	Service areas	Clean with mild detergent solution and finish with sanitizer solution as appropriate.
5	Surfaces	Remove all traces of food debris and dust as appropriate, in order to eliminate bacteria breeding areas.
6	Table/chairs	Clean to remove food debris and smears.
7	Floor	Clean as appropriate to remove all traces of dust and food particles.
8	Check	Adjust ventilation. Visual check around the entire area. Check lights and air-conditioning. Replace floral displays and linen as appropriate.

MAINTAINING CLEANING STANDARDS

One of the duties at the supervisory level of the housekeeping team is to be responsible for checking the rooms and areas immediately after the cleaning has been completed.

In a hotel, the floor housekeeper will take this responsibility. It is normal practice to do this with the aid of a checklist (see Figure 4.2), checking systematically in a clockwise direction around the room. Any problems can then be identified and the appropriate action taken. Once checked, the floor housekeeper will update the 'rooms ready' list in the office by telephoning in the code. This will automatically update the computerized list in the housekeeper's office and simultaneously update the list in the front office. This makes the reception staff's task of allocating rooms to new guest simple and accurate.

Table 4.11 Cleaning methods

A summary of cleaning methods

Method	Equipment	Process	Safety
Dry dusting	Duster	Wipe over surfaces to collect dust	Wash duster. Air dry.
Damp dusting	Duster and sanitizer in trigger spray	Spray duster and wipe over surface to remove dust.	Wash duster. Air dry.
Dust control mopping	Dust control mop	Guide over surface, keeping head on the floor surface all the time	Remove head and wash. Tumble or air dry.
Wet mopping	Bucket, wringer, hot detergent solution	Mop the floor using figure of eight movement, cleaning one section at a time.	Wash mop head, hang up to dry. Wash out bucket and wringer
Suction cleaning	Suction cleaner	Guide over the surface, cleaning one section at a time.	Empty after use.
Wet suction	Wet pick-up machine	Guide over the surface to remove slurry or water.	Empty after use. Rinse out and dry well.
Hand polishing	Soft cloth and polish	Apply polish, rub in well and buff to a shine.	Replace the lid. Wash cloth and air dry.
Machine polishing	Polish tray and applicator, polishing pad on machine	Apply polish with applicator. Buff in sections to a shine.	Discard disposable polishing head. Wash polishing pad and air dry.
Floor buffing	Buffing pad on machine	Guide over floor, buffing a section at a time.	Rinse buffing pad and drip dry.
Spray buffing	Buffing pad on machine, trigger spray	Spray over surface, buffing one section at a time.	Rinse buffing pad and drip dry.
Burnishing	Burnishing pad on machine with suction unit.	Guide over floor, working one section at a time. Ensure that the dust and debris is suctioned up thoroughly.	Wash burnishing pad and drip dry. Empty the suction unit.
Floor scrubbing	Brush/pad on machine with suction unit or wet pick-up	Scrub one section of floor at a time. Ensure that all the slurry is suctioned up.	Wash brush/pad and drip dry. Empty, rinse and dry suction unit and tank.

The checklist may also be used to grade the cleaning staff's work by using a numbered code. For example, 5 for excellent, 4 for satisfactory, 3 for mostly clean, 2 for below standard, and 1 for not clean. Cleaners should be encouraged to check any room they have cleaned in a similar manner before proceeding to the next room. This practice exercises their observation skills and helps prevent omissions and mistakes.

Figure 4.3 shows factors that are relevant to setting cleaning standards.

```
ROOM ___321___  DATE ___12/3/95___  TIME ___12.40___
CLEANER __M. Smyth__      SUPERVISOR ___J. Bell___
TASK ___Daily clean___
```

AREA	DONE	COMMENT
Walls	4	Sticky mark by door
Floor	3	Dust in corners
Bed	5	
Furniture	5	
Chairs	4	Mark on the arm
Paintwork	5	
Electrical	5	
Bathroom	3	Water marks on wall tiles

Supervisor's signature _____

Cleaner's signature _____

Figure 4.2 Room checking form

Figure 4.3 Construction of cleaning standards

WORK SCHEDULES

Work schedules (see Figure 4.4) pay a vital part in the maintenance of cleaning standards. A comprehensive work schedule will include an indication of the time allowed for each task as well as the equipment and cleaning agents to be used. The actual order that is used to complete the cleaning is of importance because it is easy to re-contaminate a surface by cleaning areas in an illogical order. For example, if the floor was suction cleaned first, then the beds made, all the dust from the bedding would fall on the clean carpet.

In order to incorporate the weekly cleaning tasks (see p. 161) it is necessary to allocate one of these weekly cleaning routines per day, into the daily cleaning schedule. For example, in the case of en-suite hotel bedrooms, daily clean the room as normal, and on:

Monday – Give extra attention to the bathroom;
Tuesday – Clean windows and paintwork as necessary;
Wednesday – Give extra attention to the floors;
Thursday – Suction clean the mattress and upholstery;
Friday – Do high-level dusting and clean inside cupboards.

This combined daily and weekly routine means that per week all the weekly tasks are covered, without the cleaners having to spend extra hours working.

Figure 4.4 Work schedule for daily cleaning of a hotel en-suite bedroom

Task	Time	Equipment	Methods
Ventilate	½ min.		Adjust curtain
			Open window
Litter	1 min.	Waste sack	Remove litter
			Take out used crockery
Bed	2 min.	Soiled linen sack	Strip bed
			Leave to air
Bathroom	3 min.	Detergent	Clean appliances
		Acid cleanser	Clean surfaces
		Cloths, brush, mop	Clean floor
Adjust ventilation	½ min.		Close window
Remake bed	3 min.	Clean linen	Remake bed
			Place clean towels in bathroom
Dust	2 min.	Duster	Work clockwise round the room
Replenish	1 min.	Crockery and dry stocks	Replenish beverage items
Suction clean	2 min.	Suction cleaner	Remove dust from floors
Check	1 min.		Check round the room
			Close and lock the door

WORK CARDS

Another way of helping staff to maintain high cleaning standards is to issue them with work cards. These cards will give the order and methods of work for an individual task, such as dry dusting or wet mopping.

Task	Dust control mopping
Equipment	Dust control mop
	Dustpan and brush
Safety	Use a floor cleaning safety sign
	Remove the head after use and wash, tumble dry

Method

1.   Remove small objects from floor area
2.   Keeping the mop head on the floor surface all the time, mop the area.
3.   Collect any accumulated dust and litter in the dust pan.
4.   Remove dust from the mop head and wash in hot detergent water, tumble dry.
5.   Replace equipment in storage area.

Figure 4.5 Front and reverse sides of a work card

ACTIVITY

Compile a work schedule for an area that your know – maybe a kitchen or a restaurant. Use your word processing skills to produce your finished schedule.

Before deciding on the work schedule you will have to:

*   Decide which surfaces and items will need to be cleaned
*   Identify the materials that they are made from
*   Select the equipment and agents to be used
*   Decide how frequently each item/surface needs to be cleaned
*   Decide on the sequence for the cleaning
*   Work out how the weekly tasks can be incorporated into the daily schedule

ACTIVITY

Use your knowledge of cleaning skills and your word processing skills to design a series of work cards for the following practical tasks:

*   Suction cleaning
*   Polishing by hand or machine
*   Floor buffing
*   Damp dusting
*   Window cleaning

SERVICING ROOMS AND REPLENISHING SUPPLIES

It is normal practice for cleaning staff to use a trolley to transport all the equipment, cleaning agents, clean and soiled linen, refuse, and room supplies. These trolleys will act as a supply station for the cleaner whilst they are cleaning their allocated rooms or areas. The use of trolleys prevents an untidy and unsafe pile of equipment and supplies being left on the floor of corridors or in the corner of areas.

Complimentary toiletries

These are supplied in most hotels. A standard allocation will be made for each guest and room maids replenish any used toiletries on a daily basis. These items are normally displayed in the en-suite bathroom, either arranged on the vanity unit or in a small bowl or basket designed especially for this purpose.

Hot beverage-making facility

This facility is supplied in the bedrooms to enable the guests to make themselves a cup of tea or coffee. An electric kettle and crockery is provided in each room. Supplies of tea bags, instant coffee, instant hot chocolate, sugar and milk are replenished on a daily basis. These are usually placed in a small bowl on the tray ready for the guests' use. Often biscuits will also be provided.

Mini-bars

Some hotels include a small refrigerated unit in the bedroom, containing miniature bottles of alcoholic beverages and carbonated drinks. Chocolate bars and small packets of salted nuts may also be included. Guests are billed for each item that is removed from the mini bar. Most are computerized, they automatically record items removed so that the guest can be accurately billed in the front office. A mini-bar steward will check each mini-bar on a daily basis and replenish the used items.

Linen

Linen may be establishment-owned and sent to a commercial laundry to be laundered or alternatively it may be hired from a linen hire company. A less common alternative for hotels is an 'on premises' laundry where the linen is establishment-owned and laundered in the premises. Leisure centres often have their own 'on premises' laundry for items such as towels and bath robes.

A poor standard of finish on any bed or table linen is unacceptable, so careful consideration of the different linen-servicing systems needs to be made. Some establishments use a combination of linen hire and another system to give them the service and flexibility that they require.

Table 4.12 A summary of the different linen-servicing systems

System	Advantages	Disadvantages
Commercial laundry	Usually a good standard of finish is achieved. Flexibility of quantity laundered to suit the business.	Money invested in a large stock of house linen and uniforms.
Linen hire	Standard contract charge. No money invested in stock.	Minimum charge paid whether linen is used or not.
'On premises' laundry	Can deal with fluctuations of demand in an emergency. Own house finish standard possible.	Labour intensive. Money invested in stock, premises and staff.

Maintenance

REGULAR MAINTENANCE

In all types of establishment maintenance is carried out on a regular basis in order to prevent faults, damage or natural wear and tear from becoming a major problem. Maintenance checks are carried out regularly at predetermined times throughout the trading year, usually by supervisory or management staff. Checklists are often used to avoid any areas or items from being omitted from the maintenance check. It is necessary to find a period when trading is slow so that the checking can be carried out without disrupting the customers.

All faults will be reported and either repaired by in-house maintenance staff or by a contractor, as soon as possible, so as to eliminate further faults developing.

PREVENTIVE MAINTENANCE

This is carried out by staff in the housekeeping section as they go about their normal duties and involves looking out for uncharacteristic signs in various areas, such as:

plumbing – taps dripping, pipes knocking or becoming blocked;
electrical – bulbs not working or flickering, flexes frayed;
fire – soot falling into the grate;
floors – carpets frayed, tiles loose, mats ragged;
windows – catches broken, glass cracked;
doors – catches broken, locks misshapen;

furniture – chipped or splintered, surface stained or damaged;
equipment – not working efficiently or parts broken;
decor – wallpaper torn or marked, tiles or mirrors cracked.

ROUTINE PROCEDURES

All the faults are reported to the housekeeper by staff in the team at the end of their shift. This enables the housekeeper to act upon the fault immediately. Poor maintenance will result in the premises becoming generally run-down, in poor staff morale and eventually in loss of trade or, worse still, accidents. Remember that the Health and Safety Act requires that premises be maintained in a good order so that they present no danger to employees or members of the public.

Often a simple proforma is used to report routine and emergency maintenance. This proforma will contain the following headings:

• the date that the fault was found
• the name of the employee who found it
• the nature of the fault itself
• the exact position of the fault
• the action taken by the employee when they found the fault

ACTIVITY

1. Use your design and word processing skills to create a proforma for maintenance reporting

2. Give your proforma a trial by asking a colleague to use it. Analyse the result, then adjust the design, if necessary. For example, you may find that the spaces in which to write, are too narrow or too short.

EMERGENCY MAINTENANCE

This is seldom necessary in a well-organized establishment, because the regular reporting procedures will identify any potential faults before they are allowed to develop into emergencies.

However, there may be an emergency beyond the management's control, caused, for example, by extreme weather conditions: snowstorms, floods, heatwaves, hurricanes or other such phenomena. Or an emergency could be the result of an accident, such as a broken window, a flooded shower or bathroom area, a small burn caused by an unprotected open fire. In all these instances, the prime concern must be the safety of all persons in the area, both guests/customers and staff. The next consideration must be the safety of the premises.

It is the duty of all employees to report all emergencies of this nature to their line manager immediately. Once this has been done there will, in most cases, be actions that can be taken by all staff. These will be organized by the management or supervisory staff on duty at the time. The area may need to be evacuated, the water turned off, debris cleared away, emergency services called, insurance companies contacted to call and assess the damage. During this period, the guests/customers must be looked after, maybe hot beverages need to be served or alternative accommodation found.

Cleaning Equipment

There is a huge range of cleaning equipment available. You will find that each manufacturer can supply all the equipment necessary for a particular establishment's requirements.

SELECTION CRITERIA

When choosing equipment it will be necessary to ascertain the:

- size of the area/surfaces to be cleaned
- types of surfaces to be cleaned
- use of the area/surfaces
- standard of cleanliness to be achieved
- time available for the cleaning process
- capabilities of the staff that are to use the equipment
- safety factors to be considered
- purchase costs involved
- cleaning and maintenance of the equipment
- size of the storage area that will be needed
- electrical equipment's mark of safety

MANUAL EQUIPMENT

Below is a summary of the principal types of manual cleaning equipment that is commonly used in hospitality and catering establishments.

- *Dust control*   Dusters, hand dusting brushes, disposable mop heads, high dusting mops/brushes; long-handled pan and brush, hand pan and brush, self-closing lobby pan and brush; carpet sweepers, dust control sweepers/mops, V sweepers, brushes
- *Mopping systems*   Buckets (single/twin), bucket wringers, handle/push types, Kentucky mops, floor squeezees, wall-cleaning mops/tools
- *Sprayers*   Hand-trigger spray bottles, power spray units, pressure sprays.
- *Window cleaning*   Window wash applicators, window squeezees, chamois leathers
- *Scrapers*   Floor scrapers, hard-bristle brushes, exterior yard brooms
- *Pads*   Abrasive hand pads, polishing pads, polish applicators/mops
- *Safety items*   Caution signs, cleaners, trolleys

ELECTRICAL EQUIPMENT

There is a vast variety of styles and types of electrical equipment. However, they can be simply classified, as in the summary list below. The main thing to remember is that the equipment should be easily used and maintained as well as being efficient. It is prudent to use only one or two manufacturers for all electrical cleaning equipment, because the servicing cost can be reduced in this way.

Summary of electrical cleaning equipment

- *Dust control*   Suction cleaners (upright/tub/cylindrical), suction sweepers
- *Wet clean*   Wet pick up/suction cleaners, high-pressure washers, scrubbing machines, spray extraction machines
- *Dry floor cleaning*   Buffing and suction machines, buffing/polishing machines

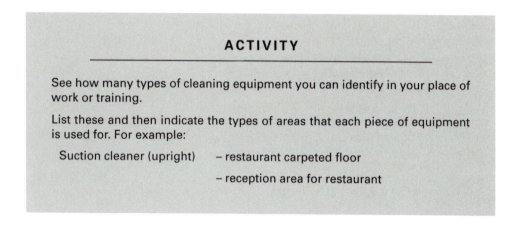

ACTIVITY

See how many types of cleaning equipment you can identify in your place of work or training.

List these and then indicate the types of areas that each piece of equipment is used for. For example:

Suction cleaner (upright)　　– restaurant carpeted floor

　　　　　　　　　　　　　　– reception area for restaurant

SAFETY RULES FOR USING EQUIPMENT

- use caution safety signs whenever cleaning public areas
- never allow flexes to trail over walkways/corridors
- make sure that you know how to use the equipment properly
- clean public areas at times when few people are about
- wear safe protective shoes and suitable protective clothes
- clean the equipment after use
- put the equipment away as soon as possible
- never leave equipment lying about
- when cleaning staircases work from the top downwards
- when cleaning lifts, keep the doors open
- check the flexes and plugs of all electrical equipment

ACTIVITY

Compile a safety checklist for two of the following types of equipment:

  (a) Upright suction cleaner

  (b) Floor-buffing machine

  (c) Wet pick-up machine

  (d) High-pressure washer

EQUIPMENT STORAGE

The following points should be remembered:
- the room should be clean and tidy
- there needs to be shelving for small items
- the room should be well lit and well ventilated
- there should be no signs of rodent infestation
- hooks are needed for long-handled equipment, hoses and flexes
- there should be a cleaners' sink with hot and cold water
- there needs to be an area in which to dry equipment after washing
- the rooms should be locked to safeguard the equipment

EQUIPMENT MAINTENANCE

In order to ensure that all electrical cleaning equipment is in perfect working order at all times, it is necessary to have it regularly cleaned and serviced. New equipment will come with a guarantee of one or more years. Any problems with this equipment will be covered by this guarantee.

It is advisable to purchase electrical equipment from one manufacturer, so that the maintenance can be arranged for all the equipment at the same time, thus reducing the charges. Some establishments take out maintenance contracts to cover all their equipment. This means that it will be serviced at regular intervals and repaired as necessary for a predetermined sum of money per annum. The maintenance of equipment is an important part of the housekeeper's duties. Staff cannot work efficiently if the equipment is broken, and standards will therefore not be maintained.

Cleaning agents

There are literally hundreds of differently named cleaning agents, each manufacturer's range carrying its brand name. The method of determining which agent is suitable for which surface is to understand the types of cleaning agents. Then it is possible to select a manufacturer's range of agents to suit the premises.

Table 4.13 below gives the primary types of agents commonly used in daily and weekly cleaning routines. For occasional cleaning tasks there are specialist cleaners available, which can be obtained as required in small quantities.

Table 4.13 Types of cleaning agent for different purposes

Equipment/area	Cleaning agent
Food areas	Liquid detergent, sanitizer, cream cleanser, hard surface cleaner
Kitchen equipment	Strong alkali detergent, powder abrasive, cream cleanser, acid de-scaler, hard surface cleaner, sanitizer
Bathrooms	Acid WC cleanser, limescale remover, glass cleaner, liquid detergent, cream cleanser
Floors	Liquid detergent, sanitizer, solvent-based detergent, mild alkali detergent, non-slip polish
Metals	Stainless steel polish, brass polish, silver polish, liquid silver cleanser
Furniture	Wax polish, spray wax-based polish, silicone-based spray polish

Table 4.14 Properties of and methods of using main cleaning agents

Type	Characteristics	Methods of use
Liquid detergent	A mix of surficants, alkaline chemicals, foaming agents, suspending agents, bleaches, conditioners, and enzymes.	Dissolve in hot water according to manufacturer's instructions, then use as required.
Sanitizer	A detergent that is mixed with a bactericidal agent and can destroy harmful bacteria.	Either dissolve in hot water and use as required or mix as instructed with cold water and use in a hand-trigger spray.
Cream cleanser	Non-scratch abrasive cream.	Use sparingly with a damp cloth. Rinse off well. Dry the surface.
Hard-surface cleanser	A liquid cleanser that will remove greasy marks on walls, shelves and flat surfaces.	Use sparingly with a damp cloth. Rub area hard, then rinse off. Dry the surface.
Strong alkali detergent	A detergent that is used for degreasing kitchen equipment. Corrosive.	Wearing gloves, wipe or spray on surface. Leave to work. Rinse off well and dry the equipment thoroughly.
Powder abrasive	A mix of pumice, bleach and detergent, which will scratch the surface.	Sprinkle onto surface. Rub with scouring pad. Rinse off well and dry thoroughly.
Acid de-scaler	Strong cleanser used to remove limescale from equipment.	Follow manufacturer's instructions. Wear gloves.
Acid WC cleanser	Strong cleanser used to remove limescale deposits from WC pans and urinals.	Sprinkle in the WC pan. Leave for 30 minutes. Brush the surface vigorously and flush.
Limescale remover	Liquid agent used to remove limescale from taps, baths, showers and sink areas.	Pour directly onto the affected area. Leave for 30 seconds then rub well. Rinse away. Dry the area well.
Glass cleanser	A liquid detergent with an acid content (vinegar) used in a trigger spray.	Spray directly onto the glass. Buff with a soft cloth to a shine.
Solvent-based detergent	A detergent used to remove solvent-based polish from floors (not PVC or thermoplastic floors).	Make to a solution by mixing with water. Mop or machine scrub over the floor. Remove slurry and rinse well.

Mild alkali detergent	A detergent used to remove water-based polish from floors.	Mix with water according to instructions. Mop or machine scrub over the floor. Remove slurry, rinse well and dry.
Non-slip polish	A water-based liquid synthetic emulsion polish, used on PVC, thermoplastic, rubber and terrazzo floor surface.	Spread by mop over the clean and dry floor surface. Leave untouched for a minimum of 30 minutes. It will dry to a shine.
Stainless steel polish	A non-toxic spray for use in food areas to give a sheen to the surfaces.	Spray sparingly over a clean dry surface and buff up with disposable paper to produce a shine.
Brass polish	A creamy liquid used to remove tarnish from unsealed brass and copper.	Apply to the surface with a soft cloth. Rub well. Rub off the polish with a clean soft cloth.
Silver polish	A liquid used to remove tarnish from silver and silver-plated items.	Apply to the surface with a soft brush or cloth. Rub well. Rub off with a clean soft cloth.
Liquid silver cleanser	A thin liquid used to remove the tarnish from silver and silver-plated items.	Dip the silver item into the liquid for a few seconds. Rinse immediately in warm water and dry well.
Wax polish	A paste or cream polish used on unsealed wooden surfaces.	Apply to the wood with a cloth, rub well in. Remove with a clean cloth and buff to a shine.
Wax-based polish	A polish applied with trigger spray to wood surfaces.	Spray sparingly onto the surface. Buff to a shine.
Silicone spray polish	A polish for gloss hard surfaces, plastic, vinyl, paintwork, ceramic tiles.	Spray sparingly onto the surface. Buff to produce a shine.
Soda crystals	Sodium carbonate, used to degrease drains and floor gullies.	Dissolve in very hot water, then pour the solution slowly down the drain. Leave for 30 minutes then flush with hot water.
Soda crystals	Used with an aluminium sheet for silver cleaning (known as Polivit clean).	Dissolve in boiling water. Pour over the aluminium sheet and place the silver over the plate. The chemical reaction will remove the tarnish from the silver.
Bleach	Sodium hypochloride. Poisonous. Use with great care. Destroys bacteria in drains and dust bins.	Use protective gloves. Mix to a solution by following instructions. Pour this onto the area. Scrub hard, then rinse well.

SAFETY PRECAUTIONS WITH CLEANING AGENTS

It must be remembered that cleaning agents are dangerous commodities if not used and stored safely. The main points to remember are listed below. Remember, if in doubt always ask your supervisor before using any cleaning agent.

• label each container properly
• store in a locked area
• never keep unused agents

- dispense easily handled quantities to staff
- use a minimum number of different agents
- instruct all staff of agents' uses
- use agents at the correct dilution
- use protective gloves if necessary
- always use the mildest agent first

STOCK CONTROL

It is necessary to have an efficient method of stock control in the housekeeping department. The items held in this section can be expensive to replace and are vital for day-to-day operations. Main items need to be coded according to their use and locality within the section. This way it is easy to identify each item of equipment and its attachments. For example, a suction cleaner could be coded 3A denoting that it is located on the third floor and is the first one on that list, the second being 3B and so on. The attachments will be coded 3A/1, 3A/2, 3A/3, according to how many attachments there are. This system makes stock control easier, and has the added advantage of aiding staff who are uncertain about the locality of equipment of the attachments that fit a particular machine.

The storage of expendables, such as cleaning agents, cloths and pads, needs to be controlled in much the same way as the consumables are controlled in the food preparation area of the establishment. They are ordered in the same manner, used in rotation and issued to staff in a controlled, organized manner. The stock of expendables needs to be:

- stored in a locked room
- issued at regular predetermined times to the staff
- stored near to the main work areas
- stored in a well lit, cool and well ventilated room
- maintained in a rodent-free zone
- stored in a shelved room to facilitate easy stock control
- labelled to facilitate safe use

DISPENSING CLEANING AGENTS

Cleaning agents are manufactured to be efficient at a predetermined dilution. It is therefore imperative that they are used in this solution in order to produce the desired finished standard of cleanliness.

Various dispensing methods are now in use.

Bulk purchase

In this case the agents are purchased in bulk drums and dispensed into easily handled containers for the staff to use. This may be economical but will be time-consuming. The large drums are heavy and need to on low shelving to facilitate easy dispensing. Spillages during this process can eliminate any savings.

Pre-packaged

In this case the agents are purchased in individual sachets or in tablet form. One sachet or tablet for a set quantity of water (often 4 litres). This means no over-usage, no wastage, and perfect stock-taking figures. However, it is more expensive to purchase agents in this manner. Some establishments use the tablet form for dangerous agents such as bleach, so that its use can be strictly controlled and the liquid bleach cannot then be mistaken for anything else, or used undiluted by mistake.

Tap dispensers

These are often seen fitted to wash-up sinks in kitchens. The bulk drum is positioned below the sink and a plastic pipe feeds it up to the tap dispenser. Whenever the detergent is required, a simple turn of the tap will dispense a measured amount into the sink with the hot water. This is a very useful way to use washing-up detergent in a food preparation or service area, as no mistakes can be made and the detergent cannot be spilt or used in too high a concentration. This method is used for all washing-up machines too.

Pump dispensers

A plastic hand-pump can be fitted to 5-litre containers. The staff can then simply use this pump to dispense the required amount of cleaning agent into their bucket or sink as required. This is an easy method of dispensing, but does not measure the quantity used by the staff. Even though one pump is usually the amount of agent recommended, staff usually pump at least twice, thinking that more agent will make their task easier. In fact the opposite result is achieved: too much cleaning agent makes the rinsing more difficult, and often leaves the finish streaky.

ACTIVITY

Looking at the chart showing different cleaning methods, decide which processes would be used in a specific room. It may be a classroom, a lounge, a restaurant or a kitchen.

1. Carry out the cleaning processes, using the logical sequences (see pp. 161–2).
2. Produce work cards for the processes that you have used.

Safety

ACCIDENT PREVENTION

It is important to work in a safe manner at all times, this is especially important in the housekeeping section of the establishment. Accidents can occur if staff are hurrying around, failing to concentrate upon the tasks in hand or not applying the safety rules of the establishment. Such careless behaviour could result in any of the following:

- floors left in a slippery condition
- wet floor surfaces
- minor accidents caused by staff running around
- equipment left where customers could trip over it
- flexes trailing long distances across floors or down stairs
- wrong dilution of cleaning agent used, causing slipperiness
- litter left on the floor
- emergency exits becoming blocked

REPORTING ACCIDENTS

All accidents to staff or guests should be reported to the management immediately. An accident report form must be completed to include all the details (see p. 183).

These reports need to be completed even if the accident appears to be of a minor nature. There could be an investigation in the future, for which the report would be useful.

AVOIDING HAZARDS

The following areas should be regularly checked to help to prevent accidents caused by needless hazards.

Residential areas
- carpets properly fitted and well maintained
- mats lying flat on non-slip surfaces
- plants and flowers on stable surfaces and never top heavy
- newspapers and magazines placed on racks or tables
- waste paper bins regularly emptied
- ash trays frequently emptied and large enough to be safe

Leisure areas
- swimming aids stored in a bin or basket at pool side
- chairs kept well away from pool side
- adequate litter bins provided and emptied regularly
- gates to tennis courts well maintained to ensure safe closure
- bins for sports equipment so that these do not spill out
- bicycle traffic kept to well defined areas

Exterior areas
- well lit approached and car parks
- level and safe paths and steps
- leaves and debris swept up regularly
- snow and ice cleared immediately
- delivery areas properly secured, empty crates stacked safely

Safety is the responsibility of all staff it is an aspect of responsibility that can never be overlooked. The list below shows how important safety is to all staff from the lowest paid to the highest paid member. It applies to all types of establishment, at all times.

Yourself

Concentrate upon what you are meant to be doing and KNOW:

• which task you are doing
• where you are to work
• what equipment you need
• how to clean the equipment to destroy harmful bacteria
• what agents you need
• how the equipment is used
• the dilution of the agent to be used
• how long the task will take
• in what sequence the tasks should be completed
• how to lift items safely
• how to reach high areas safely

Other staff

Put yourself in their position and NEVER:

• leave equipment dirty or unemptied
• leave equipment in an unsafe manner
• run about
• play jokes on staff in working areas

Customers

Your job is dependent upon your customers. You must NEVER:

• block emergency exits
• leave items of equipment lying around
• over load your trolley so that items fall off
• leave floors wet or slippery
• leave polish on surfaces
• allow flexes to trail across the floor

Signs

They all have a purpose. Therefore you must KNOW:

• all green signs are for emergencies – the safe way out
• all blue signs are mandatory instructions – must do
• all red signs are for fire fighting – fire equipment
• all red circles, plus line, mean prohibited – don't do
• all yellow triangular signs mean danger – risk, danger

Figure 4.6 Accident prevention check-list

LEGAL REQUIREMENTS

Safety regulations apply to the housekeeping department and its staff in the same way as they apply to all other sections of the establishment.

The Health and Safety at Work Act (HASAWA) 1974

This outlines the legal obligations of (a) employers, (b) employees, which may be summarized as follows:

(a) Employers are obliged to:

- ensure the health and safety of all employees
- provide a safe environment in which to work, with safe equipment and tools
- train staff to work in these areas with the equipment provided
- formulate and adhere to a safety policy

(b) Employees are obliged to:

- take reasonable care of his or her own safety, and the safety of others
- work in the manner laid down by the employer, with safety aspects always regarded

Control of Substances Hazardous to Health (COSHH) Regulations 1988

These regulations set out in detail the way in which the HASAWA regulations are met in respect of substances hazardous to health.
The regulations require that six steps are taken:

- know what products or substances are used
- assess the potential hazards of these substances
- eliminate or control these hazards
- instruct and train employees in the use of these substances
- monitor the effectiveness of the control of these substances
- keep records relating to the control and use of these substances
(See also p. 136.)

FIVE

Food preparation

Catering personnel

It is becoming increasingly necessary to have a multi-skilled work force in the catering side of the business. The traditional kitchen brigades may still be found in some large hotel and restaurant kitchens, but increasingly these traditional demarcations are being eroded in favour of a multi-experienced team. The advantage of this arrangement lies in flexibility and greater productivity. From the employee's perspective it gives a far greater opportunity to learn other skills and to advance more quickly up the promotion scale, if true skills and abilities are achieved. Table 5.1 shows staffing roles in the catering sector, divided into category A, managerial staff, category B, supervisory staff, and category C, operative staff.

It is important to remember that *all* staff are responsible for customer care, safety and hygiene. These are not therefore specifically included in the summary of duties.

Table 5.1 Catering staff by category (managerial, supervisory, operational)

Category of Staff	Establishment	Summary of duties
Managerial		
District manager	Contract catering Hotel group	Control of a group of establishments
Area catering manager	Contract catering	Control of a group of catering units
Managed house controller	Brewery-owned licensed premises	Control of a group of public houses/hotels
Purchasing director	Hotel group Contract catering	Purchasing of bulk supplies of commodities
Training manager	Large organizations	The training of all employees
Hospitality services manager	Universities Hospitals	Provision and control of catering services and staffing
Force catering manager	Police force	Provision and control of catering services
Catering manager/ officer	In-house industrial welfare establishments Leisure units	Provision and control of catering services and staffing Marketing

Management couple	Public houses Hotels-managed	Provision of all food and catering services Staffing Marketing
Domestic bursar	Universities Schools	Provision of all food and catering services Staffing
Executive/Head chef	Hotels Clubs Restaurants	Provision of all catering services Staffing
Chef/manager	In-store units Small units	Provision of all catering services Staffing
Owner manager	Privately owned hotel Public house Restaurant	Control of all catering services Staffing Marketing

Category of Staff	Establishment	Summary of duties
Supervisory		
Kitchen supervisor	In-house industrial Hospitals Schools	Control of all kitchen work and staff
Development chef	Food industry Hotel groups	Recipe development Food investigations
Chef/cook	All	Preparation of all foods, and the kitchen
Second/sous chef	Large kitchens	Deputize for chef/one section of kitchen
Chef de parti	Large kitchens	Responsible for one section of the kitchen work
Pastry chef	Large kitchens	All pastry and sweets production
Baker	Specialist units	Production of dough-based products and breads
Larder chef	Large kitchens	Cold preparation work
Store keeper	Large kitchens	Control of all goods inwards and goods outwards

Category of Staff	Establishment	Summary of duties
Operational		
Cook/chef	All	Preparation of food
Assistant cook/chef	All	Assist with the food preparation
Breakfast chef/cook	Residential establishments	Preparation of breakfasts
Store assistant	Large units	Assist with the receipt and issue of stores
General assistant	All	General catering duties
Catering services staff	All	General catering duties
Still room assistant	Hotel	Preparation and dispense of hot beverages and snacks
Kitchen porter	Large kitchens	Cleaning/carrying Washing-up Rubbish disposal

Legislation

HEALTH AND SAFETY AT WORK ACT (HASAWA) 1974

This act has implications for both the employer and the employee.

The employer
- must provide and maintain premises in a safe manner
- must provide safe premises for the handling and storage of commodities
- is responsible for the provision of instruction and training for employees
- must provide safe means of vacating the premises in normal and emergency situations
- is responsible for the provision of welfare arrangements for all employees
- is responsible for producing and implementing a safety policy

The employee
Every employee has to take full responsibility for their actions whilst at work and must:

- take care of the health and safety of themselves and others
- work in a safe manner
- follow employer's instructions
- use safety guards
- implement employer's safety practices
- wear the supplied safety clothing as required
- never use commodities or equipment in a manner likely to cause harm to others
- report any breaches of the HASAWA code of practice to the employer

The HASAWA legislation also covers the state and maintenance of the working areas, with clauses relating to:

- cleanliness of the areas
- size of the working area per employee
- ventilation facilities
- light levels in all areas
- sanitary conveniences for employees
- washing facilities for staff
- provision of fresh drinking water
- welfare facilities for employees
- accommodation and facilities for staff meals
- safety of premises especially floors and stairways
- safety measures for dangerous machines

Enforcement of HASAWA

The local authority's environmental health officer (EHO) has the power to enter premises at any time in order to enforce HASAWA. Should he/she find any aspect that contravenes the Act, an *improvement notice* will be issued, giving details of the matter(s) to be improved, altered or corrected. A specified time limit for the correction will be given, as will a three-week period for an appeal, should the employer wish to make one.

A *prohibition notice* will be issued if an inspector finds conditions or activities that are likely to cause serious injury. The cause of concern must be dealt with before normal business can continue.

HEALTH AND SAFETY FIRST AID REGULATIONS 1981

These are the regulations that make it obligatory for employers to provide first aid facilities and qualified first aid personnel in the work place. First aid boxes have a statutory minimum content, and are placed at strategic places around the work place. In a hotel they could be placed in the head chef's office, the front office, the housekeeper's office and so on. All boxes are green with a central white cross on them, and should be accessible at all times.

A record of all injuries and the treatment given to employees must be kept, usually in an accident book. That must include the following information:

- the name of the injured person
- the nature of the injury
- where the accident happened
- the time and date that it occurred
- how and when the treatment was given to the injured person
- what action was taken after the initial first aid was given
- who gave the first aid
- names of any witnesses
- any indication as to the cause of the accident

ACTIVITY

1. Compile a list of circumstances that could cause an accident in each of the following working areas:

   (a) Kitchen

   (b) Self-service cafeteria

   (c) Restaurant

2. In each case, indicate what steps could be taken to avoid such an accident.

FOOD HYGIENE (GENERAL) REGULATIONS 1970

These regulations cover all food premises and dictate the facilities and conditions that must exist in all food area. The regulations are enforced by the EHO who has the authority to inspect the premises at any reasonable hour without prior notice to the owner. The main points relating to premises and personnel are listed below.

Premises must:

- be clean, tidy, with no rubbish allowed to accumulate
- be in a good state of repair and built of suitable materials, so as to promote hygienic conditions
- be well lit
- be adequately ventilated
- not have sanitary conveniences leading directly into a food area
- have adequate hand-basins, with hot and cold running water, soap, nail brush and hand-drying facilities
- not have animals, pests or vermin in food areas
- have no food area leading directly into a sleeping area

Food handlers must:

- maintain high standards of hygiene, both personal and work-related
- wear protective clothing
- keep personal belongings out of food areas
- report to their employer an illness or infection likely to cause food poisoning
- notify the EHO if suffering from dysentery, typhoid or paratyphoid

FOOD SAFETY ACT 1990

This act strengthens the existing laws governing the production and handling of foods and aims to:

- continue to ensure that all food produced for sale is safe to eat and not misleadingly presented
- strengthen existing legal powers and penalties
- enable the UK to fulfil its role within the European Community
- keep pace with technological change

The requirements are that food throughout the food chain must not:

- have been rendered injurious to health
- be unfit for human consumption
- be so contaminated that it is unsafe to eat
- be inaccurately described if it is for sale

The Food Safety Act is enforced by the EHO, who may enter the premises at any time to investigate, and inspect any food item to ascertain its freshness.

The employer must be able to show that 'due diligence' has been taken to ensure that the Food Safety Act is being complied with. This means being able to prove that they have taken all reasonable steps and procedures to ensure that foods are stored and handled in a safe manner at all times whilst on their premises. It is for this reason that the practice of recording the temperature of refrigerators, deep freezers, chilled cabinets and holding ovens is now enforced.

Food handlers code of practice

In order to comply with the Food Safety Act and the Food Hygiene Regulations, it is necessary for all food handlers to follow a strict code of practice. Food safety training should form part of every induction course, to help handlers to appreciate the importance of the subject and of following hygienic practices. Some procedures relating to the personal hygiene of food handlers are given in Table 5.2.

Table 5.2 Personal hygiene of food handlers

Hygiene aspect	Standard	Reason
Body cleanliness	Shower/bath daily Clean short hair Clean shaven	To remove staphylococcus from the skin and to prevent body odour
Hands	Clean hands Clean short, not bitten, nails No cuts or sores	To prevent cross contamination and staphylococcus from hands, saliva, cuts and sores
Personal habits	No smoking or spitting Never touch face, ears, hair or neck	Prevention of cross contamination and staphylococcus from fingers and saliva
Protective clothing	Clean, light colour, absorbent clothing Clean socks and safety shoes	Prevention of cross contamination and the removal of body odour from perspiration
Health	No boils or skin complaints No throat or nasal infections No stomach upsets or diarrhoea	Staphylococcus is passed on easily to other workers Salmonella may be passed to other persons or into food items as they are being prepared

Food contamination

This is caused by harmful substances (e.g. chemicals) or bacteria that can affect food at any stage of its storage, preparation, cooking and service. Harmful bacteria can reach food via a human or animal carrier, or from another type of food, by direct contact or transferred from surfaces, utensils, etc. (see Figure 5.1).

CONDITIONS IN WHICH BACTERIA THRIVE

There are certain conditions in which bacteria thrive and develop quickly. It is important to know of these conditions and of the various processes by which contamination can take place, so that it is possible to take appropriate preventive action. Moist and warm (50-60°C) conditions provide an ideal environment for bacteria, which can develop under such conditions in 20 minutes. This is why it is important to cool foods quickly and keep them refrigerated, or at least in a cool well ventilated area, protected from moisture and other food safety hazards, such as flies or vermin.

DESTROYING BACTERIA

Bacteria can be destroyed by heat over 80°C, which is why it is so important to reheat cooked food or cook chilled meals thoroughly. It can be dry heat (baking, grilling, roasting, frying) or moist heat (boiling, poaching, stewing, braising, microwaving). Bacteria on surfaces, utensils or skin, can be destroyed with sanitizer or anti-bacterial soap.

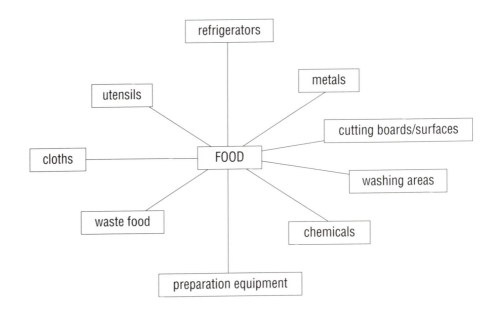

Figure 5.1 Food contamination danger areas

ACTIVITY

Compile a chart similar to the example shown below, to show the methods used to prevent food contamination.

Contamination area	Means of prevention
Refrigerators	Use separate fridges for meat, fish and cooked products.
	Use separate trays for each of these types of food.

Common causes of food contamination

CHEMICALS

Those used in the manufacture of some cleaning agents can be harmful. It is necessary to select safe cleaning agents for use in food areas and to follow the manufacturer's instructions at all times. Lubricating oil from food preparation machinery can also cause food contamination if it is allowed to leak out.

PATHOGENS

These are micro-organisms (bacteria) that are capable of causing disease in humans. Bacteria are found in many different types of areas and food products (see Figure 5.1).

POISONOUS PLANTS

Rhubarb leaves, raw red kidney beans, some mushrooms and all toadstools are poisonous. Plants (e.g. illegally grown water cress) cultivated near contaminated water can be harmful, as can plants sprayed with pesticide or herbicide immediately prior to harvesting.

METALS

Copper, zinc, tin and lead can all cause food contamination if they are allowed to come into contact with the food. Poor quality equipment and utensils should not be used.

HUMAN CARRIERS

Some people unknowingly carry harmful bacteria within their bodies. They display no symptoms themselves, but can pass the bacteria on to others through the food chain. It is for this reason that these carriers must not be allowed to work in the food industry. Prior to employment in the food industry prospective employees have to have a medical examination. This will detect such carriers.

CROSS-CONTAMINATION

This is the term used to describe the transfer of pathogenic organisms from raw food to food that is ready to be eaten. The following measures will help prevent this occurring:

- use separate areas for handling raw and cooked foods
- store raw and cooked foods separately
- use separate equipment for raw and cooked foods
- wash hands between every task
- handle foods as little as possible (use disposable gloves)
- keep equipment clean and in good repair
- keep food areas free from accumulated refuse
- eliminate all pests, flies and insects
- train all staff thoroughly and hold refresher training sessions

Food poisoning

Food poisoning is caused by eating food that looks normal but is in fact contaminated with harmful bacteria. The symptoms are sickness, diarrhoea and abdominal pains, and can develop from as soon as one hour after eating the food and up to thirty-six hours later. The illness must be treated by a doctor and can last for up to ten days. Some patients have to be hospitalized and in rare cases the poisoning can be fatal. The elderly and the young are more likely to be dangerously affected than healthy adults.

ACTION TO BE TAKEN IF THERE IS AN OUTBREAK OF FOOD POISONING

- notify the environmental health officer
- provide samples of all foods likely to have been eaten
- follow the EHO's advice
- inform all employees to report any slight stomach upset immediately

Table 5.3 Summary of food poisoning bacteria

Bacteria	Source	Cause	Foods affected
Salmonella	Raw meat Eggs Poultry	Poor preparation routines Inadequate thawing Under-cooking	Under-cooked poultry Raw egg Food that has been cross- contaminated after cooking
Campylobacter	Live animals	Poor food-handling practices Under-cooking	Food in contact with live animals Foods cross-contaminated

Clostridium
perfringens
	Raw meats
	Animal and
	  human intestines
	Soil
		Dishes cooked inadequately
		  then poorly reheated
		Unwashed salads
			Meat pies
			Pasties
			Reheated meat-based casseroles
			Unwashed vegetables

Staphylococcus aureus	Human nose, mouth and skin Septic cuts, boils and styes	Poor hygiene practices	Cooked cold meats Trifles Custards Gateaux
Bacillus cereus	Rice	Slow cooking and inadequate reheating	Rice salads Slowly re-heated rice dishes
Listeria monocytogenes	Animal intestines Milk	Poor handling practices Inadequate regeneration of cook/chill foods	Cook/chill foods Soft ripe cheeses Pâté Pre-washed salads

HIGH-RISK FOODS

Some foods are more liable to bacterial growth and/or contamination than others. This is because they provide the ideal growing conditions for the bacteria. These high risk-foods are often high in protein and are not going to be re-heated prior to consumption. For example:

- cooked meats (sliced meats, pork pies, pasties, scotch eggs, sausage rolls, pâté)
- cooked poultry (cooked chicken portions, sliced chicken, pâté)
- cooked fish (smoked fish, fish paste and fish mousse)
- eggs (fresh mayonnaise, egg custards, savoury flans)
- cooked cereals (rice, rice salads and pasta salads)
- soft cheeses (those ripened with micro-organisms and moulds)
- milk products (sauces, sweet desserts, trifles)
- salads (pre-washed leaves, fruit and cereal-based)
- sandwiches (protein-filled, salad-filled)
- cream products (synthetic and fresh cream items)

ACTIVITY

Working in groups

Collect newspaper cuttings that relate to food poisoning outbreaks and food handling practices.

Produce a scrapbook that contains these and also charts illustrating good practice for food handlers.

Preventing contamination

METHODS OF COOLING FOODS

All cooked foods that are to be stored must be cooled safely and efficiently so as to minimize the risk of contamination or bacterial growth. They should be cooled to below 50°C within a maximum of 90 minutes. Remember that the danger zone for bacterial growth is when foods are at a temperature between 50° and 63° centigrade. To minimize the growth of bacteria, foods should be placed in a cool area of between 10°C and 15°C as soon as possible after the cooking process is complete. Leaving foods to cool slowly in a hot kitchen is very dangerous. All foods should be covered with a clean muslin cloth so that the heat can evaporate and dust does not contaminate the food. Often a cooling rack is needed in order to prevent the muslin falling into the food. This is placed over a tray or pan then covered with the muslin.

Liquids

- Place in shallow clean trays to increase the surface area.
- For small volumes, place in a clean container and stand this in a cold running-water bath.

Dry items

- Place on cooling racks and allow the air to circulate freely.

Blast chilling

- Place food in a fan-assisted refrigeration cabinet, designed to lower the temperature of hot foods as quickly as possible (blast chilling).
- Ensure that food to be cooled is on shallow trays. This way it will chill more rapidly than it would if put in mass-volume containers. Foods should be no more that 6 cm deep. Joints of meat should be no larger than 2.5 kg.

ACTIVITY

In groups keep a record of the cooked foods that you have had to cool before they are refrigerated. In each case indicated (as below) the type of food, the method used to cool it down and the time taken.

Type of food	Cooling method	Time taken
6 litres soup	Shallow tray, covered, in cold room	45 minutes

KITCHEN CLEANING

In all kitchens, when organizing the cleaning routines, the following points should be taken into consideration:

What   items, surfaces, areas are to be cleaned?
When   is each to be cleaned?
Who   is to be responsible for this cleaning?
How   is each item, surface, area to be cleaned?

To ensure that cleaning is completed to the required standard work cards (see p. 166) are often used in conjunction with a cleaning schedule. The work card will specify precisely how each task is to be carried out.

Cleaning of all food preparation areas should be carried out at the end of each working shift in order to maintain clean and hygienic working conditions.

Team work is an essential component of keeping the work surfaces and storage areas clean, and the reasons for thorough cleaning of all food areas should be familiar to all staff.

Eliminate
• cross-contamination risks
• areas where bacteria can multiply
• areas that will attract pests and rodents
• hazardous working conditions

Provide
• safe and secure area for all food products
• clean pleasant working areas
• encourage hygienic practices
• clean attractive areas for customers

The cooking of food

WHY DO WE COOK FOOD?

Many foods can be eaten raw but our diet would be drastically different if we didn't cook at all. The cooking process

• adds variety
• makes some foods more digestible
• makes some foods more appetising
• makes some foods easier to eat (e.g. meat)
• destroys any bacteria that may be present
• destroys natural toxins (e.g. in kidney beans)
• reduces bulk (e.g. spinach)
• thickens and sets (e.g. egg dishes)

THE EFFECTS OF HEAT UPON FOODS

Secondly, we must look at the effects of heat upon foods to appreciate the different processes involved and how it affects the food we eat.

- **protein**   – coagulates and gradually changes to become firmer and more easily digested, although over-cooking toughens it.

- **fats**   – melt, which can be useful in cooking processes. Too much fat in the diet causes obesity and difficulty with digestion.

- **carbohydrates**   – (a) in dry heat the sugars and starches change colour from white to golden brown, then (with prolonged heat) to dark brown (caramelize), after which they burn.

                       – (b) in moist heat starches will gelatinize as the granules swell and burst, so creating a thickening agent; sugar will dissolve, become syrupy as further heat is applied and will eventually caramelize.

- **vitamins**   – fat-soluble A and D are not lost in moist methods of cookery, nor are they destroyed by heat. Vitamins B and C are water-soluble and so can be lost in moist cookery unless the liquors are utilized for sauces. Both of these vitamins are also destroyed by high temperatures, as in pressure cooking.

- **minerals**   – the breaking down of food in cooking makes it more easily digested; any minerals thus become more available to us.

Generally we can look at the methods of cookery under two headings:

- **dry**: grill, shallow fry, deep fry, bake, roast
- **wet**: boil, braise, steam, poach

In looking more closely at these processes, principles may be understood and then applied to many different types of food.

DRY COOKERY PROCESSES

Grilling

This is a fast method of cooking and so tender foods may be cooked in this way. Grilling is by radiating heat under or over a gas flame or electric grill. The food needs to be moistened with fat or oil to prevent it becoming dry whilst cooking. Pieces must also be cut evenly and turned often during grilling to ensure even heat distribution. The heat affects the surface of the food quickly so sealing in the juices, but it is very easy to overcook and dry or burn the food. Because of the radiated heat, it is possible to simply brown foods under the grill (called gratination) to assist in good presentation. For example, Cod mornay is sprinkled with grated cheese and breadcrumbs and grilled to give it that browned effect, which is pleasing to the eye and gives the surface a crunchy texture.

Grilling is suitable for snack meals, à la carte service and for cooking foods for those on fat-reduced diets.

Suitable foods for grilling

---

chops and cutlets
sausages and burgers
young, whole chickens and chicken breast
liver and kidney
fish fillets and small whole fish
tomatoes and mushrooms
steaks (rump, sirloin, fillet)

Shallow frying

There is the method of shallow frying, using a frying pan, which is perhaps what comes to mind when the term is used. There are also variants on this, using a wok or a sauté pan.

Cooking in the frying pan
This is a fast method of cookery, again suitable for tender foods. A thin layer of fat or oil is put into a shallow frying pan and food is placed in the pre-heated pan, presentation side first. Conducted heat from the base of the pan cooks the food that is in contact with it. It is advisable to turn food over once only as it may be damaged by frequent turning. This style of frying can be slow if required, in which case foods need not be coated first (e.g. onions). However, as with deep frying, fast cooking requires a coating (as for example, with fish cakes). For those on a fat-reduced diet it is possible to cook in a non-stick pan without fat, or use a very light layer of oil, applied by oil spray.

Suitable foods for shallow frying

---

fish fillets or whole, small fish
tender cuts of meat, chops and cutlet
liver and kidney
fish cakes and meat rissoles
beefburgers and sausages
onions
shredded vegetables
eggs

Cooking in a wok
The wok is a frying pan made from very thin metal in a hemi-spherical shape, which allows oils to run back to the bottom. The wok provides a very fast method of cookery, typical of the East. Foods are cut up into shreds or strips and tossed over a high flame until lightly cooked and still slightly crunchy. Foods tend to keep their colour well, their flavours are enhanced and low-fat cookery can be achieved.

Cooking in a sauté pan
Sauté is a term often used as an alternative to shallow fry. A sauté pan is heavier-bottomed than a frying pan and allows slower cooking. Meat and poultry cuts are usually sautéed, which can also involve being tossed in the pan or turned over frequently, a method which is unsuitable for delicate flesh, such as fish. Sauces can be made around the food in the sauté pan to capture the nutrients and flavour that may otherwise be lost.

Deep frying

This is a fast method of cookery, and so suitable for tender foods. It requires the total immersion of the foods into hot fat or oil. The heat from the oil penetrates the food and so cooks it. It is important to remember that raw foods such as sliced potatoes must be very well dried first or the moisture on them will cause the hot fat to 'spit'.

Suitable foods for deep frying
pieces of fish
pieces of meat and poultry
fruit
potatoes
other vegetables
dough
made-up foods

NEVER

leave a deep fryer unattended

heat the fat higher than recommended

move a friture while it is hot

allow fat to smoke – this means it is near 'flashpoint'

Except for dough and potatoes, these foods would be spoilt during frying by the oil being absorbed into the food and by loss of nutrients, unless they are sealed by coating them with milk/egg and flour, or flour and batter, or flour, egg and breadcrumbs. The reason we use protein foods, such as milk or egg is that protein coagulates as soon as it is immersed in the hot oil, forming a very effective protective coating.

Table 5.4 Temperatures for deep frying

Temperature (C)	Foods	Time
165–170°C	potato chips (blanching) white meats choux paste	5 minutes
175–180°C	whole fish doughnuts fruit fritters	8–10 minutes 4–5 minutes 3 minutes
185°C	potato chips (finishing) cuts of fish	2–3 minutes 4–5 minutes
195°C	whitebait	2–3 minutes

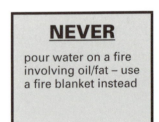

NEVER

pour water on a fire involving oil/fat – use a fire blanket instead

Baking

This term usually refers to the dry oven cooking of flour products, but can also refer to such items as potatoes and apples. Vegetables and fruit are easy to bake and require less attention than flour-based products, such as cake, for which it is important to understand the principles involved with each recipe – its balance, timing, correct temperature and effects of heat upon the product. A fan-assisted oven has a constant heat throughout its interior, and makes the art of baking much simpler.

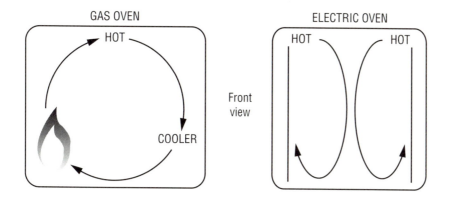

Figure 5.2 Heat flow in conventional ovens

Table 5.5 Temperatures for baking

Temperature (°C)		Regulo	Foods
110-20		s	meringues
	low		warming plates
140		1	rich fruit cakes
150		2	milk puddings
160		3	casseroles
180	moderate	4	shortpaste, fish
190		5	cakes
200		6	chouxpaste, roast
220	hot	7	bread, puffpaste
230		8	Yorkshire, scones
250	very hot	9	browning

Note: Before placing food in oven, always pre-heat the oven to the correct temperature.

Apart from making food digestible, baking creates appeal by giving foods colour and texture. Occasionally foods (e.g. bread) require a steamy condition when baking; if there isn't enough moisture in the product, a water bath can be placed at the bottom of the oven for best results. To avoid the hazard of becoming too hot and spoiling the food within them (as would occur with cream caramels) it is customary to use a water bath (bain-marie) around the vessel to lessen its temperature.

Roasting

This used to be carried out on a 'spit' over an open fire but now refers generally to the cooking of meat or vegetables in the oven in the presence of fat for basting. Radiated heat in the oven cooks the surface of the food and conducted heat from the tray cooks the item from underneath. It is very important to ensure that an even balance of heat is applied, according to the type of food, so that in cases where contact with the tray would cause food to cook too quickly, a trivet is used to hold it up. This would be necessary, for example, when roasting a best end joint of lamb, but not when roasting potatoes, for which a crispy (well cooked) finish is desired.

The fat or oil present when oven roasting can be used for basting the food to prevent it from drying out. It is also responsible for developing a specific taste, according to the type of fat used, although many foods have their own proportion of fat and so shouldn't require much added. Seasoning prior to roasting is also an important point to remember in most foods, but this may delay the colouring of meat, which may be avoided by seasoning after the initial sealing of the meat.

Care must be taken when slow roasting that flavours typical of roasting are not lost through developing a steamy atmosphere within the oven. Occasionally it may be necessary to cover foods (e.g. tougher quality meats) with tin foil when lengthening the cooking time, so that moisture is not lost. However, it is important to open the foil near the end of cooking time to develop characteristic flavours. Any cooking liquors lost from the joint may be used in accompanying sauces.

Cooking times and oven temperatures will vary according to the foods being cooked. Remember that once removed from the oven a joint of meat will continue to cook as it cools down, so a resting time is necessary before carving. Using a meat probe or thermometer stuck into the thickest part of a joint will give an internal temperature for the meat and show when it has reached cooking point.

Vegetables (potatoes, onions, parsnips and turnips can all be roasted) may be par-boiled before roasting.

Table 5.6 Temperatures for roasting

Meat	Suitable joint	Timing	Suggested temperature (C)
Beef	fore rib, rump, sirloin	20mins/500g + 20mins	200–225°
Lamb	best end, loin, leg, shoulder	25 mins/500g + 20mins	200–225°
Pork	all joint cuts	35mins/500g + 35mins	200–225°
Poultry	whole or joints	20mins/500g + 20mins	200°

WET COOKERY PROCESSES

Boiling

The boiling point of water is 100°C. Foods cooked by this method are fully immersed in water and brought to a rapid boil. Sometimes, as in the cooking of leafy vegetables, the temperature is reduced a little but the water is still 'moving' at a rapid simmer. As a rule, the foods cooked by boiling are those that will not be spoilt by the movement of the water and where a moist result is desired.

Suitable foods for boiling

---

potatoes	root vegetables
leafy vegetables	pulses
tough cuts of meat	ham and gammon
eggs	pasta and rice
shellfish	stocks

The length of time that foods will require to be boiled will vary considerably with the type and the preparation, but it must be remembered to ensure that all pieces of food are the same size so that they are cooked at the same time. It is also an important point that foods that require differing cooking times must not be mixed, e.g. potatoes and swede, as the potato will become soft and even disintegrate before the swede is cooked.

It may be necessary to use a lid during boiling to ensure that foods do not boil dry. When using a lid, check occasionally that the moisture level is retained.

Boiling from cold

Some foods are placed in cold water, then the temperature brought up to boiling point. Stocks are an example of this: at the initial boil impurities rise and it is important to refresh in cold water and reboil to ensure a clear liquid. Starting the cooking process with cold water is also safer when cooking large quantities. Unfortunately, nutrients can be lost in the lengthened cooking time unless the cooking liquor can be used in accompanying sauces.

Boiling from 100°C

Many foods are plunged into already boiling water, the advantage and disadvantage of this method are given below.

Starting cooking foods at boiling point: (a) advantages (b) disadvantages

---

(a)	Retains nutrients	(b) More dangerous
	Retains colour, texture	Must judge size of pan
	Reduced cooking time	Temporary reduction of temp.
	Cooking times more accurate	More care required at start
	Coagulates proteins quickly	

When plunging food into already boiling water it must be remembered to use a sufficiently large vessel to accommodate it all and to place it in carefully to avoid scalding splashes.

The fast boiling of some pulses for a minimum of 10 minutes is very important to remove toxins present in their skin. This can only be done by boiling as the method of heat distribution is constant and the temperature is high enough.

Braising

This is cooking in the oven or on the stove but with a lower temperature and the addition of moisture to approximately cover the food. It is a prolonged method of cookery: tougher foods are cooked in this way. Often a bed of vegetables is placed in the vessel first to prevent the protein food from coming into contact with the container, as this contact may cause the food to become dry and tough. A well-fitting lid must be employed to maintain the moisture level and create a steamy atmosphere whilst the liquid simmers so the food is both stewed and steamed. Flavours and nutrients leach into the cooking liquor so this must be used for an accompanying sauce.

The cooking liquor may consist of any or a combination of: water; stock; wine; beer.

Foods may be cut into portions or left as whole joints or pieces which will have an effect on the length of the cooking time. However, it can be said that braising can take a few hours for larger pieces.

Suitable foods for braising

---

tougher cuts of meat such as brisket of beef, venison
rabbit
breast of lamb
whole poultry
game birds
offal such as hearts and liver
vegetables such as potatoes, celery, onions and cabbage

Poaching

This method of cookery is often confused with boiling, but the difference is that the temperature of the cooking liquor is held at a slow simmer and the food is not always immersed in the liquid. Although foods cooked by poaching retain their shape, they do not take on any interesting colour and so could be looked on as unappetising. Thus the importance of a sauce made from the liquor, which not only retains the nutrients but also adds colour and interest to the finished dish.

As delicate foods are more easily digested and poaching does not require the addition of fat, menus for invalids often incorporate poached dishes.

Generally poaching is used for delicate foods which may be damaged by a faster method.

Foods suitable for poaching

Fish fillets
fish steaks
fruit
eggs
chicken breasts
asparagus

There are two types of poaching: shallow or slow poaching and deep poaching.

Shallow or slow poaching
In this method, used for example in poaching plaice fillets, the liquid level is held to a minimum and a cartouche or lid is used to trap steam, by which the food is also cooked. The liquid can be water, wine, milk or stock, or combinations of these, and may be flavoured, for example with finely cut onions and herbs. Cooking time is very short, either on the stove top or in a moderate oven; the food is then drained and sauce made, using the cooking liquor.

Deep poaching
In this method the food (for example, whole salmon or a joint of ham) is completely immersed in the cooking liquor. To avoid loss of taste it is important to poach in a well-flavoured liquor, using herbs, vegetables and seasoning. The cooking liquor is not often used for sauce as there are large amounts of it and in the case of ham it will be very salty.

When deep poaching eggs the addition of an acid (e.g. vinegar) to the water helps to speed up the coagulation of the protein so as to avoid the dispersal of the egg in the water. However, it is equally important that the eggs used should be as fresh as possible.

Poached eggs can be prepared in advance of service, trimmed to shape and held in iced water until they are required. A moment's re-dipping in hot water will soon bring them to the required temperature.

Steaming

In this method of cookery, food is held on shelves and surrounded by steam rising from boiling water in the bottom of the chamber. The steam offers a moist cooking environment that has various advantages:

- food is unlikely to be overdone
- apart from watching water levels occasionally foods can be left unattended
- nutrients are not lost as the food does not come into contact with moisture directly

One disadvantage however, is the fact that in the cooking process no colour is added to the food and it may look unappetising. For this reason, sauces are often served with steamed foods.

Foods suitable for steaming

- potatoes and vegetables
- fish portions
- sponge puddings, including Christmas pudding
- dumplings

Foods that are likely to be spoilt by the steam must be protected during the cooking process. For example, sponge pudding basins are covered with greaseproof paper and foil to keep the steam out.

A steamer is normally referred to as an 'atmospheric steamer' to distinguish it from the 'pressure steamer' in which steam builds up a pressure and so increases the temperature of the chamber and the speed of cooking.

An important point to remember when using a steamer is to use the door as a guard against a sudden rush of steam when the chamber is opened. Wait a few moments with the door ajar to allow excess steam to escape upwards before fully opening the door. In using pressure steamers, ensure that the temperature and so the pressure is lowered.

Microwaving

Really a combination of different methods of cookery according to its use, microwaving is becoming increasingly important in catering establishments for its convenience and speed although it still does have limitations due to the size of the chamber.

The oven works by creating waves similar to radio waves but of a different frequency. These waves cause moisture molecules in foods to be agitated, creating friction and resulting in heat (very much like when you rub your hands together to make them warm). Such high temperatures are reached that the food continues to cook even after the cooking period and so a resting time is often advised before service. Some microwaves are now available combined with a convection oven facility as well as the microwave. This does have some advantages but generally speed is the reason for choosing to use a microwave, and the combined method may well slow the process down again.

Suitable foods for microwaving

poached fish
quick jacket potatoes
boiling of root and pulse vegetables
casseroles (limited number of portions)
sauces
reheating portions and complete meals
'steamed' sponge puddings

One of the biggest advantages of using a microwave oven is that very little energy is used in its operation – it is thus very economic. It is a boon for fast food establishments and for cooking to order and reheating foods. A variety of foods may be cooked by microwave but it is important to recognize some of the possible disadvantages:

• drying can occur due to overcooking
• certain items explode in the oven, e.g. eggs in their shells
• fruits and dried fruit products can become dangerously hot and even flame
• protein foods do not colour, e.g. chicken, will be cooked but without being golden brown and crispy

ACTIVITY

Draw up a matrix grid to show the different methods of cookery and suitable foods for each of the methods listed. Make this as large as you can, listing suitable foods along the top, and methods of cookery down the side. Place ticks in relevant squares of the grid to indicate coincidence of food and method of cookery.

FOOD COMMODITIES

Food can be separated into distinct areas of study. This section (pp. 201–36) discusses foods under these divisions and gives an introduction to characteristics, purchasing points, storage rules, availability, uses, and nutritional values.

At the end of the section Table 5.24 gives a summary of some of these aspects.

Milk

We will be discussing cows' milk although goats' milk is becoming increasingly popular for people with allergy to dairy products. Milk is an almost complete food for humans, but also a very suitable base for bacterial growth so needs careful handling and storage.

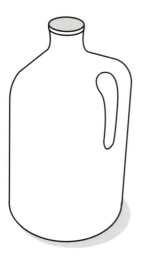

Nutritional information, for 100ml:			
FRESH MILK	whole	semi-skimmed	fully skimmed
Energy Value	280 kJ/67 Kcal	200 kJ/48 kcal	145 kJ/34 kcal
Protein	3.2g	3.3g	3.3g
Carbohydrate	4.8g	5.0g	5.0g
Fat	3.9g	1.6g	0.1g
Vitamin B^{12}	40% RDA	40% RDA	40% RDA
Minerals – calcium	15% RDA	15% RDA	15% RDA
– sodium	0.1g	0.1g	0.1g
Fibre	0g	0g	0g

*RDA – Recommended Daily Allowance

Figure 5.3 Nutritional value of milk

Table 5.7 Types of milk and their uses

Types of milk	Process	Characteristics	Uses
Fresh (pasteurized) Whole	Heated to 82°C for 15 secs	cream line keeps 48 hrs	drinks cooking milk puddings cereals
Semi-skimmed	Heated to 82°C for 15 secs	half fat content no cream line keeps 24 hrs	as above
Skimmed	Heated to 82°C for 15 secs	very low fat not dense white keeps 24 hrs	as above, for special diets
Channel Island	Heated to 82°C for 15 secs	high fat 4% rich and creamy	not used in catering very often
Sterilized	Homogenized then bottled and heated to 104°C for 30 minutes	distinctive flavour keeps 3 months unopened	not used in catering very often
Ultra-heat treated (UHT)	Homogenized, then heated to 130°C for 1 sec	changed flavour due to heating keeps 6 months unopened	cooking drinks milk puddings
Evaporated	60% water removed sterilized canned	rich flavour thick liquid	reconstitute with water or use as it is for confectionery
Condensed	More than 60% water removed	very thick non-pouring	as above
Dried	Pasteurized canned roller- or spray-dried	sweetened rich flavour usually low-fat	reconstitute with water as required for cooking and then treat as fresh

Table 5.8 Methods of storing milk

Fresh	Dried	Canned
in clean containers refrigerated for minimum time out of light (or vitamin C will be lost) away from strong smells	airtight cool dry and well ventilated store room small packs for fast rotation	cool dry and well ventilated store room will keep for number of years but once opened treat as fresh

Cream

Cream is the fat content of milk, skimmed or separated off from whole milk by centrifugal force. It can be sold in untreated form or after undergoing one of a variety of treatments (see

Table 5.9). The resulting type of cream – pasteurized, homogenized, sterilized, ultra-heat treated – must be specified on the label of the container. Cream is used to enhance food and to add enrichment to soups and sauces. When whipped, it adds volume to desserts such as mousses and ice creams.

Table 5.9 Treatments applied to cream and their effects

Process	Treatment	Effects
Pasteurized	heated to destroy harmful bacteria	keeping quality improved flavour/nutritional value unaltered
Homogenized	forced through tiny hole under pressure to give more even constitution	consistency thicker flavour unaltered
Sterilized	homogenized, then put into sealed containers and sterilized	consistency thicker distinctive flavour due to long heat process will not whip
UHT	first homogenized, heated briefly, then packaged	all bacteria destroyed flavour unaltered

Table 5.10 Types of cream and their uses

Type	Characteristics	Uses
Half ('coffee cream')	thin	pour over fruit and cereals pour into drinks
Single	18% fat content (insufficient to whip) pouring consistency	pour over fruit, cereals and desserts pour into drinks
Whipping	35% fat content will whip to twice volume doesn't overwhip easily	decoration and piping mousses spooned on desserts
Double	45% fat content will whip quickly to firm texture overwhips easily	decoration and piping ice cream production mousses spooned on desserts enriching soup/sauces
Double ultra-thick	very thick even when unwhipped unsuitable for whipping homogenized very rich texture and flavour	serve on desserts, fruit, cake and scones
Devon clotted	55% fat very thick and clotted creamy yellow, nutty flavour	as for double
Synthetic	prepared with vegetable fat available canned or dried	low-fat, low-cholesterol and dairy allergy diets

STORAGE

Fresh cream must be stored like fresh milk: in the refrigerator, for the minimum amount of time, away from strong-smelling foods and other contamination, preferably in its own sealed container.

Cheese

Cheeses originated as a method of preservation for the nutritive value of milk and has been produced throughout the world for centuries. It is now made on a large scale in this country and in many others. In some areas small quantities are produced on the farm. The processes of cheese production are shown in Figure 5.4.

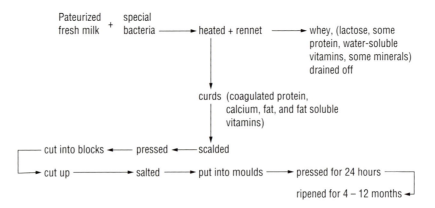

Figure 5.4 The processes of cheese production

Table 5.11 Some types of cheese, their characteristics and uses

Name	Type	Characteristics	Uses
Cottage	soft	low fat, white, lumpy very mild flavour	salads special diets
Cream	not true cheese	30-60% fat cream with less water to thicken mild flavour	cheesecake hors d'oeuvres
Cheddar	hard	mild to mature flavour firm, smooth texture	cooking pastries flavouring sauces cheeseboard
Processed	medium hard	made from mixing cheddar and other cheeses, adding colour and flavour rubbery texture ready sliced mild flavour	not often used in catering except as a sandwich filling
Stilton	blue-vein	curd innoculated with harmless bacteria to form mould veins creamy texture strong flavour	cheeseboard soups and sauces flans

STORAGE

Cheese must be stored in sealed containers, in the refrigerator, for the minimum amount of time.

USES OF CHEESE

- cheeseboard at the end of a meal, offering a variety of flavours, textures and colour for those who wish to end with a savoury taste
- gratinating: sprinkling grated hard cheese over a savoury dish and finishing under a hot grill, e.g. cod mornay
- to flavour baked products: cheese is added to pastries with seasoning
- to flavour sauces and soups: cheese is grated or diced and melted into the product. strong-flavoured cheeses are best, e.g. farmhouse cheddar, stilton
- to add colour, flavour and protein to salads, pasta dishes, fritters, baked potatoes and burgers
- to garnish dishes, e.g. on croûtes with French onion soup

ACTIVITY

1. Research and list at least three foreign cheeses under each of the following headings: hard, semi-hard, blue vein, soft.
2. Created a table to show the following information:
   - country of origin
   - type
   - characteristics
   - flavour and colour
   - culinary uses
3. Research six unusual English cheeses giving similar information.

Fats and oils

At room temperature fats are solid or creamy and oils are liquid. The main differences between them lie in:

- flavour
- colour
- melting point
- shortening ability
- oils cannot hold air when beaten

Different types of fat are selected according to the requirement. All fats have the ability to hold air when beaten, improve keeping qualities of products, enrich and soften gluten in flour to give a softer texture. The proportion and type of fat used and the method of production will alter the appearance of a finished product.

Table 5.12 Some types of fat and oil, their origin, characteristics and uses

Type	Characteristics	Uses	Origin
Fats			
Butter and unsalted butter	rich flavour adds colour difficult to cream smooth and plastic prone to rancidity	shallow frying pastries/cakes icing	milk fat
Margarine	lacks good flavour good for creaming adds colour keeps well	short, sweet and puff pastries cakes greasing trays	soya sunflower rapeseed
Lard	distinctive flavour pure white colour best shortening agent cannot cream	deep/shallow frying greasing trays hot water pie crust short pastry	pork
Suet	distinctive flavour hard and dry can be grated white colour	steamed pudding suet pastry mincemeat	from around beef kidney (vegetarian type available)
Oils			
Olive	good flavour high grade will take moderately high temperatures expensive	deep/shallow frying salad dressing mayonnaise greasing trays	olive tree
Maize or corn	very little flavour medium grade golden colour high flash/low smoke point moderately expensive	deep/shallow frying baking cold sauces	maize seed
Vegetable	very little flavour lower grade golden colour high flash/low smoke point inexpensive	deep/shallow frying greasing tins	blended: almond, sunflower, soya groundnut, palm kernel

Kosher fats are blends of margarines and shortening agents that must be used by caterers when cooking for customers of the Jewish faith who are forbidden to eat milk and meat products at the same meal.

STORAGE

Fats and oils must be kept cool. Oils will sour if kept in a warm atmosphere, as will butter. Store in a dry place away from strong smells. Do not keep oil near the deep fryer. Oils will thicken when kept in the refrigerator but will soon become liquid when warmed.

ACTIVITY

1. Find out when margarine first became popular and why.

2. Write to manufacturers to discover how various types of margarine are made. Complete a report and make comparisons of each with butter, commenting on their nutritive value, uses in cooking and availability.

3. Draw conclusions as to the preference of consuming either butter or margarine.

Meat

The amount of time, effort and cost in the rearing of animals creates a relatively expensive food. Meat is divided into these categories:

- beef
- veal (calf)
- lamb
- pork and bacon

Lean meat is the muscle of the animal. Muscles that have been much used (as in older animals) form a tougher meat and so slaughter is at a specified age. Muscle fibres are held together by a connective tissue made of two proteins called collagen and elastin. On heating, collagen turns to gelatine which tenderizes the meat. Elastin is tougher but there is less of it. Fat is found under the skin, around vital organs such as kidneys, and in between muscle fibres. The fat content helps to provide flavour and moisture during cooking.

With a dry method of cookery, such as roasting, the meat juices come to the surface and set in the heat. This gives roast meat its particular flavour. In moist cookery, such as boiling, these juices come out into the cooking liquor and so flavour is in the sauce that accompanies the meat.

NUTRITIONAL VALUE OF MEAT

Meat is considered to be important in the diet as a source of high biological protein and also contains the minerals iron, phosphorus and a little calcium and fat-soluble vitamins A and B. Vitamin C is present in lean meat.

Beef

Young males are considered the best for meat, and young un-calved cows the next best. Thus from the start farmers are rearing for meat, dairy or reproduction. The animals are slaughtered at 18 months old and the meat is hung in a cold room for 2–3 weeks to tenderize.

Purchasing points for beef are:

• bright red flesh
• marbled appearance
• firm, creamy white fat
• no unpleasant odour

A side of beef (weighing approximately 180 kg) is divided into the hind quarter and the fore quarter.

The tougher meats come from the part of the animal where the muscles work the hardest (see Figure 5.5). These are: shin, thick flank, brisket and plate.

These muscular cuts at the hind and fore of the animal require moist methods of cookery to ensure tenderness (see pp. 197–200). The tender cuts come from less muscular parts of the hind quarter (see Figure 5.5) and include: rump, sirloin, wing ribs and fillet.

These may be cooked by fast and dry methods of cookery (see pp. 192–6).

BEEF OFFAL

Not only the muscles of cattle are considered to be edible, but many organs also: tongue, heart, liver, kidney, tripe (stomach lining), tail (oxtail), sweetbread (glands) and suet (kidney fat).

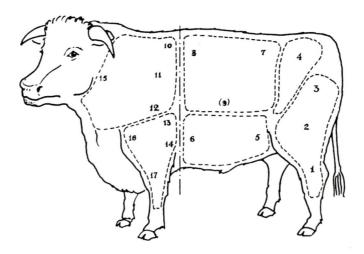

Figure 5.5 Side of beef showing the different cuts

Source: U. Jones, *Catering, Food Preparation and Service* (1986). Reproduced by permission of Hodder & Stoughton Educational.

ACTIVITY

1. Complete the chart below to show suitable methods of cookery and a menu use for each of the cuts listed.

2. Devise a similar chart to show suitable dishes using beef offal and indicating specific methods of cookery for each.

Cuts (numbered as Figure 5.5)	Suitable method of cookery	Menu example
1. Shin		
2. Silverside		
3. Topside		
4. Rump		
5. Thick flank		
6. Thin Flank		
7. Sirloin		
8. Wing rib		
9. Fillet		
10. Fore rib		
11. Middle rib		
12. Chuck rib		
13. Plate		
14. Brisket		
15. Sticking piece		
16. Leg of mutton		
17. Shank		

Veal

This is the flesh from cattle slaughtered at approximately 3 months old. Purposefully reared to maintain a very pale meat colour, the animals are fed generally with a milk diet and kept indoors. When the meat is more red it is evident that the animals have been fed solid food or grazed. Veal is also hung to ensure tenderness but for a much shorter time – approximately a week.

As with all meats, the tougher parts of the animal are suited best to a moist method of cookery but because veal is young either moist or dry methods are suitable for most cuts. For example:

- shoulder – braise or roast
- breast – stew or roast
- best end – stew or roast

Loin chops, neck cutlets and escalopes from the leg may be roasted, grilled or fried, not moist cooked.

Lamb

Traditionally seasonal, lamb is now available all year round due to imports from New Zealand. Joints of lamb provide us with a variety of familiar cuts (some shown in Figure 5.6), the most popular in catering being:

Best end • paired cutlets
- guard of honour
- single cutlets
- crown

Loin • double chops
- saddle
- single chops
- boned and rolled saddle
- whole loin

Leg • long leg (including haunch)
- short leg
- chump chop
- boned and tied

Derived from animals under 12 months at slaughter, lamb is generally tender, moist meat which cooks easily. Dry, fast methods of cookery may be used such as shallow frying and roasting. Purchasing points for lamb are:

- lean dark red flesh
- smooth skin
- white brittle fat

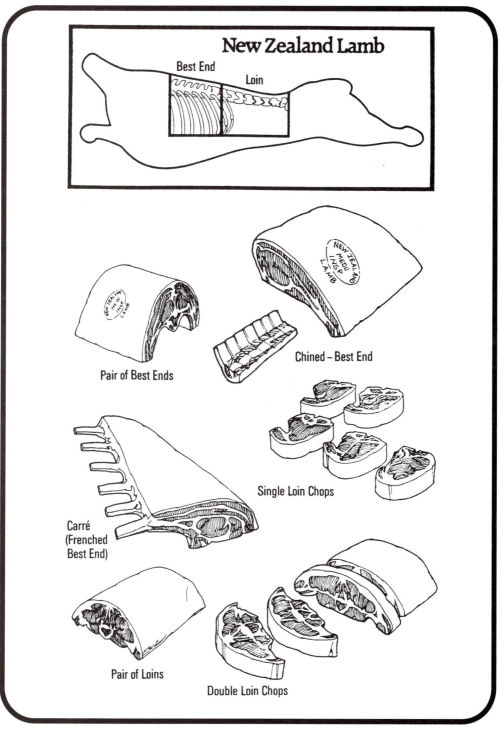

Figure 5.6 Cuts of lamb

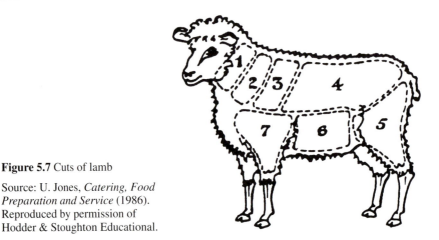

Figure 5.7 Cuts of lamb

Source: U. Jones, *Catering, Food Preparation and Service* (1986). Reproduced by permission of Hodder & Stoughton Educational.

LAMB OFFAL

Several organs of lambs are suitable for cookery and are considered to be tender meats:

- heart
- liver
- kidney
- sweetbreads (glands)

ACTIVITY

1. Complete the chart below to show suitable methods of cookery and a menu use for each cuts.

2. Devise a similar chart to show suitable dishes using lamb offal and indicating specific methods of cookery for each.

Cut (numbered as of Figure 5.7)	Suitable method of cookery	Menu example
1. Scrag end		
2. Middle neck		
3. Best end		
4. Loin		
5. Leg		
6. Breast		
7. Shoulder		

Pork

The pork sold in the UK is from Britain and Denmark. Pigs cannot eat grass alone so feed on cereals and protein, and the flavour of the flesh is dependent upon their diet. Because of the richness of the meat, pork is not considered suitable for classical cookery. The flesh is indigestible and requires acidic and sharp accompaniments as an aid to digestion.

Purchasing points for pork are:

• lean pink flesh
• white smooth fat
• smooth skin
• no unpleasant odour

Pork is used in the preparation of many meat products: For example:

• spare rib – pies
• shoulder – sausages and pies
• head – brawn
• trotters – gelatine for pies

Bacon

Is the cured flesh of a baconer pig, an animal especially bred to produce a long back and small layer of fat. Gammon is the hind leg of the baconer pig.

Gammon bacon is available in various forms:

• smoked – first salted then smoked
• green – cured in brine

Purchasing points for bacon are:

• no sign of stickiness
• no unpleasant smell
• thin, smooth rind
• white fat
• deep pink flesh

Suitable methods of cookery for bacon cuts:

• collar and hock – boil or grill
• back and streaky – grill or fry
• gammon – boil, grill or fry

Ham

Ham is the cured hind leg of the porker pig, which is especially bred to be lean. The joint is often soaked in brine or salt cured then smoked over various types of wood, which gives different flavours.

Table 5.13 Types of ham, their characteristics and methods of cookery/serving

Type	Characteristics	Suitable methods of cookery
York	long cut cured in dry salt washed dried matured 6 months	boil or bake serve hot or cold
Bradenham	soaked in molasses (giving black skin) hung for several months to mature mild sweet flavour	boil serve cold
Suffolk	salt rubbed in part covered by ale sugar and spices basted one month dried matured 4 months	boil or bake serve hot or cold
Italian	raw traditionally taken from pigs fed on parsnips dry cured matured 1 year	raw, thinly sliced serve cold

ACTIVITY

Complete the chart below to show suitable method of cookery and a menu example for each cut of pork.

Cut (numbered as on Figure 5.8)	Suitable method of cookery	Menu example
1. Leg		
2. Loin		
3. Spare Rib		
4. Belly		
5. Shoulder		

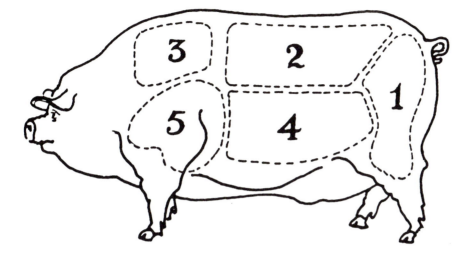

Figure 5.8 Cuts of pork

Source: U. Jones, *Catering, Food Preparation and Service* (1986). Reproduced by permission of Hodder & Stoughton Educational.

Poultry

Poultry is a term used for edible domestic fowl reared for food, such as chicken, turkey, goose, pigeon and duck. Intensive farming methods now produce a moderately inexpensive meat which is readily available. High in protein, low in fat and easily digested, poultry is available fresh or frozen. Fresh poultry must be kept in the refrigerator and used as soon as possible; frozen must be allowed to thaw thoroughly in a cool place before cooking.

The purchasing points for poultry are:

Fresh	Frozen
Soft pliable tip of breast bone	Clearly labelled
Small, flat scales on feet	Tight unbroken wrapping
Unbroken, white skin	No ice lumps
Plump meat	No softness
No unpleasant smell	Giblets may or may not be included

It is very important for all poultry to be very well cooked right through to avoid the possibility of salmonella food poisoning.

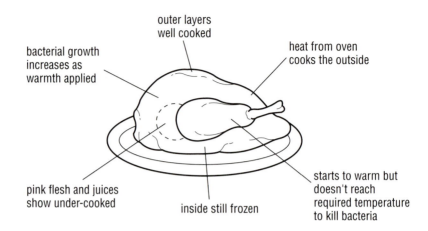

Figure 5.9 Partly cooked poultry: danger of salmonella poisoning

GIBLETS

Parts of the inside of poultry may be eaten:

- livers (used for paté and savouries)
- neck and heart (for stock, gravies and soups)

Table 5.14 Poultry convenience products: methods of processing, cooking/serving

Item	Processing	Suitable method of cookery/serving	Uses
Breaded			
Nuggets	minced flesh reformed into small oval balls	deep fry grill bake	snack buffet child meals
Kiev	chicken breast stuffed with garlic and herb butter	deep fry	luncheon dinner
Nibbles	winglet pieces panéed with spicy coating	deep fry bake	buffet snack
Steaks	minced flesh reformed into flat, round cakes	deep fry grill bake	luncheon fast food
Fingers	reshaped minced flesh into finger shapes	deep fry grill bake	child meals snack

Canned

in sauce	diced meat in velouté may have ham, peppers or mushroom added	reheat only	with rice pie filling
stuffed roll	cooked reformed meat with stuffing in centre	use cold	sandwiches salad hors d'oeuvres

Bottled

paste or paté	finely ground meat	use as spread	rolls sandwiches hors d'oeuvres
Dried	dehydrated minced or diced meat	reconstitute before use	pie filling stew curry

Eggs

This name applies not only to the egg of the hen, but to edible eggs of other birds such as geese, ducks and quail. However, hens eggs are the most widely used so they will be discussed here.

Fresh eggs are graded under EEC rules into three qualities: A, B and C. Class A are the best grade, with intact shell and perfect inside. Class B may have dirty shells or unwashed shells intact, and Class C could be cracked. These are mostly used by large-scale food processors. Eggs are also graded according to size.

Pre-packed eggs must show specific information on the box label:

- quantity
- packing date
- size
- name of producer
- quality grade
- date best before
- packing station number
- price

For caterers, there are several ways of purchasing eggs as well as in their shell! The eggs are broken, the yolk and white mixed, then pasteurized and available as:

- liquid – must be delivered regularly and stored refrigerated
- frozen – blast frozen, must be stored frozen
- dried – glucose content removed, pasteurized, dried then available as whole egg, yolk, white or egg and milk blend. Will keep on shelf providing air is excluded for 12 months.

It is important that the following hygiene rules are followed when handling raw, unpasteurized egg to avoid salmonella food poisoning:

- avoid using raw egg in products where there is only partial or no cooking such as mayonnaise, meringue, mousses, soft omelets or icecream.
- consume as soon as possible after preparation
- do not use cracked eggs
- store in a cool, dry place – preferably the refrigerator
- rotate stocks to ensure storage for minimum time
- store away from other foods that may contaminate, e.g. raw meat

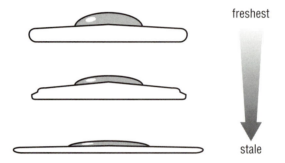

freshest

stale

Figure 5.10 Testing an egg for freshness: (a) broken onto a plate (b) unbroken, immersed in brine

As an egg ages, several changes take place

- yolk membrane weakens
- white becomes thinner
- size of the air space increases, causing the egg to float if tested in brine.
- bacteria enter the shell
- sulphur in the white reacts with phosphoric acid in the yolk, causing unpleasant odour

Table 5.15 Nutritional content of an egg

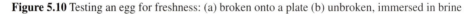

	Yolk	white
Protein (HBV)	16.5%	10.5%
Fat	33%	trace
Water	50%	88.5%
Vitamins ADEK	✔	
B vitamins		✔
Iron	✔	

ACTIVITY

Complete the chart (some boxes have been filled to start you off) to show the versatility and uses of egg in food preparation and cooking.

Uses	Description	Product example
Trapping air		
Thickening		Custard sauce
Emulsifying	especially in whisking of yolks as sauce base	
Binding		
Coating		potato croquettes
Glazing		
Enriching	add an egg or just yolk for nutritive value and colour	
Clarifier	whisked into soup, heated to coagulate holding impurities for removal – consommé	
Garnishing		

ACTIVITY

1. Make a chart showing three disadvantages to the caterer in purchasing eggs (a) in their shell or (b) in bulk out of their shell.

2. Research and discover why:

    • boiled egg yolks turn black

    • fresh boiled egg shells are difficult to remove

    • egg custards form a pitted and watery texture

    Offer remedies that can correct these problems in egg cookery

3. Make a graph to compare the nutritional content of the following foods (don't forget to take account of weights):

    • eggs

    • milk

    • cheese

    • vegetables (green)

Fish

As fish is successfully frozen or chilled, all types and sizes are available at all times of the year. Fish is highly nutritional.

- white fish contains HBV protein with vitamins A and D present in the liver (cod-liver oil is used for medicinal purposes)
- oily fish also contain HBV protein with vitamins A and D present in the flesh

Purchasing points for fresh fish are:

- no unpleasant smell
- firm, moist flesh
- bright eyes
- no whitened flesh due to 'freezer burn'

Table 5.16 Some types of fish, the forms in which they are available and suitable cooking methods

Type	Forms in which available											Suitable cooking methods						
	Smoked	Canned	Whole (gutted)	Darne	Fillet	Fingers	Cakes	Fillet in Crumb (Pané)	Fillet in Batter	Supreme	Tronçon	Poach	Deep fry	Shallow fry	Steam	Boil	Grill	Bake in 'pocket'
Salmon	✔	✔	✔	✔			✔			✔		✔			✔	✔	✔	✔
Cod				✔	✔	✔	✔	✔	✔			✔					✔	✔
Herring	✔		✔											✔			✔	
Turbot										✔	✔				✔			
Plaice			✔		✔			✔	✔			✔	✔	✔	✔		✔	✔
Trout	✔		✔											✔			✔	✔
Sardine		✔	✔										✔	✔			✔	
Pilchard		✔	✔															
Tuna		✔			✔							✔			✔			
Haddock	✔				✔			✔	✔			✔	✔					✔

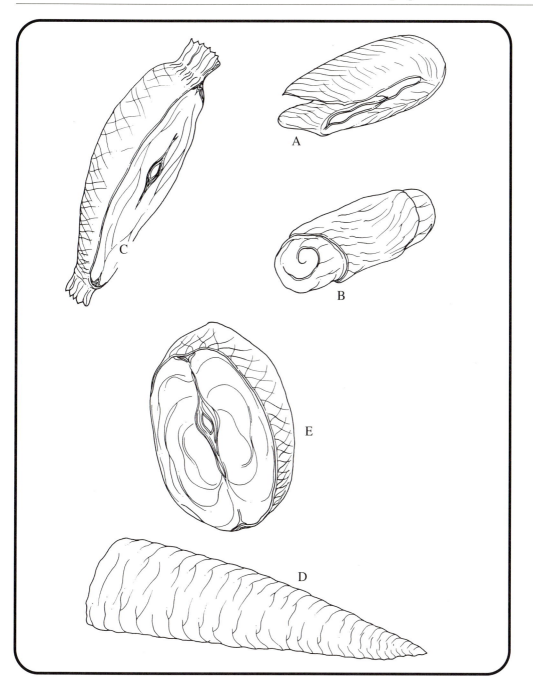

A – délice: folded fillet, presentation side outwards, e.g. plaice
B – paupiette: rolled fillet, presentation side outwards, e.g. sole
C – tronçon: a slice across a round white fish, e.g. turbot
D – fillet with edges trimmed neatly e.g. cod
E – darne: a cross-section slice of round fish, e.g. salmon

Figure 5.11 Cuts of fish

S T O R A G E

Fresh fish should be stored for minimum length of time in the refrigerator.

Frozen fish should be sealed in bags. It should be used in rotation and never re-frozen after thawing.

Vegetables

An ever greater variety of vegetables is now taken for granted all year round due to modern production methods and speed of transport from other parts of the world. Those which are not immediately available as fresh are preserved frozen, canned or dried.

Often served as accompaniments to meat or fish at any time of the day, vegetables are also the main diet of vegetarians and with increased availability of varieties this diet has greatly improved. The nutritional benefits of vegetables must not be underestimated; the important thing is to vary the vegetarian diet with a wide range of vegetables to ensure complete nutrition. Such products as tofu (from the soya bean) and Quorn (this is a trade name), which comes from a tiny plant, are of high nutritional value.

Vegetables can be classified into different types according to the part of the plant from which they come:

Type	Examples
leaves	cabbage, brussels sprouts, spinach, kale, chicory
aqueous	tomatoes, cucumber, marrow, pepper, aubergine
pulses	peas, haricot beans, lentils, broad beans
pods	French and runner beans
stems	celery, asparagus
flowers	cauliflower, broccoli, globe artichoke
roots	carrot, beetroot, swede, parsnip, turnip, radish
bulbs	onion, garlic, leek, shallot, spring onion
tubers	potato, Jerusalem artichoke

Some vegetables may be served cooked or raw but generally cooking does help to break down the structure of the plant to aid digestion. It is important to choose the correct method of preparation and cookery of each variety, not only for presentation and retention of colour but also to ensure that as many nutrients are retained as possible. Cook for the minimum time remembering that some vitamins (B and C) are water soluble and very often minerals are lost during preparation. Peel as thinly as possible because in removing skins valuable fibre is lost. It is common practice to retain cooking liquor for sauces when using moist methods of cookery. Some vegetables are rich in vitamin A (carrots and dark green vegetables), whereas none contain vitamin E. Iron and calcium is present in dark leaves, such as spinach, but the structure of the plant can render it less available to the body than other foods.

In choosing vegetables for the menu consider:

- texture – crunchy, soft, fibrous, smooth
- flavour – sharp, piquant, mild, delicate, strong
- colour – red, orange, yellow, green, brown, white

• nutritional value – a mix of vitamins and minerals
• suitable methods of cookery – dry and moist

STORAGE

Store in dry and cool conditions away from strong light. Keep vegetables away from other foods that may be contaminated by dirt before preparation. Use them in rotation and store for as short a time as possible. To obtain vegetables at their best it is advisable to purchase daily.

Purchasing points for vegetables are:

• leaves undamaged
• good, bright colour
• no sign of wilting or yellowing at edges
• smooth appearance, not wrinkly
• no unpleasant smell
• no sign of mould or decay
• no insects
• no sign of damage from spade or machinery

Cereals

Cereals are the seeds of cultivated grasses and form a staple food in nearly every country in the world. They are relatively easy to grown and cheap to cultivate in comparison to meat. The most common cereals are wheat, rice, maize, barley, oats, rye.

Most of these are included in our diet by their preparation and manufacture into popular breakfast cereals.

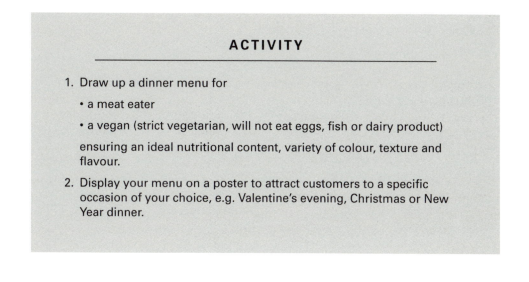

ACTIVITY

1. Draw up a dinner menu for

   • a meat eater

   • a vegan (strict vegetarian, will not eat eggs, fish or dairy product)

   ensuring an ideal nutritional content, variety of colour, texture and flavour.

2. Display your menu on a poster to attract customers to a specific occasion of your choice, e.g. Valentine's evening, Christmas or New Year dinner.

STORAGE

Cereals must be kept in cool, dry store to prevent dampness and mould growth. Wholegrains keep for less time as due to their fat content they are prone to rancidity. Keep all grains in sealed containers and use in quick rotation as insects and vermin are attracted easily.

FLOURS

Generally we think of flour from wheat, but it must be remembered that it is also available from rice and corn for use in cooking. As there are many different types of flour we must make the right choice for the purpose, so we must learn the different characteristics and uses. Familiar uses of flour are in bread, pasta, cakes and pastries.

Whole or wheatflour

- 100 per cent of the grain including the bran and germ
- adds colour and texture to the product
- is high in fibre
- more absorbent
- has limited rise in dough, producing a firm texture in the finished product
- all nutrients are retained

Wheatmeal or brown flour

- 85–90 per cent of the grain
- adds colour to product
- moderately high in fibre
- produces close texture in finished product

White flour

- 70–75 per cent of the wheatgerm
- does not add colour to product
- low in fibre
- not as absorbent as brown
- has easy lifting properties to give soft texture

NUTRITIONAL CONTENT OF FLOUR

Known to be high in starch and therefore a high energy food, flour also contains the protein glutenin which turns to gluten when water is added. Gluten is important in the production of bread, cakes and pastries as it has the ability to strengthen and hold air. Flours vary in gluten content and so are chosen for different purposes. Brown flour is also high in vitamin B and fat, which causes it to deteriorate more quickly than white and take on a sour smell.

Table 5.17 Types of flour and their uses

Type	Products	Characteristics
strong (high gluten)	yeast goods choux pastry puff pastry	structure maintained to retain gases and steam during cooking
soft (low gluten)	cakes short pastry sweet pastry roux for sauces	maintains a soft product and care should be taken to handle as little as possible to avoid toughening
self-raising	Victoria sponge cakes steamed puddings	a soft flour to which has been added 'baking powder', which is a chemical raising agent to help make the product lighter
cornflour (pure starch)	sauces cakes	used generally as a thickening agent for sweet and savoury sauces, it may be added to white wheatflour to lower the gluten content and soften the product
semolina	puddings shortbread thickening agent	the crushed endosperm of the wheatgrain, unsieved

RICE

Very similar in nutritional content to wheat, there are several types available and the choice is influenced by the dish required. Rice is a staple part of the diet in the East and has become more a part of the Western diet in recent years.

NUTRITIONAL CONTENT OF RICE

High in starch, rice is a good source of thiamin, especially wild rice. When the outer layers of the grain are removed in processing (called polishing), which renders the grains more easily cooked, much of the thiamin is lost. There is also a loss of this and other water-soluble vitamin Bs during cooking.

Long-grain (e.g. Basmati, Patna)

The grains are long and thin and are traditionally used for savoury dishes – boiled or braised in water/stock. They tend to stay separated, giving a loose, fluffy product.

Short-grain (e.g. Carolina)

Short, round grains burst easily in cooking and give off a lot of starch to create thickening and sticky texture. This rice is traditionally used for milk puddings:

- flaked: manufactured into flakes for easy cooking, traditionally used for quick milk puddings
- ground: crushed grains – used in milk puddings and as added texture in cakes and biscuits. Often confused with semolina.
- riceflour: crushed grain sifted to obtain fine powder – added to cake flours.

MAIZE

Maize (corn) is available to us 'on the cob' or as kernels. Usually boiled and served as a vegetable in Britain, in other countries corn is ground into a course type of meal flour. We produce a finer cornflour for use in baking

NUTRITIONAL CONTENT OF MAIZE

Similar to that of other cereals except for the presence of carotene which is converted to vitamin A in the body.

BARLEY

It is used primarily in the manufacture of beers and whisky by malting (this is when it is allowed to sprout, then the growth arrested by roasting). Quite a hardy plant, very little is eaten as part of our diet except as pearl barley (when the outer husks of the grain have been removed) which is used as garnish and thickening for soups and stews.

OATS

Available rolled rather than crushed, oats are used for the preparation of porridge, muesli, cakes and biscuits. They are high in fibre and relatively high in fat and protein compared to other cereals.

RYE

Often manufactured into nutritious crispbreads or as rye bread, which is dark in colour. This cereal is resistant to the cold and so is typical of the more northern countries of Europe.

SIMILAR TO CEREAL

Often thought of as cereals but not so, these products include:

Tapioca

This is a granular product almost 100% starch, made from the vegetable cassava. It is used to thicken milk puddings and in soups and stews.

Arrowroot

This is a substance, a fine powder, from the underground stems of the maranta plant. It is used as a thickening agent in glazes because when cooked it becomes clear.

Sago

This comes from the sago plant. It is granular and is used to thicken milk puddings and as a garnish for soups.

Pulses

Pulses are the dried seeds of legumes, i.e. peas, beans and lentils. There are many different types grown all over the world and nutritionally they are a valuable source of fibre, protein (LBV), vitamin B and in some cases, of fat. Produced cheaply as compared with meat, they are a valuable part of any diet, but especially for vegetarians. One of the most popular and versatile menu item today is the humble haricot bean as 'baked beans in tomato sauce'!

Table 5.18 Types of pulses and their uses

TYPE	ACTUAL SIZE	CHARACTERISTICS	USES
Haricot		Creamy white colour Slightly oval High in LBV protein	Baked beans in tomato Stews
Soya		Round Pale beige colour High in HBV protein High in fat	Ground into flour Oil extracted for cooking Made into TVP or tofu Manufacturing vegetarian products
Red kidney		Dark burgundy colour Tough skins Toxin in raw skin	Chilli con carne Bean salads
Lentil		Either red or yellow Split	Vegetarian pies, lasagne, flans, soups, stews
Pea		Whole or split Yellow or green	Soups Vegetarian dishes Pease pudding
Butter bean		Large flat oval Creamy white Bland flavour	Soups Vegetarian dishes

All the pulses except lentils must be soaked for eight hours or more before cooking when they will soften and swell. Sodium bicarbonate will speed this process and not alter the nutritional content but will alter the colour. Boil gently in minimum salted water until tender. Red kidney beans must be rapidly boiled for at least 15 minutes to destroy toxins that are present in the skin.

Do not use pulses that are over one year old as they toughen with age and are difficult to cook successfully.

Nuts

Although not eaten in large quantities, they are a valuable addition to the diet, especially for vegetarians, as they are high in starch, LBV protein, fats, vitamin B and minerals. Manufacturers include nuts in cereals and confectionery to add nutritional and energy value. Popular nuts available to us:

almond   brazil   hazelnut   peanut   walnut

coconut   pecan   cashew   chestnut   pistachio

Nuts are available to us in many forms and varieties – for eating on their own, baking and use in cooking:

For eating on their own they may be

- dry roasted
- tossed in various seasonings
- salted
- covered in chocolate or yoghurt
- mixed with raisins
- left in their shells

For use in cookery they may be purchased as:

- whole or halves
- flaked
- split
- nibbed
- ground

Purchasing points for fresh nuts are:

- shells must be intact
- no signs of dampness or mould

Storage

Nuts have limited shelf life and must be stored in cool, dry conditions and used in strict rotation as they are liable to rancidity because of their fat content.

It is important to display a notice to customers ensuring their awareness of nuts included in any dishes as some people have an allergic reaction to them.

Pulses and nuts

1. Visit your local health food shop or supermarket and discover further types of pulses. List the forms of availability, i.e. canned or dried. To give you some help to start, look out for:

   aduki beans

   blackeye beans

   chickpeas

2. Obtain samples of each and prepare a display board showing the respective names and characteristics. Write out a recipe on the word processor to include one of the pulses obtained and centre this on your board.

3. Prepare a chart to show the names, qualities, nutritional value and uses of six popular and commonly available nuts.

Fruit

Fruits encompass a wide variety of types, flavours, textures and colours and come from all over the world. Modern transportation and storage techniques have ensured most are available all year round, with the addition of homegrown produce during the season.

Table 5.19 Classification of fruits

Type	Some examples	Purchasing points
hard	apple, pear	not under-ripe or over-ripe
stone	cherry, apricot, avocado, peach	good colour, no bruises
citrus	orange, lemon, lime, grapefruit	intact, no brown or soft patches
soft	strawberry, raspberry, black or recurrants	no sign of mould growth
tropical	melon, banana, pineapple	
stem	rhubarb	

Mainly eaten for their flavour, fruits can also add nutritional value, texture, refreshment and moisture to the diet. Some are an aid to digestion in eating greasy foods and to help break down proteins e.g. apple sauce is eaten with pork. Fruits are also an invaluable source of nutrition:

- citrus fruits and blackcurrants are rich in vitamin C
- vitamin A is found in yellow fruits such as apricots
- low in fat (except avocado)
- good source of carbohydrates
- source of dietary fibre (especially bananas, figs and prunes)

Storage

Fruits need to be kept in a cool, well ventilated place and used as soon as possible. Soft fruits may be stored in the refrigerator.

Preservation of fruits

Although a wide variety of fresh fruits are available all through the year, we are also very familiar with preserved fruits as part of our diet.

Table 5.20 Forms of preserved fruit

Preservation	Suitable fruits	Uses
dehydrated	apple, pear, fig, date, grape, apricot, peach, prune, banana	fruit compôte, cakes, mincemeat
canned	apple, damson, rhubarb, cherry, mandarin, gooseberry, plum, pear	crumbles, pies, gateaux, tarts
candied	orange, lemon, lime, grapefruit	Christmas pudding, cakes, mincemeat
crystallized	peach, orange, kiwi, cherry, lemon, grapefruit	as a dessert
glacé	cherry, kiwi, orange, lemon	cake decoration
frozen	apple, gooseberry, strawberry, raspberry, melon, blackberry	puddings, flans, crumbles, pies
juices	orange, apple, grapefruit, tomato, pineapple, grape, tropical mix	chilled appetizer, mixer for cocktails
jam/marmalade	raspberry, blackcurrant, orange, strawberry, damson, apricot, plum	accompaniment, glaze, filling

Sugars

Classed as carbohydrate and energy-giving, sugars are found in many plants, fruits, stems and as honey. We can obtain sugar in our diet by eating these. There is also the processed form of sugar, which we add to our diet. This type of sugar is obtained from sugar-cane found in tropical countries and sugar-beet which is grown in the UK. Cane and beet are crushed, boiled in water and the resulting liquor crystallized out to form molasses with crystals, which are then processed to produce white sugar. This can be ground and sifted to produce various grades and types of sugar.

ACTIVITY

1. Give four examples showing fruit as a complement to meat, poultry or fish.

2. Describe the four basic methods of cooking fruit (poaching, baking, steaming, deep frying), giving examples of suitable fruit to use.

3. Pay a visit to your nearest fruiterer and discover a more unusual fruit under each of the classification headings. Give a brief description of each and write about their colour, flavour, country of origin, nutritional value and use on the menu.

4. Working in groups, peel and chop one of each of the following fruits into four pieces:

   • banana

   • apple

   • pear

   Do the following experiments with one piece of each fruit:

   • leave exposed to the air

   • wrap in polythene tightly

   • blanch in hot water

   • paint liberally with lemon juice

   Once completed, leave all pieces of fruit for at least one hour.

   Note down the results from each experiment and make a comment on the best method to prevent discolouration.

Popular types of sugar available to use are:

White sugars	Brown sugars	Liquid sugars
granulated	demerara	glucose syrup (made from starch)
caster	soft light	black treacle
icing	soft dark	golden syrup
cubes		honey

Apart from acting as a sweetener, sugars have other important functions in cooking as:

• preservative – bacteria do not grow in high sugar solutions, e.g. jam
• colouring – dark brown sugars add colour to rich cakes
• decoration – in icings
• glaze – dusted on products and heated in the oven or painted on as syrup

ACTIVITY

1. Create a chart to show the following:
   (a) different types of sugar and syrup (as many as you can);
   (b) their characteristics;
   (c) two or three examples of their use in cookery.

2. Find and write down the recipe for 'stock syrup'.

   Give three uses for this product in cookery.

- in baking – promotes aeration and colour, affects gluten, yeast and egg white
- stabilizer – in sauces prevents 'split', also promotes shine
- lowers freezing point – used in ice creams to keep them softer

Artificial sweeteners are available for those following a special diet. These are not sugar products and so do not have the properties of sugar apart from sweetening. They have no nutritive value.

Herbs

Generally herbs are used to flavour foods but some are known to have medicinal properties. Having been used for hundreds of years, the leaves and sometimes the stems of aromatic plants are chopped or crushed to release their flavour to be included in both raw and cooked foods.

Herbs are available in several different forms:

- dried – stronger flavour due to moisture removal but this is soon lost in storage, some discolouration, convenient, used for inclusion in foods rarely for decoration, inexpensive.
- frozen – prepared for use then frozen, can be used straight from the freezer, little discolouration, convenient, used for inclusion in foods, moderately expensive.
- windowsill – grown in small containers to be kept near a window and watered regularly providing fresh herbs, for decoration and inclusion into foods, inexpensive, sometimes inconvenient.
- fresh – from suppliers in crush-proof packs to be kept refrigerated, convenient, short keeping time.

Spices

Mostly grown in hot countries, spices are the dried roots, seeds and bark of plants. Used whole or crushed, they have strong aromatic flavours and before the advent of refrigerators were used to mask the flavour of poor quality and stale food. It may be suggested that they have preserving properties when used in large quantities!

Spices must be stored in airtight containers as they lose their strength with age and when in contact with air.

Table 5.21 (Right) Some popular herbs and their uses

NAME	IDENTIFICATION	USES
Bay leaf		Bouquet garni Marinades Pâtés and other meat dishes (Usually removed)
Chives		Salads Garnish for soups Cream and cottage cheese

Dill		leaves: Complements
		            fish dishes
		            Cream and cottage
		            cheese
		            Lamb, veal, chicken
		seeds: Aids digestion in
		            cabbage
		            Chutney

Sage		Stuffings Sauce Sage Derby cheese
Tarragon		Vinegar Sauces Complements chicken Game Offal

Table 5.22 (Below) Some popular spices and their uses

NAME	IDENTIFICATION	USES
Cloves	Flower buds from Myrtle tree	Pickles Baked gammon Stewed and baked fruit Mixed spice
Nutmeg	Kernel	Egg custard Fruit cakes Sauces Mixed spice (Available ready-grated)
Chillies	Red or green seed pod	Spicy casseroles Rice dishes Hot pickles (Available in powder form)
Cinnamon	Bark	Mulled wines Fruit cakes Complements apples Biscuits
Vanilla	Black seed pod of orchid	Milk puddings, custards Cakes Ice cream Sauces (Available as essence, or whole)

ACTIVITY

Select a variety of at least five commonly used herbs and spices that have not already been mentioned in the text. Either:

1. Create a chart to name, state their origin, describe them and show their uses. (You may find pictures of them in your research that you can use to illustrate your chart) or:

2. Collect a selection of fresh herbs and press them between card for about three weeks, keeping them in a warm place. These may then be mounted on a chart together with a brief written description and ideas for use.

Table 5.23 Availability of foods in a convenient form

Form in which available	Soup	Pasta	Eggs	Vegetables	Potatoes	Meat	Poultry	Herbs	Spices	Fish	Cakes & Pastry	Sauces	Dairy
Canned	✔	✔		✔	✔	✔	✔			✔	✔	✔	✔
Frozen		✔	✔	✔	✔	✔	✔	✔	✔	✔	✔		✔
Dried	✔	✔	✔	✔	✔			✔	✔			✔	
Pickled			✔	✔								✔	
Prepared				✔	✔								
Vacuum				✔	✔	✔	✔					✔	

In-house preparation	Soup	Pasta	Eggs	Vegetables	Potatoes	Meat	Poultry	Herbs	Spices	Fish	Cakes & Pastry	Sauces	Dairy
Frozen	✔	✔		✔	✔	✔	✔	✔	✔	✔	✔	✔	✔
Pickled			✔	✔								✔	
Dried		✔						✔					
Cook/chill	✔	✔		✔	✔	✔	✔			✔	✔	✔	✔

Table 5.24 Commodities summary

Commodity	Nutritional value	Purchasing points	Type or size/amount	Uses
Milk	protein (HBV) 4% vitamins A B C D fat 3.5% carbohydrate 4%	clean containers sealed containers pleasant smell fat not globular	1 pt bottle ½ ltr carton 4/6 ltr containers	sauces drinks cereals puddings
Cream	single: 18% fat whipping 35% fat double 45% fat Devon 55% fat	same as for milk	250ml carton 500ml carton 1 ltr container 5 ltr container	pouring decoration filling enriching
Cheese	protein (HBV) vitamins A B C D fat 33% calcium	no mould no cracks not greasy not runny (soft cheeses) correct smell	hard soft cream blue vein	flavouring filling gratination cheeseboard
Fats and oils	animal fat or vegetable fat/oils: vitamins A D	fats: firm good colour pleasant smell closed pack oils: clear fresh smell sealed container	250g/500g packs or tubs 15g blocks bottles or drum	greasing frying cakes/pastries sauces salad dressing
Meat (beef, veal lamb, pork)	protein (HBV) vitamins A B C iron phosphorus	bright red flesh firm white fat pleasant smell	joints or cuts half or whole side carcass	main course starter hot or cold
Offal (liver, heart, kidney, sweetbreads)	same as for meat high in iron	not sticky pleasant smell bright colour moist	portions whole organ	main course mixed grill patés pie filling
Poultry (domestic fowl)	protein (HBV)	white skin plump meat pleasant smell not sticky	whole bird quarters portions winglets	main course pastes pie filling hot or cold
Eggs (hens)	vitamins A B D E K iron protein (HBV) fat in yolk	unbroken shell pleasant smell class A label best by date	cartons of 6/12/18/24 trays of 30 crates	trap air, coat, bind, enrich, garnish, on menu, thicken, clarify
Fish	protein (HBV) vitamins A D oil in round fish	fresh smell firm flesh moist bright eyes	white: flat or round oily: round	main course pastes fillings hot or cold

(**Table 5.24** cont'd)

Vegetables	protein (LBV) vitamins A B C D carbohydrates calcium iron fibre	undamaged leaf good colour no wilting no mould no insects pleasant smell	root tuber leaf bulb flower stem fruit pod legume	accompaniment salads flavouring terrine hot or cold
Cereals	protein (LBV) carbohydrates vitamin B fibre	no mould no insects pleasant smell dry sealed containers	flour rice oats barley rye maize arrowroot	breakfast cereal cakes pastries bread garnish puddings
Pulses	protein (LBV) carbohydrates vitamin B some vegetable. fat fibre	dry no sign of mould no insects	peas, beans lentils (dried, canned, ground)	stews salads flans soups extractions for: oil, tofu/TVP pease pudding
Nuts	protein (LBV) vegetable fats vitamin B fibre	no rancid smell dry no sign of mould no insects	walnut brazil cashew pecan coconut almond pistachio	salads vegetarian decoration flavouring pastes
Fruit	carbohydrates vitamin A C fibre low in fat	unbruised good colour intact no mould	hard stone citrus soft tropical stem fresh/dried	puddings decoration filling hor or cold
Sugar	carbohydrates	dry sealed containers	granulated caster icing demerara soft brown golden syrup	sweetener colouring flavouring glaze in baking
Herbs	some medicinal	good colour no wilting no mould	dried frozen windowsill fresh	flavouring marinades garnishing
Spices	some medicinal	aromatic good colour dry	ground whole mixed essence/oil	flavouring pickles cakes, biscuits wines

Menu Planning

The following pages provide summaries of menu items, the process briefly described in their production and examples of derivatives. You may find the information useful in your studies of food preparation and cooking.

HORS D'OEUVRES AND SALADS

Hors d'oeuvres may be served for lunch, dinner or supper and a little of each combined to give variety.

Salads may be served as an accompaniment or as a dish by themselves at lunch, tea, dinner, supper and for snacks.

Dish	Process summary	Menu example
Single	Primary use of one ingredient with the addition of a dressing and garnish	Tomato Potato Beetroot
Compound	Any number of ingredients used to offer a mixed selection. May be vegetables, fruit, nuts or protein, with the addition of a dressing and garnish	Russian Nicoise Waldorf Coleslaw
Protein-based	Either single or compound but main ingredient a meat, fish, egg or dairy product with the addition of a dressing and garnish. May be served hot or cold.	Dressed crab Liver paté Smoked salmon Caviar
Fruit	Either single or compound but main ingredient fruit with the addition of a dressing and garnish. May be served hot or cold.	Grilled grapefruit Florida cocktail Mimosa salad Melon
Warm	Either single or compound selection of vegetables, proteins and fruits that complement one another which may be served hot with or without a dressing	Three-bean salad Rice salad Kedgeree Mushrooms à la greque

SOUPS

Dish	Process summary	Menu examples
Clear	Stock base, simmered with vegetables, carefully clarified with eggwhite and strained to give pure, clear soup. Various garnishes	Consommé Royal Juliènne Célestine
Broth	Stock base with finely cut vegetables, meat and cereal left unstrained in the clear soup	Scotch Minestrone Chicken

Purée	Stock base thickened with a purée of fresh vegetables or pulses by passing through a sieve. Served with croûtons.	Lentil Potato Green pea
Velouté	Flavour of stock base denotes type. Thickened with blond roux and simmered with vegetables, passed then a liaison of yolk and cream added.	Chicken
Cream	Either stock base with vegetables then passed or vegetable purée with bechamel or velouté to thicken. Finished with cream, milk or yogurt to enrich.	Tomato Mushroom Chicken Cauliflower
Bisque	Prepared from shellfish or fish stock, thickened with a roux and simmered with vegetables. Passed, enriched with cream and garnished with diced fishmeat denoting content.	Lobster Crab
Miscellaneous	Soups that are difficult to classify under the previous headings.	Mulligatawny Kidney

SAVOURY SAUCES

Type	Example	Process summary	Uses
Roux-based	bechamel (white sauce)	In a saucepan, gently cook flour and margarine for 1–2 mins. (roux) Separately, heat milk with a cloute onion. Gradually add milk to roux beating well. Various consistencies can be obtained: panada (thick), coating and pouring. Simmer well and season to taste.	Basis for cream soups Sauces eg. mornay (cheese), parsley, aurore, egg. As a binding agent for croquettes, covering sauce or accompanying sauce.
Roux-based	veloute (flavoured sauce)	Gently cook flour and margarine for longer to produce a blond roux. Gradually add hot flavoured stock beating well. Simmer well. Season.	Basis for veloute soups. Sauces eg. chicken, fish, mushroom, mutton, veal.
Roux-based	espagnol (brown sauce)	Cook flour and oil or dripping to create a browned roux (too dark will taste burnt). Cool. Add tomato puree and brown stock gradually. Add browned vegetables and bouquet garni. Simmer for 4–6 hrs, skim regularly. Pass through strainer. Equal quantities of espagnol and brown stock reduced by half produces demi-glace (half-glaze sauce)	To produce demi-glace sauce as a basis for many sauces. eg. piquant, Bercy Bordelaise, devilled, Madeira.
Miscellaneous	bread	Pour hot milk (infused with cloute onion) onto fresh breadcrumbs allowing them to swell. Consistency may be altered by varying quantities. Season.	Traditional accompaniment to roast turkey.
	mint	Wash and finely chop fresh mint with a little sugar to absorb the juices. Pour on a little boiling water to dissolve sugar and blanch leaf. Add vinegar to taste.	Traditional accompaniment to roast lamb.

apple	Wash, peel, core and slice cooking apples. Cook with very little water in a saucepan on medium heat for short time till pulped. Serve without sugar or very lightly sweetened	Traditional accompaniment to roast pork.
tomato	Gently fry root vegetables, bacon and onion in margarine. Add flour and cook to blond roux. Add tomato puree. Gradually add stock beating well. Add bouquet garni and simmer. Skim often. Season to taste.	Traditional accompaniment to fish in batter.
curry	Preparation similar to tomato sauce. Add curry spices with the vegetables.	Traditional accompaniment to kedgeree.

EGGS

Method of cookery	Process summary	Menu example
Boil	Use very fresh eggs. Hard boil: place into boiling water, simmer for 8-10 mins. Rinse in cold water to prevent black ring forming around yolk. Ensure minimum cooking time. Soft boil: place in cold water, bring to boil and simmer for 2 mins *or* place in boiling water and simmer for 3-5 mins.	Curried eggs Egg mayonnaise
Poach	Use very fresh eggs to avoid spreading white. Break into 8 cm deep simmering water (add little vinegar to help setting). Simmer for 2-3 mins. Remove with draining spoon. Trim. Reheat at service. Drain well.	Egg Florentine Egg Bombay
En cocotte	Break egg into buttered mould and place in 2 cm boiling water. Cover with tight lid. Cook for 2-3 mins till lightly set. Serve immediately.	En cocotte with cream
Shallow fry	Use very fresh eggs to avoid spreading white. Break eggs in shallow hot greased fry pan. Cook gently till lightly set. Season. Serve immediately. French fried – fairly deep hot oil in shallow pan. Shape crispy white over yolk during cooking.	
Scramble	Beat eggs with seasoning and a little milk. Cook gently in greased heavy bottomed saucepan. Stir continuously till lightly set. Add cream or butter to enrich. Serve immediately. Do not overcook.	Scrambled with ham mushroom tomatoes herbs
Omelet	Beat or whisk eggs with seasoning and a little water. Pour into hot buttered omelet pan. Agitate with fork till lightly set. Remove from heat, serve folded with or without filling or serve open finished under hot salamander.	Omelet with ham cheese Spanish
Sur le plat	Butter and season an 'eared', flat, heatproof dish. Break in an egg and cook gently on side of stove. Finish under hot salamander or in hot oven. Serve with yolk soft.	Bacon Bercy

PASTA

There are many varieties of pasta shapes, each of which can be made into numerous dishes to be served for lunch, dinner, supper or snack meal.

To cook, immerse the pasta in plenty of boiling salted water till just cooked (al dente). Wash away surface starches by refreshing in cold water to prevent sticking and reheat just before service. Drain thoroughly.

Dish	Description	Menu example
Spaghetti	Long, thin, tubular	Bolognaise
Canneloni	Short, wide straight tubes	With spinach and ricotta cheese
Tagliatelli	Long, 1cm flat strips	With springtime vegetables
Lasagne	Flat oblongs approx, 10cm × 18cm	Lasagne verde
Macaroni	Short, medium curved tubes	With cheese sauce
Ravioli	Squares filled with variety of savouries	Mushroom ravioli with tomato sauce
Farfalle	Bow shapes	With ham and peppers
Rigatoni	Short, medium slanted tubes	Mixed timpana

SAVOURY RICE

Dish	Description	Menu example
Braise	Use long grain rice. Gently fry without colour with diced onion. Add twice as much stock to rice, season and cover with cartouche. Bring to boil, place in hot oven for 15 mins till cooked. Stir in butter. Serve immediately.	Pilau rice with mushrooms, peas and pimento
Risotto	Use short grain rice and gently fry with a little onion. Add nearly twice as much stock to rice, cover with stock and simmer on side of stove. Stir often. Add more stock as rice cooks. When cooked all stock is absorbed. Risotto is more moist than pilau.	Same variations

FISH

Method of cookery	Process summary	Menu examples
Boil	Suitable for whole, white fish or portions on the bone. Cover fish with either milk or water, fish stock or combination. Court bouillon suitable for whole oily fish cooked from cold or portions into simmering liquor.	Boiled tronçon of turbot Darne of cod with parsley sauce
Poach	Suitable for small, whole fillets, supremes of larger fish and darnes. Barely cover with stock, wine or milk or combined and cover with cartouche. Cook gently on stove or in oven for minimum time. Use liquor for sauce.	Fillets of sole Duglère Plaice Veronique Cod mornay

Steam	Suitable for same cuts as poaching. Maintains full flavour, nutritional content and moisture. Held aloft in steam there is no colour added, therefore mask with suitable sauce. Délice of sole with white wine sauce.	Suprème of salmon with herb sauce Délice of sole with white wine sauce
Grill	Suitable for small whole fish, darnes, suprèmes and fillets. Gutted, whole fish have scales scraped away. Head may be left on. Pass through seasoned flour, brush with fat or pané. Grill open or closed on baking tray or on grill bars. Take care not to burn.	Sole Caprice Grilled darne of salmon Plaice St Germain
Shallow fry	Suitable for small whole fish and fillets. Pass through seasoned flour and fry in clarified butter in fry pan presentation side first. Turn once only to avoid damage.	Plaice Doria Trout meunière with almonds Sole belle meunière
Deep fry	Suitable for small whole fish, suprèmes, fine slices (goujons) and fillets. Coat for protection from the fat. Use yeast or egg batter, pané, milk or flour. Deep fry at approx, 185°C. Serve with lemon or tart sauce to aid digestion.	Fried sole with anchovy sauce Battered cod with tomato sauce Whitebait
Bake	Suitable for whole, darnes, suprèmes or fillets. Cooked on a bed of root vegetables or in a greaseproof paper 'pocket' in buttered dish in oven. Tends to be dry so avoid over-cooking.	Baked salmon with duxelle filling

SHELLFISH

Dish	Process summary	Menu examples
Lobster	Purchase alive to ensure freshness. Plunge into boiling salted water, cook for 15-20 mins. Overcooking causes flesh to toughen. Allow to cool in the cooking liquor.	Lobster Thermidor
Scampi Prawn Shrimps	Remove shells, pass through seasoned flour or pané. Fry lightly in hot, oiled frying pan or deep fry. Drain well. Place in suitable sauce or serve separately.	Scampi in tomato sauce
Mussels Scallop Oysters	When fresh, shells are tightly closed. Open shells may cause food poisoning. Scrape to remove barnacles, wash well and cook in lidded pan over fierce heat for 5 mins or till shells open completely. Check for sand and seaweeds before service.	Mussels marinière

LAMB AND MUTTON

Method of cookery	Process summary	Menu example
Roasted	Suitable for saddle, breast, leg, loin. Joint left whole on or off bone. Season, brush with oil, place on trivet. Reduce temperature of oven as necessary to cook joint through. Cook well, but may be served pink. Allow to stand before serving. Serve with aid to digestion – mint sauce or stuffing.	Roast leg with mint sauce Roast stuffed shoulder Best end boulangère

Grilled	Noisettes. Chops or fillet, kidney or thin slices of prime lamb set on skewers. Pane or seasoned and brushed with oil. Grill on greased bars or on tray under salamander. Do not overcook, may be served pink.	Mixed grill Reform Shish kebab
Braised hearts	Remove fat and excess tubes. Use suitable stuffing. Chops – pass through seasoned flour and fried off quickly. Add stock and vegetables, cover and braise on top of stove or in oven till tender.	Champvallon
Stewed	Suitable scrag end, middle neck, chump, loin, breast. Cut into even pieces. Neck left on bone. Bring to boil with vegetables for white stew and thicken with white roux. For brown, fry quickly, add mirepoix, use dark roux and brown stock.	Irish Stew Curried Navarin
Sautéed	Suitable for fillet, cutlets, kidney. Season or pane and shallow fry in hot clarified butter or oil. Firm when cooked through.	Cutlets with spaghetti napolitaine
Boiled	Suitable for leg. Place in boiling, salted water. Skim, simmer with carrots, onion, leek, celery and bouquet garni. Cook for 20 mins per half kilo. Serve sliced with a little cooking liquor.	Leg with caper sauce

BEEF

Method of cookery	Process summary	Menu examples
Roast	Suit sirloin, wing rib or fillet on or off the bone. Trim off excess fat, tie into shape. Lightly oil, season, place on trivet in roasting tin. Pre-heat moderate oven. Do not cover. Baste frequently with meat juices. Serve a little underdone. Rest before carving.	Roast beef with Yorkshire pudding and horseradish sauce
Grill	Suit rump, wing rib, fillet or sirloin. Remove sinew and excess fat. Cut into evenly thick slices, brush with oil and season. Place on pre-heated grill or under salamander and turn half way through cooking. Cook to desired degree. Test by pressing. Minced beef, seasoned, formed into flat shapes may be grilled.	Grilled sirloin steak with sauce Béarnaise Chateaubriand T-bone steak Beefburgers
Braise	Suit topside, ribs, thick flank. Trim off excess fat. Cut into evenly thick pieces or leave as a joint trimmed and tied securely. Season. Seal by fast frying. Place on lightly fried sliced vegetables, add flour if thickening and stock to cover. Bring to the boil, reduce to simmer. Cover with tight-fitting lid. Leave on stove top or in moderate oven till tender, approx. 2 hours. Use cooking liquor for sauce.	Carbonnade of beef Beef olives Goulash
Stew	Suit thick flank, shin, plate. Remove excess sinew and fat. Cut into even sized pieces. Fry quickly to brown. Add mirepoix and fry till golden. Add flour and cook till brown. Break down with tomato purée and brown stock. Season. Add bouquet garni. Cover, simmer for approx. 2 hours till tender. Remove meat, correct sauce, replace and serve. Beef may be minced and a similar method used but reduce cooking time to approx. half an hour.	Beef stew with red wine Curried beef Bolognaise sauce

| Sauteé or shallow fry | Suits rump, fillet, sirloin. Sauté may apply to a brown beef stew but using a tender quality meat, cut into thin slices. Beef is fried or sautéed quickly and served in a finished sauce. Minced beef, seasoned, formed into flat shapes may shallow fry. | Steak Diane
Beef stroganoff
Vienna steaks
American-style burgers |

VEAL

Cuts used	Process summary/Method of cookery	Menu examples
Shin	Stew: cut and saw into slices, left on bone Sauté: trim and bone out	Osso buco Veal and ham pie
Leg	Braise or roast whole: remove aitch bone, clean, trim off knuckle and excess sinew.	Roast leg with roast gravy and stuffing
Cushion (nut of leg)	Whole: bard thinly, secure with string and braise or roast. Escalopes: cut into slices against the grain and bat out thinly. Sauté or deep fry.	Veal olives Escalope of veal viennoise
Loin and best end	Whole: bone out and trim flap. Roll and secure with string. Roast. Cutlets: shallow fry or grill	Fried cutlet jardinière Crumbed cutlet napolitaine
Shoulder	Braise: bone out, may be stuffed before rolling. Tie securely and use mirepoix. Stew: bone out, remove sinew, cut into even-sized pieces.	Braised stuffed shoulder Fricassée of veal
Neck end	Stew or sauté: bone out and cut meat into even-sized pieces.	Brown veal stew
Breast	Whole: bone out, may be stuffed before rolling. Roast. Pieces may be prepared as stew.	Braised stuffed breast with gravy

PORK AND BACON

Method of cookery	Process summary	Menu examples
Roast	Suit leg, loin, spare rib, shoulder. Excess fat and sinew trimmed. On or off the bone. Skin scored, secure joint with string and season. Roasted on trivet, basting frequently. Reduce temperature and cook well. Serve with aids to digestion, e.g. apple sauce	Roast stuffed loin Roast leg of pork with sage and onion stuffing
Grill	Suit collar and hock. Bacon – all bones and rind removed. Gammon left in thick slices.	Bacon and egg Gammon and pineapple
	Pork – Small joints such as loin chops and spare ribs, seasoned, brushed with melted fat and grilled over moderate heat. Cook thoroughly. May be finished in the oven. Serve with aid to digestion.	Pork chop flamande Pork in cider

Shallow fry	Suit gammon back, streaky. Lean pork cut into even sized pieces. Fried quickly then at lower temperature to ensure well cooked. May be panéed, or sauce prepared around the pork.	Liver and bacon Escalopes of pork
Boil	Suit gammon, hock or collar. Joint left whole or boned out. Secure with string. Soak bacon in cold water for 24 hours to remove excess salt. Boil in clean water for 25 mins per half kilo.	Bacon or pease pudding

OFFAL

Name	Type	Method of cookery	Menu example
Beef	tongue	pickle, braise or boil	braised tongue with Madeira sauce
	liver	braise or stew	liver and onions
	kidney	braise or stew	steak and kidney pie filling
	tripe	simmer in milk	tripe and onions
	tail	braise or stew	haricot oxtail
Lamb	heart	braise	stuffed braised hearts
	kidney	sauté	kidney sauté turbigo
	sweetbreads	braise, sauté or grill	braised sweetbread with vegetables
Pork	head	boil	brawn or stock
	kidney	sauté or grill	mixed grill
	liver	shallow fry, braise or stew	live paté
	trotters	boil	gelatine for pies
Veal	head	boil	stock
	brains	braise or shallow fry	
	kidney	stew or sauté	mixed grill, pie filling
	liver	shallow fry	liver and bacon
	sweetbreads	braise, grill or steam	sweetbread escalope
Poultry	liver	shallow fry	chicken liver paté
	neck and stomach	boil	used for stock

POULTRY AND FEATHERED GAME

Poultry refers to all domestic fowl grown for food such as geese, turkey, chicken and duck. Feathered game refers to all birds from the wild such as partridge, pheasant and grouse. It is assumed that all birds will be obtained drawn and plucked ready for cooking.

Method of cookery	Process summary	Menu examples
Roast	Suit chicken, duck, goose, turkey, pheasant. Usually trussed to maintain shape during roasting. Moderate oven. Place on each side then onto back, basting frequently to ensure even cooking till juices are no longer pink. Serve with gravy, stuffing, bacon, bread or cranberry sauce.	Stuffed spring chicken Turkey with chestnut stuffing Duck with cranberry

Grill	Suitable for small whole chicken cut through backbone and opened, leg or chicken breast. Season, brush with melted fat and place on pre-heated grill or under hot salamander. Baste often. Grill till no sign of blood when pierced.	Devilled chicken Chicken spatchcock Grilled duck breast
Sauté	Divide bird by removing legs, winglet with breast to give some red and white meat per portion. Shallow fry quickly in seasoned fat then lower heat to cook with lid or in oven.	Chicken chasseur
Shallow fry	Suitable for breast only it cooks easily. Fry gently in butter or magarine till cooked through. Season, roll in flour or pané. Serve with reduction cream with asparagus sauce.	Chicken in cream sauce Crumbed chicken breast
Boil	Suitable for older tougher birds. Placed whole in cold water and brought to boil with vegetables, herbs, seasoning. Cook well, drain and make sauce with liquor. Cut into suitable portions.	Chicken à la king Vol au vent filling
Braise	Prepare as for sauté. Shallow fry then finish by braising in lidded pan with roux-based sauce or thickened with beurre manié. May be casseroled whole on a mirepoix of vegetables.	Chicken fricasée Coq au vin Braised duck with with cherries

VEGETABLES

Type	Examples	Suitable method of cookery	Menu example
Leaves	cabbage brussels sprouts spinach chicory	braise, boil or shallow fry	braised red cabbage stir-fry vegetables creamed spinach purée braised chicory
Vegetable fruits	tomatoes peppers aubergines	grill, bake or shallow fry	grilled stuffed tomato peppers & minced meat moussaka
Pods	peas broad beans lentils	boil or braise	peas flamande broad beans and parsley sauce lentil soup
Stems	celery asparagus	boil, deep fry, braise or steam	braised celery asparagus hollandaise
Flowers	cauliflower broccoli globe artichoke	boil, steam or braise	cauliflower mornay broccoli with almonds artichoke bottoms and peas
Roots	carrot beetroot salsify parsnip	boil, braise, roast or steam	carrots vichy boiled beetroot salsify in batter roast parsnip
Bulbs	onion garlic leek fennel	roast, shallow or deep fry, boil, braise	French fried onion garlic butter for frying braised leek fennel polonaise

Tubers	potato Jerusalem artichoke	boil, shallow or deep fry, bake, braise, roast	duchess potatoes jacket potatoes purée of Jerusalem artichokes with cream
Aqueous	marrow courgette	boil, shallow or deep fry or braise	stuffed marrow courgettes provençal
Fungi	mushrooms	shallow or deep fry or grill	mushrooms in batter stuffed mushrooms

POTATOES

Dish	Process summary	Menu examples
Boil	New – scrape away skins, wash, plunge into boiling water, salted water with mint. Cook for minimum time. With skins, wash well, pick over and boil in the same way. Old – wash, peel, wash again. Cut evenly. Bring to boil in salted water, till just cooked, drain well.	New rissolée Parsley Riced Duchess
Roast	Wash, peel, rewash, dry thoroughly. Place in roasting tray of hot oil, season and cook in hot oven for approx. 30 mins. till cooked and golden. Drain.	Roast Château
Deep fry	May be with or without skins, cut into even-sized pieces and deep fried with or without a coating of batter or crumb. Or mashed, formed into shapes and deep fried with a coating.	Chipped Pont neuf Matchstick Croquette
Shallow fry or sauté	Par-boil or steam with or without skins. Remove skins. Cut into even sized pieces (slices for sauté), shallow fry in hot fat. Drain on paper, season and serve.	Lyonnaise Noisette Parisienne
Braise	Wash, may be with or without peel, slice evenly and place in greased ovenproof dish with any onions, stock, milk or cream, cheese, bacon and seasoning to the recipe.	Savoury Fondant Berrichone Champignol
Bake	Select good sized potatoes, one per portion. Scrub well and make incision around just into skin. Place on bed of salt and bake in hot oven for approx. 1 hour till soft in centre.	May be served with butter or a variety of fillings such as cheese, chilli con carné, chicken
Steam	May be scrubbed and peeled or skins retained. Steam to retain vitamins and flavour. Season and serve. Also, preparation for sauté.	Vapeur En robe de chambre
Microwave	Wash, may be with or without peel. Cut into even-sized pieces or leave whole if even. Cook small quantities only. Easily overcooked causing rubbery texture. Use for par-cooking.	Boiled style Steamed style In jackets

FRESH FRUIT

Type	Examples	Suitable preparation	Menu examples
Hard	apple	stew: peel, core, slice with very little water in pan with tight lid. Short cooking time, sweeten.	apple sauce
		bake: remove core, score skin, stuff centre, onto tray.	baked apples with honey and sultanas
	pear	poach: peel, core and quarter poach gently in stock syrup or wine.	compôte of fruit
		raw: paint with lemon juice.	blue cheese stuffed pear
Stone	peach	poach: blanch to remove skins, halve, remove stone poach gently in stock syrup.	peach melba
	cherry	stew: wash, remove stones, with very little water in pan with tight lid, short time, sweeten.	cherry pie filling
Citrus	grapefruit	grill: wash, cut in half, cut sections, sprinkle with sugar or honey, grill till golden.	honeyed grapefruit
	lemon	blanch: remove zest in strips, plunge into boiling water for a short time.	flavouring gâteau decoration
Soft	strawberry	poach: wash and hull, pour over boiling stock syrup, leave to cool.	fresh fruit salad
	blackcurrant	microwave: little water or stock syrup with fruit in lidded dish. Short time on high.	summer pudding
Tropical	banana	shallow fry: peel off skin, pan fry in butter and sugar, flame with spirit	banana flambé
		deep fry: coat in batter.	banana fritters
	pineapple	boil: contains enzymes that prevent gelatine from setting. Boil before use to prevent this.	pineapple flan
		deep fry: coat in batter.	pineapple fritters
Stem	rhubarb	stew: remove leaves and end stalks cut into short pieces, wash, with little water in pan with tight lid. Simmer till pulped.	rhubarb crumble
		microwave: short pieces with little water in lidded dish, few minutes on high till pulped.	fruit fool

MILK PUDDINGS

Type	Process summary	Menu examples
Rice	(a) Wash rice. Place in pie dish with cold milk, sugar, nutmeg, vanilla and butter. Into moderate oven on tray for up to 2 hours till all milk absorbed and grains fully swollen. Will form skin.	baked rice pudding with fresh fruit purée
	(b) Bring milk to boil in heavy-based pan add washed rice, stir. Simmer gently, stir often till rice fully swollen and milk absorbed. Add egg yolk, butter, sugar or flavouring to enrich. Brown under salamander if liked.	empress rice
Semolina	Bring milk to boil in heavy-based pan, sprinkle on semolina grains and stir well. Simmer for 15–20 mins till thickened, stir occasionally. Add butter, sugar, flavour or egg yolk to enrich. Brown under salamander if liked.	semolina with jam sauce
Ground rice Tapioca Sago	As for semolina	
Egg custard products	Use 3 eggs to each 500ml/1pt milk or cream. Whisk eggs, sugar and flavouring in bowl and pour on heated milk. Pass through strainer into dish. Sprinkle with nutmeg if liked, place in bain-marie in moderate oven for up to 1 hour till set.	bread and butter pudding cabinet diplomat pudding crème brulée
	Cream caramels, use 4 eggs to 500ml/1pt to ensure firm consistency for successful de-moulding	cream caramels
Bavarian cream	Cream egg yolks and sugar well, whisk on hot milk, cook in clean pan to sauce anglais. Add dissolved gelatine, pass, cool till almost set. Fold in whipped cream. Fruit purée or essence may be used for flavour. (Stiffly whisked eggwhites may be folded in lastly for volume)	chocolate bavarois charlotte royale
Pastry cream	Whisk eggs and sugar very well, add flour to make smooth paste. Pour on heated milk. Return to clean pan, cook gently till thickened. Flavour as desired. Best used immediately.	chocolate pastry-cream cream St Honoré
Ice cream	A combination of double cream and milk made into sauce anglais with egg yolks, sugar and flavourings. Cool quickly and freeze, preferably in ice cream machine.	peach melba

SWEET SAUCES

Type	Process summary	Named variety
Jam	Use any flavoured jam. Add 2 parts jam to 1 part water with lemon juice and arrowroot or cornflour to thicken. Bring to the boil stirring continuously and add the diluted thickening. Re-boil, pass and adjust.	apricot strawberry raspberry

Citrus fruit	1 piece fruit to 250m/½ pt water. Boil approx. 50g/2oz sugar with water, add diluted cornflour or arrowroot, stirring. Re-boil, pass then add zest and juice of fruit.	orange lemon lime
Cornflour	Use 25g/1oz cornflour per 500ml/1pt milk. Dilute cornflour with a little cold milk and heat the rest. Combine the two stirring all the time and cook till thickened. Sweeten and flavour.	almond custard chocolate brandy
Egg custard	Use 4 egg yolks to 500ml/1pt milk. Whisk yolks with sugar, whisk on heated milk and return to pan. Cook gently to thicken slightly, do not boil. Pass and serve.	sauce à l'anglais

PASTRIES

Dish	Process summary	Menu examples
Short	Rub in half quantity of fat (lard or vegetable fat with margarine) into plain flour and mix to firm paste with water. Add a little sugar or herbs if desired. Allow to rest before use.	cornish pasties fruit pies treacle tart quiches
Sweet	Rub in ⅝ margarine to plain flour and bind with mixed egg and sugar or cream egg and sugar, add marg. fold in flour carefully. Allow to rest in refrigerator before use.	fruit flans tartlets
Rough puff	¾ quantity of large pieces of fat stirred into strong flour. Bind with cold water and a little lemon juice to form a dough. Roll and fold 6 turns allowing resting times between. Rest before use.	puff pastry items not requiring full 'lift', e.g. sausage rolls palmiers fruit turnovers Eccles cakes
Full puff	Dough prepared with little fat, strong flour bound together with lemon juice and cold water. Layered with equal quantity of fat, roll and fold for 6 turns, allow resting time between each and before use.	vol au vents gateau Pithivier jalousie pie tops
Choux	Bring water to boil with margarine, beat in strong flour all at once, cook out and cool a little. Beat in egg well to give a pipeable consistency.	profiteroles èclairs choux swans dauphine potatoes
Hot water crust	Bring water to boil with lard or vegetable fat, beat in seasoned plain flour all at once to form a soft, pliable dough. Leave to cool a little but use warm.	veal and ham pie pork pie crofters' pie
Suet	Use grated beef or vegetarian suet and stir into seasoned plain flour at a ratio of 1:2. Bind with cold water to form soft, pliable paste.	steamed fruit pudding steamed jam roll steak and kidney pudding dumplings

CAKES

Dish	Process summary	Menu examples
Rubbed-in	Varying amounts of margarine or butter to self-raising flour. May have extra baking powder added. Fat rubbed in to resemble crumbs, sugar or dried fruit added, bound with egg, milk or both.	scones rock cakes raspberry buns farmhouse fruit cake
Creamed	Usually equal quantities of margarine or butter and caster sugar beaten till fluffy. Eggs beaten in gradually and plain flour with a chemical raising agent folded in. May be flavoured.	Victoria sponge rich fruit cake queen cakes steamed sponge pudding
Melted	Margarine or butter melted with syrup or sugar and sometimes a little water or milk, but temperature must be kept low. Dried or fresh fruit, spices and flavourings may be added. Flour and egg folded in.	gingerbread parkin
Whisked	Double the amount of eggs to caster sugar whisked to a firm froth (sabayon). Plain flour folded in carefully. Warmed butter may be folded in to finish as genoese. May be flavoured.	fatless sponge swiss roll genoese

Kitchen equipment

LARGE EQUIPMENT

Large equipment can be divided into three distinct sections:

Un-powered	Powered mechanical	Powered static
tables	table mixers	cooker
benches	floor-standing mixers	refrigerator
sinks	liquidizers	steamer
racks	potato/vegetable peeler	salamander
	chip cutter	grill
	oven spit	bain-marie
		freezer
		deep fryer
		bratt pan
		jacket boiler
		griddle
		microwave

CLEANING OF LARGE EQUIPMENT

Large pieces of equipment are very expensive and so it is important that they are cared for to ensure long, efficient and safe service. The materials of stainless steel, strong plastics, aluminium and steel require regular and thorough cleaning; moving parts need greasing and electrical wiring, gas and water pipes need to be checked; see pp. 170–5. Below are suggested cleaning methods for a cross-section of large equipment.

Grill or salamander

1. Turn off heat supply. Allow to cool.
2. Scrape and scrub bars, racks and trays to remove all food particles and grease.
3. Empty grease trap. Wash or wipe clean.
4. De-grease outside areas and wipe clean.

Frequency: Dependent upon use. Do not allow grease or food particles to build up. Ideally clean after each session.

Deep fryer

1. Turn off heat supply. Allow to cool.
2. Filter oil out to remove food particles.
3. Wash inside with hot, soapy water to remove all grease.
4. De-grease outside areas and wipe clean.
5. Re-fill with clean oil.

Frequency: Dependent upon use. When oil looks dirty, has sour odour, tend to froth, looks dark. After each session if possible.

Bain-marie

1. Turn off heat supply.
2. Remove all foods. Hot wash containers ready for use.
3. Let water out carefully. Discard.
4. Wash inside and out, wipe dry.
5. Leave doors open for ventilation.

Frequency: After each session

Refrigerator (floor-standing)

1. Turn off power supply and remove all contents to another cold place.
2. If not self-defrosting, prop open the door and place drip trays on shelves.
3. Hot wash all shelves and crisper. Dry well.
4. Wipe all inside walls and floor of cabinet using odourless cleaning agent/sanitizer or washing soda in water. Remove all traces of food.
5. Replace all shelves and turn on power.
6. Wash all areas of exterior especially the handle area. Wipe with sanitizer.
7. When cooled to correct temperature, replace food.

Frequency: Check content rotation every day. Clean frequently. Defrost once a month.

Refrigerator (walk-in)

1. Leave power on. Work as quickly as possible. Remove all contents to a cold place.
2. Prop door open.
3. Hot wash all shelves. Wipe with sanitizer.
4. Wash floor. Rinse and wipe dry.
5. Close door and wait for temperature to return to normal.
6. Replace food.

Frequency: As for smaller refrigerator

Electric mixer (floor standing)

1. Disconnect power.
2. Take off bowl and attachment to hot wash. Rinse and dry.
3. Wipe down machine with hot soapy cloth to remove all food particles. Rinse and wipe dry.
4. Replace bowl. Keep attachments close by in closed container.
5. Cover machine if not in use for long periods.

Frequency: After each use or daily.

SMALL EQUIPMENT

Materials used in manufacture of small equipment

It is very important for all small equipment in the catering industry to be hard-wearing and hygienic. Items are in constant use by many different people and should they become damaged there is a risk to health and lack of efficiency. Modern materials help to ensure durability. Table 5.25 shows advantages and disadvantages of different materials.

Rules in caring for small equipment

- Always check equipment is clean before use.
- Scrape food particles away with plastic scraper.
- Rinse with jet of water if available.
- Wash or soak in hot soapy water.
- Scrub to remove stubborn stains and persistent food deposits.
- Rinse in very hot water or use a sterilizing product.
- Ideally, dry in hot atmosphere. Or dry with clean teatowel.
- Lightly oil rust-prone trays.
- Lightly bleach polyethylene to remove stains and bacteria.
- Use lemon juice or vinegar with salt to remove discolouration from copper.
- Do not plunge hot pans or trays into cold water as this will cause warp.
- Report faulty equipment promptly.
- Store utensils in a warm dry place, on neat racks or in cupboards.

SAFETY IN USING KITCHEN EQUIPMENT

Everyone in a busy kitchen is responsible for the health and safety of themselves and of others. Whilst working with both large and small equipment the importance of following rules and working with care cannot be stressed enough to ensure no-one becomes sick or is injured.

There are a few general rules to follow:

- Ensure that staff are adequately trained on equipment they may use. Post notices around the kitchen for information to staff.
- Never store on top of equipment, and ensure that staff can reach high pieces (e.g. salamanders and bakers' ovens).
- Clean all items regularly. Food deposits are unhygienic, look unsightly, and can ignite if left to burn.
- Ensure sufficient ventilation and extraction.

Table 5.25 Advantages/disadvantages of various materials used in manufacture of small equipment

Material	Equipment	Advantages	Disadvantages
Stainless steel	bowls spoons knives	stain-resistant non-rust-forming easy to clean moderately heavy	expensive heat discolours may smear
steel	baking trays frying pans omelet pans	heat resistant durable reasonable price	prone to rust must dry well heavy
copper	saucepans sauté pans moulds	attractive conducts heat well light non-rust forming	prone to attack must be lined expensive discolours
aluminium	bowls sauté pans baking trays	inexpensive may be scrubbed fairly heavy	prone to attack – become pitted
polyethylene	bowls rolling pins chop boards spoons	hard, non-porous unbreakable heat-resistant hygienic, light	may stain prone to cuts expensive
wood	rolling pins chop boards sieves, spoons mushrooms	heat-resistant easily scrubbed inexpensive	prone to crack splinter, warp, stains heavy
tin	cutters moulds	light inexpensive	prone to rust easily damaged

- Switch off all fuel supplies when not in use.
- Undertake regular maintenance checks.

For the safety of personnel and for the proper handling of food it is important that equipment should be used properly. Below are given some examples of proper use.

Refrigerator

1. To ensure the inside stays at the required temperature, open the door as little as possible.
2. Keep all foods covered to prevent them from drying, creating odours or contamination.
3. Use clean plastic, airtight containers. Do not store food in tins.
4. Store raw meats in lowest part, in case of blood spillage onto other foods.
5. Do not overfill. Arrange foods so that air can circulate.
6. Do not store strong-smelling foods (e.g. garlic, onions) or dirty foods (unwashed cabbage) in the refrigerator.

7. Check temperature control regularly (some are controlled by computer and have alarms fitted).
8. Discard stale and unwanted produce often.

Steamer

1. Follow manufacturer's instructions carefully.
2. Use the door as a shield from the steam before opening fully.
3. For pressure steamers, allow pressure to reduce before opening door.
4. Check water levels and do not allow to become dry. This is usually automatic unless a fault occurs.
5. Grease door controls occasionally to ease opening.
6. Use protective cloth or gloves to remove hot trays.

Deep fryer

1. No more than half fill with oil. Never overload – the oil may spill over.
2. Do not plunge in wet foods – the oil will froth and spit.
3. Place foods in carefully. Lay in items that may splash, such as fish, away from you.
4. Use either a spider or basket to remove foods quickly and easily.
5. Be organized and have trays on hand when removing foods.
6. Keep the temperature of the oil to the correct degree, allow recovery time between batches of food.
7. Thermostatically controlled fryers are the best. Never allow fat to smoke as this is 'flash' point (heat haze is normal).
8. Use clean, dry protective clothes and keep arms protected by long sleeves.
9. Ensure knowledge of fire procedures and placing of equipment.
10. Reduce temperature of oil during slack periods. Turn off and cover when not in use.

Mechanical mixer

1. Ensure bowl and attachments are clean before use.
2. Do not store items on top of machine, they may fall in whilst mixing.
3. Turn off motor before changing gear. Start at low speed when mixing heavy loads.
4. Turn off machine and ensure fully stopped before putting hands or equipment into bowl.
5. Check electrical connections regularly. There should be a safety cut-out.
6. Only one person should be in control of the mixer at one time.

Knives

1. Concentrate and pay close attention when using.
2. Carry in a case or pointed downwards.
3. Do not leave in sink of water to be washed as the next person will not know it is there.
4. Use correct knife for the purpose – some blades flex, some may be too small for the job.
5. Lay knives flat on the worktop, not near the edge. Remove from the work area when rolling pastry.
6. Maintain sharpness; blunt knives are inaccurate.

7. Hold handle with a fist and not with the forefinger along the blade. Use your thumb and forefinger on the sides of the blade to steady very large knives.
8. Turn fingers of the other hand into a claw when holding items so that knuckles fend the knife away from finger ends.

ACTIVITY

Research the health and safety rules for three more pieces of equipment to be found in a modern kitchen – ensure one is for a mechanical or powered piece.

Take examples from the list below or use three of your own choice.

Gas stove and oven	Microwave oven
Pressure steamer	Vegetable boiler
Pressurized deep fryer	Dish washer
Table mixer	Bain-marie
Deep freeze	Bratt pan
Combi-oven	

Holding methods

From one establishment to another there will be different types of service and different methods of ordering food, according to the type and style of menu and expectations of customers. Holding methods for foods once they are in production vary with the numbers to serve and the flow pattern of customers. For example, at a banquet all the food for each course must be produced at the same time and held at the correct temperature while the service staff are given the opportunity to collect it. Whereas, in an à la carte restaurant, the item would be cooked to order and customers would be seated at differing times.

Table 5.26 shows various methods at which they are typically used and considerations that govern their use.

Table 5.26 Holding methods

System	Description	Typical establishment	Adv/disadvantages
Buffet (hot or cold)	A wide selection of foods on a large service counter/table where the customers help themselves or are assisted.	Large hotel dining room (for functions or for breakfast service)	Within easy reach of kitchen Less staff required Large number served over shorter period Queues may form More floor space needed for movement of guests
Carvery	Hot meals presented at a hot service counter with meats carved on request and guests help themselves to other items. Starters and desserts usually served.	Pub-restaurants Some hotels	Less staff required More space needed for guests to move to carvery table Foods may deteriorate in holding Portion control more difficult
Counter	Hot and cold food and beverages served at counter for customers to self-select.	Quick service restaurant In-store cafeteria Motorway services	Wide selection possible Fast type of service Efficient back-up required Foods may deteriorate Temperature control vital Good presentation on the plate more difficult
Table d'hôte	Limited selection or fixed menu for table service.	Small hotels and restaurants Guesthouses	Variety of service styles possible Service may be slower
A la carte	Wide selection priced individually	Select restaurants Luxury hotels	All items finished to order Very little 'holding' required Can be expensive due to the need for tender cuts of meat, etc.
Sous-vide	Vacuum packed foods which are chilled quickly and regenerated within 5 days by steam	A la carte restaurants	Wide range of foods possible Economic production during slack trading periods Temperature control vital Hygienic production important
Cook-chill	Mass production of meals, fast reduction in temperature, packaged, held at 0–3°C for 5 days maximum.	Hospitals Large central kitchens	Portion control easy Little wastage Less staff required Staff may be working in cold Reheating may affect quality Strict hygiene important Temperature control vital at chilling and regeneration
Ganymede	Foods ordered in advance and served from a mobile unit heated by heat-retaining discs.	Hospital wards	Portion control accurate Quick to serve on wards Pre-ordering limits waste Patient unable to change mind

Culinary skills

Without frequent practice in the use of specialist tools and equipment, it is difficult to become confident and efficient in their use. Speed of production and safety also comes with practice.

There are traditional pieces of equipment that have been in use for many years and still remain popular. There are also new innovations in specialist tools being constantly developed to aid production and presentation techniques.

For a caterer, good, safe and efficient culinary skills are an attribute not to be underestimated. Examples:

- knife skills
- preparation and skinning of fish
- piping techniques
- cutting chicken for sauté
- boning joints
- whisking
- garnishing ideas
- carving joints of meat
- rolling pastry
- slicing and layering gateaux

ACTIVITY

Practise the skills listed below. Diagrams for guidance have been provided for (a) and (d) in Figures 5.12 and 5.13. You will need to research to find similar diagrams in the case of the other skills.

(a) Piping chocolate shapes

(b) Slicing and layering of a gateau

(c) Rolling and folding of puff pastry

(d) Cutting vegetables

(e) Cutting chicken for sauté

(f) Skinning fish

(g) Boning joints

(h) Carving joints

(i) Garnishing

Devise a checklist/record sheet so that these practices can be recorded officially.

Paper bags made with greaseproof paper are usually far the best for royal icing. Metal icing sets are difficult to control, and icing bags of calico, plastic or nylon require careful washing and often make the hands sticky.

- Use a good quality paper. Greaseproof or baking parchment sheets are the easiest to cut.

- Use a whole sheet cut across its diagonal for 2 large bags.

- Use half the sheet cut across its diagonal for 2 medium bags.

- Use a quarter of the sheet cut across its diagonal for 2 small bags

- The triangles of paper should not be equilateral

Step 1. To make the bag – hold the paper with the longest side away from you and the right angle towards you. With the palm up, take hold of the point A with the thumb and turn your hand over taking A straight down to B.

Step 2. Form a sharp point at X without a hold, then take C forward and wrap it round to AB to make the cone.

Step 3. Fold the point ABC in to secure.

Step 4. To fill the bag with icing. Hold the bag in the left hand with the thumb nearest to you. Take some icing on a thin knife and with not too much on the end, put the blade well down into the bag. Bring the knife out pressing against the thumb so leaving the icing behind the bag. Do not overfill the bag.

Step 5. Fold in the front then the sides to form a thumb press and seal

Figure 5.12 Making a greaseproof piping bag

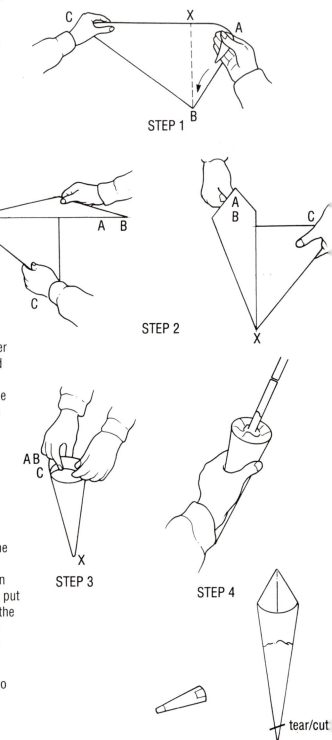

STEP 1

STEP 2

STEP 3

STEP 4

tear/cut

STEP 5

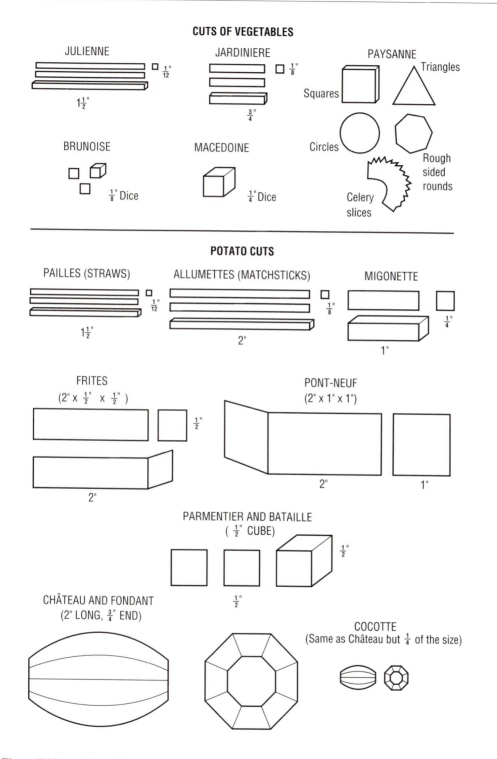

CUTS OF VEGETABLES

JULIENNE

$\frac{1}{12}$

$1\frac{1}{2}$"

JARDINIERE

$\frac{1}{8}$

$\frac{3}{4}$"

PAYSANNE

Squares

Triangles

Circles

Celery slices

Rough sided rounds

BRUNOISE

$\frac{1}{8}$" Dice

MACEDOINE

$\frac{1}{4}$" Dice

POTATO CUTS

PAILLES (STRAWS)

$\frac{1}{12}$"

$1\frac{1}{2}$"

ALLUMETTES (MATCHSTICKS)

$\frac{1}{8}$"

2"

MIGONETTE

$\frac{1}{4}$

1"

FRITES
(2" x $\frac{1}{2}$" x $\frac{1}{2}$")

$\frac{1}{2}$"

2"

PONT-NEUF
(2" x 1" x 1")

2"   1"

PARMENTIER AND BATAILLE
($\frac{1}{2}$" CUBE)

$\frac{1}{2}$"

$\frac{1}{2}$

CHÂTEAU AND FONDANT
(2" LONG, $\frac{3}{4}$" END)

COCOTTE
(Same as Château but $\frac{1}{4}$ of the size)

Figure 5.13 (top) Cuts of vegetable; (bottom) potato cuts

Glossary of terms

LARDERWORK

Bard	cover fatless meat or game with large pieces of fat or bacon to keep it moist during cooking
Bat out	flatten with a heavy object, e.g. for veal escalope
Darne	slice of round fish cut on the bone, e.g. darne of salmon
Délice	a trimmed and neatly folded fillet of fish
Dice	cut food into small neat cubes
Escalope	slice of meat taken from the best part of leg but can also be taken from neck or loin, e.g. pork escalope
Fillet	cuts of fish free from the bone, two from round fish, four from flat fish
Goujon	fillet of fish cut into thin strips
Lard	Thread strips of fat through fatless meat or game to moisten during cooking
Lardons	strips of bacon used for flavouring
Noisette	best end neck of lamb, boned and tied into a roll, cut into thick slices
Pané	to coat with flour, eggwash and breadcrumb to protect foods during frying
Paupiette	rolled fillets of fish or slices of meat
Suprème	chicken breast, or a fillet of large fish cut on the slant, e.g. suprème of turbot
Tronçon	slice of flat fish cut on the bone from large fish, e.g. tronçon of turbot or brill
Tournedos	very thick slices cut from middle of beef fillet

IN COOKING

Au beurre	cooked or finished in butter or in butter sauce
Au gratin	cooked with breadcrumb and/or cheese on top, then browned under hot salamander
Bake	cook in the oven using dry heat
Baste	spoon hot fat or liquid over food during roasting or poaching
Béchamel	white roux-based sauce made with milk and cloute onion
Beurre manié	kneaded butter and flour used for soup/sauce thickening at the end of cooking time
Beurre noisette	butter heated to turn a nut-brown colour, lemon juice and herbs added, used as sauce for fish and meat
Bind	hold lose ingredients together with a sauce of ingredient such as egg
Blanche	plunge briefly into boiling water and refresh in cold water, e.g. to halt enzyme activity and deterioration of food in advance of the cooking process or prior to freezing; to remove tomato, almond, grape, peach skins; to remove impurities from meat at start of stock
Blanquette	cooked meat dish finished with velouté sauce made from cooking liquor and blond roux, e.g. blanquette of lamb.
Blend	mix ingredients together thoroughly till smooth

Boil	cook food fully immersed in liquid at 100°C
Bouillon	a broth
Bouquet garni	parsley stalks, bayleaf, thyme and peppercorns wrapped in leek leaf or muslin and tied, to flavour stews and casseroles (removed before service)
Braise	slow moist method of cookery in sealed container in oven or on stove top, usually using mirepoix of vegetables
Brochettes	pieces of meat cooked on a skewer
Cartouche	circle of greased greaseproof paper that acts as a lid to keep in steam during slow poaching
Casserole	(verb) same as braising, in a casserole dish
Clarify	take impurities out of butter by heating and pouring off yellow liquid, or, using eggwhite to clarify soup
Clouté onion	onion studded with bayleaf and clove for flavouring milk, e.g. in preparation of béchamel
Compôte	fruit poached in sugar syrup
Cocotte	to cook in a cocotte dish on stove top or in oven
Consommé	strong, perfectly clear soup
Court bouillon	stock made from water, root vegetables, white wine or vinegar
Cuisson	natural cooked juices from fish, chicken or meat
Demi-glace	brown sauce made from mirepoix, tomato purée, mushrooms and bouquet garni
Dripping	fat that is left after roasting beef or beef bones
Duxelle	finely chopped mushrooms and onion/shallot used as stuffing.
Flambé	set alight, or flamed with alcohol
Fricassée	pieces of cooked white meat reheated in creamy white sauce with egg liaison, e.g. fricassée of chicken.
Fry	cook in hot fat in open pan (shallow): in minimum of fat (deep): completely submersed in fat
Glaze	brush with agent that will cook or dry to a shine, e.g. eggwash before cooking butter after cooking bunwash sugar syrup after baking
Grill	cook by direct heat under or over foods, on grill or salamander
Liaison	thickening and enriching agent added to sauce/soup at the end of cooking time
Marinate	soak for a long time in flavouring liquor such as wine and herbs to tenderize and flavour
Mayonnaise	cold sauce of egg yolk, vinegar and oil held in an emulsion
Mirepoix	selection of roughly cut vegetables to act as a bed for meat during braising, usually of carrots, celery, onions, turnips
Navarin	brown lamb stew
Parboil	partly cook by boiling in water

Pickle (verb)	preserve or soak for long period in acidic liquor; (noun) mixture that results from this treatment
Poach	cook very gently in shallow pan of cooking liquor
Pot roast	cook very slowly in covered pan with fat, herbs and onions
Purée	cook to pulp e.g. apple
Ragoût	thickened brown stew of large diced meat, cooked with vegetables
Roast	cook in oven with a little fat
Roux	mixture of flour and fat used to thicken sauces/soups
Sauté	shallow fry in unlidded sauté pan in small quantity of fat, more suited to foods that can be tossed or turned often during cooking
Sear	brown or seal meat by quick frying, grilling or hot oven
Simmer	cook in liquid that shows slight movement but not quite boiling (a little hotter than poaching)
Steam	gentle cooking in sealed container of steam
Trivet	support of bones or equipment to keep food away from the tray while roasting

IN BAKERY AND PATISSERIE

Bake blind	bake a pastry case empty, ready for filling
Bouchée	(Fr. *bouche*: mouth) small puff pastry case that is mouth-sized
Cream	to beat fat and sugar together till light and fluffy
Dredge	sprinkle liberally with flour or sugar
Dropping consistency	mixture drops from lifted spoon easily after one shake
Gluten	protein found in flour, adds strength to doughs and some pastries to help raise product during baking
Knead	to pummel and work a dough till smooth to develop gluten
Macerer	soak fruit in sugar syrup or liquor
Sift	shake dry ingredients through a fine mesh
Whip	fast movement with a whisk to incorporate air into a mixture

Agar-agar	produced from certain seaweeds used as jelling agent mainly by manufacturers in sweet making and pie fillings
Al dente	(It.: to the tooth) term applied to vegetables and pasta meaning the cooked substance retains some firmness (resists the tooth)
Bain-marie	a bath of hot or cold water in which to keep foods at the correct temperature
Beat	the action of aerating or loosening a mixture by rapid agitation with a heavy spoon or spatula
Brunoise	very fine dice of vegetables
Chiffonade	cut into fine shreds as in cabbage chiffonade
Conduction heat	transference of heat through metal, as in shallow fry or sauté
Convection heat	movement of heat through liquid or air as in bake or boil

Croute	slice of bread shallow-fried, used as accompaniment or garnish, or puff pastry case for fillet of beef (boeuf en croute)
Croutons	diced bread shallow-fried as accompaniment for purée soups
Curdle	separation of an emulsion caused by adding eggs too quickly when beating into fat, as in cake making
Dietary fibre	cellulose structure of foods, especially found in fruit and vegetables, that helps to expel waste from the body
Friture	a deep fryer
Gelatine	extracted from meat and bones when boiled, used as jelly in pork pies and for setting cold desserts
HBV	protein of high biological value which contains all essential amino acids, e.g. animal protein
Hors d'oeuvres	– a light course served at the start of a formal meal – or varie; various cold dishes served in small amounts as starter
Jardinière	batons of vegetables
Julienne	fine, thin strips of vegetables
Laminate	the action of rolling and folding puff pastry to form layers so trapping air and steam to create lift during baking
LBV	protein of low biological value which does not contain all essential amino acids, e.g. vegetable protein
Macedoine	diced vegetables the approximate size of peas
Mise en place	to be prepared and ready for either cooking or service
Pass	remove lumps and improve texture by passing food through a sieve or strainer
Pâté	a paste usually of meat or fish
Paupiette	olive-shaped roll of beef or small flat fish, e.g. paupiette of sole
Paysanne	thinly cut shapes of vegetables used as garnish and for soup
Prove	allow time in a warm moist atmosphere for the aeration of a yeast dough prior to baking
Radiated heat	direct heat as in using the grill
Rechauffée	a reheated dish prepared from foods left over from another menu
Retardation	slowing down of fermenting yeast by reducing the temperature or introducing enriching agents such as sugar or egg
Rub-in	the action of rubbing with fingers to disperse fat through flour to ensure even distribution and to resemble crumbs
Salamander	grill with heat source from above
Shred	cut into fine strips, e.g. cabbage
Veloute	a roux-based sauce made with blond roux and flavoured stock

SIX

Food service

Food service outlets

All food service outlets must work in partnership with the food preparation sector of the establishment. These two sectors are interdependent, neither can function without the co-operation of the other. They are normally controlled and organized by the same manager. In a hotel the food and beverage manager has responsibility for the preparation and service of all items of foods and beverages to both internal and external customers.

Principles of food service

Food service is the service of foods and beverages to internal and external customers in an efficient safe and hygienic manner, and in a way that will create customer satisfaction. Whatever the type of establishment, it is necessary for food service staff to have and be able to demonstrate knowledge of:

Systems

- what is available to serve/sell to the customer
- what the customer requires
- what the customer expectations are
- how much the customer requires
- where the customer wishes to be served
- the method of ordering/obtaining the customers' requirements
- when the customer is ready for the items they have ordered
- how the items are to be served
- what appropriate accompaniments should be offered
- how the customer is to be billed for the items and service

Safety and hygiene

- the safest and most appropriate method to carry food and beverage items
- the safe temperatures for the holding and service of foods
- the safe and most appropriate methods for the service of food and beverage items
- a high standard of personal hygiene
- clean working standards
- an awareness of the dangers of naked flames
- a knowledge of emergency exits/procedures

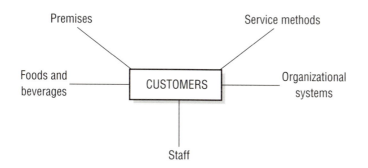

Figure 6.1 Food service outlet

In any type of food service outlet, there will be the factors shown in Figure 6.1. These factors will vary as to type within the different sectors of the industry to match varying budgetary requirements and customer expectations. For instance, the service method within any food outlet will be dependent on the:

- type of establishment
- type of customer
- type of food to be served
- staff/customer ratio
- time available
- type of premises
- type of equipment available

The service method for fish and chips, for example, will vary considerably in different types of establishment:

Establishment	Selection method	Service method
Restaurant	Table d'hôte menu	Silver service
Cafeteria	Menu board	Plated as ordered
Fish and chip shop	Price board	In paper as ordered

You can see, then, that each method of service is appropriate to the type of establishment and to the expectations customers have of that establishment.

In order for you to be able to match the appropriate food service style to each type of establishment it may be necessary to refer to the 'hospitality and catering' unit (p. 1).

Methods of food service in different outlets

HOTELS, CLUBS AND CRUISE LINERS

It is necessary to remember that each hotel has its own individual style of service and its own types of outlets. However, there are likely to be some of the following types provided for guests and casual customers.

Restaurant

This will cater for luncheon and dinner service every day. Some also cater for breakfast service if this is not taken in the guests' accommodation or in a less formal coffee shop facility. There will be a table d'hôte menu and usually also an à la carte menu for both luncheon and dinner services. The restaurant will be fully licensed.

Coffee shop

This facility will offer a less formal type of service and a flexible choice of menu that is less expensive than the hotel restaurant. The service style here may be either table, or a combination of self-service and table service. The coffee shop may be licensed to sell alcoholic beverages to diners. It is normally open all day long for beverages and snacks as well as more substantial dishes. Some may specialize in a particular type of food, such as Italian or American dishes.

Carvery

This may be a section of the main restaurant that is used for a carvery service, or it may be an entirely separate restaurant, designed for this type of service. Usually this carvery facility is available for luncheon rather than for the more formal dinner service, and there will be a combination of self- and table service. The carvery will normally be a fully licensed area.

Banqueting

This service is offered at private functions held in the hotel complex, usually in the conference rooms. The traditional banqueting service is formal in style. The numbers to be served can vary according to the facilities available, some establishments can cater for several hundred guests.

Buffet

A buffet is a more informal style of catering provided at a client's request in the conference facilities. The buffet can be a finger type, with food served as individual bite-sized morsels that are handed round to the guests as they stand and converse by food service staff. Alternatively, it can be of a more substantial nature, where the food is eaten with a fork or even a knife and fork. In this event tables and chairs would be available, with food being served from a central service table area, where guests can select from the displayed items.

Room service

This is available to residents only. A room service menu will be placed in the bedrooms, and orders from this can be telephoned to the room service department. Snacks, beverages and light meals are available on most menus. The orders are delivered to the guest's room by room service staff. The service is charged directly to the guest's account. On cruise liners the cabin stewards perform this service for passengers.

Tray service

This means the service of non-alcoholic beverages, morning coffee and afternoon tea in the lounge or conservatory areas, for residents as well as casual customers. A lounge service menu will be available. The lounge service staff will bring the requested items to the table on a tray and either place the complete tray upon the table for the guest, or take the items off the tray and lay them on the table itself.

GUESTHOUSES

A family type atmosphere and service will be found here in these small privately owned establishments.

Plated

Breakfast and an evening meal are the two meals likely to be available here. The food will be placed on the plates in the kitchen and served to the guests in a friendly, less formal style than the traditional hotel service.

Family

For the evening meal, family service may be used, where guests help themselves from dishes placed on their table.

Tray

This may be used if hot beverages are served in the lounge or garden areas. The required beverages will be brought to the guests on a tray from which they will serve themselves as and when they require.

PUBLIC HOUSES

Carvery

A separate area of the public house will be set aside for this. Food service will be a combination of table and self-service, with the meats being carved by food preparation staff or maybe food service personnel. Customers will be allocated a table, served with their beverages and then invited to select their choices from the carvery counter area. Food service personnel will assist the customers, if required, and will also clear away used crockery, cutlery and glasses as well as taking orders for and serving desserts and coffee.

Plated

In this service, the customer orders their meal from the menu, usually displayed on the bar or on a wallboard. The bar staff take the order and often request payment at the same time. Customers will be given an order number. Their order is then relayed to the kitchen, where it is plated and taken to the customer by either food service or by bar staff. Cutlery and condiments may be brought to the table at the same time as the food, or these may be placed in a suitable area of the bar for customers to help themselves. In order to save time and contamination, the cutlery is often pre-wrapped in a napkin before the service commences. Tables are cleared by either the food service or the bar staff.

Order/sale

In this service the customer selects their choice of food from a display and then pays for it at the same time. The customer then takes the food to their table and eats it. Foods offered for sale in this way range from filled rolls and sandwiches, ploughman's platters and salads to simple hot dishes such as shepherd's pie, lasagne or hot pot. Table clearing here will be carried out by the staff who serve the food in this type of service, usually bar personnel.

RESTAURANTS AND WINE BARS

Mixed

This service will be supplied by food service personnel to the customers. Choices will be made from a menu either at the table, or displayed on a wallboard. The dishes will be plated, with vegetables offered separately.

Silver service

Here the food will all be silver-served to the customers at their tables by the food service personnel. All table clearing will be carried out by the same staff, as will the service of beverages. There may be a specialist wine waiter who will advise the customers upon request, and serve the wine to the customers.

IN-STORE RESTAURANTS

Plated

In these areas, the customer will be served by food service personnel at their table and the dishes chosen will be served already plated. The service of desserts, snacks and beverages as well as table clearing will all be carried out by the food service staff.

Cafeteria

The menu here will be displayed at the entrance area. Customers will place their selected items on a tray, and pay for these before collecting cutlery and condiments and choosing a table to sit at. Some dishes and beverages will be served to the customers at the time requested, by service staff. Table clearing will also be completed on a continuous basis by the cafeteria staff.

CAFÉS

Plated

Hot and cold snacks and meals will be available here, and will be served already plated by the café staff. Staff in these small privately owned establishments often combine the food preparation with the service roles and therefore perform all the associated duties themselves.

Order/sale

In this form of service, the customer will request their choice from a menu board. Their choice of food will be given to them by the café staff and payment requested. The customer will then take their food to a table, collecting cutlery and condiments on the way. The tables will be cleared by the café staff.

FAST FOOD AND TAKE-AWAY OUTLETS

Order/sale

The food in these establishments is prepared in a systematic, controlled manner, so that it can be ready for sale instantly – hence the name 'fast food'. Customers make their choices from a large wallboard menu. The service staff take the order, collect the appropriate dishes and beverages, place these on the customer's tray, or in a take-away bag, and request payment. The customer then either takes the food to the tabled area or away from the premises. Table clearing is customer-initiated, with service staff to supplement this and ensure that the tabled area is clean at all times.

INDUSTRIAL IN-HOUSE

Order/sale

The main use of this type of service is for sandwiches, filled rolls, pastries, confectionery and non-alcoholic beverages. The customer selects the items, pays the appropriate monies and then takes the items either to a tabled area or back to their place of work.

Cafeteria

Customers make their choices as they pass the service areas. Some dishes may be plated by the cafeteria service staff others will be self-service or pre-plated. Payment is made at the end of the cafeteria's service run. Customers then proceed to collect their cutlery and condiments before selecting a table in the dining area. Table clearing here is customer-initiated, with cafeteria staff ensuring that the tabled area is kept clean and tidy for all customers.

Trolley

Here a trolley service is supplied to the employees' areas of work. The items for sale include filled rolls, sandwiches, pastries, confectionery, fresh fruit and non-alcoholic beverages.

Payment is made for items selected to the trolley sales staff. Customers eat these items at their place of work.

Vending

Vending machines are particularly useful to supplement the provision of snacks and beverages by other methods. If employees are working either in remote parts of the industrial complex or on a night or weekend shift pattern, vending can be very useful. Items for sale will include chilled sandwiches, filled rolls and pastries, confectionery, savory snack items and hot and cold beverages. Vending machines can be programmed to accept cash or tokens as the employer wishes. The machines are cleaned and replenished by catering service personnel.

OFF-SITE CATERING

Mixed

For this service, the food will be served to the customers by food service personnel. Often a pre-arranged set menu or limited choice menu is in use for this type of service. The main dish will usually be plated with the vegetables and accompaniments offered separately. All clearing and beverage service will be carried out by the food service staff.

Silver service

Here all the items served to the customers are silver-served by the food service staff. A limited or set menu will normally be in operation for this service. The service of beverages and all clearing will also be completed by the food service staff.

Buffets

These may be either finger, or fork, or full-meal style. In each case they will be served by food service personnel, possibly with food preparation personnel serving the meats in the case of a full buffet service operation. Desserts and beverages will be served and table clearing completed by the food service staff.

Order/sale

Customers select items required from those displayed, pay the sales staff the necessary sum and then take the items away to eat. Items for sale will normally include sandwiches, filled rolls, pastries, biscuits, confectionery, potato-based snacks, ice-creams, and non-alcoholic beverages. Sometimes there will be a series of these order/sale points, each selling a particular type of product: one ice-cream, one beverages, one confectionery and snack items, and one filled rolls and sandwiches. There is sometimes provision for hot snacks, such as chips, burgers and hot dogs, to be served in the same manner.

Vending

This sales facility will be filled and cleaned by catering services personnel. Vending machines will supplement the order/sale outlets and sell items such as hot and cold non-alcoholic beverages, ice cream, confectionery and potato and nut snack items.

MOTORWAY SERVICES

Mixed

This provision will be available at some service areas. The customer orders dishes from a menu at the table. The food service staff take the order, serve the customer and clear the tables. The main meal will be plated, with the vegetables served separately by the food service staff. Normally only non-alcoholic beverages are available in these dining areas.

Order/sale

These areas offer a fast-food facility to customers, where hot snacks may be purchased – beef burgers in baps with French fries being one of the most popular choices. The service is exactly the same as a fast food outlet. Customers may sit at tables provided or return to their vehicles.

Cafeteria

These are busy areas and are often planned in a free walk carousel style. Customers enter the sales area and take a tray. They then select their choices of foods from self-service wall and central carousel sales counters. These are chilled ambient or heated, as appropriate. Some main dishes and hot beverages may be served to customers by the cafeteria's service staff. Customers then proceed to the cashier to pay for their food, then collect additional crockery, cutlery and condiments on their way to the tabled area.

Vending

These machines are available to customers even when the cafeterias and order/snack sections are closed. They will be cleaned and filled by the catering services staff. Items on sale will include hot and cold non-alcoholic beverages, chilled filled rolls and sandwiches, pastries, savoury snack items and confectionery.

TRAINS

Mixed

This service will be offered to passengers who wish to have a sit-down meal service. The dining car stewards will take the passengers' orders and serve the meal in plated form, with vegetables and accompaniments offered separately. Hot, cold and alcoholic beverages will also be served by the dining car stewards. Time is often restricted by the length of the journey, so speed of service is quick. Table clearing and payment for meals is also handled by the dining car stewards.

Order/sale

There will be order/sale outlets at the railway stations. These will be there to provide light refreshments and snacks as well as hot and cold and alcoholic beverages. The buffet car service on the trains will provide an order/sale service for passengers. The items for sale here will include alcoholic and non-alcoholic beverages, sandwiches and pastries, savoury snacks, confectionery and hot filled baps. The buffet service staff will serve the customers and take their payments.

Trolley

The buffet staff will take a sales trolley down the length of the train to serve passengers in their seats, offering tea and coffee, alcoholic and non-alcoholic beverages, sandwiches, pastries and confectionery. Once the whole of the train has been served the trolley is returned to the buffet car and the staff will use a rubbish sack to collect the empty disposable cups and snack wrappings.

FERRIES

Mixed

On ferries there will be a formal restaurant service available at pre-set times for passengers. The food service personnel will take the customers' orders and serve the meal with the main course plated and the vegetables offered separately. These food service personnel will also serve beverages and clear tables. Time is usually restricted by the length of time for the crossing, so the speed of service is quick.

Order/sale

Passengers here can select and pay for beverages and sandwiches and then proceed to the lounge areas to eat the drink in comfort. Lounge service staff will clear the tables and be responsible for the cleanliness and tidiness of the lounge areas.

Cafeteria

Passengers proceed along the cafeteria service counters with their tray and select items for themselves. Some hot items and beverages may be served for them by cafeteria service staff. As soon as they have passed the cashier, they enter a tabled area where their meals can be eaten. Cafeteria service staff keep this area cleared and tidy for further customers. As time may be limited, the service here needs to be quick.

Vending

Non-alcoholic cold drinks, hot drinks, confectionery and savoury snacks may be purchased from vending machines. These are cleaned and re-filled by catering services staff.

▲ Designed to accomodate easy filling and cleaning.

Flexible drum and compartment configuration.   ▶

The MasterModule enables the operator to programme all machine settings such as prices, and retrieve sales audit information.   ▼

Figure 6.2 Vending machine

AIR TRAVEL

Airports

The facilities for catering at airports is very similar to the facilities found at motorway service areas. The only difference is that here the sale of alcoholic beverages is permitted.

In-flight tray service

Cabin staff will serve all passengers in their seats because of the restricted space inside the aircraft. Alcoholic and non-alcoholic beverages are served from a trolley which is wheeled down the aisles by the cabin staff. Meals are also served in this manner, each passenger being given an individual tray containing their complete meal and appropriate cutlery. Economy-class passengers will find their meals served in plastic dishes with plastic cutlery. Hot beverages are served from large tea and coffee pots to each passenger. Club/business-class passengers will experience a higher standard of service, and first-class passengers will have conventional style crockery and cutlery, with individual service being given by the cabin staff.

LEISURE CENTRES, MUSEUMS, THEATRES

Plated service outlets or cafeteria style outlets may be available in some of these establishments. These will be similar to those found in in-store units (see p. 268). It may also be possible to find vending and order/sale outlets here too. These will be similar to those found at off-site areas (p. 270).

HOSPITALS

Order/sale

This area will be provided for hospital staff. They can select and purchase snacks and beverages and eat these at a tabled area. The catering services staff will operate this facility and be responsible for the cleanliness of the adjacent tabled area.

Cafeteria

Cafeteria-style service will be available for hospital staff and some patients' relatives who may be staying at the hospital during an emergency. The customers will pass along the cafeteria counter and select from the self-service display areas. Some hot meals and beverages will be served by the catering services staff. After paying the cashier, customers will collect their cutlery and proceed to the tabled area. Table clearing is customer initiated with cleanliness and tidiness being the responsibility of the cafeteria services personnel.

Tray

When this type of service is used, patients' meals are trayed in the catering department and then placed in chilled or regeneration trollies and delivered to the wards. Here they are served to the patients by ward hostess personnel. Patients who are well enough to leave their bed will have their meals served at tables in the ward day room.

Trolley

Cook/chill operations are run in conjunction with a trolley service method. The chilled food for each ward is placed in the trolley and taken to the ward, where it is regenerated. Here the trolley is used as the service counter for the patients' meals. Ward hostess personnel are responsible for the service of the food to the patients in the ward day room, or if necessary, to the patient in their bed.

Vending

Vending machines are provided for out patients, visitors and staff in hospitals. Machines will be stocked with chilled filled rolls, sandwiches and pastries, confectionery and savoury snacks, hot and cold non-alcoholic beverages. These machines will be filled and cleaned by catering services personnel. Because of the number of customers who use these machines, they will normally be cleaned and filled at least twice in twenty-four hours.

SCHOOLS

Family

This style of service will be used in some boarding schools. The dishes of food are placed upon each table, and one person at each table, maybe a senior pupil or staff member, will then serve all the other people at that table. The pupils will complete any food service tasks themselves, such as fetching the food and clearing away the used plates and dishes at the end of each course.

Cafeteria

Pupils and staff will be served from a cafeteria counter. They will be served dishes of their choice by catering services personnel, and then eat this meal in the dining area. This tabled area may be permanent, or (very often) it is set out by the catering services staff in the school assembly hall and then put away by them at the end of the service time. The tables and chairs in this case are light stackable designs. Table clearing is completed by each pupil as they finish their meal.

Vending

Hot and cold beverages and savoury snacks are available, and these are cleaned and refilled by catering services personnel.

PRISONS

Cafeteria

Prisoners work within the catering section of the prison, and staff the cafeteria-style service counter for other inmates. Table clearing is completed by each prisoner when they have finished their meal. In some prisons, inmates take their meals back to their cells to eat. The meals are served in moulded partitioned trays.

RESIDENTIAL HOMES

Plated

Here the food is plated in the kitchen and given to each resident at the tables in the dining area. The residential home care staff will serve the plated meals to the residents. Some residents will also be capable of helping in this way, and will help with the table clearing as well.

Tray

Frail or unwell residents may have their meals served to them by the home care staff on an individual tray, either in their room or in the day room.

HALLS OF RESIDENCE

Order/sale

University campuses offer a range of catering facilities, some of which are fast food/take-away units and others are the more conventional food outlets. In all cases the catering services staff will be responsible for the service of the food to the students and for the cleanliness and tidiness of the tabled areas. The table clearing will be done by students.

Cafeteria

Students who do not have self-catering facilities in their halls of residence will use this facility for most of their meals. They will select their food from the self-service counters and pay the cashier before going to the tabled dining area. Some of these cafeterias run a pre-paid, voucher/ticket system as well as cash sales. Table clearing will be done by students and catering service staff will be responsible for the cleanliness and tidiness of the dining area.

Customer expectations

There are three categories of external customers in the food service sector of the catering and hospitality industry.

COMMERCIAL CUSTOMERS

These customers have a completely free choice as to which establishment they frequent. They will use the establishment for one or more of the following reasons:

- It is suitable for a business meeting.
- They have an interest in food and wines and wish to try out dishes displayed on the menu.
- Their social group uses the establishment on a regular basis so the visit becomes a sociable part of their entertainment.
- They are looking for a new experience and are attracted to the establishment by its ambience or menu.
- They use the establishment out of impulse with no other factor to influence their decision.
- It is the nearest establishment for them to visit.

VOLUNTARY CUSTOMERS

These customers are mainly industrial in-house, or in schools, university halls of residences or hostels. They can choose whether to take advantage of the catering facilities available in site. Their decision will be based upon one or more of the following factors:

- The facilities offer good value for money.

- They are convenient in terms of distance from their work place and time available for a work break.
- Their friends use the facilities.
- The choices available are compatible with their tastes.
- The facilities offer a different catering experience from their competitors.
- They promote interest in foods and a healthy life-style.

INVOLUNTARY CUSTOMERS

These customers come from sectors of the hospitality and catering industry where they have no choice about if or when they use the facilities. They will be in the following sectors: boarding schools, hospitals, prisons, HM forces, residential homes. Here the factors to be considered by the catering and food service personnel will include:

- The continual need to promote interest in the catering experience.
- The provision of a focal point in the daily routine.
- In some cases, the provision of an experience that will relieve the daily monotony of the customers' existence.

Customers from all three categories will consider the following factors:

- Ambience – decor, noise level, comfort level
- Service – efficiency, friendliness, non-intimidating
- Expectation – as good or better than previous experiences
- Knowledge – what to expect, or within their spending range
- Convenience – time available, ease of service, distance
- Product – quality, quantity, value for money, memorable

On a more specific level they will consider the falling aspects of food service:

- Staff – approachable, comprehensible, knowledgeable, welcoming
- Food – temperature, quality, taste, quantity
- Menu – choice, price, description of dishes
- Customers – noise, dress, behaviour

ACTIVITY

Using the summary above, make your own judgement on three different catering establishments that you have used as a customer.

1. Produce a grid or chart to show that you have considered all the factors above.

2. Display your work and be prepared to give a short talk about your findings.

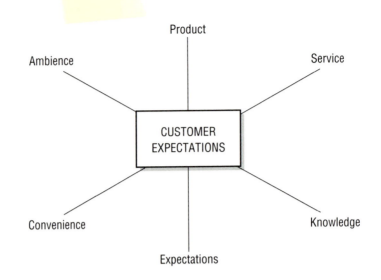

Figure 6.3 Customer expectations

From this you can see how complex the eating experience is from a customer's point of view. The food service team of staff play a vital part in the fulfilment of customer expectations. They are the key to the success of the customer's eating experience.

Staffing

It is becoming increasingly necessary to have teams of food service personnel who are multi-skilled and flexible in their ability to handle different types of food service work. This is because an increasing number of establishments are diversifying their options in order to remain competitive and financially viable. An example of this is the hospital catering service. Many of these units will cater for private functions both on the hospital premises as well as at off-site locations within their neighbourhood. The catering services staff will work in different capacities at these functions. Staff who run the cafeteria service during the working week may also work as table service staff at a private function.

This multi-skills approach means that the traditional food service brigade structure is seen less and less in the industry than in previous years. However, there are still widely recognized titles for food service personnel within different establishments. These titles have derived through the long tradition of food service both in this country and on the continent and are shown in summary form in Table 6.1.

1. Staff are categorized as: A – managerial; B – supervisory; C – operative.
2. The gender of the job titles can be either masculine or feminine. Please remember this when using the charts.

All members of staff have a responsibility for hygiene and safety as well as customer care, so these have not been included in the summary of duties.

Table 6.1 Food service personnel by category

	Establishment	Summary of duties
Category A		
Food and beverage manager	Hotel, restaurant, club, hospital, motorway services, railway, airline, liner, ferry, university	Provision and control of all food and beverage services and staff Commodity purchases
Banqueting manager	Hotel, club, university	Provision and control of all special functions and staff
Catering manager	School, prison, industrial in-house, residential home, hostel	Provision and control of all catering services, staff and commodity purchases
Domestic bursar	Hall of residence, boarding school	Provision and control of all catering services, staff and commodity purchasing
Owner/manager	Guest house, public house	Provision and control of all catering services, staff and commodity purchases
Category B		
Restaurant manager	Hotel, club, restaurant, liner	Supervision of the restaurant service and staff, and staff training Marketing
Head waiter	Restaurant, hotel, club, liner	Daily running of restaurant Staffing rotas
Bar manager	Public house, hotel, leisure outlet, liner, ferry, club, university	Supervision of alcohol sales Staffing rotas Staff training Commodity purchases
Head barman	As above	Daily provision of bar services
Steward	Liner, train, plane	Supervision of food and beverage provision Staffing rotas
Category C		
Station waiter	Restaurant	In charge of a group of tables/covers
Waiter/commis	Restaurant	Service of customers at their tables
Waiter	Public house	Service of meals and bar snacks
Carver	Carvery	Carving and service of meats
Wine waiter	Restaurant	Service of wines to customers at their table
Casual	Special functions	Service of food and drink
Floor waiter	Hotel	Room service to guests
Lounge waiter	Hotel, liner	Provision of lounge service to guests in lounge area
Cabin steward	Liner, ferry	Provision of room service to passengers in the cabins
Catering services staff	Industrial in-house, hospital, motorway service station, order/sale outlet	Service of food and drink to customers Trolley service Vending Cafeteria/table/service and direct sales

(**Table 6.1** cont'd)

Table clearers	Cafeteria, school	Clearing and cleansing tables and dining areas
Ward hostess	Hospital	Service of meals and beverages to patients on the wards
Vending staff	Industrial in-house, motorway service station, ferry, university	Cleaning and refilling of machines and surrounding area
Bar staff	Alcoholic sales area	Service of alcoholic and cold non-alcoholic drinks
Cellar man	Alcoholic sales area	Cleanliness and stock control in cellars
General assistants	Any catering outlet	General service duties and the cleanliness of the areas
Service operatives	Fast food outlet, order/sale outlet	Service of food/snacks/drinks. Cleanliness of areas
Buffet car staff	Train	Service of passengers with food and drinks, and cleanliness of these areas

Staff attributes

You can see from the summary of food service personnel duties in the various establishment (Table 6.1), that all the staff will come into direct contact with customers during their daily work. Their personal attributes and suitability for this aspect of catering and hospitality is therefore critical. Personal customer contact must be a positive and pleasurable experience at all times, if customer satisfaction is going to be gained. The following personal attributes are important for all food service staff.

AGILITY

Because of the need for speed, it is essential that food service staff are able to move quickly and effortlessly around the service areas. Well synchronized movements that cause the least amount of disturbance and expend the least amount of physical energy are a valuable asset to any food service operative.

COMMUNICATION SKILLS

The duties of food service personnel are all customer-orientated, therefore good verbal and non-verbal communication skills and positive body language are essential.

Verbal communication skills are used throughout the service period, whilst talking to customers, taking their orders and advising them on menu choices. These skills are also used when speaking to other team members and to the food production sector. Speaking to potential customers on the telephone and taking table reservations, is also part of the food service staff's duties. The ability to speak a foreign language can, in some instances, be of great benefit, and this skill is greatly encouraged by many employers.

Non-verbal communication skills are essential for all staff who have to record customer orders, even on a simple electronic order pad. Poor skills here can cause mistakes between the food ordered and that which is received from the kitchen.

Body language is a further vital aspect of communication for food service personnel. Positive body language must be practised at all times (see p. 86).

DISCRETION

While customers are eating or drinking, they may take the opportunity to discuss business or private matters with their companions. Food service personnel must practise a high level of discretion if they accidentally overhead any such conversations. Conversations between customers should never be listened to or repeated to anyone else. Conversely, directives and policy statements given to staff should never be disclosed to customers.

HONESTY

Because nearly everyone involved in food service will come into contact with cash at some time during their working day, it is essential that honesty is an undisputed attribute of all staff. Bills will have to be presented to customers and change given, tips may be received and cash sales through a till could be part of the day's duties. The strict adherence to the establishment's cash handling procedures is essential at all times.

   Honesty is also necessary when dealing with small but costly items such as light equipment, cutlery, linen and some food and beverage sales too. All such items should be strictly controlled and accounted for at the end of each working shift.

HEALTH AND HYGIENE

Personal care should be taken by all staff to ensure that they remain in good health at all times. Regular dental checks, and a healthy eating and exercise routine will help to achieve this. It is difficult to work in this fast, exacting part of the catering industry with poor health. Any illness should be immediately reported to the employer.

   High personal hygiene standards are essential for all food handlers (see p. 185). As food service personnel are in direct contact with their customers, they should have a shower or bath daily, have clean tidy hair and impeccably clean hands and finger nails. Clean, well-pressed uniform should always be worn with clean, protective non-slip shoes that will prevent unnecessary accidents. Whilst on duty the minimum amount of jewellery, make up and perfume/after shave should be worn by staff.

LOCAL KNOWLEDGE

Customers will sometimes wish to know about local services, customs, attractions, events or beauty spots. The food service personnel are the staff who frequently get asked these types of questions. In order to practise good customer care skills, it is necessary for staff to know about the local area and its amenities, or at least to be able to direct such queries to someone who can help, such as the hotel concierge or the local tourist information centre.

LOGICAL THOUGHT

In order to be an efficient member of food service staff it is necessary to be able to plan, think and work in a logical manner. It is no help to bring the customers' meal to their table before they have any plates from which to eat. Neither does it make sense to lay the tables and then proceed to clean the dining area. Working in a logical manner at all times makes it easier to remember all the stages or tasks to be completed. Flitting from one task to another is not a productive method of work.

MANIPULATIVE SKILL

Dexterity and good manipulative skills are essential attributes for food service personnel. Skills such as multiple plate clearing/stacking, silver serving and opening a bottle of wine, can all be learnt, but the manipulative ability must be there in the first place.

NUMERACY

With computerized billing and cash tills it could be concluded that numeracy would no longer be necessary. But it is necessary for staff to be able to add up a customer's bill and to give correct change. Many small establishments do not have modern cash tills that will add up the bills and work out the required amount of change. Many order/sale, cafeteria and alcoholic bar areas rely upon the staff's numeracy skills. Even with computerized tills it is necessary to be able to cash up accurately and enter the necessary sales analysis figures, as well as count up the takings and the float.

POSITIVE ATTITUDE

Demonstrating a positive attitude towards the customers at all times is a very necessary attribute. Direct contact with customers throughout the working day is a feature of this work and a positive approach is essential. Enthusiasm for the tasks to be completed and a willingness to help others are ways that the positive attitude can be demonstrated; so is punctuality and a genuine interest in the customers and the service given (see p. 303 on personal interaction).

PRODUCT KNOWLEDGE

Whether working in a restaurant, a bar, a cafeteria or an order/sale unit, it is essential that the food service staff know what they have to sell and have sufficient underpinning knowledge to be able to describe any aspect of the product or its service to the customer. Customers will at times ask for advice or recommendations about food and drinks, and the food service personnel must be able to give this information straight away. Bar staff and wine waiters in particular are expected to be able to describe wines and alcoholic drinks and give considered recommendations to the customers. Likewise, menu and dish knowledge is an essential requirement for food service personnel in all types of establishments.

PRIDE

If someone has a pride in themselves they will be alert and conscious of all that is going on around them. They will be interested in the job and in their customers and will strive to do each task to the highest standard possible. They will wear their uniform properly and it will always look clean and tidy. They will demonstrate their pride for the company that employs them by demonstrating a good knowledge of that company.

SALESMANSHIP

Every member of food service staff is, in fact, a salesman, offering dishes and beverages for sale to customers all the time. The ability to talk effectively to customers and to present products in such a manner that the customer is persuaded to purchase them is an essential skill. Positive comments should be used at all times in these instances. For example: 'Which wine would you like to choose, Sir?' is far better than 'Do you want a bottle of wine, Sir?'

TEAM SPIRIT

The teams working within the food service sector of the establishment are interdependent. In a hotel the food service team has to work with the food production team in order to obtain the food required for the customers. Staff also have to work within a team in the restaurant, where two or more staff could work together when serving a table of customers. The ability to work in and contribute to a team is an essential attribute for food service staff (see p. 96 on customer care).

ASSISTING CUSTOMERS WITH SPECIAL NEEDS

Some customers, including the elderly, physically handicapped, those with sight or hearing difficulties, large groups of customers and the young, will require more assistance from the food service. It is important for staff to be aware of the needs of these customers and respond appropriately (see p. 96 on customer care).

ACTIVITY

Keep a log over a minimum of four weeks and note down which types of customers you have given assistance to and the reasons why this was necessary. For example:

Date	Customer	Assistance given
1/11/96	Family and baby	High chair and a small plate and teaspoon provided.
4/11/96	Wheelchair customer	Moved two chairs and helped customer to the restaurant table in his wheelchair. When he left I called the lift for him.

ACTIVITY

Look at yourself and analyse your food service attributes. When you have completed this over a period of several days, ask a colleague to look at your analysis and discuss the points that you have raised. You can then do the same for their own analysis.

Use the format given below for setting out your analysis.

Attribute	Day 1	Day 2	Day 3	Day 4	Day 5	Total
Agility						
Communication						
Discretion						
Honesty						
Health/hygiene						
Local knowledge						
Logical thought						
Manipulative skill						
Numeracy skill						
Positive attitude						
Product knowledge						
Pride						
Salesmanship						
Team member						
Assisting customers						

Scoring system: 4 = good, 3 = average, 2 = poor, 1 = none.

MENU KNOWLEDGE

The menu is the sales document for an establishment, it is the method by which the potential customers can make their decision, either to purchase items from the menu, or to go elsewhere for a different choice of dishes. It is therefore of vital importance. The format of the menu should convey as much information as possible to try and attract potential customers. Menus of different styles will convey different images of the establishments that they represent (see Figure 6.4). There is a vast difference between a fast food beefburger establishment menu and that of a five star hotel restaurant. Despite such differences there will be some similarities. All menus will:

• be displayed where potential customers can read them
• have a list of the items for sale
• indicate the full price of the items on the menu
• be displayed in an attractive format
• indicate the type of establishment by their style of presentation
• include details of any special recommendations or offers
• have brief descriptions of the dishes to aid customer choice

When serving a customer, food service staff are frequently asked about dishes on the menu. Such questions as:

'What is the sauce made of?'
'What does that mean?'
'What is this dish made from?'
'How is this cooked?'
'Does this item contain garlic?'
'Does this item have mushrooms in it?'

Consequently it is necessary for all food service staff to know about every item on the menu. This means the:

• composition of each dish
• method of preparation
• method of service
• sauces and garnishes included
• accompaniments to be offered

They will then be able to give a brief description of any dish to the customer. For example, if a customer asks 'What is in the lasagne?' an unprepared food service staff might reply, 'It's pasta and beef with a cheese sauce.' This, while not incorrect, does not really tell the customer much about the dish, neither does it sound very appetizing. A better reply would be: 'It's an individual dish: pasta layered with a spicy minced beef sauce, finished with a cheese sauce and baked in the oven. It's served with a salad garnish and hot garlic bread. It's very tasty, I'm sure you would enjoy it.' Similarly when the wine waiter is selling wines, a brief description is often requested by the customer.

Figure 6.4 An example of a menu

There are various different types of menu that are used in the catering industry (see Table 6.2).

Table 6.2 Types of menu at different establishments

Menu type	Establishment	Characteristics
A la carte	Restaurant	Each dish is individually priced and cooked to order, therefore a delay is to be expected.
Table d'Hôte	Restaurant, guest house	Fixed selling price for a complete meal. Choices within each course.
Plat du jour	Restaurant, cafeteria	A specific dish offered as well as a normal menu: 'Chef's choice'.
Carte du jour	Restaurant, cafeteria	A series of dishes offered as well as the normal menu.
Function/banquets	Conference venue	Fixed price per head quoted for a menu.
Breakfast	Hotel, guest house	Choices for either continental or English breakfast.
Bar snack	Public house	Each dish individually priced.
Cafeteria	School, university, motorway services, industrial	Each dish individually priced and instantly available, displayed at entrance to the service area.
Room service	Hotel, liner	Individually priced items, prepared to order.
Lounge service	Hotel, liner	Individually priced beverages and light snacks.
Afternoon tea	Hotel, liner	Inclusive price for the complete meal.
Popular food	Fast food outlet, take-away outlet, café	Individually priced dishes and beverages.
Hospital	Hospital	Complete day's menus with choices selected by patients the day before.

ACCOMPANIMENTS

There are traditional accompaniments for the well known classical dishes that are featured on menus. For example:

Roast beef: Yorkshire pudding, horseradish sauce, roast gravy
Roast lamb: mint sauce, roast gravy
Roast pork: apple sauce, roast gravy

Customers will expect the traditional accompaniment(s) and therefore food service staff must be aware of these. Accompaniments are offered by the food service staff after they have served the dish to the customer.

ACTIVITY

Use your investigative skills to complete a comprehensive list of dishes with their traditional accompaniments, setting the information out as below. The course headings should be:

- Starters
- Soups
- Pasta and rice
- Fish
- Meats
- Puddings

Start a new page for each course. This will enable you to add further examples as you come across them. Also include the service details so that you can use these lists when you are working in the restaurant.

Meats

Dish	Accompaniments	Service details
Roast sirloin of beef	Yorkshire pudding, horseradish sauce, roast gravy	Large main plate Large knife and fork

ACTIVITY

Compile a log of service styles that you experience. See if you can cover all of the ones in Table 6.3. Compile the log from two viewpoints:

(a) as a customer

(b) as a member of staff

Customer log

Date	Service style	Establishment	Comments
25/3/96	Fast food	John's chip bar	Had to queue, but friendly atmosphere.
30/3/96	Bar snack	Public house	Self-service from a heated trolley.

Methods of service

It must be remembered that every establishment will have their own house style and routine. It is therefore not constructive to try to formalize the methods of service into a rigid framework.

The summary on p. 292 will give you an outline to work from.

The summary of establishment practices on p. 265 will give you guidance about which type of service is likely to be found in which type of establishment. Here again, this is only a guide.

Table 6.3 Summary of methods of food service

Mixed	Customer served at their table. Main dishes plated, vegetables offered separately.
Carvery	Customer's choice carved to order from heated display area. Self-service for vegetables, accompaniments, and other courses.
Silver	Complete meal served to customer at their table from platters by food service staff using service cutlery. A formal type of service.
Plated	The food is assembled on the plate in the kitchen, and then placed before the customer by food service staff.
Family	Main dishes and vegetables placed in dishes on the table for customers to serve themselves. Other courses served in the same manner, or plated.
Banquet	All tables are served simultaneously, may be full or partial silver service style. A large banquet may be served in sections, but always the top table first.
Order/sale	Customer's choice is made and payment taken.
Cafeteria	Customer selects dishes from service counters. Payment taken at the end of the service area.
Trolley	Taken to customer. Choices made and payment taken.
Tray	Order placed on a tray and taken to the customer.
Vending	Customer's choice made, payment made, and food dispensed.
Buffets	Choices made from a display area, or finger buffet may be served by food service personnel.
Room	Customer's choice delivered to customer.

TABLE LAYING

Each establishment will have its own style of lay-up and routine for its staff to follow. The diagrams in Figure 6.5 illustrate the standard lay-up for the various types of service in a formal setting. In restaurants, tables are normally laid up with flatware and cutlery at the end of the service shift, in preparation for the next meal service. They are then checked and completed at the beginning of the next service shift. For example, at the end of the dinner shift, the tables will be laid for the breakfast service.

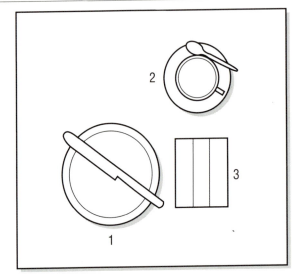

Figure 6.5a Continental breakfast cover. In some establishments all breakfast covers are laid in this style and additional cutlery is provided as required.

1. Small knife on bread plate
2. Breakfast cup and saucer, teaspoon
3. Napkin

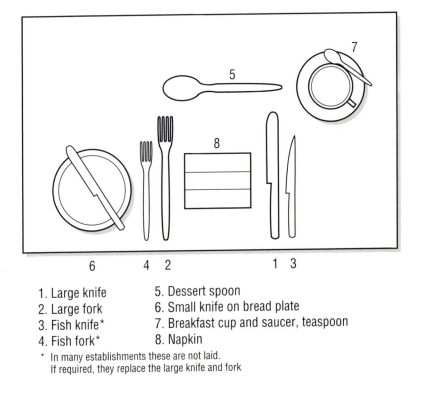

1. Large knife
2. Large fork
3. Fish knife*
4. Fish fork*

5. Dessert spoon
6. Small knife on bread plate
7. Breakfast cup and saucer, teaspoon
8. Napkin

* In many establishments these are not laid.
  If required, they replace the large knife and fork

Figure 6.5b English breakfast cover

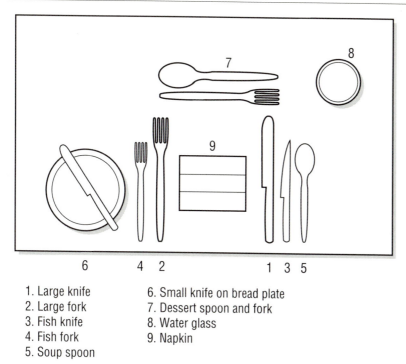

1. Large knife
2. Large fork
3. Fish knife
4. Fish fork
5. Soup spoon

6. Small knife on bread plate
7. Dessert spoon and fork
8. Water glass
9. Napkin

Figure 6.5c Table d'hôte cover

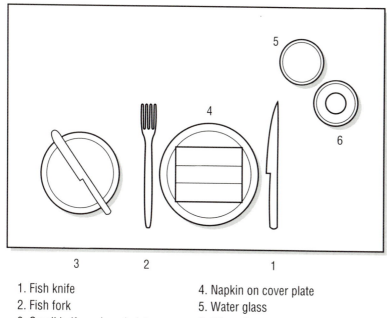

1. Fish knife
2. Fish fork
3. Small knife on bread plate

4. Napkin on cover plate
5. Water glass
6. Wine glass

Figure 6.5d A la carte cover

Tasks and considerations related to food service

With any form of food service there are always points to be considered, a summary of these is given in Table 6.4, a–f.

Table 6.4a Restaurant service

Tasks	Considerations to note
Room preparation	Cleanliness, lighting, heating, ventilation, flowers
Equipment preparation	Linen, service area equipment, trays, order pads, plate warmers, still room
Team menu briefing	Staff duties, reservations, special requests/diets, menu definitions, accompaniments, service methods
Table laying	Furniture spacing, type of service, final checking
Greeting customers	Taking coats, seating, presenting menu, offering aperitifs
Taking orders	Advise/record orders, log order, adjust cutlery
Serving/clearing	Serve from left, clear from right
Taking payment	Present bill, accept payment, log with cashier, present receipt and change
Bidding goodbye	Help with coats. Further reservations?

Table 6.4b Lounge room service

Tasks	Considerations to note
Tray preparation	Even weight distribution, non-slip cloth, liquids not likely to spill
Tray carrying	Weight appropriate to enable doors to be opened with one hand
Service	Place items on table in logical positions, minimum noise and disruption
Clearing	Place items on tray, minimum noise and disruption. Anything else required?
Taking payment	Present bill, accept payment, log with cashier, present receipt and change

Table 6.4c Buffet service

Tasks	Considerations to note
Room preparation	Furniture erected and positioned, customer flow, ventilation, heating, lighting, flowers, service areas
Team menu briefing	Staff duties, menu, service methods, times, portion control, temperatures, special requests/diets
Service area primary	Linen, service equipment, flatware, service flow
Service area secondary	Consumables, temperatures checked, presentation of the displayed dishes
Serving	Greeting, serving, presentation, accompaniments, hygiene
Replenishing	Continuous check, temperatures, hygiene, presentation
Dining area	Clearing continually, assisting guests
Service area clearing	Consumables returned, equipment cleaned/stored, linen and refuse removed, furniture dismantled/stacked, room cleaned

Table 6.4d Off-site catering

Tasks	Considerations to note
Preparation Area	Floor surface, shelter, storage areas, refuse bins, cash security, lighting, electricity/bottled gas supply
Equipment	Furniture erected/positioned, decor, service area, work/customer flow
Team briefing	Staff duties, services to be provided, times, work flow, hygiene, temperatures, security, emergency procedures
Service	Serving, hygiene, presentation
Termination Consumables	Either repackaged or destroyed
Equipment	Dismantled, ready for transportation, fuels turned off
Safety	Area checked, cash secured
Staff	Debriefed and thanked

Note: an inventory is made of all items taken to any off-site venue. It is then checked at the end of an event to ensure that no items are left behind or lost.

Table 6.4e Cafeteria service

Tasks	Considerations to note
Dining area preparation	Cleanliness, lighting, ventilation, heating, menu display, cutlery, crockery
Staff briefing	Menu, portion control, sales promotions
Service area preliminary	crockery, service equipment, chilled items, snack items, beverages
Service area secondary	Cashier/float, hot food items, temperatures, presentation, quality checking, garnishes
Service	Greeting, menu advice, selling, portion control, hygiene, presentation
Dining area	Assisting customers, clearing tables, replenishing cutlery, crockery, trays
Service area clearing away	Consumables returned to kitchen, equipment turned off and cleaned, cash balanced, paid in, staff debriefed, hygiene checked
Dining area clearing away	Crockery, cutlery, trays cleaned/stored, tables and chairs cleaned, floor cleaned

Table 6.4f Vending servicing

Tasks	Considerations to note
Cleansing	Empty refuse containers and clean/reline. Clean inside machine according to manufacturers' instructions. Clean outside of machine, and area around it. Hygiene.
Replenishing	Refill all sections, remove cash/tokens, refill cash change sections, re-lock, test before leaving

Beverage sales

There are special attributes required by staff who work in beverage sales areas. Customers frequent alcoholic sales areas because they like the products being sold and because they like the company, atmosphere and service in the establishment.

Staff must be able to demonstrate a welcoming attitude towards all customers at all times. They must therefore be staff who are sociable and communicative as well as technically skilful and knowledgeable. In order to be employed in an area that sells alcoholic beverages, it is necessary to be over eighteen years of age. A sound comprehensive knowledge of alcoholic beverages and their suitability to accompany different foods is also essential.

DISPENSE BAR

A dispense bar will be available to service a busy restaurant. It is to this bar that food service staff will go in order to be served with beverages for service in the restaurant and lounge areas. Dispense bars are usually sited between the restaurant and other bar service areas and are normally staffed by the bar staff personnel.

Food service staff will, if required, need to be able to give customers advice on the compatibility of alcoholic beverages and foods. For example, a customer may have selected grilled salmon from the menu, and require advice as to a suitable wine to accompany this. It is the role of the wine waiting staff in traditional establishments to give this sort of assistance to customers. However, in smaller units it could fall upon the table service personnel to answer such queries. It is for this reason that a basic knowledge of the wines on the restaurant list and their compatibility to the dishes on the menu is essential. This is often mentioned in the pre-service staff menu briefing in the restaurant.

Within a licensed restaurant there will be two types of alcoholic beverage service supplied. The situation where a customer requires drinks to be served whilst they are seated at the table, and the service of a bottle of wine to diners, to be drunk with their meal. The basic orders for service for these two instances are summarized below: remember each establishment will have their own house routines for these tasks.

SERVICE OF DRINKS AT THE TABLE

- Using a circular salver or tray, and an order pad, take the customers' order.
- Record the order on the order pad.
- Request the order from the dispense bar.
- Check the order and place upon the salver/tray.
- Take the order to the table.
- Serve the customers from their righthand side, ladies first, host last. If a mixer has been ordered, only pour one third into the glass, leave the remainder for the customer to add if they require more.
- Take the copy order to the cashier or, if it is to be a cash sale, present the bill to the host.
- In the case of a cash sale, collect the cash and take to the cashier.
- Present the receipt and change to the host customer, and thank the customer.

TAKING AND SERVING ORDERS FOR WINE

- Greet the customers and identify the host.
- Present the wine list to the host.
- Return and take order and/or advise the host if this is requested.
- Take the order to the dispense bar.
- Adjust the glasses at the table.
- Collect the wine from the dispense bar, using a wine cooler, if appropriate.
- Present the wine to the host.
- Open the bottle. Retain the cork for display to the host.
- Serve a taste to the host.
- When accepted, proceed to serve the wine, from the righthand side of the guest on the host's right, then the ladies followed by the gentlemen, serving the host last.
- Place the wine near the host, display the cork.
- Return to the table as the meal progresses to top up the guests' glasses.

SERVICE OF HOT BEVERAGES

Tea, coffee and milk-based drinks are frequently served in lounge areas either in the middle of the morning, at around 16.00 hours or after a restaurant meal either in the restaurant or in the lounge areas, or in cafeteria service establishments. In all establishments there will be house routines and standards to be adhered to, but the basic routines are summarized below.

Lounge service

- Order taken by lounge service staff.
- Order collected from still room area.
- Beverages carried to the lounge area on a tray.
- Each item is placed on the table adjacent to the customer (pastries or similar items may be included in this service).
- Bill presented either for authorization signature or cash payment.
- Payment or authorized bill collected and taken to cashier.
- Receipt and change collected and presented to the customer.
- When appropriate, table cleared using a tray.

Restaurant service

- Order taken by food service staff.
- Order collected from the still room.
- Order carried to the restaurant on a tray.
- Cups, saucers and spoons placed upon the table – Petit fours/chocolates may also be presented.
- Coffee poured into the guests' cups from the righthand side, ladies first, then gentlemen, then host.
- Tea is served in the pot so that the customer may help themselves. Hot water needs to be provided if there is more than one customer drinking tea.
- Bill presented for payment or authorization signature.
- Payment or authorization signature collected and taken to cashier.
- Receipt and change taken to the customer.

Cafeteria service – staffed

- Customer greeted and order taken.
- Individual pot of tea, coffee or milk-based drink dispensed.
- Order placed upon customers' tray.
- Customer proceeds to the cashier to pay.
- Customer collects cup and saucer, teaspoon and sugar, then selects a table in the dining area.

Cafeteria service – self-service

- Customer selects which beverage they require, and dispenses it into a cup/mug/pot themselves by a press button command.
- Customer takes their beverage and pays the cashier.
- Customer selects sugar, milk, spoon, and cup if necessary prior to entering the dining area.

Trolley service – trains

- Customer greeted and order taken.
- Hot water dispensed into disposable cup already containing instant coffee and whitener/tea bag and whitener.
- Cold and alcoholic beverages are dispensed with plastic 'glasses', from individual cans or miniature bottles.
- Pre-packaged snacks may be offered for sale as well.
- Total cost of sale detailed to the passenger, and payment taken, change given, passenger thanked.

Trolley service – industrial in-house

- Customer greeted and order taken.
- Beverages dispensed from insulated container.
- Pre-packaged snacks may be offered.
- Total cost of sale detailed to the customer, payment accepted, change given, customer thanked.

Bar service

- Customer greeted, order taken.
- Coffee dispensed from an automatic filter coffee pot, into a cup. Sugar and cream offered separately, *or*
- Coffee made with boiling water poured into individual cup filter placed over coffee cup. Sugar and cream offered separately.
- Payment received and change given. Customer thanked.

Food service equipment

The atmosphere within a food service area will partly be created by the furnishings and equipment and partly by the food service personnel.

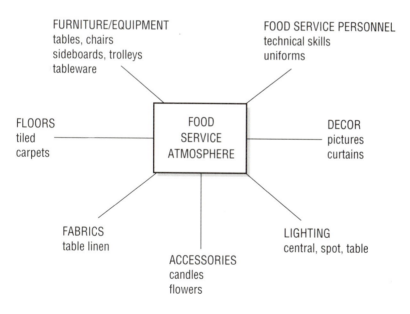

Figure 6.6 Food service atmosphere

Different food service areas will be creating entirely different atmospheres because they are catering for different types of customers and giving a different form of service. The equipment used will therefore be different as well.

For example, a comparison of an in-store coffee shop and a luxury restaurant could read as in Table 6.5.

Table 6.5 Comparison between two food service areas

Factor	In-store coffee shop	Luxury restaurant
Staff	Striped uniforms with white smocks	Traditional black and white uniforms
Decor	Modern geometrical prints in pastel colours	Rich peacock and burgundy colour scheme
Lighting	Fluorescent strips and bright spot lamps	Table lamps and subdued lighting
Accessories	Plants in entrance area	Flowers on all tables; tree in corner
Fabrics	Paper napkins	Starched linen napkins
Floors	Thermoplastic tiles	Deep pile carpet
Furniture	Fixed design light oak colour, melamine finish	Free standing, mahogany

ACTIVITY

Compile a similar comparison for yourself using two different types of food service establishments that you have visited.

Use your IT skills to word process your findings.

TABLEWARE

Similarly you will find that the types of tableware, also furniture and specialist equipment will vary according to the type of food service establishment that you are in. A transport café might serve tea in half pint ceramic mugs, whereas a luxury hotel could use porcelain cups and saucers. It is therefore important to select the type of equipment to suit the establishment and type of service.

The following aspects need to be considered before selecting flatware, cutlery and glassware for food service areas:

Intended use	Multi-purpose, specialist
Size	Portion control, type of service
Cleaning	Dishwasher proof, ease of draining dry
Storage	Space available, specialist racks available
Durability	Chip-proof, shatter-proof
Availability	Replacements, logo printing, delivery times
Compatibility	Complement existing stocks/designs
Cost	Justifiable, within budget parameters

ACTIVITY

Take an area that you have worked in and, using the list above, produce an account of the tableware equipment used in the chosen area. For example, if you have worked in a coffee shop, describe the tableware used in that area under the headings in the list above.

TABLE LINEN

The question may arise as to whether to use real linen cloths, table runners, drapes and napkins or whether to replace some or all of these with disposable items. The two main factors to be considered here are the cost implications and the customer acceptability factor:

• the cost of using real linen as compared to using disposables
• the tendency of increased use of disposables for other purposes,
  which can increase costs
• the standard of finish/service that you require
• the storage implications
• the advantage of colours and logo additions that can be achieved with disposables
• the possible benefit of the drip and place mats that are available with disposables.

FURNITURE

As in the case of tableware, when deciding on tables, chairs, sideboards and so on there are the following factors to consider:

Intended use	Fixed/movable, stackable, extend/fold up multi-purpose
Size	Width and height in proportion to rest of items, ease of moving
Cleaning	Stain resistant, melamine, varnished wood
Storage	Stackable-space available
Durability	Strong, casters, heat/scratch resistant
Availability	Replacements, additions, delivery time
Compatibility	How the items purchased will match style, height, width of existing items
Cost	Justifiable, within budget restrictions

SPECIALIST EQUIPMENT

Trolleys

These are used extensively in the food service sector and are available in many different styles, suitable for a large variety of tasks.

Table clearing	Stainless steel or aluminum frame. Sections fitted for used crockery, cutlery and waste food.
General purpose	Stainless steel, for general cleaning, equipment, transportation.
Carvery trolley	Heated top plate used to carve meats or poultry in the restaurant.
Gueridon trolley	For the completion of cooking of a dish to order in the restaurant.
Sweet trolley	May be chilled. Display and service of sweets in the restaurant.
Cheese trolley	For the display and service of cheeses in the restaurant.
Liqueur trolley	The liqueurs are displayed and served from this trolley in the restaurant.
Hors d'oeuvre trolley	For the display and service of mixed hors d'oeuvres in the restaurant.

Display cabinets

These may be mobile to enable them to be used in a variety of locations as required. They are frequently used in restaurants either for keeping hot dishes hot (e.g. breakfast) or cold dishes cold (e.g. chilled fruits yoghurts and meats). They are also used in these areas for a carvery service or a buffet service. They can be fitted in a straight line, a curved corner area, or as a circular hexagonal or oblong central display area. The only prerequisite is the supply of floor-based electrical sockets. Often a combination of heated, ambient and chilled cabinets are used. These types of cabinets are used extensively in cafeteria service areas and bar snack sections of public houses.

Table-clearing systems

In all cafeteria and popular catering establishments there will be a table-clearing system in operation. Any establishment, formal or less formal, that serves food to be eaten on the premises, will provide such a service. The effectiveness of the system will created an image of the standards of the establishment to the customer. It must therefore be unobtrusive, quiet and quick. There is nothing guaranteed to put off customers more than the sight of empty tables piled high with other people's empty, dirty crockery and cutlery. You may see some or all of the following systems being used within different establishments in your region of the country.

Table 6.6 Summary of table-clearing systems

Type	Method	Notes
Rotating shelf	Customer places tray on shelves that pass to wash-up area	Expensive to install, efficient, no unsightly trays left for customers to see
Conveyor belt	Customer places tray on moving belt	Efficient, no trays left for customers to see
Rack trolley	Customer places tray on individual tray racks	Unsightly for customers. Trays must fit racks, trolley must be changed frequently
Staff and trolley	Items cleared by staff and stacked on trolley in clearing bay area	Trolleys must be emptied frequently A labour-intensive system, as efficient as the staff will allow
Bins for disposables	Customer places all disposables in bin and stacks tray, with staff present to assist	As efficient as customers and staff will permit. Bins must be regularly emptied

Washing up machines

In the majority of establishments an automatic dish/glass washing machine will be installed. These machines are efficient and time-saving. The thoroughness of the washing process ensures protection against any possible contamination that might be possible from food particles or in saliva on forks, spoons, glasses etc. The minimum handling aspect helps reduce risk of recontamination. Whatever the size of the operation the sequence will be the same.

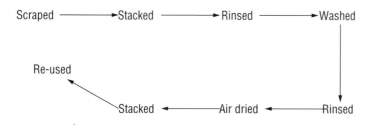

Figure 6.7 Sequence of automatic dishwasher operations

Dirty flatware and glasses will create a lasting bad impression upon the customer, so an effective washing-up system is very important. Items should also be checked for stains, chips or cracks and withdrawn if so damaged, before they reach the customer. Many establishments polish up cutlery and glassware before it is re-used, using a dry cloth and steam to produce a shine. This process, while producing welcoming tableware, also acts as a secondary checking point for damage.

Food and beverage service control

The value of the stock and the sales make this an important area of control in all establishments, of whatever size. There is no point in organizing an efficient system of food production and service if the control system is poor. The system used must be able to record the sales and the stock held, and to identify the costs incurred.

Within the food service section a cash till will be used to record all transactions, keep the cash safe and issue receipts. It will also give sales figure summaries. In order/sale units the till will most likely be a simple electric type, whereas in a bar or hotel it may be a computerized cash unit.

MANUAL CASH REGISTER

These are used in small sectors of the industry. The operative keys in the sales total, the drawer opens and the correct change is selected. These rely upon the operative being able to add up the total cost of the sale in their mind and to work out the correct change for the customer.

ELECTRIC CASH REGISTER

These cash registers will add up the sales items for the operative, and indicate the amount of change to be given. Obviously, these are preferred by the operatives as well as being more accurate. A receipt will be printed for each transaction, and a record of transactions can be obtained at the end of the sales period.

ELECTRONIC CASH REGISTER

These are used in busy trading areas. They will record all sales and identify these to each staff member. It is possible to have cash registers that will print itemized customers' bills on establishment headed paper. Some models will be programmed to the sales offered, that is in most cases the full menu breakdown. Staff will log themselves in with a code number or a key, then use the soft pad keys to record the order. The system will track the sales for each table, and add items as ordered. It can also be supplied with a stock control facility which will automatically adjust stock levels shown as items are sold. A similar system can be used in the bar and lounge sales areas.

ELECTRONIC TOUCH-SCREEN REGISTER

These are controlled by a touch-screen facility. The information is displayed upon a VDU screen and the operative simply touches the required area/box to register orders for food or drink items. The system will track the sales for each table as well as print a final bill. Stock control is an integral part of the system, reducing stock levels as items or drinks are ordered. As with the electronic register, staff are logged into the system and all sales are automatically totalled and change to be given indicated on the screen. This makes the operation accurate and quick to use. At the end of the sales period, staff sales can be quickly analysed, as can menu dish sales.

ELECTRONIC POINT OF SALE SYSTEM

This system will comprise a touch-screen and an automatic order transmission to the kitchen production area and the dispense bar. This is a quick and accurate method of controlling the operation. The orders are printed out in the kitchen and dispense bar, giving the food service staff time to adjust the table cutlery/glasses before going to collect the order. It speeds up the entire operation as it eliminates the waiting time for the staff and the customers. The transactions are totalled by table number and bills printed at the end of the service. Stock levels are automatically adjusted, and staff sales can be analysed at the end of each shift. Menu sales can also be analysed, giving an accurate picture of dish popularity.

CASH POUCH

In some quick service establishments, the food service staff wear a cash pouch around their waist. They are responsible for their own cash float and the cash transactions for their customers. In these establishments the staff must be able to total bills accurately as well as work out the correct change to be given. The process is often used in conjunction with an electronic touch-screen ordering system.

SEVEN

Basic skills: communications, numeracy and information technology

Communication

Do you ever think to yourself, 'What does that mean?' – 'What did she say?' – 'I can't read this diagram' – 'Why doesn't he explain what he means?' 'What a long preamble, I wish he would stick to the point.' If you have, then you have been at the receiving end of poor communication. You must never give cause for your internal or external customers to make any such remarks about your communication skills. Throughout the text of this book there have been references to communication skills, in particular in the customer care section (p. 93). The present section will help you to polish up these skills treated there and to develop them even further.

Verbal communication

GIVING AND RECEIVING INFORMATION

Whether speaking to internal or external customers, your prime concern must be to give and receive accurate information in a clear concise manner without causing any misunderstanding. In order to achieve this it is necessary to:

- speak clearly, with an even tone
- listen carefully
- concentrate on the conversation
- know what information you want to find out/give
- ask for clarification if you do not understand
- make a note of the main points to help you to remember

FOREIGN LANGUAGES

In the hospitality industry it is becoming desirable to have the ability to speak a foreign language. It can be very helpful to be able to put a foreign visitor at their ease by speaking in their own language. In particular, front office staff are increasingly asked for a second language at interview.

COMMUNICATION BY DISCUSSION

This method of communication will be used between yourself and other team members as well as internal customers. A discussion is different from a conversation because here you will be talking about a particular topic and putting your point of view as well as listening to other points of view. There can be two or more people having a discussion, and a discussion should normally produce a conclusion.

For example, in a restaurant the food service team could have a discussion about whether to open the doors onto the terrace before the luncheon service starts. There will be various aspects the need to be considered by the team. These could include the interior and exterior temperatures, the strength of the wind and its direction, the position of the adjacent tables and chairs and whether these are likely to be used by customers. Some team members will have one point of view whilst others will have a different opinion. These points will be talked over between the team and a conclusion reached without animosity.

ACTIVITY

Keep a log (see headings below) of work-related discussions that you have held with internal customers over a two-week period. You will find that this method of verbal communication is used frequenty

Date	Topic	Discussed with	Conclusion

Discussions will also be held with external customers. These often involve front office or food service personnel and frequently revolve around helping customers to make up their mind about a sale of a room, service or product. In these cases it is important to remember that the customer will be seeking information, advice and, maybe, reassurance so that they can make up their own mind. You should in these instances be patient and helpful so that the external customer does not feel pressured into making up their mind until they are ready to do so.

An example of this could be during the booking of a wedding reception. The bride's family will be discussing the following aspects of the plans: which menu to choose, which colour scheme for the table decorations, which wines to have available and which disco to choose for the evening. Your role here would be to give helpful information and to lead the discussions, so that each aspect is talked over and firm conclusions are reached. You would need to confirm these conclusions and make a written note of them to save any confusion in the future.

ACTIVITY

You are working in the kitchen, producing food for an in-house cafeteria. The cook wants to decide whether to prepare the apple pies in dishes that serve 10 portions, or in individual dishes. Write down the advantages and disadvantages and your conclusion. This could be the path that such a discussion would take in the kitchen between the catering services staff, who have to serve the apple pies and the cook who has to prepare them.

VERBAL COMMUNICATION BY TELEPHONE

Outgoing calls

In order to be economical with time and therefore telephone costs, it is advisable to make a note of the points that you wish to mention/ask during the telephone conversation. You should leave a space to record the answers as well. The following points are important:

- Context   Know what it is that you are calling about.
- Caller   Know the name, position and extension number of the person that you wish to speak to.
- Content   Note all the points that you wish to raise and record the answers.
- Confirm   Summarize what has been agreed and confirm this with the person you are calling.
- Close   Bid your caller good-bye and use their name, as well as thanking them for their time.

ACTIVITY

Work with a partner for this exercise.

Partner A.   You are a catering manager and wish to purchase some fillets of plaice. You are going to telephone your supplier to find out how much they will cost.

Partner B.   You are the fish supplier

- Write notes on what you wish to find out from each other.
- Role play the telephone conversation.
- Make notes on the points discussed and record the conclusion reached.
- Compare your notes after the role play has finished.

INCOMING TELEPHONE CALLS

All incoming calls must be answered promptly. External customers would not be telephoning the establishment unless they wanted something. Each call could thus represent a future sale. In order to be able to take incoming calls efficiently it is necessary to know about the establishment where you work: who people are, where they work, their responsibilities, and when they are likely to be on the premises. These facts will enable you to route enquiries to the correct person without any difficulty. (See p. 130 on front office security documents.)

The following rules should be followed when taking incoming calls:

- Speak clearly and pleasantly.
- Use good morning/afternoon/evening.
- State who you are and the name of the establishment.
- Ask how you can help.
- Listen carefully, concentrate on information you are being given.
- Make a note of the caller's name and address/organization and number.
- If you have to transfer the caller, tell them who you are going to transfer them to.
- Do not leave callers on hold for more than a few seconds without making contact.
- Record any mesages and ensure that these are forwarded promptly.
- Thank the caller before replacing the receiver.

ACTIVITY

Produce a checklist of phrases and expressions that you could use when receiving incoming telephone calls. For example: 'Good morning. Lisa speaking. How may I help you?' 'Lisa at the Red Lion speaking. Good morning.'

MESSAGE TAKING

Messages should be taken on a pro-forma message pad. This will ensure that you do not forget any important information from the caller (see Figure 7.1).

Always check that you have the caller's name and the message correctly recorded by confirming this before thanking the caller and bidding them goodbye.

When passing a message on, the following points should be remembered:

Telephone/verbal	• message form completed neatly
	• correctly spelt
	• delivered promptly, in envelope
Incoming fax	• check the machine every 20 minutes
	• deliver promptly in envelope
	• complete fax log book

```
┌─────────────────────────────────────────────────────────────┐
│                                                               │
│                      M E S S A G E                            │
│                                                               │
│   Date        . . . . . . . . . . . . . . .  Time  . . . . . .│
│   For         . . . . . . . . . . . . . . . . . . . . . . . . │
│   From:   Name . . . . . . . . . . . . . . . . . . . . . . . .│
│           Address/Company  . . . . . . . . . . . . . . . . . .│
│                                                               │
│               . . . . . . . . . . . . . . . . . . . . . . . . │
│   Tel. Number  . . . . . . . . . . .  Fax number  . . . . . . │
│   Message . . . . . . . . . . . . . . . . . . . . . . . . . . │
│                                                               │
│               . . . . . . . . . . . . . . . . . . . . . . . . │
│                                                               │
│               . . . . . . . . . . . . . . . . . . . . . . . . │
│   Urgent      . . . . . . . . . . . . . .  Please contact . . │
│   Taken by  . . . . . . . . . . . . . . . . . . . . . . . . . │
│                                                               │
└─────────────────────────────────────────────────────────────┘
```

Figure 7.1 Pro forma telephone answering pad

Non-verbal communication

This largely consists of 'body language'. In other words, it is the way that our stance and our movements give an indication of our reaction to other people and to our circumstances. Body language can convey positive or negative messages about our attitude towards people.

All the following aspects of behaviour form part of a person's non-verbal communication. It is useful for you to develop an awareness of such non-verbal communication signals so that you know how to respond in a positive manner.

- posture   standing, sitting still, tapping feet, fidgeting
- facial expression smile, blank, scowl, frown
- arms/hands   relaxed, folded, twitching, biting nails
- eyes   contact, downcast, flitting around, vacant
- space   keeps a distance, gets close, touching
- appearance   neat, untidy, scruffy
- voice   sigh, laugh, loud, quiet
- touch   handshake: firm, feeble, warm and damp, cold
- smell   body odour, perfume/after shave, cigarettes, garlic, alcohol
- gestures   hurried, calm, attention-seeking

Written communication

There are many forms of written communication used in the hospitality and catering industry, the principal ones are letters, facsimiles, memorandum, record/work cards.

ACTIVITY

Compile a list of positive non-verbal communication signals that hospitality and catering personnel should be encouraged to develop, using the list above to help you

LETTERS

In order to produce a well composed letter it is necessary to spend time planning out what facts are to be included. In addition, all letters should be:

- addressed correctly
- neat and conventionally set out
- polite and clear
- grammatically correct
- correctly spelt

Many business letters will fall into three parts (see Figure 7.2):

Context: establishing the topic/subject of the letter in context of a previous communication

Detail: the facts, set out in logical paragraphs

Conclusion: summary of proposal, and formal salutation

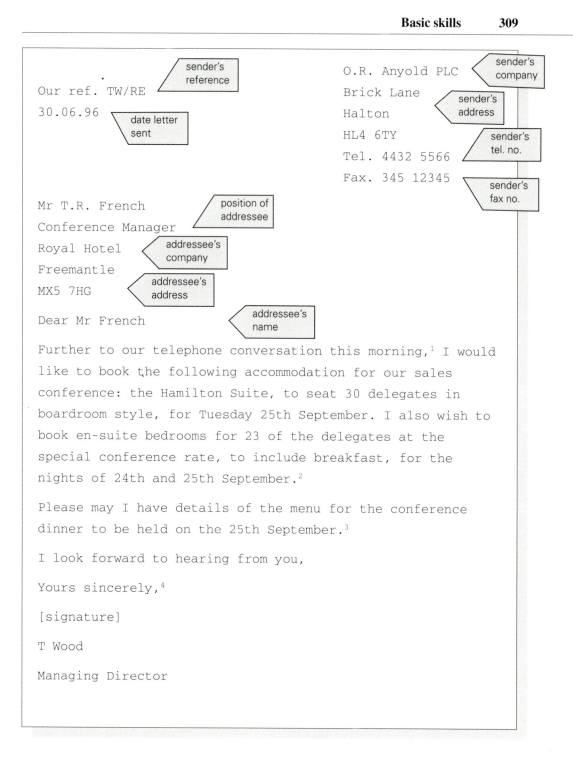

Figure 7.2 Example of a business letter

1. Context 2. Details 3. Proposal 4. Valediction

PHRASES FOR LETTER WRITING

The following list will help you to write business letters in an acceptable style.

Opening paragraph

In reply to your letter of...

Thank you for your letter regarding...

With reference to your letter of...

Further to our meeting of...

Further to our recent telephone conversation...

I wish to confirm...

The following reservation has been made...

Middle paragraph

It has become apparent that...

It is therefore necessary to...

As a consequence of this...

May I suggest that...

If this is acceptable...

It is proposed to...

Final paragraph

Should you wish for any more information...

Please do not hesitate to contact...

I look forward to meeting you...

I am certain you will enjoy your stay...

Thank you for your enquiry...

Should you require any more information...

I look forward to your early reply...

Valediction

Yours faithfully (if 'Dear Sir' or 'Dear Madam' is used)

Yours sincerely (if addressee's name is used)

FAX (FACSIMILE)

Here the written form is transmitted through the telephone network to the receiver unit. A fax number is logged in, and when the line is free the written word is transmitted. Each page of the document being sent is marked to indicate that it has been transmitted. A receipt is issued at the end of the transmission. Faxes are used extensively in the business world because written reports and documents can be instantly transmitted to any establishments that has a facsimile machine. These machines can receive transmissions 24 hours a day, provided they are switched on.

ACTIVITY

Practise your letter-writing and word processing skills by working the following examples

1. Write a reply from Mr French to Mr Wood (see Figure 7.2)

2. Write a letter from the housekeeper at the Royal Hotel Freemantle to the Everclean Laundry Boulton, questioning discrepancies between the laundry sent and the laundry received back.

Item	Laundry sent	Laundry returned
Table cloths	17	17
Napkins	42	46
Waiter's cloths	36	30
Slip cloths	18	18
Double sheets	20	19
Single sheets	15	15
Pillow cases	30	29
Chef's jackets	11	08
Chef's trousers	08	11
Tea cloths	22	22

3. (a) Write a letter from a prospective guest to the Royal Hotel Freemantle, asking about the local tourist attractions.

   (b) Reply giving the information on the countryside park at Breestone, the castle near the town centre, the folk museum in the castle grounds, the traditional market held on Thursdays, the canal long boat museum 10 miles south down the motorway, local shops and gardens in the town centre.

4. You are a receptionist working in the front office of a hotel situated in the centre of Yeovil.

   • Mrs McFreidle has asked in her letter confirming a booking how to reach the hotel. She will be travelling south down the M5.

   • Mr Lawson has asked directions to the hotel from Ottery St Mary.

   • Dr Fells has asked directions from Watchet.

In each case, write a letter giving clear directions to the hotel which is just opposite the church, with a car park in Church Row, at the rear of the premises. (You will, of course, need to refer to a road map for this exercise.)

The advantages of this method of written communication include:

- instantaneous transmission
- worldwide system
- facility to send and receive written documents
- fast and efficient communication

When conferences, exhibitions and meetings are held at a hotel complex, it is often necessary to use the hotel fax facility. In these cases the front office staff will send and receive the documents for the guests.

When sending out-going faxes for guests, the front office staff should:

- ask the guest to complete a cover sheet
- notify the guest of the charges
- transmit the fax immediately
- notify the guest if there is any delay
- return the master copy to the guest, in an envelope
- enter the transmission charge onto the guest's account

MEMORANDUM

Within an organization there are many instances when specific information has to be given to an individual employee, or to a number of employees. In these cases, the information will be written on an internal form called a memorandum – known as a memo. These are often pre-printed forms that can be handwritten. Memos are only used for internal communications. They could be used as reminders of meetings, to disseminate facts or information from a manager or supervisor to their staff.

The use of memos within an organization is encouraged because it gives a written record of the information, something that a telephone conversation does not do. The content of a memo should be concise and to the point.

MEMORANDUM

To   . . . .   From   . . . .

Reference . . . .   Date   . . . .

Figure 7.3 Example of a memorandum form

RECORD CARDS

These are used to record facts in all sections of the hospitality and catering industry. All record cards should be indexed and kept in chronological order so that the information recorded on each card can be easily accesssed.

A few examples are listed below.

Reception	Guest history cards
	Registration cards
	Previous guests' names and addresses
	Emergency contractors' names and addresses
Kitchen	Equipment maintenance records
	Recipes
	Cleaning routines for equipment and surfaces
	Suppliers' names and addresses
Housekeeping	Room redecoration records
	Equipment maintenance records
	Linen repair records
	Suppliers' names and addresses
Personnel	Staff clocking-in cards
	Staff names and addresses
	Casual staff names and addresses
	Emergency medical call-out numbers

ACTIVITY

Using the list above, and your IT skills, design four of the record cards above, one for each department.

WRITTEN INTERNAL COMMUNICATIONS

There are many examples of written internal communications within any hospitality and catering establishment. Some examples are listed in Table 7.1.

Table 7.1 Written internal communications

	Front office	Housekeeping	Food service	Kitchen
Staff rotas	✔	✔	✔	✔
Maintenance requests	✔	✔	✔	✔
Work cards		✔	✔	✔
Orders from suppliers		✔	✔	✔
Stock sheets		✔	✔	✔
Registration details	✔			
Function details	✔	✔	✔	✔
Menus			✔	✔
Recipes				✔
Order slips			✔	✔
Laundry lists		✔		
Guest accounts	✔			
Memos	✔	✔	✔	✔
Messages	✔			

ACTIVITY

Compile a chart like the one in Table 7.1 to illustrate the internal communications used within your place of work or training

CHARTS

It is often easier to put information in chart format when giving information about capacity or usage potential of different rooms. The advantages of this method of presentation are:

- figures are easily comparable
- minimum written explanation is necessary
- less space is used
- it appeals to the eye of the reader
- shading or colour can be used to help communicate the information

Areas where this presentation technique is frequently used include:

- seating configurations for conference rooms
- buffet plans for functions
- sizes and capacity of function rooms

• details of pricing structures
• staff duty rota
• menu planning cycles

Charts are also used to show the mileage between major cities. In the hospitality industry you will find that guests frequently ask the distance between two cities.

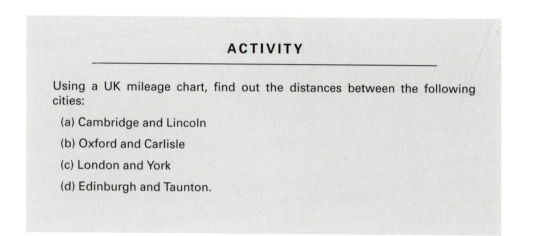

ACTIVITY

Using a UK mileage chart, find out the distances between the following cities:

(a) Cambridge and Lincoln

(b) Oxford and Carlisle

(c) London and York

(d) Edinburgh and Taunton.

MAPS

Maps are also frequently used in the hospitality industy, so it is useful to be a confident map reader.

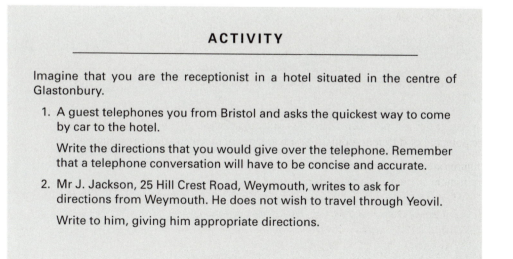

ACTIVITY

Imagine that you are the receptionist in a hotel situated in the centre of Glastonbury.

1. A guest telephones you from Bristol and asks the quickest way to come by car to the hotel.

   Write the directions that you would give over the telephone. Remember that a telephone conversation will have to be concise and accurate.

2. Mr J. Jackson, 25 Hill Crest Road, Weymouth, writes to ask for directions from Weymouth. He does not wish to travel through Yeovil.

   Write to him, giving him appropriate directions.

Numeracy

Every establishment will find it necessary to maintain accurate accounting records if their business is to succeed. These records will show details of purchases, stock, sales, expenses and overheads. From these figures an accurate picture of the current trading position can be given and forecasts can be made with regard to future trade. It is not possible to run a sound trade unless figures are faithfully and accurately maintained. The figures give an indication of whether the business is running at a profit or a loss, and which parts are more or less profitable. HMI tax inspectors and the VAT office require accurate accounts.

There are many occasions in all aspects of the hospitality industry when personnel will require numeracy skills. For example in:

- food cost control
- stock taking
- payment methods
- accommodation costs
- banking

This list in not exhaustive! Skills in basic arithmetic, percentage calculation, costing and ability to complete and calculate forecasts are all important factors which may have some influence on the success of a business. This section gives a brief description of the above-listed aspect of numeracy, with exercises to aid understanding.

FOOD COST CONTROL

A portion of each item on the menu must be costed. Before the menu for an establishment is set, it is important to consider several factors, taking into account the profit required on the sale of food, which will be different in, say, a quick service restaurant to an exclusive restaurant (Table 7.2).

Table 7.2 Differing costs in different establishments

Quick service restaurant	Exclusive restaurant
Lower customer expectations	Very high customer expectations
Minimum service	Excellent standard of service
Some trained, some untrained staff	Highly trained staff
Basic comfortable surroundings	Luxurious surroundings
Convenience produce often used	High quality, labour-intensive expensive dishes, freshly prepared
Large number of customers served	Fewer customers served

As Table 7.2 indicates, in a quick service restaurant, overheads and labour costs will be lower than in an exclusive restaurant. It is also the case that since the flow of clients is faster, the level of profit required on individual items can be lower. In the exclusive restaurant guests will expect to sit for longer after finishing their meal and have every need met by trained staff in superb surroundings. The establishment has to make a bigger profit on food served to pay for these greater overhead costs.

In every establishment it is important to standardize the menu to ensure correct costing by:

• limiting the number of food suppliers
• stock control
• ensuring accurate recipes and methods of preparation
• controlling portion size

Controlling portion size can be tricky. Sometimes photographs are used to show portion size as well as presentation. It is easier to calculate the cost of a menu item if the dish purchased is already portioned upon purchase, and for this reason many establishments prefer convenience products, for example:

• portioned gateaux
• jiggers of milk or cream
• butter portions
• 150 g frozen cod in batter portion

There are no overhead costs involved in preparation, presentation and cooking, portion control is accurate, presentation is assured and the requirement for staff training is reduced. Other methods employed in ensuring accurate portion control are:

• division into a certain number of equal size by cutting
• use of measuring equipment such as ladles, spoons and scoops
• use of particular service dishes or crockery

Whichever method is employed, it is very important to adhere to specified standards to ensure the profits calculated are actually achieved.

In calculating costs, it is usual in this industry to express figures as percentages, such as 'percentage of sales' or 'percentage of the total cost'.

Calculating gross profit (GP)

The chef's responsibility is in maintaining a percentage gross profit which has been set by the establishment. Initial costing of a menu begins with the buying of commodities. Knowing the purchasing price of items, the total cost of food is found and a profit may then be calculated and added on accordingly. This is called *gross profit*. So, the cost of the food, plus the gross profit makes the *selling price* (SP) which is *always* considered in percentage terms as *100 per cent*. This can be expressed as:

Selling price – food costs = gross profit (GP).

For example, chef has been requested to work to a gross profit of 60 per cent. He then knows that the food costs must be 40 per cent to make up to the selling price of 100 per cent. Working to the above formula, this can be expressed as:

$$100\% - 40\% = 60\%$$

Calculating net profit (NP)

The management are usually responsible for meeting percentage net profit targets set by the establishment owners. In considering the production of a menu, in reality the costs incurred are not just in the purchasing and use of commodities, but in the production of the food item to the table and in the service to the customer. The fuel used in cooking, heating and lighting of the establishment, rent, repairs and advertising costs to list but a few. In calculating *net profit, all overheads* are taken into consideration. This can be expressed as:

$$selling\ price - total\ costs = net\ profit\ (NP)$$

Another way to think of net profit is that it is 'pure profit'.
    A bad pricing policy can be devastating to the success of a business:

−overpricing causes loss of custom
−underpricing causes loss of income

For the manager's benefit, let's work out the selling price of an item, given the total cost to produce it and a percentage net profit required.

If a NP of 20 per cent is demanded on the selling price (SP) and the cost to produce it is £2.40 then that cost represents 80 per cent of SP. Therefore:

$$\frac{£2.40}{80} \times 100 = SP\ of\ £3.00$$

This sum involves finding 1 per cent of £2.40 by dividing it by 80, then multiplying 1 per cent by 100 to reach 100 per cent = selling price.
    Knowing that the total cost of the item is £2.40, deduct this from the SP. (Remember the formula! £3.00 − £2.40 = NP.) Therefore

$$NP = £0.60.$$

Calculating the selling price (SP)

As previously mentioned, it is important to remember that *selling price = 100 per cent.* It is possible to calculate a selling price given the cost of the food and a percentage gross profit or percentage net profit requested. This can be expressed as:

$$cost + profit = selling\ price\ (SP)$$

For the chef, let's work an example to find a selling price with a given gross profit:

A gross profit of 70 per cent of the selling price is requested.

Therefore the cost of the food must be 30 per cent of the selling price, making up 100 per cent in total. The ingredients cost of a dish may be £1.50

$$Cost\ (£1.50) + GP\ (70\%) = SP\ (100\%)$$

We can then work out that the cost = 30% (100%-70%), i.e £1.50 = 30 per cent. To find 1 per cent £1.50 is divided by 30:

$$\frac{£1.50}{30} = 1\%$$

Given the value of 1% it is possible to find the SP by multiplying by 100:

$$\frac{£1.50}{30} \times 100 = 100\% \text{ (SP)}$$
$$0.50 \times 100 = \text{SP}$$
$$£5.00 = \text{SP}$$

ORDERING

Food is ordered in many different units according to type, availability, style of service and staff skills. As previously discussed, weights of portions may be specified, convenience products already divided or portions marked and packets sold by weight, giving advice on number of obtainable portions. When ordering commodities it is vital to take account of for wasteage in production, which may occur for several reasons:

- poor quality
- poor culinary skills
- purchasing 'on the bone'
- shrinkage during cooking

Thus, assuming that in purchsing topside of beef there is a wasteage of 10 per cent in fat and shrinkage during cooking, then 10 per cent must be added to the total weight required before ordering.

STOCK TAKING

There are several methods used to keep a check on stock which is incoming, held in the store and used. It is important to keep a close eye on stock levels for several reasons:

• overstocking	– with overstocks value is tied up rather than being used
	– deterioration may occur
	– menu may change leaving stock not required
• understocking	– running out of menu ingredients may create a crisis, risking
	– dissatisfied customers and staff
	– loss of business
• wastage	– must be known in order to control and even eliminate
	– there must be awareness of deterioration in long-term storage
• pilfering	– needs to be recognized if, as unfortunately sometimes occurs, it is affecting stores

Bin cards

These are a popular method of stock control that have been in use for many years. They are:

- simple to understand
- easy to adjust by adding and or subtracting
- immediately show current stock levels
- enable prompt re-ordering

In a store, there is one bin card for each type of item in stock. Details are entered on the card describing:

- the commodity
- the date
- details of goods received (there will be note to sign and keep on delivery)
- goods issued
- the balance of stock left
- minimum stock level (for prompt re-ordering)

It is important to keep the bin card up to date, with all transactions being entered as they occur. There must be periodic stock checks against the bin card to ensure accuracy so, unfortunately, in the case of larger businesses they can be time-consuming to maintain.

Computerized stock control

This has become more common in recent years. Very similar to the stock control sheet, transactions are entered into the computer and the totals displayed on the screen. This is a very fast and efficient way of keeping records for all departments involved. Terminals can be included in more than one department of larger establishments, with all key personnel knowing the current stores situation. Requests can come directly through to the stores terminal, records can be updated immediately during that request, stocks re-ordered automatically and the items issued with a recorded list.

Perpetual inventories

These are maintained in the control office. All information from invoices is checked against delivery or goods received notes, purchase orders and requisitions from the food stores. On checking the card daily, it should be possible to keep accurate record of any item at any time and compare this with the physical stock. It is unusual for smaller establishments to use this method because of the cost of extra personnel to maintain the inventories.

PAYMENT METHODS

Customers pay both small or large sums for hospitality services and these may not just be in cash. Paying by cheque, credit or cash card and voucher is very much part of our society today and a convenience not to be underestimated. Providing that checks are carried out to ensure that transactions are genuine, these types of payment encourage business growth because they encourage customers to spend more easily. Accounts can be met by:

- cash – sterling
- cheque
- switch card
- credit card
- charge card
- in-house credit card
- gift vouchers
- foreign currency

ACTIVITY

1. There has been a delivery today from the grocery supplier and the storeman has to maintain an accurate record of stock. The morning production has continued as usual and goods have been withdrawn from the store.

   (a) Draw up a bin card for each commodity listed below, correctly entering all information necessary (make up your own quantities) for self-raising flour, caster sugar, butter, eggs.

   - today's date
   - name of commodity
   - amount already in stock
   - amount used this session
   - amount delivered
   - amount left on stock

2. Complete the same exercise with the following information:

   SR flour
   3.5 kg in stock
   15 kg delivered
   4.75 kg used this session
   Enter new balance of stock

   Caster sugar
   7.25 kg in stock
   15 kg delivered
   3.25 kg used this session
   Enter new balance of stock

   Butter
   5.5 kg in stock
   None delivered
   3.75 kg used this session
   Enter new balance of stock

   Eggs
   6 trays of 30 in each
   24 trays delivered
   50 eggs used this session
   Enter new balance of stock

   From your figures, can you decide whether some of the stock levels are rather high or too low if approximately 2 days stock in hand is required?

3. Research the recipe for Victoria sponge cake. Multiply the ingredients so that 56 portions can be made. Deduct these amounts of ingredients from bin cards already devised.

4. To find the cost of one portion of Victoria sponge cake: research the price of ingredients at your local grocery store, supermarket or college stores. Work out the price of producing 1 x recipe of cake and divide this by the number of portions recommended by the recipe. This figure will be the cost price per portion of the cake. Find out a selling price (see p. 318) that will give a gross profit of 70 per cent.

It is important for all hospitality staff to be aware of what is involved in the use of these different methods.

Cash

- *A float.* It is usual for a sum of money to be held as a 'float' in the paypoint till so that customers tendering cash can receive change from a large note without delay. This float is usually a set sum which must be collected, double checked and set into the correct till compartments for the start of the day's trade. At the end of the trading period it is then taken away from the total amount so as to reveal true takings.
- *Receipts and recording payments.* On tendering cash, check that the correct amount has been entered into the till. Customers are provided with a till receipt, which is duplicated within the machine. A reading is taken and the till is cleared to ensure that figures are not carried forward to the next trading session. These figures are kept and submitted for reference against monies actually received.
- *Legal tender.* This term refers to the legality of monies. Scottish notes are not, in fact, strictly legal tender in the whole of the UK but are generally accepted. When acccepting notes, check that they are not forgeries by holding up to the light and looking for the 'water mark'. There are now ultra-violet light machines available to show up the metal strip more discretely so as not to offend customers.
- *Change.* When giving change a system of counting out coins and notes is good practice, rather than just giving a handful in return. Starting with the sum to be paid, the cashier then gives the smallest coins first, counting up to the largest. For example: if £2.25 is required from a £5 note tendered, then the cashier will offer in order: 5p (£2.30), 20p (£2.50), 50p (£3) and 2 × £1 coins (£5).
- Handle just one transaction at a time.

Cheques

Instead of offering cash for payment, customers may wish to pay by banker's cheque. This is convenient for those who do not like to carry a lot of cash on them. Several points must be observed to ensure that the cheque is valid:

- *Date.* Must be correct to today's date, not post or forward dated.
- *Crossed.* Written between the lines should be 'a/c payee only' so that only the person or business named may cash it.
- *Amount.* This should be written legibly in words and given in figures in the box, and the two versions should correspond exactly.
- *Signature.* Ensure that the signature (as far as legible) is the same as the name printed at the bottom.
- *Cheque cards.* Usually cheques are only accepted with the verification of a cheque card, which is the bank's guarantee that they will pay the transaction up to the limit shown. This card will have:
    - a £50 or £100 limit shown as a hologram in the top corner
    - the hologram will also show the bank symbol or logo
    - a code number the same as that at the top of the cheque
    - an expiry date

– a card number which must be copied by the cashier onto the back of the cheque
– a signature matching that on the cheque offered

These are all methods employed to try and prevent fraud.

Debit card

Customers may offer to pay by this method. A symbol shown at the top corner of their cheque card identifies it as a debit card. The establishment registers an acceptance of receiving debit card payments and when one of the accepted cards is offered it is 'swiped' through the till and payment automatically recorded. The customer signs a receipt and the monies are removed from their account the following day.

Charge card

Again payment is made by charge card and signed for by the customer. Monies are then paid by the independent company offering the cards and the customer is billed later, usually once a month. This is very convenient for business people or frequent travellers. With this type of card, the account to the charge card company must be settled in full each time.

Credit card

This type of card is offered for payment and again 'swiped' through a special machine. Monies are received from the credit card company and customers are billed once a month in the same way as a charge card but only a percentage of the total bill need be paid. The credit card company will charge the customer interest on any outstanding payments as with any other loan.

Travellers' cheque

These are issued by banks and travel agents in the traveller's own country and provide a safe way of carrying large amounts of money when travelling. Should they get lost or stolen, they are easily cancelled and any losses are insured immediately. Travellers' cheques can be issued in specific currencies requested in varying amounts and are signed by the traveller on receipt at the bank. When accepting payment with this sort of cheque, ensure validity by comparing a second signature that the customer must give when making payment or exchanging for cash. The traveller's passport is often used to verify authenticity.

Eurocheque

Issued by banks for use in other countries, a Eurocheque may be of any specific currency. As with any other building society or bank cheque, they must be accompanied by a cheque guarantee card for validation.

Discount voucher

There is a wide variety of schemes offering vouchers, some nationwide, some company-based. They are designed to encourage repeat custom and range from offering points towards cash reductions on certain products to offering complete meals and accommodation. Some vouchers are in the form of cards which, like the phonecard, lose specific amounts each time they are used.

IN CASE OF PROBLEMS

- Keep calm and remain polite.
- Move away from earshot and avoid embarrassing eye contact.
- If it is your mistake, apologize profusely and make corrections.
- In the case of an incorrectly completed credit card slip, tear it up and start again with another.
- In the case of invalid cheques and cheque cards, explain why the item is unacceptable and suggest alternatives.
- Authorization refused. If this occurs suggest politely that the customer's credit card company will explain.
- Fraud suspected. The card company may request you to keep the card. Suggest the customer speaks to the company direct and offer a private phone. Do not return the card. Contact your superior immediately – they will take any further action required.
- Disputed bill. Check carefully and refer to any other document or orders and amend or affirm.

ACTIVITY

1. Practise the giving of change to other members of your group. Offer change by counting out backward to ensure your 'customer' has received the correct amount. Examples:

   £2 tendered to pay for £1.18 bill

   £5 tendered to pay for £1.87 bill

   £3 tendered to pay for £2.34 bill

   £10 tendered to pay for £3.55 bill

2. Practise the handling and recording of the following payment methods with the other members of your group:

   - bank or building society cheque
   - credit card
   - charge card
   - cash card

Produce a checklist to prove that you have completed all the tasks successfully

ACTIVITY

Compile a list of the items you use, or see being used every day, which rely upon technology.

Information technology

Technology, and advances in technology, influence us in all aspects of our everyday lives – at work, at home, or in our leisure pursuits. Technology is used to carry out all types of operation from everyday tasks, such as those performed by most modern watches, to complex operations such as micro-surgery via computer programs and/or mechanical equipment. Of course, the equipment must be instructed what to do, through very detailed computer programs written to cover all possibilities. Computers operate via logic.

Information technology is the use of technology to manipulate information, either text (alpha), numbers (numeric), a combination of these (alpha-numeric), pictures, graphs or diagrams (graphics), and to process this information or data quickly, efficiently, accurately and (for the computer operator) effortlessly. All the hard work has been done by the people who write the computer programs that instruct the computer.

This section will introduce you to some computer applications, which you can use to help you organize, store, retrieve and present your work in a professional way. The applications (software) used to do this will be Word for Windows, and Excel for Windows, which will offer you sufficient scope for all your needs.

THE EQUIPMENT

You should familiarize yourself early on with the components and terminology of computer technology.

Go to your college or local library, and look at the *latest* books on information technology. Advances in technology are taking place continuously, and you must try to keep up with the

---

ACTIVITY

Investigate the computer system you will be using to produce your coursework. Prepare your own notes describing simply the system and its capabilities. Make sure that you include the following items:

- type of system – i.e. standalone or networked
- information on the system specifications, e.g. memory size, and speed
- the hardware
- the operating system
- the software
- input devices
- output/storage devices
- the applications you will be using

If you come across anything you can't understand, ask your lecturer to explain. You can ask to see the manuals which come with the equipment or the applications software which will give you more information. Don't, however, get bogged down with technical details. Keep it simple.

latest developments. You will find useful up-to-date information in computer magazines and newspaper articles, which you may also find in your library.

USING APPLICATIONS*

Information Technology (IT) is a tool for you to use; with a little practice it is possible for everyone to use this tool to enhance the quality of their work. It is not necessary for you to understand everything about the equipment and the programs – only that you have a sound understanding of your equipment's capabilities, and that you have the necessary skill and expertise to exploit them. The computer software can do a lot to help you with this – but remember it can only carry out your instructions – *you* have to tell it what to do.

ABOUT WINDOWS

You have probably heard of Windows, but do you know what it is? It is a program designed to make using a computer easier, acting as a sort of interpreter between the computer's own operating system and the user (you). It is user-friendly avoiding confusing 'computerspeak'. Once you have mastered the art of using one Windows package, you can use exactly the same technique on any other Windows application because all look similar and work in the same way.

What makes Windows so easy to use? It operates on the principle of using graphic representation through which to give commands. Put simply, this means that you (the user) point to pictures (graphics) or options, through menus, in order to tell the computer what you want it to do.

One of the most useful features of Windows applications is that it permits you to work with more than one document, or more than one computer application on the same screen at the same time. It lets you open several 'windows' at once. It is as if you were sitting at your desk working on a report; you may need to get information from several files. This involves getting out the appropriate files, looking up or extracting the appropriate information and then putting the files away. This is exactly what you can do using a Windows program – you just do it via the computer screen. You do, however, have to discipline yourself to tidy up your 'desk' (your screen) when you have finished with the files. You will understand this better later, when you actually use the Windows package.

The simplest way to introduce you to Windows is to work through a few exercises and practise some of the techniques you will need to learn.

* Throughout this section of the book, where reference is made to Word or Excel, it is implicit that both packages are being used through the Windows program. The versions being referred to are:

• Microsoft Windows Version 3.1

• Word for Windows Version 2.0c (screen options to display ribbon, ruler, toolbar, horizontal scroll bar and status bar)

• Excel for Windows Version 4

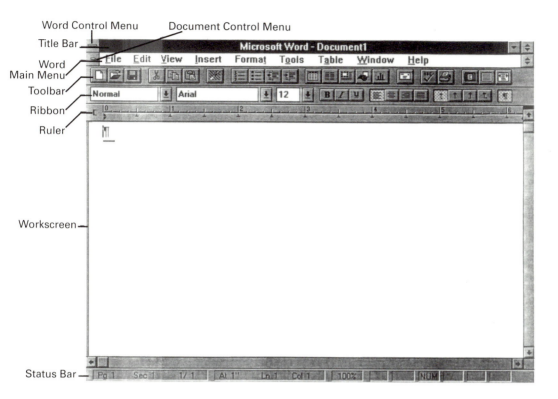

Word Control Menu Document Control Menu

Title Bar

Word
Main Menu

Toolbar

Ribbon

Ruler

Workscreen

Status Bar

Figure 7.4 Microsoft Word screen (1)

USING WINDOWS

The actual instructions you will give to get started may differ from centre to centre. It will depend upon how the program is set up, and whether you are using a standalone or networked computer. Check upon the instructions for your centre. When you have the Windows applications shown on screen, move the mouse until the arrow points to the Word icon and then double click. You will notice that the screen shows an egg timer instead of an arrow. This is to indicate something is happening – be patient. In a few moments the screen will change to the Word screen which is shown in Figure 7.4.

The Mouse. You will first have to master the technique of operating the 'mouse'. Practise until you are proficient. The mouse is your 'pointer' by which you give your instructions. You may have a special mat upon which to move the mouse, or you can simply glide it across a flat surface. You can see a ball inside the base of the mouse, and as this is moved a pointer on the screen moves similarly around the screen.

Point. Move the mouse around, to the left and right, up and down – note how the arrow on the screen moves in the same way. Note how the arrow changes to a vertical line (it looks like an elongated capital I) when it is moved away from parts of the screen which are showing the options available.

There are two buttons on the top of the mouse. You will use the left hand button to

Click. One press on the left-hand button will select the option you are pointing to.

Select. Point and click.

Double click. Press and release the left-hand button twice very quickly.

Drag. Position the arrow, press down and hold down the left-hand button whilst you move the mouse. Release the button when you reach the required position, or wish to make a selection. (This technique is usually used when you want to *highlight* a section of a document.)

The screen

You must at this point spend some time studying the screen in conjunction with the following notes. Any time you spend now will be compensated for later, when you will be carrying out operations knowledgeably instead of flicking backwards and forwards through the book to remind yourself what the different icons mean. The screen is split into sections (see Figure 7.4).

The title bar

shows the name of your document. If you are working on a new document, then Word will allocate it a number until you give it a filename.

In the left hand corner of the title bar you will see what looks like one drawer of a filing cabinet. This is your main *control menu.* Point your cursor (arrow) at this box, and click. What you will now see is one of the pull-down menus showing all the options available to you through this menu. If you have mastered the art of *dragging* (pressing down gently on the left-hand mouse button but not releasing it) you can scroll through the options and will be shown more information about each in the status bar at the bottom of the screen.

You will observe that some of the options are shown emboldened. These are the only options available to you at the moment. Try selecting (release mouse button) the 'restore' option. The screen will be adjusted – you may now see the programme manager at the bottom of the screen as an icon, or as another window. You have to get used to having several 'windows' (files or documents) open at the same time. Sometimes you cannot see them all, but they are just hidden behind the current window. Use the control menu again and select the 'maximize' option: your document will be returned to its original size. Try looking at the other options and note the information given on the status bar (I told you it was user friendly). *Be wary of pressing too quickly on an option. Make sure you read what you are going to do before you click – and actually execute your command.*

I am not going to attempt to explain the function of every option. We shall look at those you are most likely to need in more detail as we go through the exercises, and you can gradually add to your knowledge when you practise using the package.

Document control menu

(Filing cabinet drawer with smaller opening, below Word control menu.) This option will allow you to carry out instructions on the current document, i.e. manipulation of the window containing your document.

Main menu

The selections to allow you to work with your document: File, Edit, View, etc. Again, using your mouse select one of these topics. You will see a pull down menu appear showing the options available. You simply select your chosen option. For now you are just browsing through the options. Move the pointer away from the menu and click again to remove it.

The toolbar

This shows the shortcut routes to carry out many of the Word functions. As before you only need to select the option of your choice, Most of these will do exactly what the icon (picture) suggests. Have a guess at what you think each is for and then check if you are correct.

The ribbon

Shows all your options for changing the format of your document, e.g. the size and type of print you wish to use, whether it is to be underlined, emboldened, indented, etc. You can investigate, or check Appendix B for the full list of options.

The ruler

Shows the actual set up of the document, such things as margins and tab stops. When you are working on a document you will note that as you scroll through, the information on the ribbon and the ruler changes to reflect the actual format of the document at the current position of the cursor.

The workscreen

Your section, where you can insert your typewritten work ready to format before printing or saving.

Status bar

This (at the bottom of the screen) shows the position that the cursor is at in a document, e.g. page 1, line 26; whether the caps lock is on or off, and whether you are in insert or overstrike mode.

You will also notice at each corner of the workscreen, and of the Word screen are small arrows within the 'frames' (see Figure 7.5). These scroll bars are very useful tools for moving around your document.

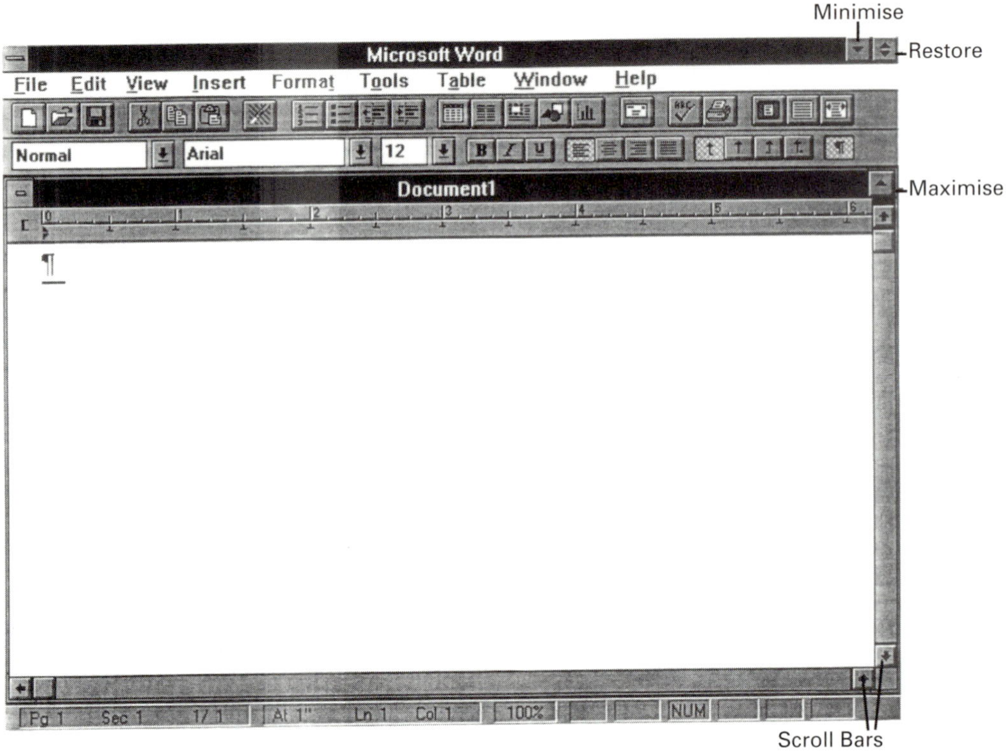

Figure 7.5 Microsoft Word screen (2)

Maximize.   Enlarge relevant window to its maximum size

Restore.   Restore relevant window to its previous size

Minimize.   Reduce the relevant window to an icon. This will be shown at the bottom of the screen, possibly behind another window. It is still running, and available to you if you select the maximize or restore options.

Scroll bars.   These enable you to move up or down your document, according to the direction of the arrow, when your document is too large to all fit in the display screen.

GETTING STARTED WITH WORD PROCESSING

Microsoft 'Word for Windows' is a very sophisticated and powerful word processing package. As well as all the usual functions of word processing – entering, saving, retrieving, editing, reformatting and manipulating information (data), Word also offers you the potential to carry out operations more usually associated with desktop publishing or spreadsheet packages: graphics, drawing, filing and many other features.

When the Word for Windows package was installed onto your computer, some instructions will have been incorporated which are known as the default settings. These are instructions such as the margin sizes, paper dimensions, type and size of print. The defaults are usually set to the options suitable for most operators. The idea is to make it easy for you to just switch on the computer and use it. You can of course amend these default settings for individual documents as you will discover shortly. If the default settings are not appropriate for the type of document the operator is creating, they can be permanently altered through the software.

CREATING A LETTER

Let us start by creating a letter (you can use the letter you composed in the Activity on p. 311). In the following directions *s* means 'select'.

Word main menu, *s* File

s New (*a 'dialogue box' will appear on the screen as in Figure 7.8*)

s Normal

Click on OK

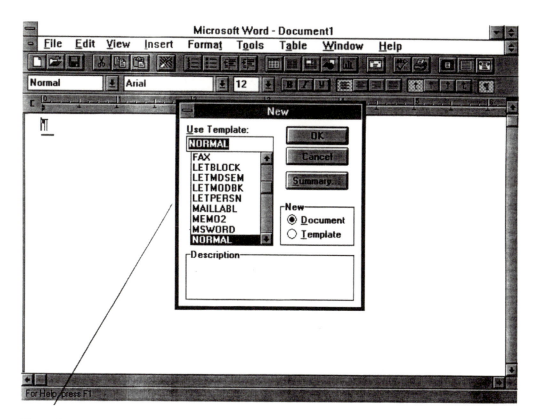

Figure 7.6 Dialogue box, showing the options available when you open a new file

You can ask the computer to automatically insert for you the date and/or time.

    s Insert

    s Date and Time

    s the option you want

    Click on OK

You will notice that when you press the space bar, or enter key, symbols appear on the screen. These symbols represent your instructions to the computer, and will not appear on your document when you print it.

    Type in your letter exactly as you would if using a typewriter but, remember, don't press Return (Enter) in the body of the letter, except where you want a new paragraph. The word-processing package will automatically start a new line for you when necessary. This is known as wraparound, or wordwrap.

Now you want to save your letter:

    s File

    s Save as

    Click on the down arrow underneath the Drives: (*box will reveal the options available*)

If you want your work to be saved on your own workdisk make sure your disk is inserted in drive a:, then (using the up or down arrows which appear to the right of the drive options you have):

    s a: in the Drive option

    position cursor in File Name box

    Click, and key in the name of your document

You can use up to eight characters, you must not use spaces or certain symbols, so it is best not to use any punctuation in the filename. *Try to make the file name meaningful* so that you can recognize what it represents when you later look at your directory. Letter1, Letter2, Letter3 will not be useful, but Conflet, Orderlet, Booklet will give you a good idea of what each document is.

    click on OK – (*Watch the status line*)

Important! Whenever you are using computers, get into the habit of *saving your work frequently*. It takes only a few seconds (you click on the save icon), but could save you hours. Make it your motto to Save and Be Sure.

Your letter is still on screen. It will now show the filename you have requested in the title bar, and this name will have been given the extension .DOC. Word attaches this extension to all filenames automatically.

To check the spelling in your letter:

    Hold down Ctrl and tap Home (*the cursor will move to the top of the document*)

    s Tools

s Spelling

Read the dialogue box and follow the prompts

Word will highlight any abbreviations, proper nouns, unusual words, etc. (see Figure 7.7). Remember it is checking your text with its own list of the most commonly used words. You must therefore ignore highlighted words which you know to be correct. For words which are incorrect:

Click on Correct word in Suggestions box

Click on Change

When you have finished spellchecking the document

Click on OK to exit Spellcheck

If you have had to make any corrections you will need to re-save the letter

s the Save icon

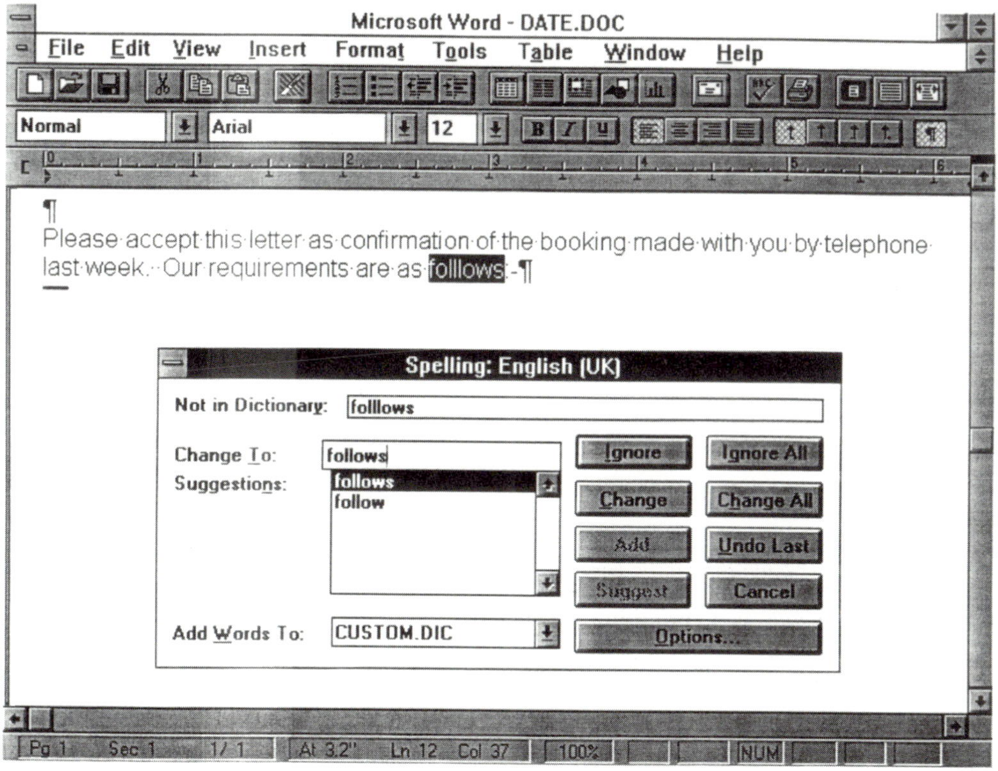

Figure 7.7 Demonstration of Spellcheck

The spellcheck has identified an error in the word *folllows*. Word is suggesting the words most likely to be what you want, from its dictionary. You select the word you want then *s* Change, or if the word you require has not been offered) position the cursor in the Change To box and key in the wanted word.

As you have previously saved this document the new version will automatically be saved, replacing the first version, under the same name.

Now read through the letter carefully. You may want to make a few amendments. If so, position the cursor where you want to carry out your amendment and click.

If you wish to delete:

Backspace key to delete to the left

Delete key to correct to the right

If you wish to substitute present text with a new version:

Insert key (look at the status bar – you will see the letters OVR when you enter overstrike mode),

Key in your correction

Tap insert key to exit OVR

If you wish to insert more text:

Position cursor where you wish insert to begin

Key in your additional text

If your letter is very short, you may wish to change the margins, to give a narrower panel with more lines for text.

s Format

s Page setup

s Left margin.

Key in the measurement figures for new margin *or*

Use the mouse and the arrow keys to select the measurement (*You will see the effect of your alteration in the Sample section of the dialogue box*).

Click on OK to confirm

Re-save you work

If your letter is a long one, you may find that Word automatically starts a new page for you when you have filled the first one. If you wish to insert the page break at a different point, position the cursor where you want to insert the break:

s Insert

s Break

s OK

ACTIVITY

Type up some reference notes, in your own words explaining what you have learned so far, and *how* to do it. You should be able to include:

Getting into the Windows package

Accessing Word for Windows

Creating a new file

Keying in text

Naming and saving your document to disk

Carrying out the spellcheck

Editing the text (inserting, deleting, amending)

Re-formatting the text (changing the margins)

Inserting a page break

Re-saving the document

Printing the document

Include a copy of your completed letter with your notes, as evidence of what you have done.

When you are sure that the letter is set out as you want it, and that there are no inaccuracies in it, you are ready to print it. Check the printing arrangements for your centre, that your computer is linked up to a printer, that it is switched on and has paper in it. Then:

s File

s Print

s OK (*if you are accepting default settings*)

It will normally be all right to accept the defaults as shown, but do look at them and make sure you understand what they mean.

By now you have learned some terms and techniques for use with any Windows package, and should, I hope, have mastered the skill of using the mouse.

CLOSING FILES AND EXITING WINDOWS

Now we shall look at closing files, and exiting the package. This is most important. You must close *all* windows you have opened before you leave the package, and you must be careful to do this *before* you remove your workdisk from the disk drive, or switch off the machine.

(*Note*: Windows will check any instruction you give to close a file if you have not saved your work.)

For each window you have opened, move the cursor to the Document control menu, and click on Close. You will move back through any open windows one at a time, and must do the same for each. Soon you will only have the Title bar left on the screen. Go to the Main control menu and again select Close. You will then be given a dialogue box which tells you that the result of your action will Exit from Windows. Click on OK and you will be returned to the screen you started with at the very beginning.

CREATING A MENU

Now let us look at some of the other files you may want to create in Word. You will probably want to create menus. This will need a little more flair. You want them to look attractive, the layout will need to be more varied than that of a letter and you might want to experiment with the appearance of the text.

Open a new file.

Type in the menu which appears on p. 286

Save this menu with an appropriate filename

Selecting text for alteration

It is essential to remember that in Word for Windows, when you want to change something which you have already keyed in, you must *select the text on which you want to work before you give instructions of what you actually want to do.* You will do this by *highlighting* the text:

s Help

s Help Index

s Search

Key in the word 'Select' in the box where the cursor is flashing. (*A list of topics will appear.*)

s Selecting Text

s Show Topics

s Selecting text with the mouse

s Go To

You should now have on screen a list showing you very clearly how to select either a word, group of words, paragraph, or document to work with. This is what I shall refer to as *highlighting* the text. You should make a note of the various methods for future reference. This will save you time later.

Do you remember how to close a window? You will need to do this to exit Help.

Your menu will still be on the screen – you opened another file to work on while keeping the first one open on your desk.

Using the notes you have made on highlighting text, try the following:

To centre the menu horizontally

Highlight the whole document

s the icon

Click

To centre the menu vertically

Highlight the whole document,

s Format

s Section Layout

s Centre

s OK

To emphasize sections of text you can underline, italicize, enlarge, embolden or change the font of selected text. (Use sparingly to emphasize the most important parts of your menu.)

To embolden text

Highlight the appropriate text

s the icon

Click

To italicize text

Highlight the appropriate text

s the icon

Click

To underline text

Highlight the appropriate text

s the icon

Click

On clicking you will see the results of your chosen alteration. If you don't like it, select an alternative. When you are satisfied with the appearance of the text, move the pointer away from the text and click once on the mouse button.

To alter typeface: font and/or size

You can make lettering larger by pointing to the downward arrow to the right of the figure on the Ribbon bar or you can select a completely different style of lettering (font) by pointing to the downward arrow to the left of this label, and then making your selection from the fonts offered (see Figure 7.8).

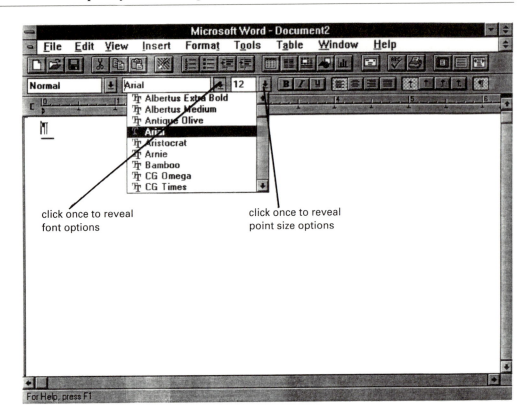

Figure 7.8 Changing font or point size

When you choose a larger size of type, the lettering increases both in width and height. Take care – letters can look out of proportion if you make them too big.

This is 10 point

this is 12 point

and this is 14 point text.

Vary the linespacing by inserting extra carriage returns where you want more space.

To insert symbols to separate the courses, position your cursor in the document where you want a symbol to appear:

s Insert

s Symbol

Click on the down arrow in the dialogue box for the choice of symbols.

Click on symbol of your choice

s OK

If you want the same symbol to appear two or three times you can *copy* as many as you like:

> Highlight the symbol
>
> *s* Copy
>
> Position your cursor where copy is to appear
>
> *s* Paste

A second copy of the symbol will appear.

You use almost the same technique to *move selected text:*

> *s* Cut
>
> Move the cursor to desired position
>
> *s* Paste

In the first case you are copying an item to a second position; in the second you are moving an item to another point in your document.

> Re-save your menu
>
> Close the file

When you want to recall a document you have previously saved, ensure that you are logged onto the correct drive (a: if you are saving to your own workdisk), then:

> *s* File
>
> *s* Open, or you can click on the icon (You will be given a list of the files stored)
>
> *s* the appropriate one (Menu)
>
> click on OK

When the file containing your menu is open, and if you still feel confident, try to improve its appearance further. You can enclose the whole menu or a section of the menu within a border.

> Highlight the text as appropriate
>
> *s* Format
>
> *s* Border
>
> From dialogue box, *s* required style of border
>
> Click on your option
>
> Click on OK

Keep working with your menu. To check the final appearance before you print it:

> *s* File
>
> *s* Print preview

You will then see the final document as it will appear when you print. If you are satisfied, you can click on print. Then re-save and close the file.

ACTIVITY

Print out two or three versions of your menu using different layouts and styles. Write up notes explaining how you achieved the different appearances. You can then use these notes for future reference. You should be able to include the new skills you have learned:

Using the Help facility

Centring vertically and horizontally

Emboldening, underlining, italics

Adjusting the point size of text and choosing different fonts

Inserting symbols

Copying

Cut and paste

Adding borders

Using the print preview

ACTIVITY

Use the Help facility to work out how to change from single line to double line spacing for a whole document. Write down your answer. Ask another student to try following your instructions to see if they work. Ask your fellow student to write a comment upon how good your instructions are.

As you have already seen, the Help facility is very user-friendly. You select Help, Help Index, Search, then key in the topic about which you want more information, and you will be prompted on what to do next. Get into the habit of reading your screen. It is usually offering useful advice.

PRESENTING MATERIAL AS A LIST

You may want to present some of your coursework in the form of a list with numbered paragraphs, in columns, or in a table. Word will make this very easy for you. For a simple list of items:

Position your cursor where you want the first item to appear

s icon

The numeral 1 will automatically be inserted for you and the cursor will jump to the first tab stop. As you type the cursor will wraparound to this position (known as indent) until you press Return. Repeat this process for each of your numbered items. Word does all the work for you. For emphasis you can insert bullet points to mark the start of each new item:

Position the cursor,

s icon

The bullet is inserted and the text is automatically indented for you. You also have the opportunity to change the style and size of the bullet symbol, if you so wish:

s Tools

s Bullets

s Numbering

s from the dialogue box

s OK then proceed as before

ARRANGING WORK IN COLUMNS OR TABLES, USING TABS

When you want to set out your work in columns across the paper, you can set 'markers' or 'tab stops' at various points across the width of the screen and by using the tab key you can 'jump' from one stop to the next without having to touch the space bar. Look at the Ruler bar on your screen. You will see it is marked out in measurements representing the width of the typing line. It is pre-set to allow you a margin at the left and right, top and bottom. You can check this if you look at the Page set-up (*s* Format, *s* Page Setup). You will also notice there are inverted Ts equally positioned along the ruler. These are pre-set (default) tab stops which you can use if they are at appropriate points. If you want to set your own tab stops at different points along the typing line:

Position the cursor at the point where you want to start typing your table.

Click on the appropriate tab in the ribbon bar

aligns the text to the left, i.e. *starts* typing from the position of the tab stop

aligns the text to the right, i.e. arranges the text to *end* at the position of the tab stop

arranges the text equally to the left and the right of the position of the tab stop

Use this for figures. It aligns at the decimal point:

10.42

122.56

1.66

Let us look at your list of dishes with traditional accompaniments (p. 288). For this exercise you need to use the align left tab stop. You will have to set your own tab stops.

Using the mouse, point to the align left tab stop

Click to select

Move the pointer to the first point on the ruler bar where you want a tab to be set (2″ for this exercise) Click again

Move to the position where you want your next tab stop (4.5″)

Click again

You will notice that the default tabs in front of your manually set stops will disappear each time you set a new one. If you find you have set the stops incorrectly, you can move a tab stop from one position to another by dragging it along the ruler bar.

You are now ready to type in your table. You must type across the page line by line and use the tab key to move between the columns. Type your text as follows:

Dish [TAB]	**Accompaniments** [TAB]	**Service details**
Roast sirloin [TAB]	Yorkshire pudding [TAB]	Large mains plate
of beef [TAB]	Horseradish sauce [TAB]	Large knife and
[TAB]	Gravy [TAB]	fork [TAB]
and so on		

Some of your work would look better presented in the form of a table, for example your bookings diary (p. 140); this too is very easy.

Type in the text as usual until you reach the point in your document where you want to insert the table:

s Table

s Insert Table (*you will be prompted to specify the number of rows and columns you want: try something simple at first.*)

s 6 rows and 5 columns,

s OK

Your table will be prepared instantly and displayed on the screen ready for you to insert your text.

Table 7.3 Using tabs and borders for tables

ROTA	Restaurant	Restaurant	Diner	Diner
Monday	John	Sally	Mary	Louise
Tuesday	William	Daniel	Lucy	Abigail
Wednesday	Sally	Louise	Nina	Ben
Thursday	Adam	Nina	Dominic	Mary
Friday	Mary	Abigail	John	Sally

You move around the boxes (known as cells) by using the tab key, or the cursor control keys. You can adjust the width of the columns by dragging the vertical lines separating them to the left or right. The pointer on screen will look like ◀▶ when it is selecting the separator lines. To insert/delete cells, rows or columns select Table again, and then select the option you require. You should, by now, feel confident enough to try this out for yourself.

The rows will expand in depth if you position your cursor in the appropriate cell and press Enter.

The gridlines you see on the screen separating the cells will *not* appear in the printed table unless you instruct the computer to insert borders. You have already tried using this option. Your instructions will be different this time. To insert borders around all the cells:

Highlight the whole table

s Format,

s Border,

s Grid

s the type of border you require,

s OK

Your table will now have the gridlines printed when you print the document.

It takes a little practice to get the tables just right. Experiment! Now try to work out how to shade the cells. If you have been reading the screen this should be quite easy. Don't forget to save your original document so that if you decide you don't like the changes you have made, you can clear the screen without saving any changes and start again.

ACTIVITY

You have now learned some of the more advanced presentation functions of the Word package. Print a copy of the best examples of your coursework, and a reference sheet explaining the techniques you have used.

DRAWING

In order to give your work a really professional look, you could try to incorporate pictures into some of the documents.

If your Word program has been loaded to allow you access to the MS (Microsoft) Draw application, open a new file and then click on the icon.

You will be presented with a new screen which looks like that in Figure 7.9.

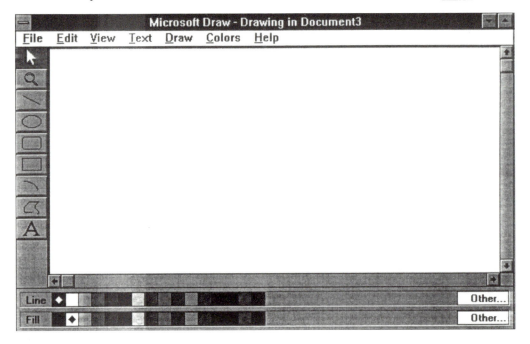

Figure 7.9 Microsoft Draw screen

Now that you have acquired some skills with using a Windows package you should enjoy experimenting with this drawing package. Along the top you have the menu option, which should now be familiar to you. Down the left-hand side of the window are the different icons showing the 'Tools' you can use for drawing different shapes. Spend a little time finding out what the various tools can do. Along the bottom of the screen are the line and fill options, for shading in the outlines and shapes you have drawn. If you have access to a colour printer, you can really use these to enhance your drawing.

The Draw package has (as you might have suspected) a very good help guide, and if you want to spend a few minutes looking through this, you will find all you need to know. Select Help, make your selection, then follow the prompts. When you have finished creating any drawing, you have to exit from Draw:

s File

s Exit and return to [your document]

s Yes

This will 'embed' the drawing in the document which is still open behind the Draw window. Dont forget to save the document.

Experiment! When you feel ready, try the Activity below.

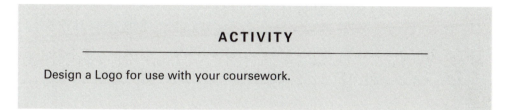

ACTIVITY

Design a Logo for use with your coursework.

GETTING STARTED WITH SPREADSHEETS

In almost every aspect of business, computers have been introduced to streamline and speed up the manipulation of data. This is probably seen at its most spectacular when spreadsheets are used. Their main function – the manipulation of numeric data – makes them a vital tool for any business. Spreadsheets convert seemingly unintelligible sets of figures into visual representation at the touch of a button.

What is a spreadsheet? It is a grid into which the operator can insert text, numbers and formulae in order to take the drudgery (and margin for error) out of working with figures. Spreadsheets are used for all types of mathematical operations. Think of the calculations you might want to carry out in the hotel and catering industry: costing purchases, calculating profit margins and overhead costs, projecting future profits and expenditure, seasonal variations, efficient stock management, the effects of VAT changes, etc.

How can the spreadsheet do this for you? Once again, remember you don't need to know everything about how it works. What you must understand is what it can do, and *how* you can do it!

We are using the Excel spreadsheet operated in the Windows environment, so you are already used to this. You may need to check back on some of the instructions contained in the earlier section. Appendix shows Toolbar buttons.

Let us look at a simple spreadsheet. Using your centre instructions, load the Windows software onto your computer, and when your screen shows the Windows applications select the icon for Microsoft Excel. When Excel is loaded, you will see that the workscreen consists of 'boxes' (known as cells).

The Grid is made up of columns labelled A, B, C etc across the screen, and rows labelled 1, 2, 3 etc., down the side of the screen. You can identify any particular cell by reading the co-ordinates across and down, e.g. B3, E5.

You can only see the top left corner of your worksheet (spreadsheet) Imagine it is a large sheet of paper covering your whole desk and you are looking at one section of it. To see the rest you have to use your cursor control buttons to scroll to the right and down, or some shortcuts to see other parts of the sheet. Look in the reference box in the formula bar above the worksheet. At present it is displaying A1 (the current active cell – so called because this is where your cursor is at the moment). Watch the contents of this box change as you move around the worksheet. Try these:

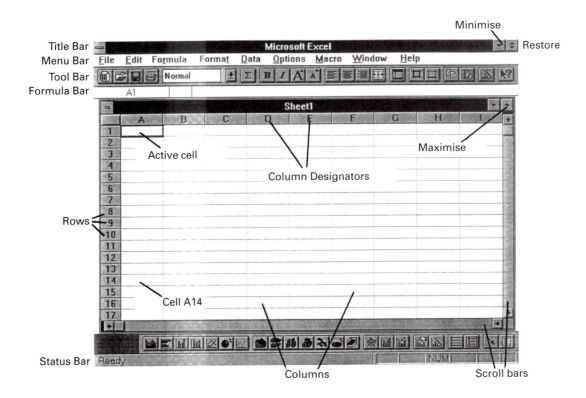

Figure 7.10 Microsoft Excel spreadsheet

Hold down Ctrl

Tap the cursor control key showing the down arrow

This will move you to the last row – or the last row where there is an entry if you have data entered into the spreadsheet. (Look at the reference box.)

Ctrl + right arrow – will move you to the last column

Ctrl + left – you are back in the first column

Ctrl + up – you are back at the top

You can also use the scroll bars to move around the worksheet, either gradually with each single click on the mouse button, or continuously if you keep your finger depressed. Or you can use the PageUp, PageDown keys to move around the sheet a page at a time. If you want to go straight to a particular cell:

s Formula

s Goto

Give the cell address e.g. K33

s OK

Creating a spreadsheet

We are going to start by creating a spreadsheet to show the profits made by a small guesthouse for the first quarter of the financial year.

You have the information displayed in Table 7.4.

Table 7.4 Guesthouse expenditure and income, April–June 1996

		April	May	June
3		April	May	June
4				
5	OUTGOINGS			
6	Rent	200	200	200
7	Electricity	250	250	250
8	Salaries	3000	3000	3000
9	Grocery	150	350	245
10	Cash and Carry	400	400	380
11				
12				
13	INCOME			
14	Accommodation	1750	2450	4250
15	Restaurant	1200	1100	2200
16	Coffee shop	500	550	600

First we want to enter the **title**. Move to cell A1. (The active cell is indicated by a border around it.) Type in the title and watch the information appear in the reference box as you type it. Don't worry if the title is too long to fit into the cell – it will spill over into the next. If you make a mistake whilst typing it in, backspace and correct your error. Tap Enter, and your title will be placed in the worksheet.

We now want to enter the column labels (headings or titles of the individual columns). Now we *do* want each label to fit into its own cell. After you have typed them in we can decide which columns, if any, need to be widened.

Click your cursor in cell D3

Type in April

Tap the right arrow key

The text will appear in D3 and the cursor will move to E3.

Repeat the process to key in the labels May and June. Now you need to enter the **labels for the rows**.

> Click your cursor in cell A5
>
> Type in OUTGOINGS
>
> Tap the down arrow key

The text will appear in A5 and the cursor will move to A6. Continue entering the rest of the row labels.

If you want to use figures as a label, for example a date, 10/10/1996, insert " before you key in the actual information. This indicates that the data is to be treated as text and not as figures.

Check what you have entered so far. If you have made any keying-in errors you can amend them by activating the appropriate cell (click in it) and then either key in the whole entry again and press Enter (the new data will replace the original when you do this) or move your pointer to where the cell contents appear in the formula bar (arrow changes to a vertical line), click at the point where the error occurs and then edit the text as you have previously learned.

If you have any row labels which are too long to fit into their cells, widen the row column. Obviously the width of column A will need to be sufficient to accommodate the longest row label, Cash and Carry.

> Click on the main column heading letter, e.g. A, B etc. (known as the column designator) and the whole column will be highlighted. You can adjust several columns at once by pointing to the first column designator, and dragging to highlight all the columns you wish to adjust. This is known as highlighting or painting the range
>
> s Format
>
> s Column width
>
> Key in required width

An easier way to adjust the width of the columns is to drag the separator line between two columns to the new required position (you have used this technique before).

Now we come to the **entering of numeric data**. Position cursor in appropriate cell, key in the figures, and then complete the entry as before by pressing one of the arrow keys to move to the next cell in that direction, or pressing Enter to complete the entry.

Continue to enter the rest of the information onto your spreadsheet as shown in the example.

You will have noticed that as you type in text it is automatically left aligned, and as you type in figures these are automatically right-aligned. It is best to keep the figures right aligned but it sometimes looks better if you realign the column labels. To **change the alignment**:

> Position the cursor in cell D3
>
> Drag to highlight the cells D3, E3 and F3
>
> s Format
>
> s Alignment (Horizontal)
>
> s Centre
>
> s OK

Your column headings will now be centred. Save your worksheet with an appropriate filename. The Excel software will automatically attach the extension .XLS to each spreadsheet file you save.

We now come to the most significant part of the exercise: **entering formulae**. The formulae are the real secret of success of the spreadsheet: it is through these that you actually instruct the software to perform calculations. It is, therefore, most important that you think carefully when you are designing and setting up your own spreadsheets, to ensure that you include all the information you will need to be able to carry out the calculations you want. You can carry out calculations by instructing the computer to 'link up' various cells, and carry out your instructions using the contents of the cells. This sounds a bit complicated, but let us say for example, that we wanted to calculate the total expenditure for the guesthouse for April. It would be very simple to add up the figures we have inserted, and key in the answer. *Excel will do the hard work for you.* All you need to do is tell it to add up the **contents** of the cells, and show the **result** in the totals cell. The calculations can be very simple, such as adding or multiplying the contents of two cells, or can involve very complex mathematical functions. By instructing Excel to manipulate the contents of the cells, any subsequent changes you make to those contents will cause the calculations to be updated to include your changes.

N.B. You must enter an equals sign (=) as the first character of any formula; this instructs Excel that instead of entering the data into the cell, you want it to perform a calculation.

Let us enter the formulae you will need to complete the worksheet you have keyed in. First we want to **total the outgoings** for April to June.

> Position your cursor in cell D11
>
> Tap =
>
> Type in SUM (
>
> Move the cursor to D6
>
> Press the mouse button and drag the cursor across all the cells containing information to be added in this formula (*a dotted line will appear around the cells*)
>
> Type in the final bracket).
>
> Look at the formula bar. *Your formula should read =SUM (D6:D10*)
>
> *If it does not:*
>
> > Click against the × on the formula
> >
> > Start again
>
> *If it does:*
>
> > Either click on ✔ or press Enter

The answer to your sum will appear in cell D11 (4000). Using the sum function has the same effect as typing the formula =D6+D7+D8+D9+D10, but is much easier and quicker to use – especially if you want to add the contents of 20 or 30 cells. An even quicker way to do this is to use the Sigma function.

Position the cursor in cell E11

s $\boxed{\Sigma}$ *(Excel will offer you the formula for the range of cells most likely to be those required)*

Tap enter if it is correct

Amend if not correct.

You have now calculated the total outgoings for April and May, and you want to do the same for June. Instead of entering the formula again, you can **copy (or replicate) the formula** to the appropriate place(s).

s cell D11

s Edit

s Copy

Paint the range where you want the same formula to be inserted (in this case only F11)

s Edit

s Paste to insert the formulae to the new position(s)

N.B. Excel will copy the formula, but adjust the cell references to make them relative to the cells in the columns to which you have moved them. Look at the formulae (in the formula bar) in these cells. In cell D11 the formula is sum(D6:D10), in cell E11 sum(E6:E10), in F11 sum(F6:F10) and so on.

Using what you have just learned, now insert the formulae to calculate the totals for income into cells D17 to F17 of your spreadsheet. Re-save the spreadsheet.

Other mathematical functions

Symbols for other mathematical functions are:

+   Addition e.g. =A1+B1
-   Subtraction e.g. =A1-B1
∗   Multiplication e.g. =A1•B1
/   Division e.g. =A1/B1

You may have to use these in future calculations.

Show, in a column to the right of the spreadsheet the total outgoings, and the total income for the three-month period. Insert suitable formulae to calculate these figures. Check at the bottom of the page to see if you have inserted the correct formulae.

Show, in a row at the bottom of the spreadsheet, the profit per month. In order to do this you will have to deduct the outgoings from the income. You will need to use a subtraction formula to do this. Think about the formula you want before you try to insert it.

Activate cell D18

Tap = *s* cell D17

Tap − *s* cell D11

If the formula now in the formula bar is what you want

Tap Enter

Instruct Excel to enter the total profit for May and June

Re-save the spreadsheet. It should now look like Figure 7.11. To print out your spreadsheet first check that you are linked up to a printer, that it is switched on and that there is paper in it.

  s File

  s Print preview

  If you are happy with the preview:

  s Print

GUEST HOUSE - PROFITS APRIL 199 - JUNE 199						
			April	May	June	
						TOTAL
OUTGOINGS						
Rent			200	200	200	
Electricity			250	250	250	
Salaries			3000	3000	3000	
Grocery			150	350	245	
Cash and Carry			400	400	380	
			4000	4200	4075	12275
INCOME						
Accommodation			1750	2450	4250	
Restaurant			1200	1100	2200	
Coffee Shop			500	550	600	
			3450	4100	7050	14600
MONTHLY PROFIT			-550	-100	2975	

Figure 7.11 Spreadsheet for guesthouse accounts, April–June 1996

Imagine that the data for the three-month period from July to September (Figure 7.14) has now become available.

You will need to insert three more columns to accommodate the new information, but you have two columns with no data in them so we can tidy up the worksheet first.

  Position your cursor on column designator for column B

    Drag across B and C (both columns should be 'painted')

    s Edit

    s Delete (the empty columns will be deleted, and the information from columns to the right will be re-positioned)

    Position your cursor on column designator for E

    Click

    s Edit

    s Insert (*a new column will be inserted and the present contents of column E will be moved to the right*)

Table 7.5 Guesthouse expenditure and income July–September 1995

	JULY	AUGUST	SEPTEMBER
Rent	200	200	200
Electricity	275	275	280
Salaries	4000	4000	4000
Grocery	275	345	455
Cash and Carry	500	500	600
Accommodation	8900	12500	12000
Restaurant	4000	5000	4500
Coffee shop	1000	1200	1100

Insert two more columns in the same way then enter the new data in the correct position, enter the appropriate formulae to calculate the totals for the period July to September.

CREATING CHARTS

Recall your guesthouse spreadsheet to the screen. You have been asked to produce some information for presentation at the managers' meeting, showing the profit made over the last six-month period. It would be very easy for you to print out a copy of the spreadsheet, showing the figures for each month and the total profit. It would, however, be much more impressive if you could produce the information in a chart or graph form – it gives an instant picture of the ups and downs of the profits over the last six months. You can convert the information from your spreadsheet to a very effective chart within minutes.

Highlight the range of cells containing profit figures: A18:G18

s File

s New

s Chart

s OK

A column chart has been plotted for you. Excel has taken the information contained in the cell references you highlighted (the data series) and converted that information to a visual representation. Excel will select an appropriate scale to cover the figures contained in your range.

Now you can use your mouse pointer to select other options from the special chart options menu displayed at the bottom of the screen. As soon as you select a different option, your chart changes to reflect your new choice. (N.B. For some of the options you need to give different information – you will get a message telling you if the option is not available.)

Your chart is displayed on screen, and is now the active window, but your original spreadsheet is still current – it is 'behind' the chart. Practise using the mouse to change the size of the windows, and move them around the screen, so that you have both windows side by side on the screen. You can do this by positioning the mouse on the right or left edge of one of the windows (you will see that the arrow changes to a double headed horizontal arrow) or on a corner of the window (arrow changes to a two-headed diagonal arrow). Press the left-hand button and drag the edge of the window in the required direction. You might need to use the Restore option to reduce the chart window before you try this.

To move from the spreadsheet to the chart or vice versa, click anywhere in the document you want to be the active window. The title bar of the active window will appear emboldened (or coloured if you have a colour screen). Save your chart:

s File

s Save

s a:

Name your chart (*Excel will automatically add the extension .XLC*)

Close the chart window. Your spreadsheet is still on screen: maximize the window containing it. Now we'll try to create a second chart showing how the income has been generated – to give the comparison between the different sources of income. We want to label the six-month periods, and insert a title. We have to select two data ranges, and omit other data which appears between them in the spreadsheet:

Highlight the first range B3:G3 (the labels)

Hold down Ctrl and highlight the second range: A14:G16

s File

s New

s Chart

s OK

The bar chart will be produced instantly for you, showing the six monthly sets of income, labelled along the X-axis, as requested. From the chart tool bar at the bottom of the screen:

s and the legend (label for the different types of income) will be added

If you want to insert a chart title:

s Chart

s Attach text

s Chart title

s OK (Chart is now ready for you to key in the title)

Type in your title (which will appear at the top of the chart in the formula bar, so that you can edit if necessary)

Tap Enter (the title will be placed on the chart)

Save your chart

Close all the windows you have opened, but keep the Excel program loaded

IMPORTING FROM EXCEL INTO WORD

Minimize the Excel window. You should now be able to see the program manager either as the current window or as an icon at the bottom of the screen. Load the Word package,

If Program Manager is the active window, you can immediately load Word; if it is an icon, maximize this window, and then load Word. Open a new file in Word and then type up the following report until you come to the words 'as the following chart shows'. Then follow the instructions carefully to import the Excel chart into the Word document. When you have done this, continue typing the rest of the report.

Report on the comparative income generated during the period April to September

As expected, the income from the accommodation has grown rapidly over the last quarter – a result of the exceptionally good holiday season. The restaurant, too, is showing a healthy profit, and as the reputation of our new chef spreads, we anticipate that this increase will be maintained. Although the coffee shop is showing a profit, it is below our expectations, as the following chart shows:

(Insert chart here)

This is an area which we feel could be improved. We would like to invest some capital in upgrading the decor of the coffee shop, and widening the 'snack' menu service to encourage our younger clientele to visit it for a mid-day snack; as they seem to prefer these surroundings to the more formal restaurant facilities.

Inserting the chart

Insert two carriage returns

Minimize the Word window (*You should be able to see the Excel icon at the bottom of the screen; if you have Program Manager on screen, the Excel icon is behind it, so you will have to minimize the Program Manager window*)

Maximize the Excel window

Retrieve the Income chart you prepared earlier (*You will be asked if you wish to update references to unopened documents. If you select Yes, this instructs Excel to check and update the spreadsheet to which the chart is linked. This is another example of the capabilities of the Excel software; when you are updating information in one document your changes can be incorporated into any other linked documents, if you request it. This is quite an advanced concept. If you select No, the check and update will not take place. You are not going to make any changes*): s No

s Edit

s Copy (*a dotted line is inserted around the chart*)

Minimize the Excel Window

Maximize the Word window

s Edit

s Paste (*a copy of the chart is now imported (embedded) into your Word document. You will see the message {EMBED ExcelChart\s\•mergeformat} showing that this has been done*)

Continue typing the rest of the report

What you have done is to copy the chart from the Excel document into 'Clipboard' – a temporary storage place – and then imported it by pasting it into the Word document.

Save and Print your final document

Close your files in both packages

ACTIVITY

Design and create a spreadsheet to calculate the accounts of guests shown on the tabular ledger you have been asked to produce (see p. 145). You will have to insert formulae to *add* the contents of all the cells showing costs incurred, and formulae to *deduct* the contents of all the cells showing payments made, or reductions to the account. Print out your spreadsheet.

Security

It is most important to develop and follow good practice when handling the storage and retention of computerized records. Hours and hours of work can be lost at the press of a button, or as a result of a power cut – even months of work if a fire or theft occurs. It would be difficult, and surprising, for someone to steal the contents of a filing cabinet, but a personal computer (which may hold the contents of your filing cabinet) is a different matter.

Some safeguards you can employ to protect your information:

- Save your work frequently *while* keying it in.
- Always back up your files. This means keeping a second copy of *all* your work on floppy disks. Check on your centre policy for creating backup disks. Don't wait until you have lost your work once before you learn this lesson!
- Store backup disks in a fireproof cabinet in a different location from the main storage.

Limit access to the equipment by:

- allowing only authorized personnel into the computer room(s).

Limit access to the data by:

- using passwords to restrict entry to certain applications or to specific files.

As you have found, in order to use a package you need to know how to access it; once you are into the package you need to know which file to ask for. Passwords can be 'built in' to the software (similar to personal identification numbers used for access to personal banking information) to allow access only to authorized staff. You can introduce different access levels – with a password at each level – to further safeguard the data.

If you are choosing a password for your own documents, try to choose something not too obvious – your date of birth, or initials backwards, for example, could easily be obtained by someone with determination.

Health and safety

You will already be familiar with the legislation affecting employees at work. There are several matters specifically relating to the use of computers and to keyboard operators, of which you should be aware.

Though the advent of computers has enabled offices to streamline equipment, and newer developments have reduced some of the early problems associated with technological equipment, the computerized office is still a relatively new phenomenon, and potential problems are still being identified. Some of the problems associated with using computers are given in Table 7.6.

Table 7.6 Possible health hazards and their causes

Eye strain, headaches, fatigue, backache	Caused by poor lighting, glare or reflection from the screen, over-long spells of work at the computer, poor seating or poor arrangement of the equipment
RSI (repetitive strain injury)	This affects the fingers and wrists of operators using keyboards regularly for long periods of time
Noise	Older equipment, e.g. printers, were very noisy, emphasized by being sited in small offices
Stress	Can result from heavy workloads coupled with unrealistic deadlines, monotonous repetitive jobs, lack of training on new equipment or with new applications
Radiation	There is no conclusive evidence to confirm that any damage occurs, but pregnant women are advised not to spend long periods at computer screens, as a precaution

In addition to the specific points mentioned above, the operators must remember that they are operating electrical equipment, and must take the usual precautions to avoid putting themselves or their colleagues at risk.

ACTIVITY

1. Contact your local Health and Safety Executive and request information leaflets relevant to working with IT in offices.

2. Name the legislation which specifically affects people who work with IT equipment.

3. Indicate three different potential health problems associated with working on computers.

4. Describe, briefly what could be done to avoid these problems.

5. Consider your own work area – equipment, arrangement of furniture, etc. – and compile a chart and on it record marks you would award (out of 10) for each item.

Appendix A: Toolbar buttons

Create new document

Open an existing document

Save the current document

Cut – remove highlighted text, store on clipboard

Copy – copy highlighted text, store on clipboard

Paste – insert text from clipboard at point of cursor

Undo – undo the last instruction

Produce text in numbered paragraphs

Produce text in bulleted list

Move left indent one tab stop to the left

Move left indent one tab stop to the right

Inset a table

Change column format

Insert a frame

Starts the Microsoft Draw program

Starts the Microsoft Graph program

Create an envelope

Starts the Spelling Check

Print the current document

Zoom display to view the whole page

Zoom to 100% (full size)

Zoom to display whole page width

Appendix B: Ribbon bar buttons

B   **Bold text**

I   **Italic**

U   **Underline**

     Justify to the the left

     Centre

     Justify to the right

     Justify to the left and the right

     Left tab

     Centre tab

     Right tab

     Decimal tab

¶   **Display/Hide screen codes**

`Normal`   **Current paragraph style**

`12`   **Current point size**

`Times New Roman`   **Current font**

Appendix C: Excel toolbar buttons

Create new worksheet

Open an existing document

Save current document

Print current document

Cell style

List options for cell style

Sum function button

Bold text

Italic

Increases font size

Decreases font size

Justify to the left

Centre

Justify to the right

Centre text across selected columns

Apply last table format set

Apply border round selected cells

Add or remove border at bottom of cell

Copy selected cells to clipboard

Pastes format only from cells copied

Create or edit chart

Help

Index